The Works of Ibn Wāḍiḥ al-Yaʿqūbī

Volume 1

The Works of Ibn Wāḍiḥ al-Yaʿqūbī

An English Translation

VOLUME 1

Edited by

Matthew S. Gordon
Chase F. Robinson
Everett K. Rowson
Michael Fishbein

BRILL

LEIDEN | BOSTON

This paperback was originally published in hardback as Volume 152/1 in the series *Islamic History and Civilization*.

Cover illustration: Sour orange (*nāranj*), al-ʿUmarī, *Masālik al-abṣār*, fol. 212r, detail (BnF, Department of manuscripts, Arab 2771).

The Library of Congress Cataloging-in-Publication Data is available online at http://catalog.loc.gov
LC record available at http://lccn.loc.gov/2017470540

Typeface for the Latin, Greek, and Cyrillic scripts: "Brill". See and download: brill.com/brill-typeface.

ISBN 978-90-04-40098-6 (paperback, set, 2019)
ISBN 978-90-04-40102-0 (paperback, vol. 1, 2019)
ISBN 978-90-04-40103-7 (paperback, vol. 2, 2019)
ISBN 978-90-04-40104-4 (paperback, vol. 3, 2019)
ISBN 978-90-04-35608-5 (hardback, set, 2018)
ISBN 978-90-04-36414-1 (e-book, vol. 1)
ISBN 978-90-04-36415-8 (e-book, vol. 2)
ISBN 978-90-04-36416-5 (e-book, vol. 3)

This book is printed on acid-free paper and produced in a sustainable manner.

Printed by Printforce, United Kingdom

Contents

VOLUME 3

Acknowledgements

We extend our deepest appreciation to Dr. Lawrence Conrad for his friendship, scholarly example, and leadership in the project through its first years. We would be badly remiss in not acknowledging his vital contribution, not only in helping to launch the project but, again, in guiding it through its first stages.

The original contributors included Drs. Camilla Adang and Lutz Richter-Bernberg, and we would thank both of them for their initial participation. Dr. Andrew Marsham—now a Reader in Classical Arabic Studies at the University of Cambridge—participated, as a doctoral candidate at the Oriental Institute, in our meetings at the University of Oxford. Our thanks go to him for keeping invaluable minutes of the meetings and in contributing to their organization. Dr. Hans Hinrich Biesterfeldt provided expert advice regarding the section on the Greeks in the *History*. Many colleagues, the majority in the fields of Arabic, Islamic, and Middle Eastern studies, responded over many years to numerous queries on H-Mideast-Medieval, via email, and in person. We are grateful to one and all and regret only that we cannot acknowledge each of these persons individually.

The editorial team wishes also to express deepest appreciation to the National Endowment for the Humanities for its support of this project. Our conviction is that this project reflects precisely the NEH's contribution to the intellectual and cultural life of the United States and, indeed, the global community, and at a moment in history when communication across cultural, religious and regional divisions is so pressingly important.

We also extend lasting thanks to Maurits van den Boogert, Pieter te Velde, and the staff of Brill Publishing, for their invaluable role in this project. Our thanks go also to Alan Hartley for meticulously proofreading the text, and to Jacqueline Pitchford for preparing the index.

Finally, to the contributors who remained with the project to its completion—Drs. Leila Asser, Paul Cobb, Elton Daniel, Fred Donner, Sidney Griffith, and Wadad Kadi—here, finally, are your contributions in print. Our appreciation to each of you can only fall short of what is due.

The Editors

If I might add a personal note, I am, first of all, deeply grateful to my three co-editors, Drs. Robinson, Rowson, and Fishbein. Each in turn contributed immeasurably to the completion of this project. Dr. Robinson, to whom I turned early on for support and ideas, has provided these on a consistent basis over the many years. He not only contributed one section of the translation of the *Taʾrīkh* but also served as a wise and generous host to our meetings at the Oriental Institute at the University of Oxford. Dr. Rowson has been a constant source of guidance, both on the editorial front and in grappling with myriad questions of Arabic translation. He also played a critical part in handling the trickiest section of the *Taʾrīkh*, Ibn Wāḍiḥ's account of the transmission of Greek-language material. And, without the participation of Dr. Fishbein, I very much doubt the project would have reached a successful conclusion. At several late and critical points in the project, he took on the translation of sections of the *Taʾrīkh* as well as the *Mushākala*. I also very much appreciate his part in translating the short but valuable anecdotes, attributed to Ibn Wāḍiḥ, from Ibn al-Dāya's *Mukāfaʾa*. His skills as editor, translator, and scholar of early Islamic history and letters inform every page of this project.

Lasting thanks as well to my colleagues in the Department of History at Miami University. I am especially grateful to Drs. Allen Winkler, Charlotte Goldy, Carla Pestana and Wietse de Boer—each of whom served in turn as chair of the department over the past two decades—and their patient backing for my work on this project. Dr. Andrew Cayton, who probably heard more about the project than he deserved, will forever be missed by us all.

Finally, the members of my family—Susan, Jeremiah and Katharine—will no doubt share my relief and astonishment that the project is finally complete. To Susan there is no expression of gratitude appropriate enough for these many years of encouragement, companionship, and love.

Matthew S. Gordon

List of Contributors

The Geography (*Kitāb al-Buldān*)
(Pagination Based on Leiden Edition of 1892)

	Contributor	Topics/Regions
232–308	Elton Daniel	Baghdad, Samarra, Iran and the East, governors of Khurāsān.
308–373	Paul M. Cobb	Iraq, Arabia, Syria, Egypt, North Africa, and al-Andalus

Fragments

Paul M. Cobb, Matthew S. Gordon, Michael Fishbein

The Book of the Adaptation of Men to Their Time and Their Dominant Characteristics in Every Age
(*Mushākalat al-nās li-zamānihim wa-mā yaglibu ʿalayhim fī kull ʿaṣr*)

Michael Fishbein

The History (*Taʾrīkh*)

	Contributor	Historical period/topics
		VOLUME I (ed. Leiden) (pagination based on the Houtsma [Leiden] edition)
2–89	Sidney H. Griffith	Adam, Old Testament Prophets, Israelites, Jesus, Ancient Near Eastern Kings.

(cont.)

	Contributor	Historical period/topics
90–106	Michael Fishbein	Kings of India.
106–204	Lutz Richter-Bernburg, Everett K. Rowson, Michael Fishbein	The Greeks, Greek and Roman Kings.
204–246	Lawrence I. Conrad	Kings of China, Egypt, North Africa, Ethiopia and Yemenite Kings of al-Ḥīra.
246–315	Lawrence I. Conrad, Michael Fishbein	Kinda War to the pre-Islamic Arabs.
	VOLUME II (ed. Leiden)	
2–98	Michael Fishbein	Introduction, the Prophet Muḥammad (to his son Ibrāhīm).
98–186	Fred Donner	The Prophet Muḥammad (cont.) and the Caliphs Abū Bakr and ʿUmar.
186–303	Wadad Kadi (al-Qāḍī)	The Caliphs ʿUthmān and ʿAlī, and the Umayyad Caliphate to Muʿāwiya II.
303–403	Chase F. Robinson	The Marwānid (Umayyad) Caliphs to Ibrāhīm ibn al-Walīd.
403	Matthew S. Gordon, Michael Fishbein	Ibrāhīm ibn al-Walīd
404–524	Layla Asser, Matthew S. Gordon	Marwān II (Umayyad Caliphate) to Hārūn al-Rashīd (ʿAbbāsid Caliphate)
524–625	Matthew S. Gordon	Al-Amīn to al-Muʿtamid (ʿAbbāsid Caliphate).

Introduction: The Yaʿqūbī Translation Project

Matthew S. Gordon

Given the early date of the works of Ibn Wāḍiḥ al-Yaʿqūbī (fl. late third/ninth century) and their remarkable historiographic value, the decision to translate them came easily.[1] The execution of the project, however, has been over two decades in the making. It is with relief, gratitude, and a bit of wonder that we bring it to fruition.

The Yaʿqūbī Translation Project began as correspondence in 1994 with Lawrence (Larry) Conrad, then at the Wellcome Institute in London. To my innocent proposal to translate al-Yaʿqūbī's *Taʾrīkh* (*History*), Dr. Conrad gently responded that even a seasoned Arabist would find it a daunting task. We soon decided to invite a small group of colleagues to take part in a collaborative project to translate all that survived of al-Yaʿqūbī's oeuvre. This includes not only the *Taʾrīkh*, but also his work of geography, the *Kitāb al-Buldān* (*The Book of Countries*), a short political essay, the *Mushākalat al-nās li-zamānihim* (*The Book of Adaptation of Men to Their Time*), and a set of short fragments scattered across various later medieval Arabic-language works. Dr. Conrad and I divided the texts into manageable sections and assigned them to our collaborators.

To kick start the project, we held three meetings, each in conjunction with the annual gathering of the Middle East Studies Association (1997, 1998, and 1999). Two further meetings of the editors and contributors followed in July 2001 and 2002; these were held in Oxford University, with financial support from the British Academy. In 2003, we were pleased to receive a generous five-year grant from the National Endowment for the Humanities.

Changes in editorial leadership occurred thereafter. Dr. Chase Robinson, who first joined the project as a contributor, agreed to become a co-editor in 2000. Following the departure of Dr. Conrad from the project in 2006, Dr. Everett Rowson agreed to replace him. Finally, in 2008, Dr. Michael Fishbein accepted our invitation to serve as copy editor, and subsequently assumed responsibility for the final draft of three sections of the *Taʾrīkh* as well as a new translation of the *Mushākala*. The completion of the project is due in largest measure to the contributions of Drs. Rowson and Fishbein in this later phase of the project.

---

1 I am grateful to Drs. Fishbein and Robinson for their close comments on a draft of this introduction.

 | DOI: 10.1163/9789004364141_002

The aim of the project was clearly stated from the start, that is, to serve two groups of readers. In the first group are scholars in related fields who, in most cases, are unable to read al-Yaʿqūbī in the original Arabic. These include historians of Late Antiquity; scholars whose work treats regions neighboring the premodern Islamic world (for example, Armenia and the Caucasus region, Central Asia, India, Saharan Africa, and southern Europe); and world historians, concerned as they are with broad, hemispheric trends. We also hope that the translation will benefit historians and other scholars conducting comparative study from outside the fields of Arabic and Islamic studies—for example, on the formation of dominant religious communities; the shaping and decline of empire; or the role played by complex urban centers in premodern history. Al-Yaʿqūbī's interests being so broad, we do not doubt that historians will find much to draw on from his writings.

The second group of readers consists of students of early Near Eastern and Islamic history. An increasing number of colleges and universities offer degree programs in Middle East and Islamic studies at the undergraduate and graduate levels. Many more offer courses in these areas within departments of history, political science, religious studies, and other fields. Those of us who teach Middle Eastern, Arab, and Islamic history rely on texts in translation (from Arabic as well as the many other languages of the Near East and Islamic worlds), but are often faced with the difficulty of locating material that is both compelling and accessible. Students often struggle with the ornate and intricate styles that are characteristic of much of early Arabic/Islamic prose. A virtue of al-Yaʿqūbī's writing is his direct, unadorned language; a well-annotated translation of his works should find a ready audience in our students.

Interest in the translation of al-Yaʿqūbī's writings was sparked in part by the eager welcome met by the translation of al-Ṭabarī's *History*, which was completed in 2007 and has become an invaluable resource for scholars and students alike.[2] We trust that the works of al-Yaʿqūbī—a slightly earlier contemporary whose approach and background contrast with those of al-Ṭabarī—will prove a useful complement.

Al-Yaʿqūbī and His Writings

Ibn Wāḍiḥ al-Yaʿqūbī appears only rarely in the Islamic biographical literature: a detailed account of his life cannot be written. Although no secure death

2 Please see the Bibliography for a full citation.

date can be established, it seems likely that he died shortly after 295/908. The biographical essay contained in this volume treats the available information, including invaluable references by Ibn Wāḍiḥ himself. Here it suffices to point out that al-Yaʿqūbī was of notable Iraqi birth and education, and that he spent much of his professional life in the employment of provincial governing families of the late third/ninth-century ʿAbbāsid empire. His own statements indicate that he worked in Armenia, perhaps at an early point in his career, and that he took up subsequently with the Ṭāhirid family in the Iranian province of Khurāsan. We have no direct evidence, but it seems that Ibn Wāḍiḥ then made his way to Egypt following the fall of the Ṭāhirids around 258/872. There he lent his skills to the administration of the Ṭūlūnid state (254–292/868–905), which was among the first autonomous regional dynasties to challenge the ʿAbbāsid state, founded roughly a century earlier.

The content and style of the *Taʾrīkh* and the *Kitāb al-Buldān* bespeak a busy life of travel and service on the part of a cosmopolitan scholar and imperial bureaucrat, an impression that is strengthened by indirect evidence contained in what was apparently an independent work on fragrances (the fragments of which are included in our translation). The two major works provide exceptional detail on matters provincial (for example, his accounts on late first/seventh and early second/eighth-century Armenia and third/ninth-century Egypt) and metropolitan (for example, his descriptions of early Baghdad and Samarra, the two capitals of the ʿAbbāsid empire). Our sense of the physical and socio-political fabric of the early Islamic Near East is enhanced immeasurably by his writings.

That later Muslim biographers say little about al-Yaʿqūbī likely relates to the early fate of his books: while scholars of subsequent generations made use of the *Buldān*—Ibn al-ʿAdīm in the seventh/thirteenth century is a case in point—Ibn Wāḍiḥ's *History* appears to have mostly fallen into oblivion; the meager manuscript tradition is discussed in the accompanying essay. This may have had to do with his sectarian identity. Al-Yaʿqūbī's religious views were clearly Shīʿite, but they seem to conform neither to the Imāmi Shīʿite tradition that would prevail later, nor to what would become the Zaydī Shīʿite tradition. Sean Anthony, in an essay published in *al-ʿUṣūr al-Wuṣṭā* (2016), argues convincingly that Ibn Wāḍiḥ likely held to a relatively hard-line theological view that was in conflict with a quietist, proto-Imāmi viewpoint then predominant in Iraqi cities.[3] Writing as he did before 'classical' Shīʿism crystallized, al-Yaʿqūbī held religious views that later Muslims likely found difficult to categorize.

3 For the full citation, please see the Bibliography in this volume.

Because his *History* is a digest that only rarely contains unique information, it may also be the case that it was considered expendable by scholars and scribes of the Arabic/Islamic historiographical tradition. Paradoxically, the limited circulation of his work may also have been a function of his cosmopolitanism: his geographical and historical coverage is as wide as his accounts of Islamic history can be selective and succinct. The breadth of his vision is clear from the *History* and *Geography*, as it is from his minor works, both preserved (the likely volume on fragrances and aromatics) and lost (a history of the Byzantines and an account of the Arab conquest of North Africa).

The *Taʾrīkh* (*History*)

The text, of which we possess two manuscripts, is a universal chronicle consisting of two parts: a pre-Islamic section covering a variety of empires and peoples that is primarily sequential in organization, and an Islamic-era section that tracks the history of the Islamic polity from the prophet Muḥammad's day until roughly 259/872–873.

Dr. Rowson discusses the two closely related manuscripts in the essay contained in this volume. Each—one from Cambridge, the other from Manchester—is missing the title page and introductory material; in its present form, each begins with Adam and Eve already on the scene, but it is safe to assume that the text originally began with Creation. It then treats the Patriarchs and Prophets of ancient Israel, followed by an account of Jesus and the Apostles. (Previous translations of the sections dealing with ancient Israel and Jesus are now obsolete in several respects.) Subsequent portions of the *History* treat Assyria, Babylon, and India; the Greek and Persian Empires, including valuable comments on the transmission of Greek philosophical, medical, and other texts; various other regions and their dominant communities (Turks, Chinese, Egyptians, Berbers, and Abyssinians); and, finally, a portion on the pre-Islamic Arabs that includes comments on the Arabs as the progeny of Abraham's son Ismāʿīl (Ishmael).

The presence of this material underscores the value of Ibn Wāḍiḥ's work to historians working in a variety of fields. For one thing, al-Yaʿqūbī does preserve unique material; for example, the Biblical passages appear to have come directly from then available Syriac texts. For another, the *History* reflects an ambitious cosmopolitan view of history. Nothing in what survives of the contemporaneous Christian world approaches the *History* in its command of ancient and late antique history; the quantity of direct quotations from Jewish, Christian and Greek texts is striking. And, from early medieval Islamic letters, only the work of ʿAlī ibn al-Ḥusayn al-Masʿūdī (d. c. 345/956), the well-known Baghdadi polymath, compares favorably with that of al-Yaʿqūbī in this regard.

The second half of the *History* contains a concise narrative of Islamic and Middle Eastern history, beginning with a biography of the Prophet Muḥammad and proceeding with his immediate successors (the so-called 'Rāshidūn' caliphs, a designation that does not occur, however, anywhere in these texts), followed by the Umayyad and ʿAbbāsid rulers to about 259/873. Throughout, al-Yaʿqūbī follows a fairly consistent scheme: he begins with each ruler's accession and (often) the horoscope for the date of accession, then provides a brief narrative of the major events of his reign; the circumstances of the caliph's death; a list of the major officials and religious scholars active during his reign; and a brief assessment of his character and male progeny. Ibn Wāḍiḥ's employment of horoscopes ought not be viewed as a bow to superstition; instead, it reflects—and, perhaps, champions—the broad cultural tastes of his still Late Antique readership.

As an example of caliphal history, there is nothing extraordinary about the work, although the author was certainly a gifted digester. But compared to those who followed him in this form—such later authors as Ibn al-ʿImrānī (d. 580/1184) and ʿAlī ibn Anjab ibn al-Sāʿī (d. 674/1276) can be cited among other medieval and premodern writers—he succeeds in covering an astonishing amount of political history. This is why the text ought to be so useful for students with little background in Islamic and Arab history: within a historiographic tradition that was frequently prolix and complex, the *History* delivers a coherent and concise narrative of the early Islamic period.

Ibn Wāḍiḥ distinguishes himself from other historians in a number of respects. As already suggested, he proposes a Shiʿite reading of Islamic history, which is made clear in his accounts of the Prophet's life and the First Civil War of 656–661, and especially so in his generous obituaries of the descendants of the Prophet's son-in-law and cousin, ʿAlī ibn Abī Ṭālib. History here, as elsewhere, both describes and prescribes. And, unlike most contemporaneous historians, al-Yaʿqūbī also dispenses with the chains of transmission and the multiple, overlapping and/or inconsistent accounts that are so characteristic of the prevailing traditionalist historiography, exemplified by al-Ṭabarī himself. The only gesture towards expertise and indication of his Islamic source material comes in a brief bibliography, which stands at the beginning of the Islamic section of the *Taʾrīkh*. The result is an altogether clearer authorial voice. Finally, we have already noted his broad vision of history and culture. A single example suffices: premodern Muslim learned men were no more comfortable with astronomy than were premodern rabbis, and thus al-Yaʿqūbī's inclusion of the caliphs' horoscopes suggests a readership beyond the religious elite. Topics such as these—the author's Shīʿite sympathies, his method, and intended audience—deserve further investigation.

The *Kitāb al-Buldān* (*Geography*)

As indicated by the available Arabic editions (Leiden, 1892, and Beirut, 1988), and a partial French translation by Gaston Wiet (Cairo, 1937), we possess only an incomplete version of the work.[4] S. Maqbul Ahmad and André Miquel have situated the text in the formative period of Arabic geographical scholarship.[5] Arab/Islamic geography, as a body of knowledge and praxis, emerged in the second/eighth century, and retained its vitality from that point on in all languages of the Islamic realm into the premodern period. The rise of geographical writing in Arabic is to be situated against the backdrop of the multivalent transmission of ancient Greek, Pahlavi, and Sanskrit writings. That process probably began, in the case of the Sanskrit texts, through Pahlavi, and in the case of the Greek, through Syriac. It did so in the late Umayyad and early ʿAbbāsid period—the middle decades of the second/eighth century—in large measure through patronage offered by the caliphal court.

Mathematical geography likely appeared first, with the translation and adaptation of Ptolemy's *Geography*. The development of a more practical or applied "administrative geography" can be tied to the concerns of ʿAbbāsid imperial governance. Ibn Wāḍiḥ's text is among the exemplars of this trend, along with the works of Ibn Khurdādhbih, al-Iṣṭakhrī, Ibn Ḥawqal, and al-Maqdisī (Muqaddasī). Of particular concern to Ibn Wāḍiḥ would have been to provide his fellow regional functionaries with the kind of information required to carry out their administrative duties. In this sense, the *Buldān* is properly described as an 'imperial' digest. Composed perhaps in the final decade or so of the third/ninth century, by which time the author may have been in residence in Egypt, it provides detailed (if formulaic) descriptions of the major towns and cities of the contemporary ʿAbbāsid Empire and the chief features of the principal routes linking one population center to the next. The text comments on distances; agricultural infrastructure, production, and yield; local crafts and products; and the religious and ethnic composition of local populations.

The *Buldān* thus offers much practical data, and Ibn Wāḍiḥ's eye for detail is impressive. To cite one example, his description of Samarra (the ʿAbbāsid

4 I wish to thank Dr. Jean-Charles Ducène for his helpful comments on al-Yaʿqūbī as geographer.

5 For full citations, please see the Bibliography in this volume.

capital for much of the third/ninth century) reads as if one were led by its author on a walking tour of the city, this at a fairly late point in its history as the imperial hub (and at a point when the ruling dynasty was facing crushing fiscal and political challenges). He provides a brief history of the city's foundation and comments on the distribution and recipients of land grants that gave rise to its military and urban character. He also identifies the location of the houses of Samarra's elite families; the size and location of its major cantonments; the city's main markets, bathhouses, and mosques; and, finally, its annual tax yield. Several generations of archaeologists who have worked on the ruins of ʿAbbāsid Samarra testify to the value of al-Yaʿqūbī's account. The *Buldān* begins with a no less valuable description of Baghdad, the original ʿAbbāsid center, and, within a few years of its founding, the cultural and commercial axis of the early Islamic world.

Three manuscripts of the *Buldān* are known, as Dr. Rowson points out. The work was translated into French by Gaston Wiet in 1937 as *Les Pays*, but a new translation is in order. Wiet's version of the text is occasionally inaccurate, and, published early in the previous century, the volume is difficult to find. It is also out of date: seventy years of research on Islamic urbanism are behind us and the archaeological record alone sheds new light on the text. The version proposed here will provide the full text in English translation, additional fragments discovered in other early Arabic texts, and a more complete annotation than provided by Wiet. Because the *Geography* sets the scene for some of the events narrated by the *History*, the two texts are complementary.

The Mushākala (*The Adaptation of Men*)

The title of the essay, the shortest of al-Yaʿqūbī's extant works, suggests a work of socio-political theory. It consists, in fact, of a collection of pithy anecdotes arranged chronologically by caliphal reign. The intent seems to be to highlight the conduct and tastes of the caliphs, beginning with Abū Bakr, as a model for their clients and followers, and, indeed, the wider Islamic community—for the better, when people adopted their virtues, and for the worse, when people embraced their vices.

In some sense, it is a work of panegyric: the dynasts set the style and tone for imperial society. William Millward, in his treatment of the work, noted its resemblance to the type of early Arab/Islamic letters known as the *Awāʾil* literature, that is, a genre that concerns itself with 'firsts'—archetypal or prototypical examples of deeds and conduct. Millward's full and still useful translation appeared in the *Journal of the American Oriental Society* (1964). The decision to retranslate the essay here was informed principally by the wish to provide a more accessible translation consistent with the style and level of annotation of the other works of al-Yaʿqūbī included in this project.

Ibn Wāḍiḥ al-Yaʿqūbī: A Biographical Sketch

Sean Anthony and Matthew S. Gordon

Historians of the early Islamic world have long recognized the importance of the historical and geographical works of Ibn Wāḍiḥ al-Yaʿqūbī. The earliest printed editions were published in Europe in the latter half of the nineteenth century. The Arabic text of al-Yaʿqūbī's *Taʾrīkh* (*History*) was first edited by Martijn Theodor Houtsma and published by Brill in 1883.[1] Several reprints appeared in the Arab world after the publication of Houtsma's edition, the two most widely used published in Beirut (Dār Ṣādir, 1960) and Najaf (al-Maktaba al-Ḥaydariyya, 1964). The incomplete Arabic text of al-Yaʿqūbī's geographical work, the *Kitāb al-Buldān* (*The Book of Countries*), was edited by M. J. de Goeje, with quotations from fragments discovered in other works.[2] De Goeje published the edition in 1892, also with Brill, in volume VII of his groundbreaking series of Arabic geographical treatises, the *Bibliotheca Geographorum Arabicorum* (BGA).[3] The *Taʾrīkh* and the *Kitāb al-Buldān* remain indispensable staples of the source material utilized in the modern study of Islamic history.[4]

The works of Ibn Wāḍiḥ date to the third/ninth century and, therefore, represent some of the earliest historical and geographical writings to survive in Arabic literature. Not only does his corpus contain early specimens of these categories of Arabic writing, it is also of an exceptional quality. His chronicle endeavors to do no less than cover the entire stretch of human history, from the creation of Adam and Eve to the dramas of early Islamic history and the political fortunes of the ʿAbbāsid caliphate and the luminaries who served the

1 *Ibn Wāḍiḥ qui dicitur al-Jaʿqūbī Historiae*, 2 vols. For a discussion of the manuscripts of this work, see Everett Rowson's essay in this volume and T. M. Johnstone, "An Early Manuscript," 189–195.

2 The present translation of the work includes two new sets of fragments not identified by de Goeje.

3 De Goeje had already published portions of the *Buldān* as part of his Ph.D. thesis (Leiden University, 1860). See Jan Just Witkam, "Michael Jan de Goeje," 4. The following year, however, the first edition of the *Buldān* was published by T. G. J. Juynboll, *Kitābo'l-boldān* (*Sive librum regionum*) (Leiden: Brill, 1861). All citations of the *Buldān* hereafter refer to de Goeje's edition published in the BGA.

4 Less influential is al-Yaʿqūbī's brief treatise, *Mushākalat al-nās li-zamānihim*, which was discovered and edited by William G. Millward (Beirut: Dār al-Kitāb al-Jadīd, 1962). Millward produced a translation of the work in 1964 ("The Adaptation of Men"). Michael Fishbein's new translation appears in this volume.

 | DOI: 10.1163/9789004364141_003

dynasty in his own day. If his corpus is relatively small compared to the writings of his peers, among them the historians al-Balādhurī (d. 279/892) and al-Ṭabarī (d. 310/923), it is rarely derivative.

And al-Yaʿqūbī's voice is distinct. Unlike al-Ṭabarī, for example, a paragon of early Sunnī historiography, al-Yaʿqūbī in his chronicle reflects a worldview that modern scholars have occasionally characterized as recognizably Shiʿite. His work, however, defies such facile sectarian categorization.[5] A keen observer of ʿAbbāsid society, al-Yaʿqūbī offers penetrating and discerning descriptions of the political, cultural, and geographical landscape of his own era. His is the perspective of a man whose ken is the endlessly fascinating, and often perilous, world of the ʿAbbāsid-era bureaucrat and writer.

Sadly, despite the significance of his work, there is little that can be known for certain about al-Yaʿqūbī and his life. His family history and personal biography have long been recognized as difficult, if not impossible, to reconstruct with certainty. Prior attempts by modern historians to do so have been characterized by frequent missteps, as recent scholarship has made clear.[6] So, for example, the statements that he was born in Baghdad and that he spent his childhood in Armenia appear to be little more than informed guesses.[7]

It would be best to begin by letting Ibn Wāḍiḥ speak for himself. In a rare and fragmentary autobiographical note that begins his *Kitāb al-Buldān*, he gives us our best insight into his life and the sort of experience that shaped his work. He represents himself as follows:

> When I was in the prime of youth, possessed of an adventurous spirit and a sharp mind, I took an interest in reports about countries and about the distance from one country to another; for I had traveled since childhood, and my travels had continued uninterruptedly and had taken me to distant places. So whenever I met someone from those countries, I asked him about his homeland and its major city[8] ... Then I verified

5 The question is addressed in more detail in S. W. Anthony, "Was Ibn Wāḍiḥ al-Yaʿqūbī a Shiʿite Historian?"

6 See Elton Daniel, "Al-Yaʿqūbī and Shiʿism Reconsidered," 209–231, and Anthony, "Was Ibn Wāḍiḥ al-Yaʿqūbī a Shiʿite Historian?"

7 The first statement appears to have originated with Gaston Wiet. See the introduction to his French translation of the *Kitāb al-Buldān* (*Les Pays*), viii, xvi. It is repeated by Muhammad Qasim Zaman in his article on al-Yaʿqūbī in the *EI*². The second comment, regarding Armenia, was perhaps first made by Carl Brockelmann: see his brief comments on al-Yaʿqūbī in the *Geschichte der arabischen Litteratur* (GAL), 2nd edition, 226–227.

8 De Goeje read the Arabic term as *miṣr*—understood here in the sense of administrative

> everything he told me with someone I could trust, seeking assistance by questioning men of one nationality after another until I had asked an enormous number of people during the pilgrimage season and at other times, from both eastern and western lands. I wrote down their reports and related their stories.[9]

Al-Yaʿqūbī states all of this, however, without informing his readers of the trajectory of these journeys or where he began them. His comments suggest a figure who was curious, highly literate, and well-travelled, but offer little else. It certainly helps al-Yaʿqūbī's case that the contents of the *Taʾrīkh* and the *Buldān* reflect a life's work of this kind. His accounts of contemporary cities and monuments stand out as among the most vivid extant descriptions in the Arabic geographical literature. A striking example is his description of the recently founded caliphal capital at Samarra and its expansion in the reign of al-Mutawakkil (r. 232–247/847–861): modern archaeology has largely affirmed the accuracy of much of his account of the palatial city.[10]

The small amount of additional information on Ibn Wāḍiḥ derives from two sources: first, the accounts of other historians, geographers, and scholars who cite his work or (far more rarely) write about him; and, second, what can reasonably be inferred from a close reading of his own extant writings. Each of these sources poses distinct challenges of interpretation, but reading them carefully in aggregate suggests the basic outlines of his life.

The longest biographical notice for al-Yaʿqūbī appears in the *Muʿjam al-udabāʾ* by Yāqūt al-Ḥamawī (d. 626/1229), a biographical dictionary of Arabic belletrists and authors of a variety of backgrounds. Yāqūt wrote the entry almost entirely from information transmitted by a predecessor whose own text no longer survives, the Egyptian historian Abū ʿUmar al-Kindī (d. 350/961). The entry is exceedingly laconic. It includes al-Yaʿqūbī's name and lineage (*nasab*); notes that he was a client (*mawlā*) of the Banū Hāshim (the clan of Quraysh to which both the Prophet and the ʿAbbāsid caliphs belonged); lists select titles from his oeuvre; and records his death as taking place in the year 284/897.[11]

---

center—but the context suggests that the original might have read *mudun*, the Arabic plural of "city."

9 Al-Yaʿqūbī, *Buldān*, 232–233.

10 Alastair Northedge, *Historical Topography*, 29–30, 267–273. Northedge suggests that al-Yaʿqūbī resided in Samarra for only a limited time, perhaps the 860s, and knew the city mostly in a private capacity.

11 Yāqūt al-Ḥamawī, *Muʿjam al-udabāʾ*, 2:557.

Yāqūt also refers to him as *al-akhbārī*, indicating that he was known as an historian (a purveyor of historical reports, or *akhbār*), and calls him *al-'Abbāsī*, revealing that he was not merely a client of the Banū Hāshim but also a client of the ruling caliphal house, the 'Abbāsids.

Yāqūt attributes the following works to Ibn Wāḍiḥ, adding that he authored many others as well: a large book called *Kitāb al-Ta'rīkh* (*The History*); a single volume called *Kitāb Asmā' al-buldān* (*The Names of Countries*); a small book called *Kitāb Fī akhbār al-umam al-sālifa* (*Stories of Nations Past*); and *Kitāb Mushākalat al-nās li-zamānihim* (*The Adaptation of Men to Their Times*). Arguably, all these works can be regarded as extant in some fashion, especially if one regards the *Kitāb Fī akhbār al-umam al-sālifa* as referring to the first volume of the work known today as *Ta'rīkh al-Ya'qūbī* inasmuch as it deals with pre-Islamic history.

Yāqūt's entry is our best source on al-Ya'qūbī's life. Unfortunately, it seems to err on at least one count: the date of Ibn Wāḍiḥ's death. Citations of al-Ya'qūbī's poetry on the fall of the Ṭūlūnid dynasty of Egypt (see below) and his own reference to the 'Abbāsid caliph al-Muktafī (r. 289–295/902–908) prove that he must have lived beyond the latter's death in 295/908.[12] Yāqūt, perhaps, is not entirely to blame for botching the death date, as he derives it from his source, the Egyptian historian al-Kindī. The root of the error appears to be confusion between Ibn Wāḍiḥ and a similarly named figure who appears in biographical dictionaries of the scholars of Prophetic reports (*ḥadīth*). These works record a minor Egyptian scholar named Abū Ja'far Aḥmad b. Isḥāq b. Wādiḥ b. 'Abd al-Ṣamad b. Wāḍiḥ al-'Assāl ('the honey merchant'). He, too, is described as a client (*mawlā*) of Quraysh and as having lived and died in third/ninth-century Egypt. The same works also report the honey merchant's death date as falling in Ṣafar 284/March–April 897—a date matching the death date that Yāqūt records for al-Ya'qūbī exactly.[13]

The biographical literature places *this* Aḥmad b. Isḥāq b. Wāḍiḥ al-'Assāl squarely in the orbit of contemporary Egyptian *ḥadīth* scholars. He appears, for example, as a minor *ḥadīth* scholar and authority in the works of al-Ṭabarānī (260–360/873–970), as having transmitted traditions from the Egyptian scholar

12 On the Ṭūlūnid references, see Wiet, *Les Pays*, viii; Ḥusayn 'Āṣī, *al-Ya'qūbī*, 50–51; Daniel, "Al-Ya'qūbī and Shi'ism Reconsidered," 209 and n. 2. The verses are treated in greater detail below. On the references to al-Muktafī, see al-Rāghib al-Iṣfahānī, *Muḥāḍarāt al-udabā'*, 2:534.

13 Al-Sam'ānī, *al-Ansāb*, 9:291 (citing the *Kitāb Ghurabā'* of the Egyptian scholar Ibn Yūnus al-Ṣadafī, d. 347/958), and al-Dhahabī, *Ta'rīkh al-Islām*, 6:668.

Saʿīd b. al-Ḥakam b. Abī Maryam (d. 224/839)[14] and Ḥāmid b. Yaḥyā al-Balkhī (d. 242/857), a scholar who resided in Tarsus but who had a large number of Egyptian students.[15] Aḥmad b. Isḥāq b. Wāḍiḥ al-ʿAssāl also makes scattered appearances as a *ḥadīth* transmitter in the works of the Andalusian scholar Ibn ʿAbd al-Barr (d. 463/1071). The latter transmits these traditions from the Egyptian scholar ʿAbdallāh b. Jaʿfar b. al-Ward (d. 351/362),[16] who cites Aḥmad b. Isḥāq b. Wāḍiḥ as an authority for reports from Abū Dāwūd al-Sijistānī (d. 275/889), the compiler of the *Sunan*, the famous Sunnī *ḥadīth* collection.[17] The impression left by these references is that Ibn Wāḍiḥ al-ʿAssāl—the honey merchant—was a minor *ḥadīth* transmitter known locally in Egyptian scholarly circles. But is he to be identified with al-Yaʿqūbī, the historian and geographer? There is good reason *not* to do so, but it requires us to broaden the scope of our analysis.

A method that modern historians use in gleaning further biographical details about al-Yaʿqūbī relies on the scattered references to his writings in the works of later medieval authors. Viewed collectively, these texts strongly recommend against identifying the author of the so-called *Taʾrīkh al-Yaʿqūbī* with the honey merchant. These citations indicate that, although our Ibn Wāḍiḥ certainly lived and worked in Egypt in the late third/ninth century, he was unlikely to have been of Egyptian origin like the honey merchant. The citations also indicate that the chronological scope of Ibn Wāḍiḥ's life makes a death date of 284/897 for the author of the *Buldān* and the *Taʾrīkh* untenable.

In reading these later references, two points are to be kept in mind. First, few medieval Muslim scholars seem to have read al-Yaʿqūbī's chronicle; citations of the *Taʾrīkh* are rare. The earliest confirmed citations of this kind appear in a fifth/eleventh-century work, *Kitāb al-Dhakhāʾir wa l-tuḥaf* (*The Book of Gifts and Rare Treasures*),[18] and in a treatise on Qurʾānic exegesis by the theologian al-Shahrastānī (d. 548/1153), who cites al-Yaʿqūbī's sectarian account of ʿAlī b. Abī Ṭālib's collection of the Qurʾān.[19] By contrast, scholars such as Ibn al-ʿAdīm

14 Al-Mizzī, *Tahdhīb al-Kamāl*, 10:393. Cf. these traditions in al-Ṭabarānī, *al-Muʿjam al-kabīr*, 2:73; 7:70; 9:99; 10:26–27, 191, and 12:47, 91.

15 Al-Ṭabarānī, *al-Muʿjam al-ṣaghīr*, 1:25; cf. al-Mizzī, *Tahdhīb*, 5:325–357, for Ḥāmid b. Yaḥyā's Egyptian pupils.

16 Originally from Baghdad, Ibn al-Ward settled in Egypt later in life; see al-Dhahabī, *Siyar aʿlām*, 16:39.

17 Ibn ʿAbd al-Barr, *al-Tamhīd*, 7:142.

18 Ibn al-Zubayr, *Kitāb al-Dhakhāʾir*, 245 (§359) = *Book of Gifts and Rarities*, tr. al-Qaddūmī, 225; cf. al-Yaʿqūbī, *Tārīkh*, 1:24–25.

19 al-Shahrastānī, *Mafātīḥ al-asrār*, 1:24 ff., calling the work *Taʾrīkh Ibn Wāḍiḥ*. Cf. al-Yaʿqūbī,

(d. 660/1262), al-Qazwīnī (d. 682/1283), and al-Maqrīzī (d. 845/1442) cite al-Yaʿqūbī's geographical work, *Kitāb al-Buldān*, far more frequently.[20]

The discrepancy—the difference in the number of times that medieval scholars refer to al-Yaʿqūbī's *Taʾrīkh* and the *Kitāb al-buldān* respectively—raises a second important point. The modern convention of referring to the author of these works as 'al-Yaʿqūbī' is simply that—a modern convention. The designation derives from the version of his name that appears on the colophon of the extant manuscripts of his works. Medieval authors who do cite al-Yaʿqūbī call him by many names: Ibn Wādiḥ, Ibn Abī Yaʿqūb, Aḥmad b. Wāḍiḥ, and Aḥmad al-Kātib.[21] The last of these versions of his name is very helpful: the term *kātib* indicates that he was known to be a secretarial scribe or bureaucrat by profession and, hence, a member of the cosmopolitan secular elite of ʿAbbāsid society.

At no point do medieval sources refer to al-Yaʿqūbī as "the honey merchant" (*al-ʿassāl*). Most notably, al-Yaʿqūbī's contemporary and fellow geographer Ibn al-Faqīh al-Hamadhānī (d. c. 289–290/902–903), cites the author of the *Kitāb al-Buldān* as 'Ibn Wādiḥ al-Iṣfahānī,' indicating that the author was at one point in his career known for being of Iranian rather than Egyptian extraction.[22] Elton Daniel has dismissed Ibn al-Faqīh's reference as isolated, but in fact, it is not. Abū Manṣūr al-Thaʿālibī (d. 429/1039), a fifth/eleventh-century Arab scholar, includes "Aḥmad b. Wāḍiḥ" in a long list of literary elites who hailed from Iṣfahān.[23] Moreover, if Ibn Wāḍiḥ indeed hailed from Iṣfahān, this would

Taʾrīkh, 2:152–154, and Th. Nöldeke et al., *The History of the Qurʾān*, 220 (2:9–11). Earlier citations of the *Taʾrīkh* might be found in the Leiden manuscript of an anonymous history of the ʿAbbāsids called *Dikhr Banī ʿAbbās wa-ẓuhūrihim* (Leiden Or. 14.023), which cites al-Yaʿqūbī's *Taʾrīkh* directly. See al-Sāmarrāʾī, "Hal kataba l-Tanūkhī kitāban fī l-Taʾrīkh?" 531. For a description of the manuscript, see Jan Just Witkam, 15:11.

20 Ibn al-ʿAdīm, *Bughyat al-ṭalab*, 1:88, 107–108, 123, 141, 150, 156, 173, 219, 263, 265, 478; al-Qazwīnī, *Āthār al-bilād*, 187 (citing al-Yaʿqūbī, *Buldān*, 333–334). See Daniel, "Al-Yaʿqūbī and Shiʿism Reconsidered," 216 n. 43 for references to al-Yaʿqūbī's *Kitāb al-Buldān* in al-Maqrīzī's *Khiṭaṭ*.

21 For these variants, see the material collected by de Goeje in BGA, 7:361–373.

22 Al-Hamadhānī, *Mukhtaṣar Kitāb al-buldān*, in de Goeje, ed., BGA, 5:290–292; cf. Yāqūt, *Muʿjam al-buldān*, 1:222. The passage displays the same familiarity with the pre-Islamic history of the Persian Sasanid dynasty that characterizes al-Yaʿqūbī's chronicle. Shiʿite sources know of an Aḥmad b. Yaʿqūb al-Iṣfahānī, but he is a figure of the mid-fourth/tenth century who died in 354/965 and, therefore, too late to be identified with the author of al-Yaʿqūbī's chronicle. See al-Khaṭīb al-Baghdādī, *Taʾrīkh Madīnat al-Salām*, 6:479–480; al-Majlisī, *Biḥār al-anwār*, 45:105, 88:267, and 92:225.

23 Al-Thaʿālibī, *Yatīmat al-dahr*, 3:299 (citing the lost *Kitāb Iṣfahān* of Ḥamza b. al-Ḥusayn al-Iṣfahānī, d. between 350/961 and 360/970).

accord well with his suggested familiarity with the Ṭāhirid dynasty of Iran. This familiarity is attested, however, only in a single, internal reference: al-Yaʿqūbī states in his *History*, referring to a document—the well-known letter written by Ṭāhir b. al-Ḥusayn on the execution of the caliph al-Amīn in 198/813—that he intended to place the letter in "a separate book."[24]

The reference is, in fact, only one of very few indications of the locations in which al-Yaʿqūbī apparently lived and worked outside of Egypt and North Africa (see below). A second reference occurs in the fragmentary passages that de Goeje collected for the *BGA*, although he opted only to provide the opening phrase.[25] The passage derives, again, from al-Hamadhānī. It places our author in Armenia at some undisclosed point in time:

> Aḥmad b. Wāḍiḥ al-Iṣbahānī mentioned that he resided for a long time in the land of Armenia, worked as a secretary for a number of its kings and governors, and had never seen a land more abounding in amenities or richer in wildlife than it.[26]

It is worth pointing out that, while such references come to us directly from Ibn Wāḍiḥ, none are at all clear. The one reference says nothing of where he might have worked for the Ṭāhirids, if, in fact, he did: he might well have done so in Iraq, where members of the illustrious family held key administrative positions.[27] The reference regarding Armenia is more helpful, although it seems impossible to date his sojourn in the province or identify the officials under whom he served. It is also difficult to understand what is meant therein by "kings": did al-Yaʿqūbī provide services to local notables and in what capacity? It is very difficult to know.

The role of Egypt in al-Yaʿqūbī's career seems clearer; the indications, including citations of his writings, suggest a long tenure there during the latter portion of his life. These indications can be subtle. For instance, the early sections of the *History* rely on an early Arabic translation of a Christian work, *The Cave of Treasures*. The Arabic translation of the work was also utilized by the Cop-

24 Al-Yaʿqūbī, *Taʾrīkh*, 2:537.

25 *BGA*, 7:314.

26 Al-Hamadhānī, *Mukhtaṣar Kitāb al-buldān*, 290–291. Carl Brockelmann's comment on our author's childhood in the province, noted earlier, occurs in his entry on al-Yaʿqūbī in *EI*[1]. It is repeated in later biographical sketches: see Lawrence I. Conrad, "al-Yaʿqūbī," 12:717; Camilla Adang, *Muslim Writers*, 36; and Muhammad Qasim Zaman in *EI*[2], s.v. al-Yaʿḳūbī.

27 See the article by C. E. Bosworth in *EI*[2], s.v. Ṭāhirids.

tic historian, Eutychius of Alexandria (d. 940 CE), a fact that points to the two authors sharing a common Egyptian milieu.[28]

Other indications, especially his familiarity with the Ṭūlūnids, the semi-autonomous dynasty of late third/ninth-century Egypt, would seem more telling. The Egyptian official and historian, Ibn al-Dāya (fl. early fourth/tenth century), knows al-Yaʿqūbī as an administrator of the land-tax (*kharāj*) for Aḥmad b. Ṭūlūn in Barqa (modern-day al-Marj in northeastern Libya) during the rebellion of Ibn Ṭūlūn's son al-ʿAbbās in 265/878.[29] The reference is our clearest indication that he earned his livelihood as a member of the secretarial class. Al-Yaʿqūbī also provides a detailed entry on Barqa in his geographical work, a fact that lends Ibn al-Dāya's assertion more credence.

Additional evidence suggests that al-Yaʿqūbī fondly remembered at least some moments of his tenure with the Ṭūlūnids and that he ultimately lived to see the dynasty's collapse. The historian al-Maqrīzī (d. 845/1442) ends his account of the Ṭūlūnid dynasty with an anecdote about how, on the night of ʿĪd al-Fiṭr in 292 AH (5 August 905), Aḥmad[30] b. Abī Yaʿqūb found himself pondering what had befallen the Ṭūlūnids. In his sleep, he heard a spectral voice (*hātif*) declare, "Kingship, glory, and glamor vanished with the Ṭūlūnids' departure (*dhahaba l-mulk wa-l-tamalluk wa-l-zīna lammā maḍā Banū Ṭūlūn*)."[31] These sentiments towards the Ṭūlūnids are affirmed in several lines of poetry that an earlier Egyptian historian, al-Kindī, attributes to al-Yaʿqūbī in his *Kitāb al-Wulāt*:[32]

If you would know the grandeur of their kingdom,
  turn aside and enjoy the Great Square's green expanse.[33]
Behold these palaces, what they contained;
  delight your eyes with the beauty of that garden.
But ponder well: a lesson lies there, too,
  that tells you of the fickle ways of Time.

---

28 Sidney Griffith, *The Bible in Arabic*, 186.

29 Ibn Saʿīd, *al-Mughrib fī ḥulā l-Maghrib*, 122: *kāna yatawallā kharāj Barqa.*

30 Reading "Aḥmad" for "Muḥammad" in the printed text, a reading supported by al-Kindī's *Kitāb al-Wulāt* cited below.

31 Al-Maqrīzī, *al-Mawāʿiẓ wa-l-iʿtibār fī dhikr al-khiṭaṭ* (ed. London), 1:2, 112 and n. 1.

32 Al-Kindī, *Kitāb al-Wulāt*, 250.

33 The Great Square (*al-Maydān*) is probably to be located in al-Qaṭāʾiʿ, the new city north of al-Fusṭāṭ founded by Ibn Ṭūlūn to be the seat of government. See al-Balawī, *Sīrat Aḥmad b. Ṭūlūn*, 54.

The evocative call of these verses to ponder the urban topography of al-Fusṭāṭ under the Ṭūlūnid dynasty—and, specifically, it seems, the Ṭūlūnid center at al-Qaṭāʾiʿ—speaks to the authenticity of their attribution, inasmuch as they mirror the rich depictions of urban landscapes in the *Kitāb al-Buldān*. Yet, they reveal more, too, about al-Yaʿqūbī's attitudes towards the fortunes of the Ṭūlūnids in Egypt. If, at first, nostalgic for the glory days of the Ṭūlūnids, by the poem's end al-Yaʿqūbī seems to welcome the ʿAbbāsid assault that brought the Ṭūlūnid reign to an end. On this ʿAbbāsid victory, he subsequently declares:[34]

> Egypt, like a bride, was escorted to the house of Prophethood and Guidance,[35]
> and torn away from Satan's partisans.

The poem's seemingly contradictory turn against the Ṭūlūnids, and the effort to extol the ʿAbbāsids, has confused modern scholars.[36] The volte-face against the Ṭūlūnids may reflect a desire on al-Yaʿqūbī's part to find acceptance and patronage with the caliphal family to whom his ancestors had long been attached.

The laudatory manner in which Ibn Wāḍiḥ describes the ʿAbbāsids as "the house of Prophethood and Guidance" brings us to another aspect of his biography, one that is often misrepresented: his family's multi-generational attachment to the ʿAbbāsid dynasty and his purportedly 'Shiʿite' take on Islamic history. The 'Shiʿism' intended here refers to a commitment to the descendants of the Prophet's household and his clan, the Hāshimites, seen as possessing a unique claim to the sacral leadership of the Islamic community, in major part because of their kinship with the Prophet. Al-Yaʿqūbī is quoted directly, stating that his grandfather was a slave-client (*mawlā*) of the ʿAbbāsid caliph al-Manṣūr,[37] so his connection to the ʿAbbāsid house appears certain. His family, in fact, seems to have served the dynasty in a bureaucratic capacity over at least three generations, a fact likely reflected in the itineracy to which al-Yaʿqūbī seems to refer in the passage quoted earlier.

There are further indications of his abiding interest in the Hāshimites that could be broadly construed as rooted in a pious reverence for the Prophet's clan and its descendants. The Shiʿite historian, Abū l-Ḥasan al-Masʿūdī (d. 345/956),

34 Ibid. Cf. the article by M. Gordon in *EI*², s.v. Ṭūlūnids, and Thierry Bianquis, "Autonomous Egypt," 107–108.

35 That is, the ʿAbbāsids, as related to the family of the Prophet.

36 See, for example, Hassan, *Les Tulunides*, 272–273.

37 Ibn al-Dāya, *al-Mukāfaʾa*, 66.

lists among the sources for his massive *Murūj al-dhahab* a certain *Kitāb al-Taʾrīkh* of one Aḥmad b. [Abī?] Yaʿqūb al-Miṣrī. The text, he says, "concerns the stories of the ʿAbbāsids" (*fī akhbār al-ʿAbbāsiyyīn*).[38] It is tempting to view this as a reference to al-Yaʿqūbī's extant chronicle. Indeed, Houtsma, the chronicler's first editor, succumbed to the temptation, identifying al-Yaʿqūbī's *History* as precisely the work cited by al-Masʿūdī.[39]

But the evidence works against Houtsma. First, the work that modern scholars known as *Taʾrīkh al-Yaʿqūbī* is by no means so narrow that one would characterize it as primarily about the ʿAbbāsids—al-Yaʿqūbī's chronicle is a universal, not a dynastic, history. The ninth/fifteenth-century Egyptian historian al-Maqrīzī also knows of a certain Aḥmad ibn Abī Yaʿqūb al-Kātib who composed a *Kitāb al-Buldān* and "a book on the history of Hāshimites, which is large (*kitāb fī taʾrīkh al-hāshimiyyīn wa-huwa kabīr*)."[40] This hypothesis finds further confirmation in the fact that the fourth/tenth-century historian Ibn al-Dāya includes extensive quotes that are likely to be from the same history mentioned by al-Masʿūdī and al-Maqrīzī.[41] None of Ibn al-Dāya's quotations from what appears, in other words, to have been a specific work by al-Yaʿqūbī on the ʿAbbāsids, resembles any passage found in his extant *History* either in content or style. The latter work mostly adopts a detached and economical style of narrative prose; the passages quoted by Ibn al-Dāya, by contrast, are often anecdotal vignettes and intimate portrayals of episodes in the ʿAbbāsid court. The book on the ʿAbbāsids would thus appear to be no longer extant.

The quotations of al-Yaʿqūbī recorded by Ibn al-Dāya are an underutilized resource for mapping al-Yaʿqūbī's family history. A number of these passages ultimately rely on the testimony of al-Yaʿqūbī's ancestor (*jidd*): Wāḍiḥ the *mawlā* of the ʿAbbāsid caliph al-Manṣūr. Because so much misinformation exists about this Wāḍiḥ in the secondary literature, one must first understand

38 Al-Masʿūdī, *Murūj al-dhahab*, 1:16.

39 See the preface to Houtsma's edition of the *Historiae* (Histories), 1:vi. Houtsma, realizing that al-Yaʿqūbī's *History* could not be described as primarily about the ʿAbbāsids, but intent nonetheless on showing that al-Masʿūdī was indeed referring to al-Yaʿqūbī's *History*, argued that al-Masʿūdī somehow mangled the title, which, so Houtsma argued, originally was *Taʾrīkh* [*al-Yaʿqūbī*] *al-ʿAbbāsī* (The History of/by al-Yaʿqūbī the ʿAbbāsid, i.e., the client of the ʿAbbāsids), turning it, by "lapse of memory," into *Taʾrīkh al-ʿAbbāsiyyīn* (The History of the ʿAbbāsids) and then into *Taʾrīkh fī akhbār al-ʿAbbāsiyyīn*.

40 Al-Maqrīzī, *Kitab al-Muqaffā al-kabīr*, 1:738.

41 See Ibn Dāya, *Mukāfaʾa*, 45–48, 61–62, 66, 83–85, 119–120, 144–145; Ibn ʿAsākir, *Taʾrīkh madīnat Dimashq*, 68:209.

who this Wāḍiḥ was *not* in order to arrive at a more precise understanding of who he actually was.

Al-Yaʿqūbī's ancestor, Wāḍiḥ, is certainly *not* the same person as another *mawlā* named Wāḍiḥ who briefly ruled Egypt as governor in 162/779.[42] This notorious Wādiḥ, known as Wāḍiḥ al-Maskīn (the Destitute), was a slave-client (*mawlā*) of the ʿAbbāsid prince Ṣāliḥ b. al-Manṣūr and head of the later ʿAbbāsid postal network (*al-barīd*) in Egypt. Chroniclers often denounce this Wāḍiḥ al-Maskīn as a "vile Shiʿite (*rāfiḍī khabīth*)," and he is always reviled as such in accounts that relate the aid he rendered to the ʿAlid rebel Idrīs b. ʿAbdallāh upon his escape from ʿAbbāsid pursuers to the distant Maghrib in 169/785. For his perfidy, Wādiḥ al-Maskīn was beheaded and crucified either by the caliph Mūsā al-Hādī (r. 169–170/785–786),[43] or Hārūn al-Rashīd (r. 170–193/786–809) soon after his accession to the caliphate.[44] As Daniel demonstrates,[45] this Wāḍiḥ turns out to have been a eunuch (*khaṣī*) and, hence, is unlikely to have been Ibn Wāḍiḥ's ancestor.[46]

Al-Yaʿqūbī mentions nothing, in his extant works, about Wāḍiḥ al-Maskīn's involvement in the escape of the fugitive Idrīs from the ʿAbbāsids. He does mention, however, a Wāḍiḥ who was a client (*mawlā*) of the ʿAbbāsid dynasty. In the past, scholars have assumed that al-Yaʿqūbī glossed over Wāḍiḥ's misdeeds in Egypt because he was identical with his ancestor, a family member, and thus wished not to impugn his reputation. But, if Wāḍiḥ al-Maskīn was a eunuch, again, this cannot be the case. But does one actually find a direct mention of al-Yaʿqūbī's ancestor Wāḍiḥ either in his *Taʾrīkh* or in his *Buldān*? The answer is probably not.

In the *Buldān*, for instance, al-Yaʿqūbī discusses the founding of Baghdād by the caliph al-Manṣūr and includes details on a certain Wāḍiḥ—whom he refers to as "the slave-client (*mawlā*) of the Commander of the Faithful"—and also notes the land-grant (*qaṭīʿa*) issued him by the caliph, which was located near the start of Baghdād's Anbār Road.[47] While al-Yaʿqūbī does state earlier in his

42 Al-Kindī, *Wulāt Miṣr*, 121, and al-Ṭabarī, *Taʾrīkh*, 3:493.

43 Al-Ṭabarī, *Taʾrīkh*, 3:560–561.

44 Al-Balādhurī, *Ansāb al-ashrāf*, 2:540–541. Al-Ṭabarī, *Taʾrīkh*, 3:561, recounts the story in which Wāḍiḥ is executed during the caliphate of al-Rashīd as well but favors the earlier date under al-Hādī. On the accounts of the flight and death of Idrīs b. ʿAbdallāh, see now Najam Haider, "The Community Divided," 459–475.

45 Daniel, "Al-Yaʿqūbī and Shiʿism Reconsidered," 217–221.

46 Ibn Taghrībirdī, *al-Nujūm al-zāhira*, 2:40.

47 Al-Yaʿqūbī, *Buldān*, 246–247.

Buldān that his ancestors (*salafī*) settled in Baghdād and that one of them even managed its affairs,[48] he does not explicitly provide their names.

In his *History*, al-Yaʿqūbī also mentions a *mawlā* of al-Manṣūr named Wāḍiḥ, whom he designates as among the freedmen who served al-Manṣūr as governors of a province.[49] But al-Yaʿqūbī does not specify where this Wāḍiḥ ruled as governor, although later in the author's chronicle, the reader learns that it was Armenia and Azerbaijan. The passage indicates that when the ʿAbbāsid governor of Armenia, al-Ḥasan b. Qaḥṭaba, failed to repel an uprising of a mountain people known as the Ṣanāriyya (Georgian *Tsʿanar*),[50] al-Manṣūr sent his general ʿĀmir b. Ismāʿīl al-Ḥārithī, who handily defeated them and pursued them as far as Tiflīs. When the army withdrew, al-Manṣūr appointed his *mawlā*—Wāḍiḥ—to the governorship of Armenia and Azerbaijan, a position he retained through al-Manṣūr's reign, that is, at least to 158/775.

This Wāḍiḥ appears in Yaʿqūbī's chronicle as the governor of Egypt as well. It is a brief reference: he mentions the monetary and material support that the caliph al-Mahdī (r. 158–169/775–785) requested from Wāḍiḥ for renovations to the Kaʿba and its environs in Mecca sometime after the caliph undertook a pilgrimage there in Dhū l-Ḥijja 160/September 777.[51] This is certainly the same Wāḍiḥ al-Maskīn who first ruled briefly as Egypt's governor and subsequently managed its postal network (*barīd*), a position he notoriously used to help the fugitive Idrīs escape ʿAbbāsid agents.

Elton Daniel was the first scholar to highlight the problems underlying the (ultimately untenable) identification of al-Yaʿqūbī's ancestor Wāḍiḥ with the Wāḍiḥ al-Maskīn who served the ʿAbbāsids. To Daniel modern historians also owe the brilliant insight into the most likely identification of al-Yaʿqūbī's ancestor.[52]

It seems most likely that the Wāḍiḥ who was al-Yaʿqūbī's ancestor was, rather than an ʿAbbāsid governor or provincial administrator, a household steward (*qahramān*) who served the dynasty from the caliphate of al-Manṣūr to that of Hārūn al-Rashīd. This can be determined by reading Ibn Dāya's quotations from al-Yaʿqūbī's likely lost history of the ʿAbbāsid house, in which he cites his

48 Ibid., 226: *salafī kānū [min] al-qāʾimīn bihā wa-aḥaduhum tawallā amrahā*.

49 Al-Yaʿqūbī, *Tārīkh*, 2:462, "*ʿummāluhu min mawālīhi*".

50 On the identification of the people called 'al-Ṣanāriyya' by Arabic writers, see V. Minorksy, "Caucasica IV," 506.

51 Al-Yaʿqūbī, *Taʾrīkh*, 2:476–477.

52 Daniel, "Al-Yaʿqūbī and Shiʿism Reconsidered," 221.

ancestor Wāḍiḥ as an authority,[53] alongside instances in which a certain Wāḍiḥ appears as an authority for historical reports in the annals of al-Ṭabarī.[54]

Although al-Ṭabarī does not cite al-Yaʿqūbī as his source for Wāḍiḥ's historical reports,[55] the reports closely resemble those found in Ibn Dāya's history insofar as they are primarily anecdotal and relate detailed accounts of the intimate and courtly lives of the ʿAbbāsid caliphs. The last anecdote that Ibn Dāya records from al-Yaʿqūbī—on the authority of his grandfather Wāḍiḥ—also gives us an indication that he outlived the notorious Wāḍiḥ al-Maskīn, for it concerns the skillful treatment of Hārūn al-Rashīd by the famed Christian physician Jibrīl b. Bukhtīshūʿ (d. c. 215/830).[56]

Such is the material that modern historians use in reconstructing the biography of Ibn Wāḍiḥ al-Yaʿqūbī. Taken together these scraps of data leave the impression that he was deeply enmeshed in the bureaucratic circles of the ʿAbbāsid era and keenly interested in the history of its elites: in particular, members of the ruling ʿAbbāsid dynasty, and the world they inhabited. His career spanned a geography that stretched from Iṣfahān to al-Fusṭāṭ, across which he seems to have witnessed the waxing and waning of the fortunes of such regional dynasties as the Ṭāhirids of Iran and the Ṭūlūnids of Egypt. All of his works bear the stamp of these experiences and are enriched by them.

The same data tell us little about al-Yaʿqūbī's ideological proclivities. The oft-vaunted connection to the ʿAbbāsids has been cited as evidence for his Shiʿite sympathies, but in fact, these notices offer us little by way of insight into his religious views. One only gains hints, first, of his Shiʿite disposition and, second, the sort of Shiʿism he espouses, from the portions of his *History* that discuss the conflicts over the leadership of the early Islamic community in the wake of Muḥammad's death. There one finds that al-Yaʿqūbī grappled with key questions regarding the role of the Prophet's kinsmen in the leadership of the community. The thrust of his comments strongly suggests that he held to rather hardline Shiʿite views.[57]

---

53 Ibn Dāya, *Kitāb al-Mukāfaʾa*, 66, 84, 119.

54 Al-Ṭabarī, *Taʾrīkh*, 3:405, 408, 523–524.

55 Al-Ṭabarī's source is "ʿAlī b. Muḥammad", which may refer to either one of two third/ninth-century historians, ʿAlī b. Muḥammad al-Nawfalī or ʿAlī b. Muḥammad al-Madāʾinī. On these figures, respectively, see Sebastian Günther, "al-Nawfalī's Lost *History*," 241–266, and Ilkka Lindstedt, "The Role of al-Madāʾinī's Students," 295–340.

56 Ibn al-Dāya, *Kitāb al-Mukāfaʾa*, 144–145; cf. the article by Lutz Richter-Bernburg in EIr, s.v. Ebn Boḵtīšūʿ.

57 For further details, see Anthony, "Was Ibn Wāḍiḥ al-Yaʿqūbī a Shiʿite Historian?"

Even given this knowledge about al-Yaʿqūbī, one remains in the dark as to which particular Shiʿi community he belonged. Certainly staunch Shiʿite loyalties would not have precluded al-Yaʿqūbī from enjoying an illustrious career in the upper echelons of the ʿAbbāsid-era commonwealth, as the history of the famously Shiʿite Nawbakhtī family amply suggests.[58] Yet al-Yaʿqūbī's interest in the scions of the Hāshim tribe can just as easily be attributed to his family's attachment to the ʿAbbāsids as it can to any purported sectarian allegiances. Even then, although his attachments to the ʿAbbāsids were real, they were not absolute. Al-Rāghib al-Iṣfahānī (d. early 5th/11th century) cites verses attributed to al-Yaʿqūbī where he seems to welcome the death of the caliph al-Muktafī (r. 289–295/902–908), stating "when [the caliph] died, his harm lived on (*lammā māta ʿāsha adhāhu*)."[59] These lines of poetry cited by al-Rāghib al-Iṣfahānī are also the last indication one finds of al-Yaʿqūbī. Nowhere does mention of his death date occur.

58 Cf. the article by S. W. Anthony in EIr, s.v. The Nawbaḵti Family.

59 Al-Rāghib al-Iṣfahānī, *Muḥāḍarāt al-udabāʾ*, 2:534.

Manuscripts, Printed Editions, and Translations of al-Yaʿqūbī's Works

Everett K. Rowson

We are fortunate that three of al-Yaʿqūbī's works have been preserved, although not in optimal form, and that they have received considerable scholarly attention.

The *Taʾrīkh* (*History*)

Two surviving manuscripts of this work are known. The first is a manuscript now in Cambridge, England, (Qq. 10) that was signed and dated by its copyist in the year 1096 of the Islamic calendar, corresponding to 1685 C.E. Believed at the time to be the only surviving manuscript of the work, it was the basis for M. Th. Houtsma's standard Arabic edition.[1] The second manuscript, which is undated but clearly much older, was first identified by Alphonse Mingana in his catalogue of the Arabic holdings in the John Rylands Library in Manchester, England (Arabic 801, R46158), published in 1934. On the basis of the manuscript's script, T. M. Johnstone proposed in 1957 a mid-fourteenth-century date for the Manchester manuscript, and also concluded that the two manuscripts belong to the "same family."

Lawrence Conrad has since argued that the Manchester manuscript is a direct ancestor of the Cambridge manuscript, and further work by the present translators and editors has only strengthened this argument; it now appears certain that the Cambridge manuscript is a *direct* copy of the Manchester manuscript. There are several reasons for this conclusion. The Manchester manuscript is acephalous—that is, it has lost its first folios, with the title page and the beginning of the text, and begins in mid-sentence. (A later intervener has helpfully added a line identifying author and title at the top of the first surviving page.) The Cambridge manuscript has the same acephalous text, but clearly as a *copy*, beginning mid-page with an introductory line praising God, followed immediately by the mid-sentence text (and without comment on the

1 Please see the Bibliography for the full citation of this and all other works referenced in this essay.

 | DOI: 10.1163/9789004364141_004

problem). Both manuscripts at their conclusion report that "here is finished *what survives* of the *History* ..."

Exactly what is going on with the Manchester manuscript is unclear—perhaps the copyist was himself working from a manuscript that had lost both its initial and final folios?—but the direct dependence of Cambridge on Manchester seems unquestionable. Furthermore, nowhere, with a single exception, does the Cambridge manuscript offer any textual evidence independent of the Manchester manuscript. The one exception is a marginal note concluding an account of a Shīʿī rebel with the added words "until he was killed, God have mercy on him." It would be normally assumed that this addition comes from another manuscript of the work, but its uniqueness, as well as the very large number of lacunae in the text of both manuscripts, with no other marginal supplementation from elsewhere, renders that assumption unlikely. Finally, it seems that all the (many but minor) departures by the Cambridge manuscript from the Manchester text can be explained by misreadings or guesses where the latter is illegible, due either to poor penmanship or to damage to the page, or in a few cases simple sloppiness on the part of the Cambridge scribe. If Cambridge were a third- or fourth-generation descendant of Manchester, one would expect non-obvious textual divergences, but those seem to be lacking.

The upshot is that our sole *real* exemplar of the text of the *History* is the Manchester manuscript. The Cambridge manuscript's interpretations of hard-to-read words and phrases of the Manchester manuscript can be useful at times; and Houtsma's valiant attempts to restore order to the Cambridge text where it clearly lacks it are repeatedly (but not universally) validated by the Manchester text. The present translation accordingly pays attention to Cambridge and Houtsma (as well as Carlo von Landberg's 1886 review of Houtsma's edition) but prioritizes Manchester as our only independent source for text readings.

The Manchester manuscript is not wonderful. The script is crabbed; it frequently lacks disambiguating dots; as already noted, there are distressingly frequent lacunae; and it is missing a true colophon at the end, which would have provided information on the date of copying and identified the copyist, although this lack is clearly not due to loss of its final folio. (A later owner has used the remaining space on the last page to copy out a passage from the tenth-century C.E. quasi-philosophical *Epistles of the Brethren of Purity*.) The entire text is divided into ten parts, almost certainly on the basis of (equal) length, which presumably reflect either the state of the copyist's original (ten separate volumes?) or that of an earlier manuscript ancestor; in the Manchester manuscript, the breaks between them (e.g., "here ends the sixth part and begins the seventh part") never fall at the end of a page or folio. These divisions seem unlikely to go back to al-Yaʿqūbī himself, notably because the unquestionably original division of the work into two books, Pre-Islamic and Islamic, falls haphazardly midway through Part 4.

Marginalia are quite copious in the Manchester manuscript, and appear in at least three different hands and probably more. The majority concern textual questions, and many are clearly the result of the original copyist's collating his completed copy against his original and correcting mistakes. Whether other textual corrections and additions actually depend on other manuscripts is impossible to say, but the "outside" contribution to emending the text is surely minimal. Other marginalia offer supplementary information (apposite verses, genealogical information, and the like), or, very occasionally, critical comments on the content of the text ("this cannot be correct, for the following reason"). At one point, where the invention of chess is mentioned, a half-page has been bound into the text which has a poem on chess on one side, totaling sixty-four words, with those words distributed on the squares of a chess board on the other side. In two cases—the birth of Jesus and the birth of Muḥammad—al-Yaʿqūbī's horoscopes are diagrammed in the margin.

The Manchester manuscript seems to have been owned by a succession of fairly militantly Shīʿī partisans. While some aspects of the fraught question of al-Yaʿqūbī's Shīʿī allegiance seem to have a solid textual base (such as his references to the "caliphate" of al-Ḥasan ibn ʿAlī and other Shīʿī imams, versus those to the "days" of the Umayyad and ʿAbbāsid caliphs), others depend on manuscript evidence more directly attributable to copyists and owners. The Manchester manuscript regularly follows any mention of the Umayyad caliph Muʿāwiya with "may God have mercy on him," but with impressive thoroughness these pious wishes have been blotted out by a later owner and replaced with an interlinear "may God curse him." (At the point where Muʿāwiya attains full power the interlinear vitriol expands to "may God not have mercy on him, and upon him be the curse of God, the angels, and human beings, all of them, amen, amen, amen.") The same treatment is applied, with somewhat less consistency, to other Shīʿī nemeses, notably Muʿāwiya's son and successor Yazīd.

The Cambridge manuscript is fairly slavish in its reproduction of the Manchester manuscript. The ten-part division is copied with only minor variations. The "curses" on Muʿāwiya and other Shīʿī enemies are mostly simply incorporated into the text, sometimes relegated to the margins, but almost never ignored. Manchester's textual marginalia are almost uniformly incorporated into the Cambridge text, without comment. Non-textual Manchester marginalia are often reproduced as marginalia but not infrequently ignored (or possibly unknown, if they post-date the Cambridge copying). Cambridge seems to be half-hearted about horoscope diagrams: it reproduces the one for the birth of Jesus, but not that for the birth of Muḥammad; it supplies one for the *hijra* that is not in Manchester, as well as one for the accession of Muʿāwiya. Short phrases identifying the topic of the text ("the martyrdom of al-Ḥusayn" and the like) are quite frequent but not regular; these seem to have been supplied by a later reader. As with the Manchester manuscript, there are a number of later hands contributing not only to the marginalia but also to interlinear material. The colophon, which includes both the date of copying and the identity of the copyist, is followed by two further folios, in a different hand, copying out an excerpt from the famous grammatical *Maqṣūra* poem by the ʿAbbāsid littérateur Ibn Durayd (d. 312/933).

The only respectable publication of the *History* is still that of Houtsma from the nineteenth century. There have been repeated republications of the text, based on Houtsma's edition, from Beirut. A Persian translation in two volumes by Muḥammad Ibrāhīm Āyatī first appeared in Tehran in 1964 and has been much reprinted. A French translation by André Ferré of the first section of the *History*, dealing with "Adam to Jesus," appeared in 2000. None of the post-Houtsma editions or translations have taken account of the Manchester manuscript.

The *Kitāb al-Buldān* (*Geography*)

The *Geography* is preserved, but only very imperfectly, in three known manuscripts, now in Munich (259), Berlin (Oct. 1833), and Istanbul (Topkapı, Ahmet III, 2403/2). It seems clear that both the Berlin and Istanbul manuscripts depend, directly or indirectly, on the Munich one. The latter has a colophon dating it to the year 607 of the Islamic calendar (1211 C.E.). We know from what is preserved of the text that al-Yaʿqūbī structured his work to begin with Baghdad and Samarra, followed by four "quarters" of the world: Eastern, Southern, Northern, and Western. A very large lacuna has deprived us of much of the Southern quarter (and part of what survives is mislabeled the Northern quarter), all of the Northern quarter, and the first part of the Western quarter. The critical edition of the text prepared by M.J. de Goeje (1892) offered fragments of the missing text in the form of quotations in later works. These have been translated here into English by Paul Cobb, who also found and translated yet further fragments, from both the pre- and post-lacuna sections of the work. Further fragments, from Ibn al-Dāya's *Mukāfaʾa*, have been translated by Matthew Gordon and Michael Fishbein and are likewise included here.

Gaston Wiet published an annotated French translation of the text in 1937. A Persian translation was produced by Muḥammad Ibrāhīm Āyatī in 1964–1969, which has since been reprinted.

The *Mushākala* (*The Adaptation of Men*)

This short work is preserved in a single manuscript, Istanbul Murad Mulla 1433, folios 79b–86b, datable from the hand to the ninth/fifteenth century, although a much more recent (nineteenth-century?) manuscript, Istanbul Fatih 5347, folios 73b–75a, reproduces about a third of the text, without significant variants from the Murad Mulla text. The work has been published twice, by William Millward (1962) and by Muḥammad Kamāl al-Dīn ʿIzz al-Dīn (1980?). Millward also published (1964) an annotated English translation, which has been useful for the new translation by Michael Fishbein presented here.

The Book of the Adaptation of Men to Their Time and Their Dominant Characteristics in Every Age

Mushākalat al-nās li-zamānihim wa-mā yaglibu ʿalayhim fī kull ʿaṣr

In the Name of God, the Merciful, the Compassionate
May God Bless Our Master Muḥammad

∴

The Book of the Adaptation of Men to Their Time and Their Dominant Characteristics in Every Age

The shaykh, imam, Qur'ān scholar, and very learned Aḥmad b. Abī Yaʿqūb b. Jaʿfar b. Wāḍiḥ—may God have mercy on him—said: As for the caliphs and kings of Islam,[1] Muslims in every age have been followers of the caliph, traveling his path, pursuing his course, acting in accordance to what they saw from him, and not departing from his habits, deeds, and words.

Abū Bakr was, after the Messenger of God—God's blessings and peace be upon him—the most abstemious of men, the most humble and sparing in his clothing. While he was caliph, he wore a wrap (*shamla*) and a coat (*ʿabāʾa*). The nobles of the Arabs and the kings of Yemen once came to him wearing crowns, brocaded cloaks (*burūd*), and striped garments (*ḥibar*); when they saw his humility and clothing, they took off what they were wearing, did as he did, and followed in his footsteps. Among those who came to Abū Bakr was Dhū l-Kalāʿ, the king of Ḥimyar, wearing his crown and surrounded by his relatives and retainers—he had ten thousand slaves serving him in his domains.[2] When he saw how Abū Bakr dressed, he said, "It is not fitting for us to do otherwise than the successor (*khalīfa*) of the Messenger of God—God's blessings and peace be upon him—does"; whereupon he took off what he had been wearing

1 The text begins abruptly, without the customary preliminary section of praise of God and the Prophet, and with a formula (*ammā ... fa*) that usually signals transition from one subject to another. This may indicate that the essay originally began with such a preface, now lost, and with a section, also lost or suppressed, on how people before Islam, Arab and non-Arab, conformed to the habits and practices of their rulers.

2 Parallel (with fuller wording): al-Masʿūdī, *Murūj*, 3:40–41 (§1512). Dhū l-Kalāʿ Samayfaʿ b. Nākūr (not to be confused with the earlier Dhū l-Kalāʿ listed by al-Yaʿqūbī, *Taʾrīkh*, 1:225, among the "kings" of Yemen), was the leader of a powerful South Arabian tribe on the eve of Islam. He converted in response to a mission that Muḥammad, in his final illness, sent to Yemen and remained loyal to Islam after the Prophet's death. Having sided with Abū Bakr against apostates in Yemen, he came to Medina in response to Abū Bakr's call for men to fight in Syria. (Presumably, this anecdote refers to this time.) He fought in various battles against Byzantine forces, settled in Syria, and died fighting for Muʿāwiya at Ṣiffīn in 37/657.

and imitated Abū Bakr. He was even seen in the market of Medina carrying a sheepskin on the back of his neck. "You've disgraced us!" said his kinsmen and tribesmen. "Will you, our lord, carry a sheep amid the Emigrants (*Muhājirūn*) and Helpers (*Anṣār*)?" He replied, "Did you want me to have been a proud tyrant in pagan times (*al-jāhiliyya*) and a proud tyrant in Islam as well?"

Al-Ash'ath b. Qays, the king of Kinda, used to wear a crown and be greeted as a king.[3] When, after apostatizing, he returned to Islam, and Abū Bakr married him to his sister, Umm Farwa bt. Abī Quḥāfa, he became so modest after being proud and so humble after being haughty that he would wrap himself in a worn-out cloak and, with his own hand, smear pitch on his camel's skin, imitating Abū Bakr and casting away the habits he used to have in pagan days.[4]

Abū Bakr—may God have mercy on him—permitted no noble to act extravagantly. Once he received a report that Abū Sufyān had done something he disliked.[5] He summoned Abū Sufyān and began shouting at him, while Abū Sufyān stood submissive and humble before him.[6] Abū Quḥāfa,[7] who had become blind, approached, led by his attendant; when he heard Abū Bakr shouting, he asked his attendant, "At whom is Abū Bakr shouting?" "At Abū Sufyān b. Ḥarb," he replied. Abū Quḥāfa said: "Abū 'Atīq![8] Will you raise your voice to Abū Sufyān? You have gone too far." Abū Bakr replied, "Father, God has raised some men through Islam and lowered others."

'Umar b. al-Khaṭṭāb—may God have mercy on him—despite his humility and the coarseness of his clothing and food, was strict in matters relating

---

3 On the checkered life of this prince of the originally South Arabian tribal confederacy of Kinda, see the article by Khalid Yahya Blankinship in *EI*³, s.v. al-Ash'ath, Abū Muḥammad Ma'dīkarib b. Qays b. Ma'dīkarib.

4 Pitch was used to prevent wounds from becoming infected and to promote healing.

5 Abū Sufyān b. Ḥarb was an influential Meccan leader. Originally hostile to Muḥammad, he converted at or shortly before the conquest of Mecca, fought afterward on the Muslim side, and, according to some reports, was appointed by the Prophet as governor of Najrān. His son, Mu'āwiya, established the Umayyad line of caliphs. The report here fits other reports that relations between Abū Bakr and Abū Sufyān were cool. See the article by Khaled M. G. Keshk in *EI*³, s.v. Abū Sufyān.

6 Parallel, al-Mas'ūdī, *Murūj*, 3:41 (§1513).

7 Abū Bakr's father.

8 Addressing his son: Abū 'Atīq, a nickname for Abū Bakr, literally means "father of one set free," or simply "man set free," referring to a report that Muḥammad promised Abū Bakr that he would be free (*'atīq*) from the fire of hell. (See Ibn Sa'd, *Ṭabaqāt*, III/1, 120, 133.) The parallel in al-Mas'ūdī has the variant, *yā 'atīq Allāh* (O one set free by God).

to God. His governors and everyone else in his presence or away from him imitated him, and none of the Companions of the Messenger of God—God's blessings and peace be upon him—did otherwise. He used to wear a woolen tunic (*jubba*) and wrap himself in a coat (*ʿabāʾa*).[9] He would smear his camel with pitch and carry a water skin on his back for his family. His governors, the commanders of the garrison cities—God had granted them victories, favor, and power and had enriched them and protected them—went barefoot; they would remove their shoes and not wear boots, and they wore coarse garments. When they came before him, they came unkempt, dusty, coarse-garmented, and emaciated in complexion. If he saw them otherwise than such, or it was reported to him, he reprimanded them for it. Their mounts were camels, more than horses, imitating ʿUmar, his way of acting, and how they had been in the time of the Messenger of God—God's blessings and peace be upon him.

Abū ʿUbayda b. al-Jarrāḥ, the commander of Syria—God had granted him victory over it—was seen wearing an ill-smelling woolen tunic (*jubba*). Abū ʿUbayda said, "I have sat beside the Messenger of God—God's blessings and peace be upon him—wearing something that smelled stronger than this, but he did not object."[10]

Salmān al-Fārisī was ʿUmar b. al-Khaṭṭāb's governor of al-Madāʾin.[11] He used to wear the coarsest of garments and ride a she-ass with a pack saddle and a halter rope of palm fiber. When Salmān was about to die, Saʿd b. Abī Waqqāṣ came and said to him, "Give me your parting advice, Abū ʿAbdallāh." "Yes," he replied: "Be mindful of God with your thoughts when you are about to do something, and with your tongue whenever you speak, and with your hand whenever you distribute." Salmān began to weep, and Saʿd asked him, "Abū ʿAbdallāh, what is making you weep?" He replied, "I once heard the Messenger of God—God's blessings and peace be upon him—say that in the Hereafter there is a pass that can be crossed only by those who travel light, and I see all this baggage around me." (Saʿd said,) "We looked and saw nothing in his room other than a water skin, a drinking cup, a cooking pot, and a ewer."[12]

---

9 Parallel, al-Masʿūdī, *Murūj*, 3:48 (§1525).

10 Parallel, al-Masʿūdī, *Murūj*, 3:49 (§1528).

11 Al-Yaʿqūbī, *Buldān*, 321, notes that the tomb of this Companion of the Prophet, said to have been the first Persian convert to Islam, was located at al-Madāʾin. The historicity of Salmān's governorship of al-Madāʾin is uncertain. See the article by G. Levi Della Vida in *EI*^{2}, s.v. Salmān al-Fārisī.

12 Parallel, al-Masʿūdī, *Murūj*, 3:49 (§1527). The Arabic terms are *idāwa* (a small leather bag

ʿUmar b. al-Khaṭṭāb put ʿUmayr b. Saʿd al-Anṣārī in charge of the military district of Ḥimṣ. He stayed for a year and then returned on his camel in the same state as when he had departed from ʿUmar. So ʿUmar said, "Woe to a people over whom you were set in charge! Didn't they recognize what you were entitled to?"—or something of the sort.

ʿUmar b. al-Khaṭṭāb performed the pilgrimage. Then he asked his son ʿAbdallāh, "How much did we spend on our pilgrimage?" "Sixteen dinars," he replied. Whereupon ʿUmar said, "We have been extravagant with this money."[13]

ʿUthmān b. ʿAffān—may God have mercy on him—was known for magnanimity and generosity, for loyalty to his kinsmen and promoting his relatives, and for acquiring property; and people modeled themselves on his actions. ʿUthmān built his home in Medina and spent a huge sum of money on it. He built it of stone and put panels of teak on its doors. He acquired properties in Medina, wells, and herds of camels. According to ʿAbdallāh b. ʿUtba:[14] "On the day he died, ʿUthmān b. ʿAffān left with his treasurer 150,000 dinars and 1,000,000 dirhams. His estates were Biʾr Arīs,[15] Khaybar, and Wādī l-Qurā, whose value was 200,000 dinars; and he left horses and herds of camels."[16]

In the days of ʿUthmān, the Companions of the Messenger of God—God's blessings and peace be upon him—acquired wealth and built houses.

---

to hold water), *rakwa* (a small leather drinking vessel), *qidr* (a cooking pot), and *miṭhara* (a vessel holding water for performing ablutions).

13 Parallel, al-Masʿūdī, *Murūj*, 3:77 (§1582); Ibn Saʿd, Ṭabaqāt, III/1, 222, with an *isnād* beginning with Muḥammad b. ʿUmar (al-Wāqidī).

14 Al-Yaʿqūbī indicates only the final authority for this report. The parallel in Ibn Saʿd, *Ṭabaqāt*, III/1, 53 indicates that the report was part of the work of Muḥammad b. ʿUmar al-Wāqidī. ʿAbdallāh b. ʿUtba b. Masʿūd al-Hudhalī, an early Muslim (born during the lifetime of the Prophet, died c. 74/693–694) was known as a jurist (he served as *qāḍī* of Kufa in 67/686–687), an authority on Qurʾān readings (he was the nephew of ʿAbdallāh b. Masʿūd), and a transmitter of traditions. See Ibn Ḥajar, *Tahdhīb al-Tahdhīb*, 5:211–212.

15 Thus in the printed editions of the text. According to Yāqūt, *Muʿjam al-buldān*, 1:430, s.v., Biʾr Arīs was a well in Medina into which the Prophet's ring fell and from which ʿUthmān tried unsuccessfully to retrieve it. However, a well inside Medina hardly fits the category of "estate" (*ḍayʿa*, pl. *ḍiyāʿ*). The parallel in Ibn Saʿd, *Ṭabaqāt*, III/1, 53, reads *bi-Barādīs* (as corrected by the editor Sachau from manuscripts that read *Bīrādīs*); and a marginal note in one of the manuscripts of Ibn Saʿd identifies Barādīs as "an orchard on the outskirts of Medina, outside of al-Baqīʿ" (Sachau's note ad. loc.).

16 Parallel, al-Masʿūdī, *Murūj*, 3:76 (§1579).

Al-Zubayr b. al-ʿAwwām[17] built his renowned house in Basra; in it there are markets and shops.[18] Al-Zubayr also built a house in Kufa, one in Egypt,[19] and one in Alexandria. The value of al-Zubayr's wealth amounted to 50,000 dinars. He left a thousand horses, a thousand slaves, and real estate in Egypt, Alexandria, Kufa, and Basra.[20]

Ṭalḥa b. ʿUbaydallāh[21] built houses and estates valued at 100,000 dinars. His daily income in Iraq was fully 1,000 [dinars],[22] and his income in Syria was 10,000 dinars [a year].[23] He built his house of gypsum, baked bricks, and teakwood, and left a huge fortune in gold and silver.

ʿAbd al-Raḥmān b. ʿAwf[24] built his house and made it spacious. He had 1,000 camels, 10,000 sheep, and 100 horses. One-fourth of the eighth of his wealth amounted to 84,000 dinars.[25]

---

17 Al-Zubayr b. al-ʿAwwām, a cousin of Muḥammad and one of the earliest converts to Islam, was a member of the six-man conclave (*shūrā*) that chose ʿUthmān to succeed ʿUmar. Later, he was killed at the Battle of the Camel, near Basra, in 36/656, fighting against ʿAlī. He was known as one of the wealthiest of the Companions of the Prophet. See the article by I. Hasson in *EI*², s.v. al-Zubayr b. al-ʿAwwām.

18 Or, "in it there *were* markets and shops" (the Arabic clause has no explicit verb). The question is whether the complex (*dār*, here translated as "house," can also refer to an estate or even to an entire district) included markets and shops from the beginning, or whether they were a later addition. The parallel in al-Masʿūdī, *Murūj*, 3:76 (§1579) suggests the latter, but is also ambiguous: "He built his house in Basra—the one known at this time, namely the year 332 (943–944)—occupied by merchants, persons of wealth, purveyors of naval equipment, and others."

19 That is, in al-Fusṭāṭ (Old Cairo).

20 Parallel, al-Masʿūdī, *Murūj*, 3:76 (§1579); Ibn Saʿd, *Ṭabaqāt*, III/1, 77, with *isnād* beginning with Muḥammad b. ʿUmar (al-Wāqidī).

21 On the career of this very early convert to Islam, who was also a member of the conclave (*shūrā*) that chose ʿUthmān to succeed ʿUmar and who died at the Battle of the Camel in 36/656, see the article by W. Madelung in *EI*², s.v. Ṭalḥa.

22 Supplied from the parallel in al-Masʿūdī, *Murūj*, 3:77 (§1580).

23 Addition from Ibn Saʿd, *Ṭabaqāt*, III/1, 157, where the report has an *isnād* beginning with Muḥammad b. ʿUmar (al-Wāqidī).

24 An early Meccan convert who emigrated first to Abyssinia and then to Medina. He fought in most of the battles of the Medinan community, and later was a member of the *shūrā* (conclave) to determine a successor to the caliphate after the murder of ʿUmar. He died in 32/652–653, during the caliphate of ʿUthmān, and was renowned for his wealth. See the article by Wilferd Madelung in *EI*³, s.v. ʿAbd al-Raḥmān b. ʿAwf.

25 Reading *rubʿ thumn mālihi*. The meaning is clarified by two reports in Ibn Saʿd, *Ṭabaqāt*, III/1, 96f. At his death, ʿAbd al-Raḥmān b. ʿAwf left four wives. Assuming that the later Islamic rules for quota-heirs prevailed at the time (see the article by J. Schacht in *EI*², s.v. Mīrāth, as well as Sachau's note to Ibn Saʿd, *Ṭabaqāt*, III/1, 77), a widow, assuming that

Sa'd b. Abī Waqqāṣ[26] built his house in al-'Aqīq.[27] He plastered it[28] and gave it balconies.[29]

According to Sa'īd b. al-Musayyab:[30] Zayd b. Thābit[31] left so much gold and silver that it had to be broken up with pickaxes, as well as property, estates, and springs amounting to 150,000 dinars.[32]

Ya'lā b. Munya al-Tamīmī[33] left 500,000 dinars, plots of land, estates, and loan credits with a value of 300,000 dinars.[34]

Al-Miqdād[35] built his palace at al-Jurf[36] of unbaked bricks; he stuccoed it inside and out, and gave it balconies. No men had done this during the time of 'Umar; they did it only after him.[37]

---

there were surviving sons or daughters, would receive a eighth of the estate; since 'Abd al-Raḥmān left four widows, each would have received "one-fourth of the eighth." According to the first report, this came to 80,000 (sc. dinars) for each. According to the second report, "Tumāḍir bt. al-Aṣbagh received one-fourth of the eighth; she went away with 100,000; she was one of the four." The parallel in al-Mas'ūdī, *Murūj*, 3:77 (§1580) reads *al-ray' min mālihi* (the income from his property/wealth after his death amounted to 84,000 dinars), which is less likely to be the correct reading.

26 An early convert who commanded the Arab armies in the conquest of Iraq. He, too, was a member of the conclave (*shūrā*) that chose 'Uthmān to succeed 'Umar. See the article by G. R. Hawting in *EI*², s.v. Sa'd b. Abī Waḳḳāṣ.

27 A valley to the west of Medina; a report in Ibn Sa'd, *Ṭabaqāt*, III/1, 105, with an *isnād* beginning with Muḥammad b. 'Umar (al-Wāqidī) locates Sa'd's al-'Aqīq estate 10 Arab miles from Medina.

28 Arabic *shayyadahā*, which can also mean "he built it tall."

29 Parallel, al-Mas'ūdī, *Murūj*, 3:77 (§1581).

30 Sa'īd b. al-Musayyab (b. c. 15/636, d. c. 91/709) was one of the so-called "seven jurists of Medina." See the article by Ch. Pellat in *EI*², s.v. Fuḳahā' al-Madīna al-Sab'.

31 A Medinan convert who served as Muḥammad's scribe and later as 'Uthmān's treasurer. He seems not to have pledged allegiance to 'Alī, and later served under Mu'āwiya. See the article by M. Lecker in *EI*², s.v. Zayd b. Thābit.

32 Parallel, al-Mas'ūdī, *Murūj*, 3:77 (§1581).

33 Commonly known as Ya'lā b. Umayya (Munya was his mother's name), he was a Companion of the Prophet, served as 'Umar's governor of Najrān, and fought on the side of al-Zubayr and 'Ā'isha at the Battle of the Camel in 35/656. See Ibn Ḥajar, *Tahdhīb al-Tahdhīb*, 11:399–400.

34 Parallel, al-Mas'ūdī, *Murūj*, 3:77 (§1582).

35 Al-Miqdād b. 'Amr al-Bahrā'ī (also known as al-Miqdād b. al-Aswad), a Companion of the Prophet, later served as military commander under 'Umar and 'Uthmān. He died in 33/653–654. See the article by G. H. A. Juynboll in *EI*², s.v. al-Miḳdād b. 'Amr.

36 About 3 Arab miles north of Medina, according to a report in Ibn Sa'd, *Ṭabaqāt*, III/1, 115, and Yāqūt, *Mu'jam al-buldān*, 2:62, s.v.

37 Parallel, al-Mas'ūdī, *Murūj*, 3:77 (§1582).

ʿAlī b. Abī Ṭālib—peace be upon him—was occupied all his days with fighting. However, he never wore a new garment, never acquired an estate, and never contracted for property,[38] except what he had in Yanbuʿ and al-Bughaybigha,[39] from which he gave alms to the poor. People have preserved his sermons; he delivered 400 sermons that were preserved from him, and they are the ones that circulate among people and that they use in their own sermons and speeches.[40]

Then came Muʿāwiya b. Abī Sufyān.[41] He built palaces, constructed houses, and raised screens.[42] He acquired guards, acquired a police force (*shurṭa*), established chamberlains,[43] and built rulers' compartments (*maqṣūras*) in the mosques. He rode good-looking mounts with padded saddles. He wore silk and brocade. He acquired crown lands[44] and estates. *Ṭirāz*[45] was made for him in Yemen, Egypt,[46] Alexandria, and al-Ruhā.[47] His family, children, and officials acquired what he acquired and did as he did.

---

38 Arabic *wa-lam yaʿqid ʿalā māl*. The meaning is unclear. If one adds one word, to read *wa-lam yaʿqid* [*nafsahu*] *ʿalā māl*, it would mean "he never set his heart on wealth."

39 The reading is uncertain, as the Arabic ductus is completely undotted in the manuscript. Support for the reading can be found in Yāqūt, *Muʿjam al-buldān*, 1:696, s.v., which lists al-Bughaybigha as a property belonging to ʿAlī. The parallel in al-Masʿūdī, *Murūj*, 3:172 (§1744), omits the second place name and refers only to ʿAlī's property in Yanbuʿ.

40 Parallel, al-Masʿūdī, *Murūj*, 3:172 (§1744).

41 On Muʿāwiya b. Abī Sufyān, the first of the Umayyad caliphs (r. 41/661 to 60/680), see the article by M. Hinds in *EI*², s.v. Muʿāwiya I.

42 Arabic *sutūr* (curtains, screens) could refer to the *maqṣūra*, an enclosed compartment for the ruler near the *miḥrāb* of the mosque, introduced to protect the ruler from attempts on his life. Muʿāwiya is sometimes credited with its introduction; e.g., al-Ṭabarī, *Taʾrīkh*, 1:3465. However, since the *maqṣūra* is mentioned specifically later in the sentence, this reference may be to screens or curtains in the audience chamber.

43 Arabic *ḥujjāb*, pl. of *ḥājib*, referring to the official who controlled access to the ruler, so that only approved persons might approach him. See the article by D. Sourdel in *EI*², s.v. Ḥādjib.

44 Arabic *ṣawāfī*, originally conquered Sasanian crown lands retained by the caliph on behalf of the community. In the reign of Muʿāwiya attempts were made to identify former Sasanian crown lands in Iraq; these were appropriated by the caliph and often redistributed to members of the Umayyad family. See the article by A. K. S. Lambton in *EI*², s.v. Ṣafī.

45 *Ṭirāz* (from a Persian word meaning 'adornment') referred to ornamental bands of cloth with woven or embroidered inscriptions. Garments with these panels were worn by rulers and other high officials and could be bestowed as robes of honor. See the article by Yedida K. Stillman and Paula Sanders in *EI*², s.v. Ṭirāz.

46 That is, al-Fusṭāṭ (Old Cairo).

47 Ancient Edessa, modern Urfa in southeastern Turkey.

ʿAmr b. al-ʿĀṣ built his house in Egypt and acquired estates for himself.[48] On his estate at al-Ṭāʾif called al-Waht he planted one million grapevines, and his income from the yield was 10 million dirhams. On the day of his death he left 300,000 dinars. When he was about to die, he said, "Would that it were only 100,000 dinars."[49]

ʿAbdallāh b. ʿĀmir b. Kurayz, Muʿāwiya's governor of Basra, did as he did. He dug canals, erected houses, built palaces, and acquired estates, property, and gardens in Basra, Mecca, and al-Ṭāʾif.

Ziyād,[50] Muʿāwiya's governor of Iraq, did this in Kufa, Basra, and the rest of Iraq. He acquired estates and built and constructed buildings. On the day of his death, Ziyād left 6 million [dirhams and 100,000][51] dinars. Muʿāwiya took them; Muʿāwiya usually did this to his governors, but sometimes he shared equally with the heirs.

Maslama b. Mukhallad, Muʿāwiya's governor of Egypt, did the same.[52] He acquired estates in Egypt that he set aside as trusts (*waqf*) for his family. On the day of his death he left 100,000 dinars and 1 million dirhams.

---

48 On the career of ʿAmr b. al-ʿĀṣ, Muʿāwiya's governor of Egypt, see the article by Khaled M. G. Keshk in *EI*[3], s.v. ʿAmr b. al-ʿĀṣ.

49 The parallel in al-Yaʿqūbī, *Taʾrīkh*, 2:263–264, provides a fuller context: "When ʿAmr came to die, he said to his son: 'Your father wishes that he had died at the raid of Dhāt al-Salāsil [i.e., during the lifetime of the Prophet]. I have involved myself with affairs for which I do not know what excuse I shall have before God.' Then he looked at his fortune and seeing its magnitude he said: 'Would that it were dung! Would that I had died thirty years ago! I made Muʿāwiya's worldly fortune thrive, while I spoiled my religion; I preferred my worldly life and abandoned my afterlife; my integrity was blinded, and now my time of death has come. I seem to see Muʿāwiya taking possession of my fortune and making my succession evil for you.'"

50 That is, Ziyād b. Abīhi (Ziyād "the son of his father," because of his uncertain parentage), was officially recognized by Muʿāwiya as the son of Abū Sufyān and hence as Muʿāwiya's half-brother. He later became Muʿāwiya's governor of Iraq and became famous for his restoration of order to the chaotic province. See the article by I. Hasson in *EI*[2], s.v. Ziyād b. Abīhi.

51 The bracketed words are a marginal addition in the MS. The question of Ziyād's fortune and its disposition remains unclear. A curious passage in al-Balādhurī, *Ansāb al-Ashrāf*, IV/1, 282 (ed. Iḥsān ʿAbbās), reads: "Ziyād died only owning less than 10,000 dirhams; of clothing he left only two shirts, two waist-wrappers, and two pairs of drawers. He used to say, 'As long as our power lasts, all the world is ours; when it departs from us, what will suffice us of the world will be the least of it.'"

52 Maslama b. Mukhallad became governor of Egypt sometime after the death of ʿAmr b.

ʿUqba b. ʿĀmir al-Juhanī, who also was Muʿāwiya's governor of Egypt, created estates in Egypt. He bequeathed some of them in perpetuity,[53] and he built a house in Egypt[54] of stone and plaster. He left 30,000 dinars and 700,000 dirhams.

Ḥuwayṭib b. ʿAbd al-ʿUzzā[55] sold a house to Muʿāwiya for 40,000 dinars. Someone said to him, "Abū Muḥammad, forty thousand?"[56] He replied, "And what are 40,000 dinars for a man with six dependents?" Muʿāwiya used to say, "I have split apart the kingdom."[57]

Yazīd b. Muʿāwiya[58] was devoted to the chase, hunting animals[59] and dogs, entertainment, and carousing over wine; these things then dominated his companions. It was in his time that singing made its appearance in Mecca and Medina, musical instruments were used, and nobles drank openly.[60]

---

al-ʿĀṣ (two other governors, ʿUtba b. Abī Sufyān and ʿUqba b. ʿĀmir, intervened); see the article in *EI*², s.v. Maslama b. Mukhallad.

53 Arabic *wa-ḥabbasa baʿḍahā*. That is, he made some of them inalienable trusts either for his family or for charitable purposes.

54 That is, al-Fusṭāṭ (Old Cairo).

55 A leader of the Quraysh, who converted only after Muḥammad's conquest of Mecca. He is said to have been married at one time to Muʿāwiya's sister Āmina (al-Balādhurī, *Ansāb al-Ashrāf*, IV/1, 1) and to have lived to the age of 120.

56 The interlocutor addresses Ḥuwayṭib familiarly by his *kunya*, Abū Muḥammad. The parallel in al-Balādhurī, *Ansāb al-Ashrāf*, IV/1, 61 (where the sum is given as 45,000 dinars) clarifies the context: "Some men congratulated Ḥuwayṭib," i.e., for having become rich from the sale. Ḥuwayṭib replies that such a sum was nothing for a man with so many dependents (seven in al-Balādhurī's account, which comes from al-Madāʾinī). The anecdote also appears in the *Kitāb al-Bukhalāʾ* by al-Jāḥiẓ (ed. Ṭāhā al-Ḥājirī, Cairo, 1967), 150, where the interlocutor's remark is phrased, "You've become very wealthy!" To which Ḥuwayṭib replies, "What's the use of 45,000 with six children?" In a version in al-Ṭabarī's appendix of biographies (ed. Leiden, 3:2329, coming from al-Wāqidī) there is an extra detail: the exchange between Ḥuwayṭib and the interlocutor is set years after the sale, by which time Ḥuwayṭib "was among the recipients of the monthly [rations] of food." (Trans. by Ella Landau-Tasseron in *The History of al-Ṭabarī*, XXXIX, 46).

57 The reading of the MS (*anafataqtu l-mulk*) is unclear, and in the absence of a more detailed parallel, one can only speculate about the meaning.

58 On Yazīd b. Muʿāwiya, the second Umayyad caliph (r. 60/680 to 64/683), see the article by G. R. Hawting in *EI*², s.v. Yazīd (I) b. Muʿāwiya.

59 Arabic *jawāriḥ*, referring to cheetahs, falcons, and the like.

60 Parallel, al-Masʿūdī, *Murūj*, 3:265 (§1918).

Then came ʿAbd al-Malik b. Marwān.[61] He was stern, resolute, and miserly, fond of poetry, boasting, encomium, and praise.[62] In his days the "stallions" among the poets were Jarīr, al-Farazdaq, al-Akhṭal, and others.[63] Poetry flourished in the days of ʿAbd al-Malik. The poets praised the military commanders and tribal dignitaries and sought rewards.

ʿAbd al-Malik had a penchant for shedding blood and acting in haste, and his governors were of similar character: al-Ḥajjāj in Iraq, al-Muhallab in Khurāsān, Hishām b. Ismāʿīl al-Makhzūmī in Medina, ʿAbdallāh b. ʿAbd al-Malik in Egypt, Mūsā b. Nuṣayr al-Lakhmī in the Maghrib, Muḥammad b. Yūsuf al-Thaqafī (al-Ḥajjāj's brother) in Yemen, and Muḥammad b. Marwān in the Jazīra and Mosul. All of them were tyrannical, unjust, violent, and headstrong. Al-Ḥajjāj was one of the most unjust of them and most given to shedding blood.

Al-Walīd b. ʿAbd al-Malik was tyrannical, stubborn, and unjust.[64] His governors in all lands were of similar character. ʿUmar b. ʿAbd al-ʿAzīz[65] used to say, "With al-Walīd in Syria, al-Ḥajjāj in Iraq, ʿUthmān b. Ḥayyān in the Ḥijāz, Muḥammad b. Yūsuf in Yemen, Qurra b. Sharīk in Egypt, and Mūsā b. Nuṣayr in Ifrīqiya, the world was full of injustice." Nothing of al-Walīd's manner of acting deserves notice except for his building of mosques, for it was he who built the mosque of Damascus.[66]

Then came Sulaymān b. ʿAbd al-Malik b. Marwān.[67] He was an epicure and a glutton beyond all measure, a wearer of fine clothing and garments of brocade: tunics, cloaks, trousers, turbans, and hats. His family members would enter his presence only in brocades, and similarly his governors, companions, servants, and those in his household. It was his costume when he was riding, when he was

---

61 Al-Yaʿqūbī omits the brief reigns of Muʿāwiya b. Yazīd (r. briefly in 64/683–684) and Marwān b. al-Ḥakam (r. 64/684 to 65/685). On ʿAbd al-Malik b. Marwān, the fifth Umayyad caliph (r. 65/685 to 86/705), see the article by H. A. R. Gibb in *EI*², s.v. ʿAbd al-Malik b. Marwān, and Chase Robinson's book-length treatment, *ʿAbd al-Malik*.

62 Parallel, al-Masʿūdī, *Murūj*, 3:291 (§ 1973).

63 Arabic *fuḥūl al-shuʿarāʾ*, a term reserved for poets who could overcome their rivals in poetic contests.

64 On al-Walīd I (r. 86/705 to 96/715), see the article by Renate Jacobi in *EI*², s.v. al-Walīd.

65 That is, the successor of al-Walīd's successor. Later historians often cited ʿUmar b. ʿAbd al-ʿAzīz as the only truly pious Umayyad caliph. Hence, his pronouncement about al-Walīd carries particular weight as being a denunciation of a member of his own family.

66 That is, the Great Umayyad Mosque of Damascus. Its beauty is praised by al-Yaʿqūbī, *Kitāb al-Buldān*, 326. Parallel, al-Masʿūdī, *Murūj*, 3:365 (§ 2114).

67 Ruled 96/715 to 99/717; see the article by R. Eisener in *EI*², s.v. Sulaymān b. ʿAbd al-Malik. Parallel, al-Masʿūdī, *Murūj*, 4:6–7 (§ 2154).

holding audience, and when he was in the pulpit. None of his servants would enter his presence except in brocade, even the cook, who would come before him in a tunic and tall hat, both of brocade.

Then came ʿUmar b. ʿAbd al-ʿAzīz b. Marwān.[68] He governed with humility, devoutness, asceticism, religion, and seeking the friendship of people of virtue. He removed al-Walīd's governors and appointed the most righteous people he could find. His governors followed his path, and the people were relieved of the oppression and injustice that they had been suffering.[69] He abandoned the cursing of ʿAlī b. Abī Ṭālib—peace be upon him—from the pulpit,[70] and replaced it with: "O Lord, forgive us and our brothers who preceded us in belief, and do not set in our hearts rancor toward those who believe. Our Lord, surely Thou art merciful and compassionate."[71] People have followed this custom in the Friday sermon until the present day.

Then came Yazīd b. ʿAbd al-Malik.[72] He was the first caliph to acquire a singing slave-girl and the first over whose affairs a woman gained control. Ḥabbāba, his singing slave-girl, used to appoint and dismiss, set free and imprison, command and forbid. Along with this, he was swift to shed blood and seize property, and his governors reverted to their former injustice.

Then came Hishām b. ʿAbd al-Malik b. Marwān.[73] He was harsh, rough, crude, and miserly. He amassed wealth, developed agriculture, and sought excellence in everything made for him in the way of clothing and furniture, severely punishing any shortcomings in this regard.[74] It was in his time that figured silk was made.[75] People in the days of Hishām all followed his lead in

---

68 Ruled 99/717 to 101/720 and held up by later historians as the only truly pious Umayyad caliph; see the article by P. M. Cobb in *EI*², s.v. ʿUmar (II) b. ʿAbd al-ʿAzīz.

69 Parallel, al-Masʿūdī, *Murūj*, 4:17 (§ 2171).

70 A practice said to have been originated by Muʿāwiya and continued by his successors.

71 Qurʾān 59:10.

72 Ruled 101/720 to 105/724; see the article by H. Lammens and Kh. Y. Blankinship in *EI*², s.v. Yazīd (II) b. ʿAbd al-Malik.

73 Ruled 105/724 to 125/743; see the article by F. Gabrieli in *EI*², s.v. Hishām.

74 Parallel, al-Masʿūdī, *Murūj*, 4:41 (§ 2219).

75 Arabic *al-khazz al-raqm*. The exact meaning, apart from the fact that the material must have been either entirely or partly of silk, is unclear. It may be a way of referring to the bands known as *ṭirāz* embroidered with the caliph's name, or it may refer to striped cloth of silk. Yedida Stillman and Paula Sanders in *EI*², s.v. Ṭirāz, note that Hishām was the first Umayyad caliph mentioned as having *ṭirāz* factories and that he was known as "a dandy and a great lover of fine robes, textiles, and carpets."

withholding what was in their hands, lack of generosity, and abstaining from charity, so that it was said that no time had ever been seen more difficult for the people than his. This was because he discontinued the generosity, subsidies, rewards, and gifts that the caliphs used to bestow. People used this as a pretext, followed his course, and imitated him. Abū Sālim al-Aʿraj once said to him: "You are nothing but a market; whatever sells briskly with you gets carried to you."[76]

Al-Walīd b. Yazīd b. ʿAbd al-Malik[77] was a devotee of wine, amusement, music, and listening to singing. He was the first to import singers from the provinces; he consorted with entertainers and made a public show of wine, entertainments, and music. The singer Ibn Surayj lived in his days, as well as Maʿbad, al-Gharīḍ, Ibn ʿĀʾisha, Ibn Muḥriz, Ṭuways, and Daḥmān.[78] Vocal music

---

76 Abū Sālim appears to be a mistake for Abū Ḥāzim al-Aʿraj (full name Salama b. Dīnār), who is listed by al-Yaʿqūbī, *Taʾrīkh*, 2:396, as one of the learned men in Hishām's reign. The meaning of the saying is unclear. The first two pronouns are plural and probably refer to the Umayyads as a whole; the third pronoun, singular, probably refers to Hishām personally: "You (Umayyads) are a market such that to you (Umayyads) gets carried (only) what sells briskly (i.e., is in demand) with you (Hishām)." It may have something to do with the sharp reply with which this Medinese jurist is said to have met a caliphal invitation to come to Damascus. The anecdote is given by Ibn Ḥajar, *Tahdhīb*, 4:144, but unfortunately the caliph is identified as Sulaymān, not Hishām. In any case, the caliph is supposed to have sent al-Zuhrī to invite al-Aʿraj to come to Damascus. The jurist replied: "If he has any need, let him come; as for me, I have no need for him." This is as if to say: "What I have (viz. learning) would not be in demand in your market" (where only gourmet food and luxury garments are in demand). But this interpretation is conjectural.

77 Al-Walīd II ruled 125–126/743–44, then was deposed and killed. He is best known for his poetry; see the article by Renata Jacobi in *EI*², s.v. al-Walīd.

78 Al-Yaʿqūbī's chronology, placing all of these singers in the time of al-Walīd II, is wrong, as most of them were active before his reign. The mistake may have been caused by al-Walīd II's reputation for dissoluteness. Although some sources place the death of Ibn Surayj as late as 126/744, most connect him with al-Walīd b. ʿAbd al-Malik (al-Walīd I), who invited him from the Ḥijāz to Damascus, and place his death in 96/714, before the caliphate of al-Walīd II (see the article by J. W. Fück in *EI*², s.v. Ibn Suraydj). Maʿbad b. Wahb is reported to have been invited to court by al-Walīd II, but died shortly after his arrival in 125/743 or 126/744; his heyday was in the reigns of al-Walīd b. ʿAbd al-Malik and Yazīd b. ʿAbd al-Malik (see the article by H. G. Farmer and E. Neubauer in *EI*², s.v. Maʿbad b. Wahb). Al-Gharīḍ is usually said to have died in 98/716–717, although some reports show him living at the court of Yazīd b. ʿAbd al-Malik sometime between 101/720 and 105/724 (see the article by H. G. Farmer in *EI*², s.v. al-Gharīḍ). Ibn ʿĀʾisha is said to have been invited to Damascus by al-Walīd b. Yazīd, then a prince, sometime during the caliphate of Hishām b. ʿAbd al-Malik, and to have died before al-Walīd II became caliph (see the article in *EI*², s.v. Ibn ʿĀʾisha). On Ibn Muḥriz, who may or may not have appeared at the court of al-Walīd II, see the article in *EI*², s.v. Ibn Muḥriz. Ṭuways rose to fame as early as the reign

became the rage among the nobility, and people acquired lutes. Al-Walīd was profligate, dissolute, and shameless.[79]

Then came Yazīd b. al-Walīd b. ʿAbd al-Malik.[80] His days were not long enough for his character and ways of acting to become widely known, except that he professed the doctrine of *iʿtizāl* and would argue in its defense.[81]

Then came Marwān b. Muḥammad b. Marwān b. al-Ḥakam.[82] He was at war during all his days; except that he was the first caliph to display *ʿaṣabiyya* openly and to incite it among the people.[83] His secretary was ʿAbd al-Ḥamīd b. Yaḥyā b. Saʿd, the author of the epistles.[84] At the beginning of his career he had been a teacher, and he was the first to write lengthy epistles and to make use of elaborate doxologies in the sections of his letters.[85] People took up this usage after him.

---

of ʿUthmān and died in 92/711 (see the article by H. G. Farmer and E. Neubauer in *EI*², s.v. Ṭuways). Daḥmān was a pupil of Maʿbad, and so may have been active in the reign of al-Walīd II (see the article on Maʿbad already cited).

79 Parallel, al-Masʿūdī, *Murūj*, 4:50 (§ 2238).

80 That is, Yazīd III, who died of natural causes after a rule of approximately six months in 126/744. See the article by G. R. Hawting in *EI*², s.v. Yazīd (III) b. al-Walīd (I).

81 *Iʿtizāl* (standing aside, remaining neutral) became the designation of the school of thought espoused by a group of thinkers collectively called Muʿtazila (see the article by D. Gimaret in *EI*², s.v.). It would be anachronistic to ascribe membership in this school to Yazīd III, but he was known for supporting the doctrines of the Qadariyya, a predecessor of the latter school, which emphasized man's free will, as opposed to God's predetermination of human actions. See the article by J. van Ess in *EI*², s.v. Ḳadariyya. The parallel in al-Masʿūdī, *Murūj*, 4:58 (§ 2254) simply says that Yazīd followed the doctrine of the Muʿtazila (*qawl al-Muʿtazila*) and then lists the components of this doctrine.

82 The last of the Umayyad caliphs, Marwān II ruled from 127/744 to 132/750; see the article by G. R. Hawting in *EI*², s.v. Marwān II.

83 *ʿAṣabiyya* literally means "loyalty to one's kinship group," from *ʿaṣaba*, meaning one's relations in the male line. Here the word is used in the larger sense of tribalism, although ascribing its rise to such a late date is not accurate, since rivalries and fighting between various tribal alliances had been endemic long before this time. However, al-Masʿūdī, *Murūj*, 4:66 ff. (§ 2267 ff.) has a long section on the rivalry between the tribal groupings of Yamāniyya and Nizāriyya during the days of Marwān.

84 ʿAbd al-Ḥamīd is generally accounted the founder of Arabic epistolary prose. Six of his long compositions survive, the most famous of them being his epistle of advice to Marwān's son and heir ʿAbdallāh and his epistle setting forth the dignity of the secretarial office. See the article by Wadād al-Qāḍī in *EI*³, s.v. ʿAbd al-Ḥamīd b. Yaḥyā al-Kātib.

85 Literally, "he used *taḥmīdāt*." These were elaborate passages of praise to God, full of Qurʾānic allusions and other literary devices. J. D. Latham in his article "The Beginnings of Arabic Prose Literature: the Epistolary Genre," in *Arabic Literature to the End of the Umayyad Period*, 173, calls them "congratulatory 'Te Deums' in which the author gives thanks and praises to God for some victory won for Islam by the addressee."

An Account of the ʿAbbāsid Caliphs

Abū l-ʿAbbās came to power as Commander of the Faithful; he was ʿAbdallāh b. Muḥammad b. ʿAlī b. ʿAbdallāh b. al-ʿAbbās b. ʿAbd al-Muṭṭalib.[86] His first action that people imitated was to deliver the sermon (*khuṭba*) on the pulpit standing—the Umayyads had delivered it seated. The people therefore acclaimed him, saying, "O descendant of the uncle of the Messenger of God, you have revived the practice (*sunna*) of the Messenger of God—God's blessings and peace be upon him."[87] He was quick to command the shedding of blood:[88] al-Ashʿath[89] shed it in the Maghrib, and Ṣāliḥ b. ʿAlī[90] in Egypt; Ḥāzim

86 Known by his sobriquet "al-Saffāḥ" ("the Spiller," sc. of blood) to which al-Yaʿqūbī will soon allude, he came to power in the revolution that overthrew the Umayyads. He was proclaimed caliph in Kufa in 132/749 and ruled until his death in 136/754. The genealogy here traces his ancestry to the Prophet's uncle, al-ʿAbbās b. ʿAbd al-Muṭṭalib, from whom the dynasty took its name and claim to legitimacy. See the article by S. Moscati in *EI*², s.v. Abū ʾl-ʿAbbās al-Saffāḥ.

87 Parallel, al-Masʿūdī, *Murūj*, 4:94 (§ 2308).

88 An intriguing parallel to al-Yaʿqūbī's section on the character of the ʿAbbāsid caliphs occurs in al-Masʿūdī, *Murūj*, 5:211–215 (§ 3445–3458). Al-Masʿūdī reports a conversation between a courtier of the Caliph al-Qāhir (r. 320/932 to 322/934) and an otherwise unknown antiquarian/historian (*akhbārī*) Muḥammad b. ʿAlī al-ʿAbdī (accepting the alternate reading for the printed al-Miṣrī; cf. Rosenthal, *A History of Muslim Historiography*, 2nd ed., 58–59) al-Khurāsānī (still alive, according to al-Masʿūdī, ibid., 5:215 [§ 3458], in 333/944–945). At the caliph's command, this courtier gives a series of character sketches of the ʿAbbāsid caliphs from al-Saffāḥ to al-Mutawakkil that so closely echoes al-Yaʿqūbī (who died c. 292/905)—the remainder of this paragraph, for example, occurs in al-Masʿūdī almost verbatim—that the material must have come directly from al-Yaʿqūbī's work, from one of its immediate sources, or from a subsequent author who quoted al-Yaʿqūbī. Unfortunately, the *isnād* in al-Masʿūdī is of no help in determining whence this Muḥammad b. ʿAlī drew his material, which occasionally presents a fuller text than that in the *Mushākala*.

89 In al-Masʿūdī, *Murūj*, 5:211 (§ 3445), he and the following people are identified as governors appointed by al-Saffāḥ. Al-Ashʿath is Muḥammad b. al-Ashʿath al-Khuzāʿī (not to be confused with two other figures who shared the name "al-Ashʿath" ["having unkempt hair"]), a military commander who served the ʿAbbāsids in a variety of capacities from the time of Abū Muslim until his death in 149/766. His activity in North Africa involved the retaking in 144/761 (hence not under al-Saffāḥ, but under his successor al-Manṣūr) of the city of al-Qayrawān in Ifrīqiya, which had been occupied by the Ibāḍiyya, a Khārijite group. See the article in *EI*², s.v. al-Ḳayrawān.

90 A member of the ʿAbbāsid family, Ṣāliḥ b. ʿAlī b. ʿAbdallāh b. al-ʿAbbās served twice as governor of Egypt (for a year beginning in 133/750 and again in 136–137/753–55). See the article by A. Grohmann and H. Kennedy in *EI*², s.v. Ṣāliḥ b. ʿAlī.

b. Khuzayma shed it, and Ḥumayd b. Qaḥṭaba shed it in Iraq; ʿAbdallāh b. ʿAlī shed it in Syria; Dāwūd b. ʿAlī shed it in the Ḥijāz; and his brother Yaḥyā b. Muḥammad shed it in Mosul. Nevertheless, he was generous, free, and open-handed with money.

Then came Abū Jaʿfar al-Manṣūr ʿAbdallāh b. Muḥammad.[91] He was the first Hāshimite to sow division between the descendants of al-ʿAbbās b. ʿAbd al-Muṭṭalib and those of Abū Ṭālib b. ʿAbd al-Muṭṭalib, so that people took to saying, "an ʿAbbāsī," or "a Ṭālibī."[92] Previously, it had been the affair of all the Banū Hāshim.[93] He was the first caliph who acquired astrologers and acted in accordance with the stars.[94] He was the first caliph who translated ancient Persian books and rendered them into the Arabic tongue.[95] In his days the book *Kalīla and Dimna*[96] was translated; the book *Sindhind*[97] was translated;

---

91 The second ʿAbbāsid caliph, r. 136–158/754–775. See the article by H. Kennedy in *EI*², s.v. al-Manṣūr.

92 That is, people began to differentiate politically between ʿAbbāsīs, those who supported the ʿAbbāsids' claim to authority based on their descent from the Prophet's uncle, al-ʿAbbās b. ʿAbd al-Muṭṭalib b. Ḥāshim, and Ṭālibīs, those who supported the claims of the descendants of ʿAlī b. Abī Ṭālib.

93 That is, supporters of the right of close relatives of the Prophet to the caliphate had made common cause, not distinguishing between descendants of al-ʿAbbās (the ʿAbbāsids) and those of Abū Ṭālib (the Ṭālibids). The text as printed translates, "It was said, 'That was the name of all the Banū Hāshim.'" Millward, in his edition of the Arabic text, notes that the word *ism* (name) is unclear in the MS. The parallel in al-Masʿūdī, *Murūj*, 5:211 (§3446), reads *amr* (thing, affair), which is graphically similar, makes more sense, and has been translated here. For *qīla* (it was said), al-Masʿūdī reads *qablu* (previously), which also has been used as the basis for the translation.

94 The parallel in al-Masʿūdī names three astronomers/astrologers at this point (Nawbakht, Ibrāhīm al-Fazārī, and ʿAlī b. ʿĪsā) with information about each. If they were originally part of al-Yaʿqūbī's essay, one might infer that the text of the *Mushākala* has been truncated. Another possibility is that they occurred in al-Yaʿqūbī's source or were added by a subsequent transmitter between al-Yaʿqūbī and Muḥammad b. ʿAlī.

95 Al-Yaʿqūbī's language gives the mistaken impression that al-Manṣūr personally translated the books. Al-Masʿūdī is more careful: "He was the first caliph for whom books were translated from the Persian language into Arabic."

96 Originally an Indian (Sanskrit) mirror for princes in the form of an extended series of beast-fables, translated from Middle Persian by Ibn al-Muqaffaʿ sometime before 139/756, when al-Manṣūr had him put to death.

97 An Indian astronomical treatise whose Sanskrit title probably ended with the word *Siddhānta* (perfected). Cf. al-Yaʿqūbī, *Taʾrīkh*, 1:92: "Scholars have said that the first of the kings of India under whom they became united was Brahman .... He was the first person who discoursed about the stars. From him was derived knowledge of them and the first book,

the books of Aristotle were translated, and the *Almagest* of Ptolemy, the book of Euclid, the book *Arithmetic*,[98] and the rest of the non-Arabic books on the stars, computation, medicine, philosophy, and other things, and people examined them. In his days, also, Muḥammad b. Isḥāq b. Yasār set down the books of the *Maghāzī*;[99] they had not been collected or well known before that. He was the first caliph who built a city and settled in it: the city of Baghdad. A horoscope was cast for him about the time to commence building it, and he was told that no caliph would ever die there. Abū Jaʿfar interested himself in scholarship and transmitted *ḥadīth*. In his days, the sciences that people studied and the traditions they transmitted became numerous. He was the first caliph who appointed his clients (*mawālī*) and slaves (*ghilmān*) as officials and advanced them over the Arabs. After his death, the caliphs who were his descendants followed his example.

Al-Mahdī[100] was generous, munificent, noble, and open-handed with money; and the people in his time followed his example. People in the days of al-Mahdī lived in ample circumstances.[101] Whenever he rode out, bags of coins were carried with him; anyone who asked him for a boon received it from his own hand, and the people imitated him. His objective was to kill the Manichaeans,[102] because they had become numerous. Among the things that Ibn al-Muqaffaʿ had translated were books by the dualist Mānī, by the dualist

---

which the Indians call the *Sindhind*, which means 'Eon of Eons.'" See the article by D. Pingree in *EI*², s.v. Sindhind.

98 Arabic *Arithmāṭīqī* (transliterating the Greek title), a treatise by the mathematician Nicomachus of Gerasa, whose book is summarized in al-Yaʿqūbī, *Taʾrīkh*, 1:140–143, where he is mistakenly identified as Nicomachus the father of Aristotle.

99 *Maghāzī* is the usual term for the Prophet's military expeditions and raids from Medina. Since the work of Muḥammad b. Isḥāq included the Prophet's earlier life in Mecca, the word may here have a broader connotation. (See the article by M. Hinds in *EI*², s.v. Maghāzī.) The parallel in al-Masʿūdī mentions the three sections of Ibn Isḥāq's work explicitly: "In his days, Muḥammad b. Isḥāq set down the books of the *Maghāzī*, the *Siyar* ("ways of acting"), and Reports of the Inception (of the Prophet's mission)."

100 Al-Manṣūr's son, the third ʿAbbāsid caliph, who ruled from 158/775 to 169/785. See the article by H. Kennedy in *EI*², s.v. al-Mahdī.

101 Arabic *ittasaʿa l-nās ... fī maʿāyishihim*. The parallel in al-Masʿūdī, *Murūj*, 5:212 (§2447) reads *fa-ttasaʿū fī masāʿīhim*, "and so they were expansive in their (good, charitable) efforts," which better fits the context.

102 Arabic *zanādiqa* (pl. of *zindīq*), the usual designation for Manichaeans, followers of the religion founded by Mānī (b. 216 CE, put to death c. 274) although it could designate various other sects considered heretical. See the article in *EI*², s.v. Zindīḳ.

Ibn Dayṣān,[103] and by others, and there were the works of Ibn Abī l-ʿAwjāʾ,[104] Ḥammād ʿAjrad,[105] Yaḥyā b. Ziyād,[106] and Muṭīʿ b. Iyās,[107] whereby they had filled the earth with books by heretics. The Manichaeans became numerous and their books spread among the people. He was the first caliph who commanded the theologians to compose books against the heretics. He rebuilt the Sacred Mosque as it is to this day, and he rebuilt the Mosque of the Messenger of God—God's blessings and peace be upon him—which had been destroyed by earthquakes.[108]

Then came Mūsā b. al-Mahdī.[109] He was a tyrant. He was the first caliph before whom men marched with drawn swords, halberds, and strung bows. His governors imitated him and followed in his ways.

Then came Hārūn al-Rashīd b. al-Mahdī.[110] He was constant in performing the pilgrimage, conducting military campaigns,[111] and building cisterns and

---

103 Better known by the Syriac version of his name, Bar Dīṣān, or its Greek version, Bardesanes, he was active in Edessa and died in 201 CE. His extent works display a syncretistic religion that fuses Christian and dualistic elements. See the article by Patricia Crone in *EI*[3], s.v. Dayṣanīs.

104 Correcting the printed text, which has Ibn Abī l-ʿArjāʾ. Ibn Abī l-ʿAwjāʾ, a member of a prominent family, lived at Basra and later at Kufa, where he was put to death in 155/772. Muslim historians depict him as "a man of dangerous heterodoxy, who, on his own admission, invented numerous traditions, falsified the calendar and spread Manichaean propaganda by means of insidious questions relating to the problem of suffering and of divine justice, and who was a believer in the eternity of the world and in metempsychosis." (G. Vajda in *EI*[2], s.v. Ibn Abī ʾl-ʿAwdjāʾ.)

105 Ḥammād ʿAjrad (d. c. 161/777–778), was a poet known for his satires and libertine verses, but he was also accused of religious heterodoxy (*zandaqa*). See the article by Ch. Pellat in *EI*[2], s.v. Ḥammād ʿAdjrad.

106 Yaḥyā b. Ziyād was a poet and member of the same circle as Muṭīʿ b. Iyās, who wrote an elegy for him as "his companion in debauchery" (thus Ch. Pellat in *EI*[2], s.v. Muṭīʿ b. Iyās).

107 Muṭīʿ b. Iyās (d. 169/785 at Basra) was a poet and member of a circle whose libertine manner of living eventually attracted charges of religious heterodoxy. See the article by Ch. Pellat in *EI*[2], s.v. Muṭīʿ b. Iyās.

108 The parallel in al-Masʿūdī, *Murūj*, 5:212 (§ 3447) differs in one detail: "He began to rebuild the Sacred Mosque and the Mosque of the Messenger of God—God's blessings and peace be upon him—as the two are to this day, and he rebuilt Jerusalem (*Bayt al-Maqdis*), which had been destroyed by earthquakes."

109 The fourth ʿAbbāsid caliph, Mūsā al-Hādī, ruled from 169/785 until his sudden death in 170/786. See the article by D. Sourdel in *EI*[2], s.v. al-Hādī Ila ʾL-ḥaḳḳ.

110 The fifth ʿAbbāsid caliph, Hārūn al-Rashīd, ruled from 170/786 until 193/809. See the article by F. Omar in *EI*[2], s.v. Hārūn al-Rashīd.

111 Arabic *ghazw*, conducting military expeditions into "infidel" (that is, Byzantine) territory.

forts on the road to Mecca and Medina and in Mecca, Medina, Minā, and ʿArafāt.[112] He built eight forts like those at Ṭarsūs and elsewhere, and built housing for troops stationed on the frontiers. His family, governors, companions, and secretaries imitated him; there remained no one who did not build a house in Mecca, a house in Medina, and a house in Ṭarsūs, to imitate him and do as he had done. The ones who did this the most and left the finest legacy were his wife, Umm Jaʿfar bt. Jaʿfar b. al-Manṣūr, followed by his viziers the Barmakids, and others of his clients, officials,[113] and secretaries. Moreover, al-Rashīd was the first caliph to play at polo and bowls and to shoot arrows in the game called *birjās*,[114] and he promoted people skillful at these things. He was the first caliph to play chess and backgammon; he promoted players and granted them pensions. He was the first caliph of the Banū Hāshim who acquired singing girls.[115] People one and all imitated him and followed his path. His viziers were from the Barmakid family.[116] Yaḥyā b. Khālid[117] loved philosophy, theology, and speculation. There were many theologians in his days; they argued, debated, and wrote books. Among them were Hishām b. al-Ḥakam,[118] Ḍirār b. ʿAmr,[119] and

112 The road to Mecca and Medina is the famous Darb Zubayda (Zubayda's Highway, named for al-Rashīd's wife Umm Jaʿfar Zubayda bt. Jaʿfar b. al-Manṣūr). It ran from Kufa to Mecca, with a branch to Medina. See the article by Saad A. al-Rashid and M. J. L. Young in *EI*², s.v. Darb Zubayda.

113 Arabic *quwwād*, pl. of *qāʾid*; in modern usage generally restricted to military leaders, but in earlier usage more general. See Dozy, *Supplément*, 2:417, s.v.

114 A version of this game of skill or military exercise, documented from the time of al-Muʿtaḍid (r. 279/892 to 289/902), involved a contestant on horseback having to get his lance-point through a metal ring fixed to the top of a wooden column, thereby demonstrating his skill at controlling his horse and aiming his weapon. See the article by C. E. Bosworth in *EI*², s.v. Istiʿrāḍ/ʿArḍ.

115 The piety of the Hāshimites as close kin of the Prophet was often contrasted with the dissoluteness of the Umayyads (al-Yaʿqūbī has already mentioned music or singing girls in connection with the Umayyad caliphs Yazīd b. Muʿāwiya, Yazīd b. ʿAbd al-Malik, and al-Walīd b. Yazīd b. ʿAbd al-Malik). Therefore, the development of a hedonistic culture at the ʿAbbāsid court was in a way unexpected.

116 On this family of Iranian origin that produced a series of secretaries and viziers for the early ʿAbbāsid caliphs, see the article by Kevin van Bladel in *EI*³, s.v. Barmakids.

117 Yaḥyā b. Khālid b. Barmak was al-Rashīd's vizier from 170/786 to 187/803.

118 A Shīʿī theologian (d. 179/795–796) associated with the imams Jaʿfar al-Ṣādiq and Mūsā l-Kāẓim, and later with a circle of theologians who held disputations in the presence of Yaḥyā b. Khālid al-Barmakī. See the article by W. Madelung in *EI*², s.v. Hishām b. al-Ḥakam.

119 A prolific Muʿtazilī theologian (d. c. 200/815) who took part in the debates organized by Yaḥyā b. Khālid al-Barmakī. See the article by J. van Ess in *EI*², s.v. Ḍirār b. ʿAmr.

Muʿammar b. ʿUmar.[120] He also delved into books of alchemy.[121] The Barmakids were generous, noble, bountiful, and beneficent. Their officials and people one and all imitated them, so much so that the days of al-Rashīd, due to the multitude of benefactors then living, used to be called "wedding-party days." The deeds of the Barmakids are famous and renowned, but there was no one in al-Rashīd's entourage who was not a benefactor, either by nature or by imitation. Al-Rashīd was the first caliph to write in the headings of letters: "And I pray that He will bless Muḥammad, His servant and messenger—God's blessings and peace be upon him." The caliphs after him followed his example. He was the first caliph to wear the tall Ruṣāfī cap.[122] He was the first caliph who wrote in white on the black banners, "There is no god but God, Muḥammad is the messenger of God."[123]

As for Umm Jaʿfar bt. Jaʿfar b. al-Manṣūr, she was always trying to outdo al-Rashīd in everything, be it serious or frivolous.[124] As for the serious, there were the beautiful monuments that had no equal in the realms of Islam. She excavated the spring at ʿAyn al-Mushāsh and channeled its water twelve Arab miles to Mecca, spending 1,700,000 dinars on it. Then she constructed cisterns, fountains, and places for ablutions around the Sacred Mosque. She built hostels and cisterns at Minā, fountains at ʿArafāt, and dug wells at Minā on the road from Mecca. For the upkeep of these things, she designated as charitable endowments (*waqf*) in perpetuity estates with an annual revenue of 30,000 dinars. She built hostels in the frontier districts and established hospitals, and she designated as endowments in perpetuity for the frontiers, the poor, and the destitute estates with a revenue of 100,000 dinars. As for the things whereby

---

120 Thus in the printed text, but probably a mistake for the well-known Muʿtazilī theologian Muʿammar b. ʿAbbād (d. 215/830) also associated with the court of Hārūn al-Rashīd. See the article by H. Daiber in *EI*², s.v. Muʿammar b. ʿAbbād.

121 Arabic *al-kīmiyāʾ* (the ultimate source of the English word "alchemy"). See the article by Regula Forster in *EI*³, s.v. Alchemy.

122 Arabic *al-qalansuwa al-ṭawīla al-ruṣāfiyya*, named for the al-Ruṣāfa quarter of Baghdad on the east bank of the Tigris, a military center and the location of al-Mahdī's great palace. On the *qalansuwa* headgear, see the article by W. Björkman in *EI*², s.v. Ḳalansuwa. On al-Ruṣāfa, see the article by C. E. Bosworth in *EI*², s.v. al-Ruṣāfa.

123 The banners of the ʿAbbāsids since the beginning of their revolution were black. This seems to imply that the banners originally had no writing on them and that the addition of this motto was an innovation.

124 Parallel, often more elaborately worded, to this section on al-Rashīd's wife in al-Masʿūdī, *Murūj*, 5:213 (§ 3450).

kings seek ease and pleasure, she was the first person in Islam to have utensils of gold and silver inlaid with jewels made. She wore such fine variegated silk[125] that a single dress made for her cost 50,000 dinars. She was the first to employ a private bodyguard (*shākiriyya*) consisting of mounted servants and slave-girls, who would come and go on her errands, carrying her messages and letters.[126] She was the first to have palanquins made from silver, ebony, and sandalwood, their top and fastenings being of gold and silver, lined with variegated silk (*washy*), sable, brocade, cloth of silk and wool (*khazz*), cloth of silk and cotton (*mulḥam*), and cloth of the sort called *dabīqī*.[127] She was the first who had gowns made with pearls interspersed with jewels, as well as ambergris candles. The people imitated Umm Jaʿfar in all her works.

Then came Muḥammad al-Amīn.[128] He was the son of al-Rashīd, and his mother was Umm Jaʿfar. He promoted eunuchs,[129] favoring them and elevating their estates. When Umm Jaʿfar saw his weakness for eunuchs, she obtained some slender, fair-faced slave girls, cut their hair into bangs and short at the temples and the back of the neck, dressed them in sleeved tunics and waistbands—she was the first to do this—sent them to him, and put them on display to the people. As a result, courtiers and ordinary folk acquired slave girls, cut their hair short, dressed them in sleeved tunics and waistbands, and called them "page girls" (*ghulāmiyyāt*). Muḥammad's days, until he was killed, were short.

Then came al-Maʾmūn as Commander of the Faithful, the son of al-Rashīd.[130] At the beginning of his caliphate, under the influence of al-Faḍl

125 Arabic *washy*, which can refer either to variegated silk or to cloth of gold.

126 On such private bodyguards and militias see the article by Khalīl ʿAthāmina in *EI*², s.v. Shākiriyya.

127 That is, cloths of the sort for which the Egyptian town of Dabīq, near Damietta, was famous. The city specialized in the manufacture of fine textiles embossed with gold, as well as multicolored linen. See the article in by G. Wiet in *EI*², s.v. Dabīḳ.

128 The sixth ʿAbbāsid caliph, ruled from 193/809 to 198/813, when he was overthrown by his brother al-Maʾmūn in a civil war. See the article by Michael Cooperson in *EI*³, s.v. al-Amīn, Muḥammad.

129 The word for eunuchs used here is *khadam*, which can also mean servants. The parallel in al-Masʿūdī refers specifically to the favor granted to Kawthar, who was almost certainly a eunuch. For an obscene poem implying that al-Amīn had sexual relations with Kawthar, see al-Ṭabarī, *Taʾrīkh*, 3:804–805 (trans. M. Fishbein, *The History of al-Ṭabarī*, *XXXI*, 58–59). In any case, the remainder of the paragraph leaves little doubt about what is implied.

130 ʿAbdallāh b. Hārūn, surnamed al-Maʾmūn, the seventh ʿAbbāsid caliph, ruled from 196/812

[b. Sahl],[131] he occupied himself with astrology, emulated the ways of the kings of the Persians, and was fond of reading ancient books. But when he arrived in Iraq, he put these things aside and professed the doctrines of Justice and Monotheism.[132] He associated with theologians, jurists, and literary men, brought them from the provinces, and granted them subsidies. There were many theologians in his days, and each wrote a book to defend his own doctrine and refute his opponents. He was the most generous of men in granting pardon, the most able of them, the most liberal with wealth, and the most lavish with gifts. As for his clemency, he pardoned Ibrāhīm [b.] al-Mahdī, who, after having been his governor of Basra, cast off his allegiance, claimed the caliphate for himself, styled himself Commander of the Faithful, and made war on al-Ma'mūn's supporters.[133] He pardoned al-Faḍl b. al-Rabīʿ, the person who had induced Muḥammad [al-Amīn] to remove al-Ma'mūn as heir apparent and had sent armies to fight him; al-Ma'mūn subsequently guaranteed his safety, but he became disloyal and called on the people to swear allegiance to Ibrāhīm b. al-Mahdī.[134] He pardoned Ismāʿīl b. Jaʿfar b. Sulaymān, who had cast off his obedience and had said the most scurrilous things about him.[135] He par-

(when he was proclaimed caliph by his supporters during the lifetime of his brother, al-Amīn, whom he overthrew in a civil war) to 218/833. See the article by M. Rekaya in *EI*², s.v. al-Ma'mūn. Parallel, al-Masʿūdī, *Murūj*, 5:214 (§ 3453).

131 Al-Faḍl b. Sahl, al-Ma'mūn's tutor and trusted advisor, was instrumental in his rise to power. When al-Ma'mūn became caliph, al-Faḍl became both vizier and military commander (hence his title *Dhū l-Ri'āsatayn*, "the Man with Two Commands"). He continued to exercise authority until his assassination in 202/818. See the article by Hayrettin Yücesoy in *EI*³, s.v. al-Faḍl b. Sahl.

132 Arabic *al-ʿadl wa l-tawḥīd*, shorthand for the main Muʿtazilī doctrines.

133 In 202/817, Ibrāhīm b. al-Mahdī was involved in an abortive revolt sparked by opposition to al-Ma'mūn's naming of ʿAlī al-Riḍā as his heir. The revolt was effectively quashed by 204/819. In fact, Ibrāhīm spent several years in hiding, was imprisoned after being discovered, and was pardoned only in 210/825–826, whereupon he returned to Baghdad and devoted himself to poetry and music. See the article by D. Sourdel in *EI*², s.v. Ibrāhīm b. al-Mahdī.

134 As vizier to al-Amīn, al-Faḍl b. al-Rabīʿ was responsible for al-Amīn's decision to deprive his brother al-Ma'mūn of the succession rights specified in al-Rashīd's testament and proclaim his own son heir apparent. After al-Amīn was defeated in the civil war, al-Faḍl b. al-Rabīʿ went into hiding, but emerged to support the abortive revolt of Ibrāhīm b. al-Mahdī. He was later granted pardon. See the article by D. Sourdel in *EI*², s.v. al-Faḍl b. al-Rabīʿ.

135 Ismāʿīl b. Jaʿfar b. Sulaymān, al-Ma'mūn's governor of Basra, refused to accept the naming

doned Nu'aym b. Ḥāzim, who had kept fighting him for a number of years.[136] He pardoned 'Īsā b. Muḥammad b. [Abī] Khālid, who had broken his oath of allegiance time after time and had fought al-Ma'mūn's supporters and had killed the latter's chief of police.[137] He pardoned the "volunteer" Sahl b. Salāma, who wore wool, hung a copy of the Qur'ān around his neck, and commanded people to depose al-Ma'mūn and that no one should grant him obedience.[138] He pardoned the Khārijite Mahdī b. 'Alwān, who styled himself Commander of the Faithful, fought against al-Ma'mūn's supporters, and whom al-Ma'mūn captured without any pledge or promise of safety.[139] He pardoned the poet Di'bil, who had composed the most scurrilous sort of satire against him.[140] He pardoned 'Ubayd[allāh] b. al-Sarī b. al-Ḥakam, who had taken control of Egypt and continued fighting for a number of years.[141] He pardoned the 'Alid Muḥam-

of 'Alī al-Riḍā as heir apparent in 201/817 and called for the deposition of al-Ma'mūn. He was later pardoned. See the account in al-Ya'qūbī, *Ta'rīkh*, 2:545.

136 Nu'aym b. Ḥāzim was another dignitary who refused to accept al-Ma'mūn's naming of 'Alī al-Riḍā. Al-Ma'mūn then sent him to fight against Ibrāhīm b. al-Mahdī, but Nu'aym went over to the latter's side. He was later pardoned. See Michael Cooperson, *Classical Arabic Biography: The Heirs of the Prophets in the Age of Al-Ma'mūn*, 193–194.

137 On the part played by 'Īsā b. Muḥammad b. Abī Khālid in the revolt of Ibrāhīm b. al-Mahdī and his later service to al-Ma'mūn, see al-Ya'qūbī, *Ta'rīkh*, 2:547–548, 564.

138 Arabic, Sahl b. Salāma *al-Muṭṭawwi'ī*. The epithet is derived from Qur'ān 2:158, 184: "And whoso volunteers good (*man taṭawwa'a khayran*), God is All-grateful, All-knowing." And, "Yet better it is for him who volunteers good (*man taṭawwa'a khayran*) ..." In 201/817, Sahl b. Salāma al-Anṣārī led a popular pietistic movement in the al-Ḥarbiyya quarter of Baghdad that challenged the government's authority. See the account in al-Ṭabarī, *Ta'rīkh*, 3:1008–1012, 1023–1025, 1034, 1035–1036 (trans. C. E. Bosworth, *The History of al-Ṭabarī*, XXXII, 55–60, 75–78, 90, 92); also the article by Wilferd Madelung, "The Vigilante Movement of Sahl b. Salāma al-Khurāsānī and the Origins of Ḥanbalism Reconsidered."

139 On the revolt of Mahdī b. 'Alwān in 202/817–818 or 203/819, see al-Ya'qūbī, *Ta'rīkh*, 2:548; al-Ṭabarī, *Ta'rīkh*, 3:1016–1017.

140 On the poet Di'bil (a *nom de plume* of 'Alī b. Muḥammad al-Khuzā'ī), who lived from 148/765 to 246/860, see the article by L. Zolondek in *EI*², s.v. Di'bil. One of Di'bil's satires of al-Ma'mūn is cited at al-Ṭabarī, *Ta'rīkh*, 3:1155–1156 (trans. C. E. Bosworth, *The History of al-Ṭabarī*, XXXII, 248–249).

141 'Ubaydallāh b. al-Sarī b. al-Ḥakam had been commander of the guard (*ṣāḥib al-shurṭa*) in Egypt since 205/820–821, but declared himself governor in 206/822, resisting al-Ma'mūn's attempts to replace him. In 210/825–826, al-Ma'mūn sent 'Abdallāh b. Ṭāhir with an army to dislodge him. Although there was fighting, 'Ubaydallāh was treated very leniently afterward. See al-Ya'qūbī, *Ta'rīkh*, 2:560–561; al-Ṭabarī, *Ta'rīkh*, 3:1086–1087, 1091, 1096–1098 (trans. C. E. Bosworth, *The History of al-Ṭabarī*, XXXII, 159–160, 164, 171–173).

mad b. Jaʿfar b. Muḥammad, who had rebelled in Mecca and had styled himself Commander of the Faithful.[142] He pardoned Zayd b. Mūsā b. Jaʿfar, who had rebelled at Basra and had renounced allegiance to al-Maʾmūn.[143] He pardoned the ʿAlid Ibrāhīm b. Mūsā b. Jaʿfar b. Muḥammad, who had rebelled in Yemen and had fought against al-Julūdī.[144] He pardoned all who had usurped authority:[145] Rabāḥ b. Abī Ramtha, who had taken control in Diyār Rabīʿa; al-ʿAbbās b. Zufar al-Hilālī, who had taken control at Qūrus in the military district of Qinnasrīn; Naṣr b. Shabath[146] al-ʿUqaylī, who had taken control in Diyār Muḍar, despite his having fought for a long time; ʿUthmān b. Thumāma al-ʿAbsī, who had rebelled against him in the Ḥijāz; al-Ḥawārī b. Ḥiṭṭān al-Tanūkhī, who rebelled in Ḥāḍir Tanūkh;[147] and others whom it would take too long to mention in this book. He once said, "Pardoning has been made so attractive to me that I do not think I shall be rewarded for it."

As for his generosity and open-handedness: On a single day he ordered that 1,500,000 dinars should be given to three individuals—500,000 dinars to each. Once, when money ran short in the treasury, he assembled his companions and said: "The money has run short, and that has harmed us and our friends. Go and get us a loan from the merchants in the amount of 10 million dirhams until the revenues come in and we repay." But Ghassān b. ʿAbbād[148] stood up, recounted the favors al-Maʾmūn had bestowed on him, and offered 30 million dirhams, saying, "I have them on hand." Ḥumayd b. ʿAbd al-Ḥamīd al-Ṭūsī[149] said the same, and each of his companions present at the gathering stood up

---

142 This revolt, which took place in 200/815, receives a short notice in al-Yaʿqūbī, *Taʾrīkh*, 2:540, 544; to which one can add the longer account in al-Ṭabarī, *Taʾrīkh*, 3:989–994 (trans. C. E. Bosworth, *The History of al-Ṭabarī, XXXII*, 30–37).

143 On the revolt of this ʿAlid, surnamed Zayd al-Nār ("Zayd of the Fire" due to the large number of houses of ʿAbbāsids and their supporters he ordered to be burnt down) in 200/815–816, see al-Yaʿqūbī, *Taʾrīkh*, 2:500, 540, 546; al-Ṭabarī, *Taʾrīkh*, 3:986–987 (trans. C. E. Bosworth, *The History of al-Ṭabarī, XXXII*, 26–27).

144 On this revolt, which took place in 200/815–816, see al-Yaʿqūbī, *Taʾrīkh*, 2:544–546; al-Ṭabarī, *Taʾrīkh*, 3:987–988 (trans. C. E. Bosworth, *The History of al-Ṭabarī, XXXII*, 28–29). ʿĪsā b. Yazīd al-Julūdī was one of al-Maʾmūn's military commanders.

145 The following list should be compared to al-Yaʿqūbī, *Taʾrīkh*, 2:539–541.

146 MS Shabīb, corrected on the basis of the form found elsewhere: e.g., al-Yaʿqūbī, *Taʾrīkh*, 2:541, and al-Ṭabarī, *Taʾrīkh*, 3:975 and *passim*.

147 *Ḥāḍir Tanūkh* means "the settlements of (the tribe) Tanūkh"; according to al-Yaʿqūbī, *Taʾrīkh*, 2:541 (where the name appears as Ḥanṭān), the area was near Aleppo.

148 Subsequently governor of Khurāsān and then of Sind. More about his generosity will be mentioned shortly by al-Yaʿqūbī.

149 The general who was largely responsible for the defeat of Ibrāhīm b. al-Mahdī; more about

and offered what he had, until what they offered him amounted to 156 million dirhams. He accepted nothing from any of them and rewarded them well. Once the revenues were late. When news arrived that the land-tax revenues from Fārs[150] had arrived, he rode out to look at it and then distributed all of it, so that there remained only enough to pay the army, and he commanded al-Muʿallā b. Ayyūb to take charge of it.[151]

Al-Maʾmūn's companions, ministers, secretaries, and officials imitated[152] his actions, walked in his ways, and followed his path. Among them was al-Ḥasan b. Sahl.[153] He was the noblest, the most generous, and the most benevolent of men, the most comely of them in the face of misfortune and affliction,[154] and the most patient in giving everyone what he asked. Ḥumayd b. ʿAbd al-Ḥamīd al-Ṭūsī was generous, open-handed, and beneficent. He set aside estates with a yearly revenue of 100,000 dinars as charitable trusts (*waqf*) for the benefit of those belonging to noble families[155] and relatives of powerful people.[156] He would turn no one away. Ghassān b. ʿAbbād was open-handed: on a single day he distributed 13 million dirhams. Whenever anyone asked him to speak to al-Maʾmūn about some need, he gave it to him from his own funds and spoke to al-Maʾmūn. ʿAbdallāh b. Ṭāhir was a person of great manliness, patience, and courtesy.[157] On a single day he commanded that three of his compan-

---

his generosity will be mentioned shortly by al-Yaʿqūbī. See the article in *EI*², s.v Ḥumayd b. ʿAbd al-Ḥamīd.

150 The major province of southeastern Iran.

151 The incident is narrated at greater length in al-Ṭabarī, *Taʾrīkh*, 3:1143–1144 (trans. C. E. Bosworth, *The History of al-Ṭabarī, XXXII*, 234–236), where al-Muʿallā b. Ayyūb appears as the official in charge of distributing pay to the army.

152 Reading with ed. Cairo, *yataqayyalūn*, rather than ed. Beirut, *yataqabbalūn* (accepted); the words differ by only one diacritical dot.

153 The brother of the vizier al-Faḍl b. Sahl, he served al-Maʾmūn as secretary and governor in Iraq. See the article by D. Sourdel in *EI*², s.v. al-Ḥasan b. Sahl.

154 Arabic *ajmalahum li-nāʾibatin wa-fādiḥah*. Although the sense is ambiguous, this may refer to al-Ḥasan's reaction to the assassination of his brother in 202/818, or it may simply refer to his readiness to relieve the misfortunes and afflictions of others.

155 Arabic *ahl al-buyūtāt*: "originally denoted those that belong to Persian families of the highest nobility (Nöldeke, *Geschichte der Perser und Araber zur Zeit der Sassaniden*, 71), then, the nobles in general" (*EI*², s.v.).

156 Arabic *dhawī l-aqdār*. For *aqdār* as "powerful people," see Dozy, *Supplément*, 2:321.

157 On the career of this general, who served al-Maʾmūn in Iraq, Egypt, and Khurāsān, where he ended his days (d. 230/844) as a virtually independent ruler, see the article by C. Edmond Bosworth in *EI*³, s.v. ʿAbdallāh b. Ṭāhir.

ions should be given 300,000 dinars—100,000 dinars apiece—and that three persons should be given 150,000–50,000 dinars apiece. ʿAlī b. Hishām was the most generous and manly of people; whenever he traveled, his kitchen would be loaded onto 700 camels.[158] Aḥmad b. Yūsuf, his secretary, was a person of great manliness.[159] The people in general were of praiseworthy character. Once, when the troops rioted in Baghdad and raised an uproar because their pay was late, Faraj al-Rukhkhajī went out to them and guaranteed them a year's wages, which he paid them from his own money.[160]

Al-Maʾmūn was the first caliph who wrote the words "In the Name of God, the Merciful, the Compassionate" in the directions or addresses of his letters.[161] He was the first caliph who assigned an Inspection Bureau to the army.[162] He was the first caliph who dated his letters with the name of his secretary; previously they had been dated only with the name of the clerk who wrote them (*muḥarrir*). These formalities[163] remained in use.

Then came al-Muʿtaṣim, who was Muḥammad b. Hārūn al-Rashīd.[164] He followed the path of al-Maʾmūn in religious doctrine. His dominant interests

---

158 ʿAlī b. Hishām al-Marwazī was a prominent Khurāsānian entrusted with the governorship of Baghdad by al-Ḥasan b. Sahl, and later with the governorship of al-Jibāl by al-Maʾmūn. He was executed in 217/832. See al-Ṭabarī, *Taʾrīkh*, 3:998, 1107–1109 (trans. C. E. Bosworth, *The History of al-Ṭabarī*, XXXII, 42, 192–194).

159 He was al-Maʾmūn's private secretary. See the article by D. Sourdel in *EI*², s.v. Aḥmad b. Yūsuf.

160 Faraj al-Rukhkhajī, a *mawlā* originally from Sīstān, is reported as heading an army sent by al-Maʾmūn to Egypt (al-Yaʿqūbī, *Taʾrīkh*, 2:556) and also served as overseer of the caliphal private domains. See the references cited by C. E. Bosworth, *The History of al-Ṭabarī*, XXXII, 107n.

161 Arabic *ʿunwānāt* (pl. of *ʿunwān*): the introductory portion of the letter, containing the designation of the sender and the addressee, each of whom received increasingly elaborate honorific formulas under the ʿAbbāsids. See the article by W. Björkman in *EI*², s.v. Diplomatic.

162 Reading with the MS and ed. Cairo, *dīwān al-ʿarḍ*, rather than the emendation proposed by Millward, *dīwān al-farḍ* (paymaster's department). On this bureau, concerned with reviewing, inspecting, and classifying troops, see the article by C. E. Bosworth in *EI*², s.v. Istiʿrāḍ/ʿArḍ.

163 Reading with ed. Cairo, *al-rusūm*, instead of Millward's *al-rumūz* (signs, symbols).

164 The eighth ʿAbbāsid caliph, Muḥammad b. Hārūn, whose full regnal name al-Muʿtaṣim Bi ʾllāh (He Who Holds Fast to God) recalls the language of Qurʾān 4:146 and 22:78, ruled from 218/833 to 227/842. See the article by C. E. Bosworth in *EI*², s.v. al-Muʿtaṣim Bi ʾllāh.

were horsemanship and imitating the Persians. He wore garments with narrow sleeves, and so the people narrowed the sleeves of their garments. He wore large boots and square caps; he was the first to wear such a cap, and people began wearing them in imitation of him.[165] They were named after him: people would say "a Muʿtaṣimī cap." He was the first caliph who rode on uncovered saddles[166] and used Persian utensils, and the people imitated him. In his time there was no one among his viziers, officials, and secretaries who was characterized by generosity, open-handedness, or benevolence except al-Ḥasan b. Sahl, despite his limited circumstances,[167] and Ibn Abī Du'ād;[168] the latter was a man of great merit and courtesy. Ibn Abī Du'ād had the greatest influence over his affairs and was favored by him.

Then came Hārūn al-Wāthiq, the son of al-Muʿtaṣim.[169] His path in religion and in the doctrine of God's justice was the same as that of his father, al-Muʿtaṣim, and of his uncle, al-Ma'mūn. He made this clearly apparent, tested people for it, punished those who disagreed with him, and imprisoned those who showed recalcitrance in the matter. He wrote to the judges near and far that they should test such persons as had been previously certified as of good character and not accept the testimony of anyone who did not adhere to his doctrine.[170] This doctrine became dominant among the people and by means

---

165 Arabic *al-shāsh al-murabbaʿa* and *shāshiyya murabbaʿa*. Similar language occurs in the parallel in al-Masʿūdī, *Murūj*, 5:214 (§ 3454), where al-Muʿtaṣim is said to have worn *al-qalānis wa-l-shāshiyyāt* (*qalansuwas*, tall hats already mentioned above, and *shāshiyyas*). The latter are a bit mysterious, but the word appears to refer to a style of cap. See Dozy, *Supplément*, 2:802. Millward translated "scarf" (p. 342), but this seems less likely.

166 Arabic *al-surūj al-makshūfa*: the meaning is unclear. One might conjecture that they were unpadded saddles. On al-Muʿtaṣim's love of polo, see al-Ṭabarī, *Ta'rīkh*, 3:1326–1327 (trans. C. E. Bosworth, *The History of al-Ṭabarī*, XXXIII, 212–213).

167 This may allude to the fact that al-Ḥasan b. Sahl, who has already been mentioned as active during the reign of al-Ma'mūn, retreated from public life after the assassination of his brother, al-Faḍl b. Sahl, and held no office under al-Muʿtaṣim, although he lived until 236/850–851. See the article by D. Sourdel in *EI*², s.v. al-Ḥasan b. Sahl.

168 Aḥmad b. Abī Du'ād began his career at the court of al-Ma'mūn, and, recommended by the latter, was made chief *qāḍī* after al-Muʿtaṣim's succession to the caliphate. As such, he was instrumental in enforcing adherence to the Muʿtazilī doctrines favored by al-Ma'mūn and al-Muʿtaṣim. See the article by John P. Turner in *EI*³, s.v. Aḥmad b. Abī Du'ād.

169 Abū Jaʿfar Hārūn b. al-Muʿtaṣim, who took the regnal name of al-Wāthiq Bi 'llāh (He Who Trusts in God), was the ninth ʿAbbāsid caliph. He ruled from 227/842 to 232/847. See the article by K. V. Zetterstéen, C. E. Bosworth, and E. van Donzel in *EI*², s.v. al-Wāt̲h̲iḳ Bi 'llāh. Parallel in al-Masʿūdī, *Murūj*, 5:214 (§ 3455).

170 "Such persons as had been previously certified as of good character" translates a single

of it they sought favor with Ibn Abī Du'ād and the judges. During his time there was no one to whom entreaty was made except Ibn Abī Du'ād. Al-Wāthiq was a heavy eater with a great capacity for food, abundant in almsgiving, and seeking the good of the members of his family in every land.[171]

Then came Ja'far b. al-Mu'taṣim al-Mutawakkil.[172] He rescinded the doctrines to which al-Wāthiq had adhered and publicly professed the doctrine of the Sunna and the Community.[173] He released anyone who had been imprisoned for not affirming that the Qur'ān had been created.[174] He forbade disputation, and he commanded all the scholars of *ḥadīth* whom he had released to resume transmitting *ḥadīth*. The people therefore abandoned that doctrine; those who had been upholding it repudiated it, and disputation and debate disappeared.[175] Among the things he innovated was the building of impoundments[176] and gated porticos, and so the people in Samarra all built in this way.

Arabic term, *al-'udūl*, literally, "just persons" or "persons of good morals." Testimony could be accepted only from persons vouched to have good morals, but such persons also performed a variety of other court functions. See the article in *EI*², s.v. 'Adl.

171 Arabic *kathīr al-akl wāsi' al-ṭa'ām* (much of eating, capacious of food). One parallel in al-Mas'ūdī, *Murūj*, 5:214 (§ 3455) substitutes *wāsi' al-'aṭā'* (idiomatic for "liberal of giving") for the last part of the phrase; another parallel in al-Mas'ūdī, *Murūj*, 4:364 (§ 2832) is slightly longer: Al-Wāthiq was *kathīr al-akl wa l-shurb, wāsi' al-ma'rūf, muta'aṭṭifan 'alā ahl baytihi, mutafaqqidan li-ra'iyyatihi* (much of eating and drinking, capacious/wide of beneficence, attached to the members of his family, seeking the good of his subjects).

172 The tenth 'Abbāsid caliph, he was the brother of al-Wāthiq and took the regnal name al-Mutawakkil 'Alā 'llāh (He Who Puts His Trust in God). He ruled from 232/847 until his assassination in 247/861. See the article by H. Kennedy in *EI*², s.v. al-Mutawakkil 'Alā 'llāh.

173 Arabic *al-qawl bi-l-sunna wa l-jamā'a*: a way of referring to the emerging self-definition of Sunni orthodoxy, based on the Prophet's Sunna (as transmitted through *ḥadīth*), as opposed to the Mu'tazilī doctrines based on philosophical premises, and on the consensus of the community regarding Muḥammad's successors (as opposed to Shi'ī doctrines about the necessary location of the imamate in Muḥammad's closest family members).

174 A favorite doctrine of the Mu'tazilī school, used as a litmus test during the Miḥna (on which see the article by M. Hinds in *EI*², s.v. Miḥna).

175 Parallel up to here in al-Mas'ūdī, *Murūj*, 5:214 (§ 3456); the remainder of the paragraph has parallels in al-Mas'ūdī, *Murūj*, 5:5–6 (§ 2873–2875).

176 Arabic *ḥubūs* (pl. of *ḥabs*). The usual meaning, "prisons," does not fit the context. Meanings connected with canals and other waterworks can be found in Freytag's *Lexicon Arabico-Latinum* and in Kazimirski's *Dictionnaire Arabe-Français*. This appears to be a reference to the canal-building projects undertaken by al-Mutawakkil in connection with the building of his new administrative center a few miles north of Samarra to be called al-Ja'fariyya; see al-Ya'qūbī, *Buldān*, 266, for a description of them.

He preferred wearing garments of *mulḥam*[177] over all other garments, and so that was his clothing and the clothing of everyone great and small in his residence. The price of *mulḥam* rose in his time because of its quality. His days were good, cheerful, and prosperous. However, he was the first caliph to display frivolity and to give free rein to levity and joking in his presence, along with things we have omitted to mention. These things spread among the people; they became accustomed to them and followed his lead. Al-Mutawakkil was not someone who could be described as benevolent or generous. The person with the greatest influence over him and who most enjoyed his favor was al-Fatḥ b. Khāqān;[178] he was a man whose beneficence was not to be expected, but from whom no evil needed to be feared. ʿUbaydallāh b. Yaḥyā b. Khāqān was his vizier; he was a seeker of safety, possessing manly virtue (*murūʾa*) with regard to himself, but having no beneficence toward anyone, though people feared no evil from him. He used to be attacked by people's saying that he had no truth. Aḥmad b. Isrāʾīl[179] used to say, "We learned lying from him."

Then came Muḥammad al-Muntaṣir,[180] the son of al-Mutawakkil. His days were not long enough for his ways to become known, other than the fact that he was stingy. Aḥmad b. al-Khaṣīb was his secretary and vizier; he was a man of little good, much evil, and intense ignorance.[181]

Then came al-Mustaʿīn, who was Aḥmad b. Muḥammad b. al-Muʿtaṣim.[182] He was the first caliph to widen the sleeves of garments, making them three spans and the like. He made the *qalansuwa* headgear smaller and shortened

---

177 *Mulḥam* cloth was "a fabric with a silk warp and a woof of some other stuff" (Y. K. Stillman in *EI*², s.v. Libās).

178 On his career, see the article by Matthew S. Gordon in *EI*³, s.v. Fatḥ b. Khāqān.

179 Secretary and later vizier to al-Mutawakkil's son al-Muʿtazz (al-Yaʿqūbī, *Taʾrīkh*, 2:595, 616, 617).

180 Al-Muntaṣir came to power by engineering his father's assassination before the latter could change the succession to bypass him. He ruled for only six months in 247/861 and 248/862, before dying of natural causes, although some reports (al-Ṭabarī, *Taʾrīkh*, 3:1496–1497) suggest that his demise was speeded by poisoning. See the article by C. E. Bosworth in *EI*², s.v. al-Muntaṣir.

181 Known as Aḥmad b. al-Khaṣīb al-Jarjarāʾī. On his career, see the article by D. Sourdel in *EI*², s.v. al-Djardjarāʾī. The noncommittal, if not downright negative assessment of al-Muntaṣir given here should be compared with the laudatory description of his character in al-Masʿūdī, *Murūj*, 5:50–51 (§ 2992), where al-Muntaṣir's excellence is contrasted with the "little good, much evil, and intense ignorance" of his vizier.

182 On the reign of this caliph, who was installed by the Turkish commanders in Samarra after the death of al-Muntaṣir in 248/862 and who abdicated amidst civil war in 251/866, see the article by K. V. Zetterstéen and C. E. Bosworth in *EI*², s.v. al-Mustaʿīn.

it.[183] No manner of acting of his in which the people followed him is known, nor any character traits in which people imitated him. He was distracted from everything else by the attempts to disobey and depose him.

Al-Muʿtazz, who was Abū ʿAbdallāh b. al-Mutawakkil, was the first caliph who rode out with gold ornaments; the caliphs used to ride out with light ornaments of silver on their belts, swords, saddles, and reins.[184] When al-Muʿtazz rode out with gold ornaments, the people followed his example. No particularly praiseworthy or blameworthy character traits of his are known.

Then al-Muhtadī, who was Muḥammad b. al-Wāthiq, came to power.[185] He hewed to a moderate path in religion.[186] He presided over the *maẓālim* courts, signed documents in his own hand, and gave precedence to people of learning.[187] He used to say: "O Banū Hāshim, let me walk in the ways of ʿUmar b. ʿAbd al-ʿAzīz, that I may be among you as he was among the Banū Umayya."[188] He reduced the wardrobe and furniture. People suspected that he followed his father in professing the doctrine that the Qurʾān was created.[189]

And [then came] al-Muʿtamid, who was Aḥmad b. al-Mutawakkil.[190] Before he had ruled very long, he lost control of his affairs. He was fond of pleasure and

---

183 The same detail is mentioned by al-Masʿūdī, *Murūj*, 5:90 (§ 3102).

184 On the reign of al-Muʿtazz, raised to power in 252/866 and deposed in 255/869, see the article by C. E. Bosworth in EI², s.v. al-Muʿtazz Bi ʾllāh. The detail on his use of gold ornaments is similarly mentioned in al-Masʿūdī, *Murūj*, 5:90 (§ 3102).

185 Or, "was brought to power"—the Arabic verb can be read as active or passive. He ruled from 255/869 until his murder in 256/870. See the article by K. V. Zettersteen and C. E. Bosworth in EI², s.v. al-Muhtadī.

186 The MS reading (*wa-dhahaba ilā l-qaḍāʾ fī l-dīn*) "he inclined to judgment in religion" makes little sense. The parallel in al-Masʿūdī, *Murūj*, 5:98 (§ 3130) reads (*dhahaba fī amrihi ilā l-qaṣd wa-l-dīn*) "he inclined in his affairs toward frugality and religion." Al-Masʿūdī follows with a list of ostentatious practices that he abolished. One can explain *al-qaḍāʾ* as a miscopying of *al-qaṣd*. The translation assumes that al-Yaʿqūbī originally wrote *wa-dhahaba ilā l-qaṣd fī l-dīn*.

187 The *maẓālim* courts were special courts in which petitions and complaints were heard. Al-Yaʿqūbī, *Taʾrīkh*, 2:617, also mentions this detail; similarly al-Masʿūdī, *Murūj*, 5:92 (§ 3111).

188 That is, just as ʿUmar b. ʿAbd al-ʿAzīz was remembered as having been the most pious of the Umayyad caliphs, so al-Muhtadī wished to be remembered among the ʿAbbāsids (here referred to as the Banū Hāshim). Al-Masʿūdī, *Murūj*, 5:92 (§ 3111) also cites these words.

189 That is, that he followed his father al-Wāthiq in supporting the Muʿtazilī school of theology that had been repudiated by al-Mutawakkil. Al-Masʿūdī, *Murūj*, 5:99–101 (§ 3132–3138), relates an anecdote that would substantiate this claim.

190 Al-Muʿtamid ruled nominally from 256/870 to 279/892, but, as al-Yaʿqūbī notes, he soon "lost control of his affairs" and was a mere figurehead, while real power lay in the hands of others. See the article by H. Kennedy in EI², s.v. al-Muʿtamid ʿAlā ʾllāh.

devoted himself to enjoyments. His brother Abū Aḥmad took charge of affairs, eventually depriving him of power and imprisoning him. He was the first caliph who was subdued, confined, and deprived of power.[191]

Then came al-Muʿtaḍid, who was Aḥmad b. Abī Aḥmad b. al-Mutawakkil. He was an astute, resolute man.[192]

---

191 Parallel in al-Masʿūdī, *Murūj*, 5:119 (§ 3193). The brother, Abū Aḥmad, took the title of al-Muwaffaq.

192 Al-Muʿtaḍid ruled from 279/892 until his death in 289/902. He was in fact the son of the brother, Abū Aḥmad, who had usurped al-Muʿtamid's authority. Contrast this laconic description of him as "astute and resolute" with the account of his love of cruelty in al-Masʿūdī, *Murūj* 5:138 (§ 3245). See the article by H. Kennedy in *EI*^{2}, s.v. al-Muʿtaḍid Bi ʾllāh.

The Geography

Kitāb al-Buldān

MAP 1 *The Muslim World circa 287/900*

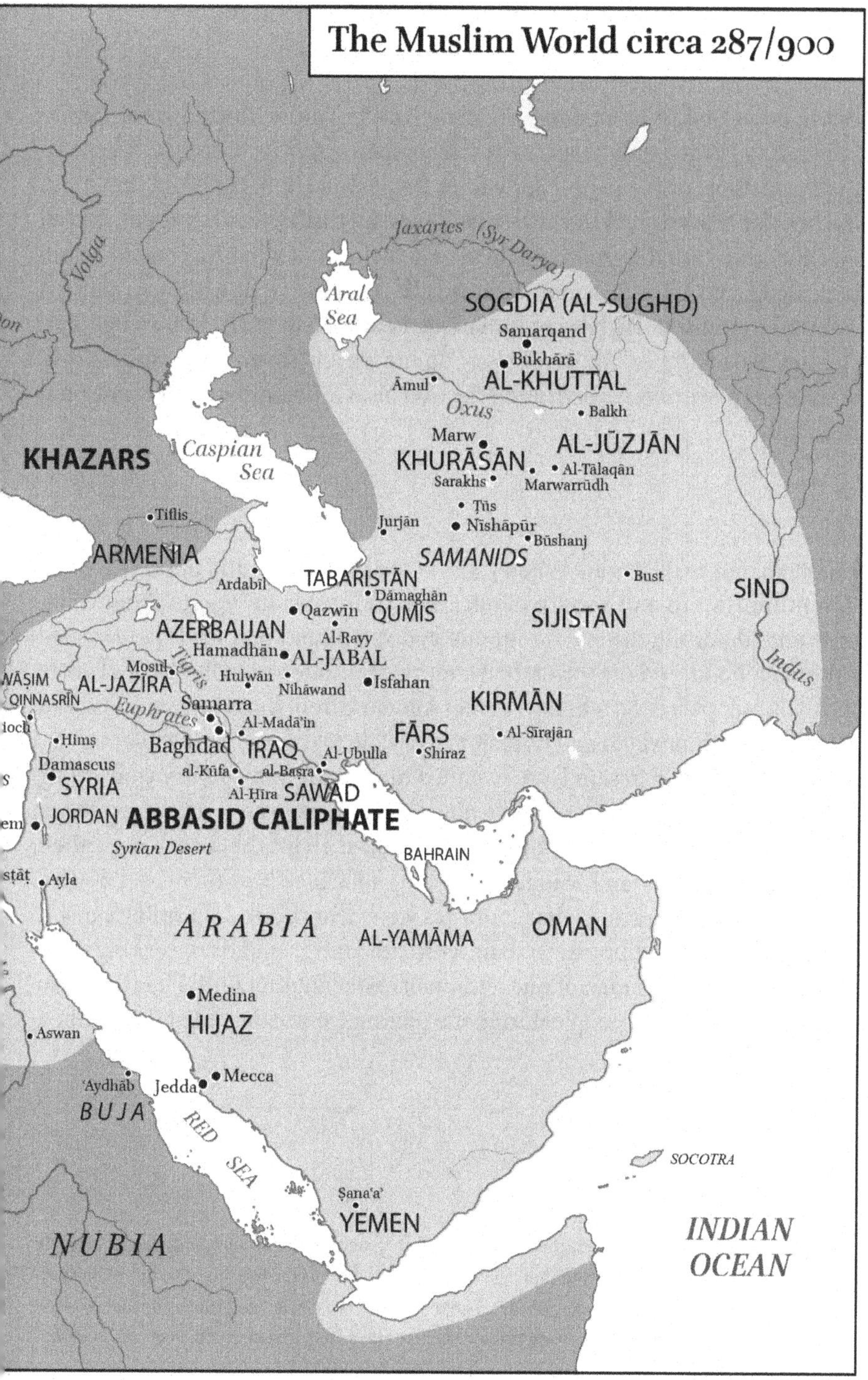
Jaxartes (Syr Darya)
Volga
Aral Sea
SOGDIA (AL-SUGHD)
Samarqand
Bukhārā
Āmul
AL-KHUTTAL
Oxus
Balkh
Marw
AL-JŪZJĀN
KHAZARS
Caspian Sea
KHURĀSĀN
Al-Tālaqān
Sarakhs
Marwarrūdh
Tiflis
Ṭūs
Jurjān
Nīshāpūr
Būshanj
ARMENIA
SAMANIDS
Ardabīl
TABARISTĀN
Bust
Dāmaghān
SIND
Qazwīn
QUMIS
AZERBAIJAN
Al-Rayy
SIJISTĀN
Hamadhān
AL-JABAL
Indus
Mosul
Tigris
Hulwān
Nihāwand
Isfahan
AL-JAZĪRA
QINNASRĪN
Euphrates
Samarra
KIRMĀN
Al-Madā'in
FĀRS
Al-Sīrajān
Ḥimṣ
Baghdad
IRAQ
Al-Ubulla
Shīraz
Damascus
al-Kūfa
al-Baṣra
SYRIA
Al-Ḥira
SAWAD
JORDAN
ABBASID CALIPHATE
Syrian Desert
BAHRAIN
Ayla
ARABIA
AL-YAMĀMA
OMAN
Medina
HIJAZ
Aswan
Mecca
'Aydhāb
Jedda
BUJA
RED SEA
SOCOTRA
Ṣana'a'
YEMEN
INDIAN OCEAN
NUBIA

The Muslim World circa 287/900

In the Name of God, the Compassionate, the Merciful: Lord, Assist [Us]!

Praise be to God, Who opened His Book (the Qur'ān) with (the word) *praise* (*ḥamd*), and Who made praise to be a recompense for His blessings, accepting the invocations of the people for whom He has affection. He is the Creator of the highest heavens and the lowest lands and all that is between them, as well as what is beneath the ground;[1] Who had knowledge of what He created before it existed,[2] and Who designed whatever He brought forth without a pattern external to Himself. He has comprehended each thing in His knowledge, and counted it by number.[3] To Him belong dominion and sovereignty and majesty, and He has power over everything. May God bless Muḥammad the Prophet and his family.

∴

Aḥmad b. Abī Yaʿqūb[4] said: When I was in the prime of youth, possessed of an adventurous spirit and a sharp mind, I took an interest in reports about countries and about the distance from one country to another; for I had traveled since childhood, and my travels had continued uninterruptedly and had taken me to distant places. So whenever I met someone from those countries, I asked him about his homeland and its major city;[5] if he told me about the place of his home and where he resided, I questioned him about that country concerning ... his birth[6] ... what its crops and who its inhabitants were, whether Arabs or non-Arabs ... what its people drank. I even asked about their clothing ... their religions and beliefs, and who held power [and leadership] there[7] ... how distant that country was and what countries were near it and ... for riding camels. Then I verified everything he told me with someone I could trust, seeking assistance by questioning men of one nationality after another until I had asked an enormous number of people during the pilgrimage season and at other times,

---

1 Cf. Qurʾān, 20:6 (and *passim*).

2 Cf. Qurʾān, 67:14.

3 Cf. Qurʾān, 19:94; 72:28.

4 That is, al-Yaʿqūbī, the author of the work.

5 Arabic *miṣr*, which can mean either "major city" or "province." It has been translated variously here, according to the meaning that best matches the sense in English. See also below, note 10.

6 Thus in the text: *lidatihi* ([*bi*]*ladatihi*?). The text is defective in several places in this section.

7 The text and its exact meaning are not clear here. The editor, de Goeje, suggests *al-ghālibīna ʿalayhi wa l-mutaraʾʾisīna fīhi*, which parallels the phraseology used later in this section.

from both eastern and western lands. I wrote down their reports and related their stories, and I recounted which of the caliphs and commanders had conquered each country and had garrisoned each province, and the amount of its land tax and what is collected on its revenue and property. | I continued writ- 233
ing down these reports and composing this book over a long period of time. I attached each report to its proper country, and everything I heard from trustworthy inhabitants of the major cities to what I already knew. I realized that no creature could encompass the entirety of it and that no human being could reach the end of it. But even a religious law need not be learned completely, neither is a religion made perfect only by full comprehension. Scholars of the science of religious jurisprudence sometimes say,[8] "A Summary of the Book of Such and Such a Jurist"; similarly, authors who compose literary works, such as books of lexicography, grammar, the Prophet's military campaigns, historical reports, or biographies, sometimes say, "A Summary of Such and Such a Book." Thus we have composed this book as a summary of information about the countries; therefore, if someone finds any information about a country we have mentioned not included in our book, this is because we have not intended to include everything. The philosopher[9] once said, "My quest for knowledge is not a desire to cover every detail, however remote, nor to command every last point, but rather to know what it would be wrong to ignore and what no intelligent person would contest." Thus I have reported the names of the provinces, military districts, and rural districts; what is to be found in each province in the way of cities, regions, and counties;[10] who inhabits it, who holds power there, and who has assumed authority there among the Arab tribes and non-Arab nationalities; the distances from country to country and province to province; which of the leaders of the armies of Islam conquered it and the date of that

---

8 That is, they sometimes title a book.

9 Arabic *al-ḥakīm* (the sage). The quotation, with some variants, is attributed to Aristotle by Ibn Abī Uṣaybiʿa, *ʿUyūn al-anbāʾ fī ṭabaqāt al-aṭibbāʾ*, s. v. Arisṭūṭālīs; it also appears in al-Yaʿqūbī, *Taʾrīkh*, 2:3.

10 Arabic administrative terminology is not always clear and could be translated in various ways. In this sentence and elsewhere, al-Yaʿqūbī seems to have his own specialized vocabulary in this regard; the following English equivalents are used as consistently as possible in the translation: "province" or "major city" for *miṣr* (pl. *amṣār*); "military district" for *jund* (pl. *ajnād*); "rural district" for *kūra* (pl. *kuwar*); "region" for *iqlīm* (pl. *aqālīm*); "county" for *ṭassūj* (pl. *ṭasāsīj*). Also, terms for administrative units varied from one part of the Islamic world to another in response to the different terminology that the Muslims inherited from earlier empires. *Jund*, for example, was used only for the military districts of Syria-Palestine; *tassūj* only for administrative divisions in Iraq.

according to year and time; the amount of its land tax (*kharāj*); its lowlands and mountains; its terrain and its waterways; how hot or cold its climate is; and its water for irrigation and drinking.

Baghdad[11]

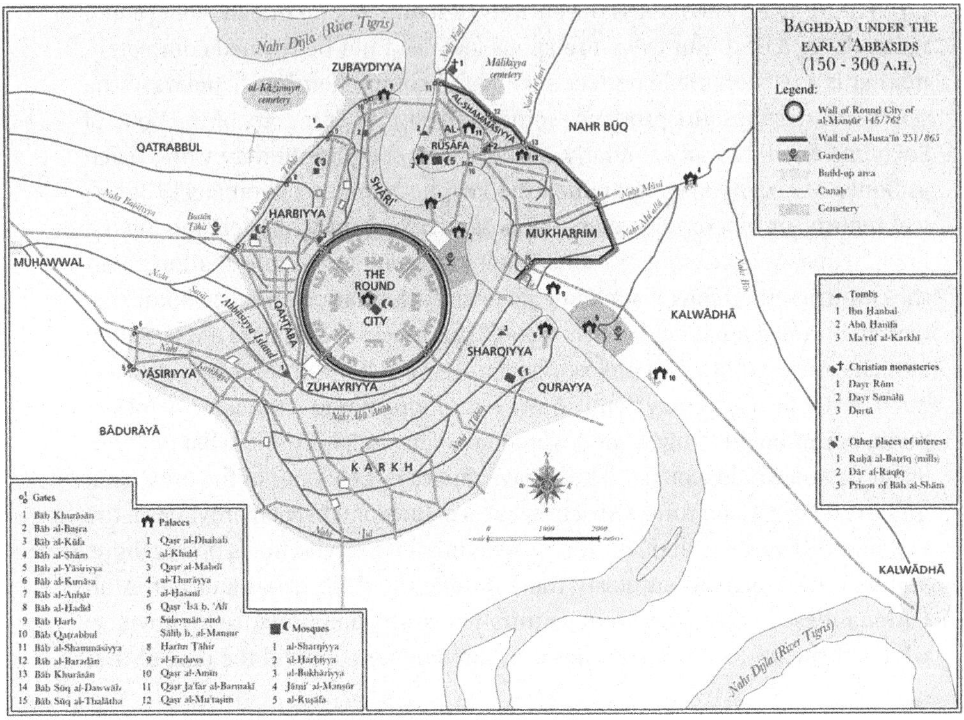

MAP 2 *Baghdad under the Early ʿAbbāsids (150–300 A.H.)*

I have begun with Iraq because it is the center of the world, the navel of the earth; and I report about Baghdad because it is the center of Iraq and the greatest city, one which has no peer in the east or the west of the earth in size, importance, prosperity, abundance of waters, and salubrious climate, and because it is inhabited by all varieties of mankind and urban and rural folk who
234 have immigrated to it from all countries | near and far. People from the remotest

11 Al-Yaʿqūbī's description of the ʿAbbāsid capital and its relation to various parallel texts have been studied in detail in Guy Le Strange, *Baghdad during the Abbasid Caliphate*, and Jacob Lassner, *The Topography of Baghdad in the Early Middle Ages*.

parts of the world have preferred it to their homelands; people from every country have residential quarters there and places for trade and for business. What can be found together in no other city in the world comes together there. The two great rivers, the Tigris and the Euphrates, flow along its borders, so that goods and provisions come to it by land and by water with such ease that every object of trade which can be exported from the east or the west, whether from Islamic or non-Islamic lands, makes its way there. So many goods are imported to it from India, Sind, China, Tibet, the country of the Turks, Daylam, the country of the Khazars, Ethiopia, and other countries that there may be more of a commodity there than in the country from which it was exported. Indeed, so much can be found and obtained there that it is as if earth's bounties had been conveyed there, the world's riches amassed there, and the blessings of the universe perfected there.

Moreover, Baghdad is the city of the Banū Hāshim[12]—their capital and the seat of their power—where no one had preceded them and no kings other than they had resided. In fact, my ancestors were residents there, and one of them was its governor.[13] Its name is famous, and its reputation is renowned. It is the center of the world because, according to what the geographers[14] universally say and what has been included about it in the books of the ancient scholars, it is in the fourth clime, which is the central clime, where the weather balances out over the times and seasons.[15] Thus it is extremely hot at the height of summer and extremely cold in winter, but it is moderate during the seasons of autumn and spring. In the transition from autumn to winter, the change in temperature is not abrupt, and neither is the change during the transition from spring to summer. Each season moves in this way from one kind of weather to

---

12 That is, the ʿAbbāsids, so called because they traced their ancestry to the Prophet's uncle, al-ʿAbbās b. ʿAbd al-Muṭṭalib b. Hāshim.

13 This statement suggests that it should be possible to identify which of al-Yaʿqūbī's ancestors were among these early residents (*al-qāʾimīna bihā*) of Baghdad and in charge of the city (*tawallā amrahā*); however, no such individuals can be definitely identified. It is possible that Wāḍiḥ, *mawlā* of the caliph al-Manṣūr, mentioned below in the *Geography* by al-Yaʿqūbī (ed. Leiden, 247) as one of the supervisors in the construction of Baghdad, was his ancestor (see pp. 18–21 of the Introduction to this volume).

14 Arabic *ḥussāb*: literally, "calculators" (of latitude).

15 Al-Yaʿqūbī is alluding to the classical theory that divided the world by latitude into seven climes (*iqlīm*), the fourth being the one where the features of the other six are in equilibrium. On the concept and its use by Muslim geographers and astronomers, see André Miquel, *La géographie humaine du monde musulman.*

another, from one time to another. The weather thus becomes balanced, the
soil is good, the water is sweet, the trees thrive, the fruits are excellent, the seed-
235 crops flourish, the excellent things (of the earth) are plentiful, | and tapped
(water)[16] is near its source. Because of the equitable climate, the fertility of the soil, and the sweetness of the water, the character of the people is good. Their faces shine and their minds are opened, so that they surpass all other people in learning, understanding, refinement, perception, common sense, commerce, crafts, and business. They are clever in every subject of discussion, competent in every occupation, skillful at every craft. No scholar is more learned than their scholars; and no one is more versed in *ḥadīth* than their traditionists, better at disputation than their theologians, more knowledgeable of Arabic than their grammarians, more correct than their Qurʾān reciters, more adroit than their physicians, more skillful than their singers, more talented than their artisans, better calligraphers than their scribes, clearer than their logicians, more pious than their worshippers, more godfearing than their ascetics, more learned in jurisprudence than their judges, more eloquent than their preachers, more artful than their poets—or more roguish than their profligates!

Baghdad was not a city in ancient times—I mean in the days of the Kisrās[17] and the Persians—it was only a village in the rural district of Bādūrayā.[18] The capital which the rulers preferred from among the cities of Iraq was al-Madāʾin,[19] which is about seven farsakhs[20] from Baghdad and is where the palace (*īwān*) of Kisrā Anūshirwān is located. There was nothing in Baghdad at that time except a monastery at the place where the Ṣarāt canal flows into the Tigris—the place

16 Arabic *mustanbaṭ*. According to Lane, 8:2759, this signifies "water that comes forth from a well when it is first dug"; al-Yaʿqūbī may mean that wells do not have to be dug deep nor water carried far from its source.

17 Arabic *al-Akāsira*, pl. of *Kisrā*. This was originally the proper name of one Persian king (Khusraw), but became the generic Arabic term for the rulers of Sasanian Iran.

18 An agricultural area southwest of Baghdad which provided much of the city's food supply. See the article by M. Streck in *EI*², s.v. Bādūrayā; and Peter Christensen, *The Decline of Iranshahr*, 96, 102.

19 Ctesiphon.

20 The farsakh (Persian *farsang*) was a unit of distance. Originally it was the distance that could be covered on foot in a mile; later it was fixed at 3 Arab miles (*mīl*), equivalent to 5.985 km (3.719 English miles); see the article by W. Hinz, in *EI*², s.v. Farsakh, and idem., *Islamische Masse und Gewichte*, 62–63.

is called Qarn al-Ṣarāt.[21] It is the monastery which is named the Old Monastery (*al-Dayr al-ʿAtīq*) and is still standing in the same place today; the Catholicos, leader of the Nestorian Christians, resides there.

There was also no Baghdad in the days of the Arabs when Islam came, for the Arabs founded Basra and Kufa. Saʿd b. Abī Waqqāṣ al-Zuhrī founded Kufa in the year 17,[22] while he was governor (*ʿāmil*) for ʿUmar b. al-Khaṭṭāb. ʿUtba b. Ghazwān al-Māzinī, of the tribe of Māzin Qays, founded Basra in the year 17, while he was governor for ʿUmar b. al-Khaṭṭāb. The Arabs staked out their lots in these two cities, although all their notables, dignitaries, and prosperous merchants have now moved to Baghdad.

The Umayyads did not reside in Iraq, because they were resident in Syria. Muʿāwīya b. Abī Sufyān was governor of Syria for twenty years | under ʿUmar b. 236
al-Khaṭṭāb and ʿUthmān b. ʿAffān. He and his family with him took up residence in the city of Damascus. When he came to power and assumed sovereignty, he established his residence and his court in Damascus, where his power and supporters and partisans were. The Umayyad kings after Muʿāwīya resided there because they had been brought up there, were acquainted with no other places, and only its people were favorably disposed to them.

When the caliphate passed to the clan of the uncle of the Prophet—God's blessing be upon him and his family—among the descendants of al-ʿAbbās b. ʿAbd al-Muṭṭalib, they recognized, thanks to the excellence of their discretion, the soundness of their intelligence, and the perfection of their judgment, the merit of Iraq: its grandeur, its spaciousness, and its centrality in the world. It is not like Syria with its pestilential climate, cramped towns, barren soil, continuous epidemics of plague, and uncouth people. Neither is it like Egypt with its tainted air and frequent outbreaks of pestilence, owing to its location between a damp and putrid river full of vile vapors that give rise to maladies and spoil food, and arid, barren mountains where, owing to their dryness, salinity, and sterility, nothing green can grow and no spring of water can gush up. Nor is it like Ifrīqiya, distant from the peninsula of Islam and from the sacred House of God,[23] with coarse, often hostile, people; nor like Armenia, remote, bitterly cold, infertile, and surrounded by enemies; nor like the harsh, tough, icy, rural districts of al-Jabal,[24] home of the hard-hearted Kurds; nor like the

21 The Ṣarāt canal branched off the ʿĪsā canal west of Baghdad near the town of al-Muḥawwal and ran east and south to the Tigris just below the Basra Gate; see Le Strange, *Lands*, 66–67.

22 17 A.H. = January 23, 638 – January 12, 639.

23 That is, the Arabian Peninsula and the Kaʿba in Mecca.

24 Al-Jabal (the Mountain; often in the plural, al-Jibāl, the Mountains), was the province

land of Khurāsān far to the east, surrounded on all sides by rabid enemies and battle-hungry warriors; nor like the Ḥijāz, which is so lacking in the things one needs and so limited in means of livelihood that its people must get sustenance from elsewhere, as God—may He be glorified and exalted—has informed us in His Book in the words of Abraham His friend—peace be upon him: "Our Lord,
237 I have made some of my seed to dwell in a valley where is no sown land."[25] | And it is not like Tibet, which has such wretched climate and food that the complexion of its people has become altered, their bodies shriveled, and their hair frizzed.

Realizing that Iraq is the most excellent of countries, the ʿAbbāsids chose to establish their residence there. The Commander of the Faithful Abū l-ʿAbbās, who was ʿAbdallāh b. Muḥammad b. ʿAlī b. ʿAbdallāh b. al-ʿAbbās b. ʿAbd al-Muṭṭalib,[26] resided at Kufa at first; then he moved to al-Anbār and built a city on the banks of the Euphrates and named it al-Hāshimiyya.[27] Abu l-ʿAbbās—may God be pleased with him—died before the city was completed.

When Abū Jaʿfar al-Manṣūr (who was also named ʿAbdallāh b. Muḥammad b. ʿAlī b. ʿAbdallāh b. al-ʿAbbās b. ʿAbd al-Muṭṭalib) became caliph, he built a city between Kufa and al-Ḥīra that he named al-Hāshimiyya. He stayed there for a time, until he decided to dispatch his son Muḥammad al-Mahdī to fight the Slavs in the year 140.[28] Then he went to Baghdad and stopped there and asked, "What is the name of this place?" Told that it was Baghdad, he said: "By God, this is the city that my father Muḥammad b. ʿAlī foretold to me that I would build and that would be where I and my descendants after me would reside. The kings in the time of the Jāhiliyya and Islam neglected it, so that God's plan and decree could be implemented by me, the reports be proven correct, and the signs and prophecies be made clear. In any case, it is an island between the Tigris and the

stretching from the mountains that rise from the northeast of Iraq across northern Iran to Rayy on the east and Isfahan on the southeast. See the article by L. Lockhart in *EI*^{2}, s.v. Djibāl; Le Strange, *Lands of the Eastern Caliphate*, 185 ff.

25 Qurʾān, 14:37.

26 Usually known as al-Saffāḥ; he was proclaimed caliph in Kufa on 12 Rabīʿ II 132 (November 28, 749).

27 In honor of Hāshim, the father of ʿAbd al-Muṭṭalib, the common ancestor of the ʿAbbāsids and the Prophet Muḥammad.

28 140 A.H. = May 25, 757 – May 14, 758. This bears no resemblance to other Arabic accounts of the founding of Baghdad (e.g., al-Ṭabarī, *Taʾrīkh*, 3:271–272), which attribute al-Manṣūr's desire to move to a new capital to the revolt of the Rāwandiyya in al-Hāshimiyya. There is also no corroboration of any raid by al-Mahdī against "the Slavs" in this year.

Euphrates, the Tigris to its east and the Euphrates to its west, a thoroughfare for the world. Everything that comes on the Tigris from Wāsiṭ, Basra, al-Ubulla, al-Ahwāz, Fārs, Oman, al-Yamāma, al-Baḥrayn, and places adjacent to them can come upstream to Baghdad and anchor there; similarly, whatever comes from Mosul, Diyār Rabīʿa, Azerbaijan, and Armenia and is carried on boats on the Tigris, or whatever comes from Diyār Muḍar, al-Raqqa, Syria, the districts on the (Byzantine) frontier, Egypt, and the Maghrib and is carried on boats in the Euphrates can be unloaded and stored here. It will be an emporium | for the 238
people of al-Jabal, Isfahan, and the districts of Khurāsān. Praise be to God who has reserved it for me and caused all those who preceded me to neglect it. By God, I will build it and dwell there to the end of my life, as will my descendants after me. It shall be the most prosperous city on earth. Then I will build four cities after it, and none of them shall ever be laid waste." He did build them: he built al-Rāfiqa, although he did not give it its name, and he built Malaṭya, al-Maṣṣīṣa, and al-Manṣūra in Sind.[29]

Then he directed that engineers and experts in construction, surveying, and the division of plots be assembled, until he had laid out his city, known as the City of Abū Jaʿfar. He assembled architects, workmen, carpenters, blacksmiths, and excavators, and when enough of them had gathered, he assigned them wages and provisions. He wrote to every country to send whoever was there who understood anything about construction, and 100,000 skilled workers and craftsmen of various kinds came. A number of authorities have reported that Abū Jaʿfar al-Manṣūr did not commence construction until he had 100,000 skilled workers and laborers. He marked out the city in the month of Rabīʿ I 141.[30] He made it a round city, and apart from it no other round city is known

29 The most likely interpretation of this sentence is that al-Rāfiqa had been conceived (but not actually built) by al-Saffāḥ, who gave it its name. Al-Yaʿqūbī himself says elsewhere (*Taʾrīkh*, 2:430, 445) that al-Rāfiqa, a suburb of al-Raqqa, was founded by Abū l-ʿAbbās al-Saffāḥ, but al-Ṭabarī, *Taʾrīkh*, 3:276 attributes it to al-Manṣūr. Cf. Wiet, *Yaʿḳūbī: Les Pays*, 10, n. 4. In any case, it is fanciful to say that al-Manṣūr founded these cities. Al-Manṣūra, because of its name, was often misidentified as one of his constructions (see the article by Y. Friedmann in *EI*², s.v. al-Manṣūra). He did carry out some reconstruction at Malaṭya (Melitene) and al-Maṣṣīṣa (Mopsuestia) as part of his program to fortify the frontier with Byzantium; see Guy Le Strange, *Lands of the Eastern Caliphate*, 120, 131.

30 July 12 – August 11, 758. This can only refer to a preliminary layout of the site; by most accounts construction did not begin until 145/762; see the next note.

in all the regions of the world. The foundations of the city were laid at a time chosen by the astronomers Nawbakht and Māshāʾallāh b. Sāriya.[31]

Before the foundations were laid, great bricks were made. Each complete square brick was one *dhirāʿ*[32] by one *dhirāʿ* and weighed two hundred *raṭl*s;[33] the half-bricks were one *dhirāʿ* long and half a *dhirāʿ* wide and weighed one hundred *raṭl*s. Wells were dug for water, and the canal was made which comes from the Karkhāyā canal, which is the canal which comes from the Euphrates. The canal was completed and made to run into the city to provide water for drinking, brick-making, and moistening clay.

He gave the city four gates: one he named Bāb al-Kūfa, one he named Bāb al-Baṣra, one he named Bāb Khurāsān, and one he named Bāb al-Shām. Each gate was distant from the next by five thousand *dhirāʿ*s, calculated according to the "black *dhirāʿ*,"[34] as measured from the outer bank of the moat. Each gate had a large, splendid, double door made of iron, neither half of which could be
239 closed | or opened except by a group of men. A horseman carrying a banner or a lancer bearing a long lance could enter without lowering the banner or tipping the lance. The enclosure wall was made of great bricks, the like of which had never been seen before, of the size we have described, and of clay. He made the width of the base of the enclosure wall 90 black *dhirāʿ*s, decreasing as the wall

---

31 Nawbakht (a Persian name meaning "New Fortune") was the first of a famous family of astrologers and theologians in the early ʿAbbāsid period; Nawbakht supposedly gained great influence with the future caliph al-Manṣūr by predicting his rise to power. See the article by L. Massignon in *EI*², s.v. Nawbakht. Māshāʾallāh b. Sāriya (or Atharī) al-Baṣrī, probably of Persian Jewish ancestry, was a celebrated astronomer and author of scientific treatises. See the article by J. Samsó in *EI*², s.v. Māshāʾ Allāh b. Atharī or b. Sāriya. The text of the horoscope as recorded by al-Bīrūnī, *al-Āthār al-bāqiya*, 270–271, yields the date 3 Jumādā I 145/30 July 762 for the foundation of the city. Two other astrologers not mentioned here, ʿUmar al-Ṭabarī and Muḥammad al-Fazārī, also participated in casting the horoscope; al-Yaʿqūbī mentions them below (ed. Leiden, 241).

32 The *dhirāʿ* (cubit or ell) in the ʿAbbāsid period could be measured in several different ways, ranging from a "legal" cubit of approximately 54 cm to a "great" cubit of 66 cm or more; see W. Hinz, *Islamische Masse und Gewichte*, 54–64.

33 The *raṭl* was a unit of weight that varied according to the commodity being measured. The official *raṭl* of Baghdad has been estimated as equivalent to approximately 401.7 g. See the article by W. Hinz in *EI*², s.v. Makāyil.

34 The length of the "black" cubit has been estimated at 54.04 cm (see the article by W. Hinz in *EI*², s.v. Dhirāʿ); Le Strange, *Baghdad*, 18, calculated 5000 black cubits to be equivalent to 2,500 yards (2,285 m); Wiet, 12 n. 7 suggests 2,466 m (at .49326 m per cubit).

rose to measure 25 *dhirāʿ*s at the top.[35] Its height was 60 *dhirāʿ*s, including the battlements. Around the wall was a large, strong rampart (*faṣīl*). Between the (face of the) enclosure wall and the (face of the) rampart was a space of 100 black *dhirāʿ*s. The rampart had great towers and round battlements. Beyond the rampart and surrounding it was a high embankment, perfectly constructed and sturdy, made of baked bricks and quicklime (*ṣārūj*). The moat next to the embankment was filled with water from a channel which branched off the Karkhāyā canal. Beyond the moat were the grand avenues.

He gave the four gates of the city great vestibules, each of them vaulted (*āzāj*), 80 *dhirāʿ*s long, and having a ceiling of baked brick and gypsum (*jiṣṣ*), so that when he entered one of the vestibules from the rampart, he reached a courtyard (*raḥba*) paved with stone, and then (another) vestibule on the great enclosure wall, which had large, splendid, double doors made of iron, neither half of which could be opened or closed except by a group of men. All four gates were like that. After entering one of the vestibules on the great enclosure wall, he passed through a courtyard to an arcade (*ṭāqāt*) with a ceiling of baked brick and gypsum in which were Greek skylights, through which sunlight could penetrate but rain could not. The residences of the pages[36] were there. Each of the four gates had an arcade, and each of the city gates on the great enclosure wall had a large, domed room with a gilded ceiling, around which were reception rooms and benches where one could sit and look out on everything that went on. One ascended to these domed rooms via arched (stairways), some of which were constructed with gypsum and baked brick and some with large mud bricks. The arches were built with some higher than others, and the interiors of these were for the horseguards (*rābiṭa*) and bodyguards. On the exterior, | a ramp accessible to riding animals went up 240
to the domes over the gates; there were gates on the ramp which could be locked. Upon exiting from the arcade, one reached a courtyard and then a large vaulted vestibule made of baked brick and plaster with an iron double door;[37] one went out via the door to the grand courtyard. All four arcades were constructed according to the same plan. In the middle of the courtyard

35 Cf. al-Yaʿqūbī, *Taʾrīkh*, 2:449.

36 Arabic *ghilmān* (pl. of *ghulām*) has the basic meaning of "young man, youth, or boy," but can also mean "slave." Its precise meaning in this context is ambiguous. See the article by D. Sourdel in *EI*², s.v. Ghulām.

37 According to Lassner, *Topography*, 292 n. 25, this should be translated as "two doors" (in contrast to the double door of the main portal), but the context seems to justify using "double door" in this case also.

was the palace—its gate was named the Golden Gate—and next to the palace was the congregational mosque. There were no other buildings or houses or residences around the palace for anyone, except a structure on the side of Bāb al-Shām for the bodyguard and a large gallery on columns constructed of baked brick and gypsum; the chief of the security forces used to be stationed in one and the head of the bodyguard in the other—today it is used for performing the prayer. Arranged around the perimeter of the courtyard were the residences of al-Manṣūr's young children and the household slaves in attendance, the treasury, the armory, the chancery, the finance ministry, the ministry of the privy seal, the ministry of the army, the ministry of supplies, the ministry of court servants, the public kitchen, and the ministry of stipends (*nafaqāt*).

From one arcade to another there were streets and lanes[38] known by the names of (the caliph's) military officers and clients or the residents of each street. Between Bāb al-Baṣra and Bāb al-Kūfa were Police Street (Sikkat al-Shuraṭ); al-Haytham Street; Dungeon Street (Sikkat al-Muṭbaq), on which lay the large prison named the Muṭbaq, solidly built with sturdy walls; Women's Street (Sikkat al-Nisāʾ); Sarjis Street; al-Ḥusayn Street; ʿAṭiyya Street, Mujāshiʿ Street; al-ʿAbbās Street; Ghazwān Street; Abū Ḥanīfa Street; and Narrow Street (al-Sikka al-Ḍayyiqa).

Between Bāb al-Baṣra and Bāb Khurāsān were Guardsmen Street (Sikkat al-Ḥaras), al-Nuʿaymiyya Street, Sulaymān Street, al-Rabīʿ Street, Muhalhil Street, Shaykh b. ʿAmīra Street, al-Marwarrūdhiyya Street, Wāḍiḥ Street, Watercarriers Street (Sikkat al-Saqqāʾīn), Ibn Burayha b. ʿĪsā b. al-Manṣūr Street, Abū Aḥmad
241 Street, | and Narrow Lane (al-Darb al-Ḍayyiq).

Between Bāb al-Kūfa and Bāb al-Shām were al-ʿAkkī Street, Abū Qurra Street, ʿAbdūya Street, al-Samaydaʿ Street, al-ʿAlāʾ Street, Nāfiʿ Street, Aslam Street, and Manāra Street.

From Bāb al-Shām to Bāb Khurāsān were Muezzins' Street (Sikkat al-Muʾadhdhinīn), Dārim Street, Isrāʾīl Street, a street now known as al-Qawārīrī (I have forgotten for whom it was named), al-Ḥakam b. Yūsuf Street, Samāʿa Street, Ṣāʿid the Client of Abū Jaʿfar Street, a street known today as al-Ziyādī (I have forgotten for whom it was named), and Ghazwān Street.

---

38 Arabic *al-sikak wa l-durūb*: Here, *sikka* (a relatively wide, straight path) will be translated as "street"; *darb* (usually a relatively narrow and irregular path running through an urban quarter, often with a gate at each end) will be translated as either "lane" or "neighborhood," depending on the context. Both will be distinguished from the *shāriʿ* (a major road or avenue).

These streets between one arcade and another were inside the city and within the enclosure wall. On each of these streets resided the (caliph's) high-ranking military officers who were trustworthy enough to reside with him, his high-ranking clients, and those people whom he needed to handle important matters. There were stout gates at both ends of every street. None of the streets connected with the wall of the courtyard where the caliphal palace was located; the wall was around the courtyard and the streets were concentric to it.

The men who laid out the city were ʿAbdallāh b. Muḥriz, al-Ḥajjāj b. Yūsuf,[39] ʿImrān b. al-Waḍḍāh, and Shihāb b. Kathīr, in concert with Nawbakht, Ibrāhīm b. Muḥammad al-Fazārī,[40] and al-Ṭabarī,[41] the astronomers who made computations.[42] (Al-Manṣūr) divided the areas outside the wall into four quarters and put one of the engineers in charge of each of the quarters. He assigned the head of each quarter a certain amount of land to be distributed among the holders of estates, as well as an amount of land to construct markets for each suburb.

He entrusted all the quarter from Bāb al-Kūfa to Bāb al-Baṣra and Bāb al-Muḥawwal and Karkh and what adjoined them to al-Musayyab b. Zuhayr, al-Rabīʿ the (caliph's) client, and ʿImrān b. al-Waḍḍāh the engineer. He entrusted the quarter from Bāb al-Kūfa to Bāb al-Shām and the avenue on the road to al-Anbār as far as the suburb | of Ḥarb b. ʿAbdallāh to Sulaymān b. Mujālid, 242 Wāḍiḥ the (caliph's) client, and ʿAbdallāh b. Muḥriz the engineer. He entrusted the quarter from Bāb al-Shām to the suburb of Ḥarb and its environs and the avenue of Bāb al-Shām and what was adjacent to it as far as the furthest bridge over the Tigris to Ḥarb b. ʿAbdallāh, Ghazwān the (caliph's) client, and al-Ḥajjāj b. Yūsuf[43] the engineer. He entrusted from Bāb Khurāsān to the Tigris bridge,

39 According to Wiet, 17, n. 3, this is a copyist's error and should be read Arṭāt rather than Yūsuf (cf. al-Ṭabarī, 3:276). However, the text consistently gives the name as Yūsuf.

40 Sic. Wiet, 17, n. 4, apud Nallino, suggests reading Ibrāhīm b. Ḥabīb, but the astrologer in question was most likely his son, Muḥammad b. Ibrāhīm b. Ḥabīb al-Fazārī. See David Pingree, "The Fragments of the Works of al-Fazārī," *JNES* 29 (1970), 103–123.

41 Abū Ḥafṣ ʿUmar b. Farrukhān al-Ṭabarī, a protégé of the Barmakids and translator of works from Pahlavi into Arabic. See Ullmann, *Natur- und Geheimwissenschaften*, 506–507; David Pingree, "ʿUmar ibn al-Farrukhān al-Ṭabarī," in *Dictionary of Scientific Biography*, xiii, 538–539; idem, "The Liber Universus of ʿUmar ibn al-Farrukhān al-Ṭabarī," *Journal for the History of Arab Science* 1 (1977), 8–12.

42 Arabic *al-munajjimīn aṣḥāb al-ḥisāb*, literally "astronomers/astrologers masters of computation"—both astronomers and astrologers were referred to as *munajjim*.

43 See note 39 above.

stretching along the avenue by the Tigris to Baghayyīn and Bāb Quṭrubbul,[44] to Hishām b. ʿAmr al-Taghlibī, ʿUmāra b. Ḥamza, and Shihāb b. Kathīr the engineer.

He assigned the superintendent of each quarter what should go to each dignitary and his comrades and what to allot for stores and markets in each suburb. He ordered them to make the stores spacious, so that there should be in each suburb a general market uniting the various trades; to make in each suburb streets and lanes (both thoroughfares and cul-de-sacs) in proportion to the number of its houses; and to name each alley after an official residing in it, a prominent man who resided there, or the nationality of the people who lived there. He specified to them that they should make the width of the avenues 50 black *dhirāʿ*s and the alleys 16 *dhirāʿ*s. In every suburb, market, and alley, they were to build enough mosques and baths for the people in each district or neighborhood. He ordered them all to take from the estates of the military generals and officers a specified amount of land for merchants to build on and reside and for tradesmen and visitors.

The first of his relatives to whom he granted an estate outside the city was ʿAbd al-Wahhāb b. Ibrāhīm b. Muḥammad b. ʿAlī b. ʿAbdallāh b. al-ʿAbbās; it was opposite Bāb al-Kūfa, on the lower Ṣarāt (canal), which comes from the Euphrates. His suburb became known as ʿAbd al-Wahhāb's Little Market (Suwayqat ʿAbd al-Wahhāb). His palace there has now fallen into ruin, and I have heard that the Little Market has also fallen into ruin.

He granted as an estate to al-ʿAbbās b. Muḥammad b. ʿAlī b. ʿAbdallāh b. al-
243 ʿAbbās b. ʿAbd al-Muṭṭalib | the island between the two Ṣarāt (canals). Al-ʿAbbās made it into a plantation and farm, the famous and well-known al-ʿAbbāsiyya, which yields harvests all year round, both summer and winter. After making the island into a plantation, al-ʿAbbās obtained another estate for himself on the east bank. The two branches of the Ṣarāt join at the end of al-ʿAbbāsiyya. The great mill known as the Patrician's Mill (Raḥā l-Baṭrīq) was there; it had 100 millstones and yielded income of 100 million dirhams a year. A dignitary (*biṭrīq, patrikios*) who had come to (al-Manṣūr) from the Byzantine emperor designed it, and it was named for him.

He granted an estate to the Sharawīs, who were clients of Muḥammad b. ʿAlī b. ʿAbdallāh b. al-ʿAbbās, this side of ʿAbd al-Wahhāb's Little Market, adjacent to Bāb al-Kūfa. They were its gatekeepers, and their chief was Ḥasan al-Sharawī.

---

44 Le Strange, Wiet, and others vocalize this name as Qaṭrabbul; however, Ibn al-Athīr, *Lubāb*, 3:45, explicitly gives it as Quṭrubbul.

He granted an estate to al-Muhājir b. ʿAmr, head of the ministry of charities (*dīwān al-ṣadaqāt*), in the square which faced Bāb al-Kūfa, where the ministry of charities was located. Opposite it was the estate of Yāsīn, chief of the courier service (*al-najāʾib*) and the couriers' hostel. Outside the couriers' hostel was the clients' stable.

He granted an estate to al-Musayyab b. Zuhayr al-Ḍabbī, chief of the police (*shurṭa*), to the right of Bāb al-Kūfa as one enters the city, in the direction of Bāb al-Baṣra. Al-Musayyab's mansion and the Mosque of al-Musayyab, with the tall minaret, were there.

He granted an estate to Azhar b. Zuhayr, al-Musayyab's brother, behind al-Musayyab's estate, on the *qibla* side by the Ṣarāt. Azhar's house and Azhar's garden are still there at the present time. The estate of Abū l-ʿAnbar, al-Manṣūr's client, was adjacent to the estate of al-Musayyab and his family on the *qibla* side.

The estate of the Companions[45] was on the Ṣarāt; they were from all the Arab tribes, such as Quraysh, the Anṣār,[46] Rabīʿa, Muḍar, and Yemen.[47] The houses of ʿAyyāsh al-Mantūf and others were there.

Then came the estate of Yaqṭīn b. Mūsā, one of the dynasty's major supporters and a leader of its propaganda mission (*daʿwa*). After that, you cross the Grand Ṣarāt formed by the confluence of the two Ṣarāts, upper and lower. There is an arched bridge across it built of baked bricks and gypsum, | sturdy and mas- 244
sive, which is called the Old Bridge (al-Qanṭara al-ʿAtīqa) because it was the first thing that he built, and he ordered that it should be sturdily constructed. After the bridge, you turn right—toward the *qibla*—toward the estate of Isḥāq b. ʿĪsā b. ʿAlī and his compounds and mansions spread along the Grand Ṣarāt on the east bank. The great highway runs between the mansions and the Ṣarāt. From the estate of ʿĪsā b. ʿAlī, (you go) to the estate of Abū l-Sarī al-Shaʾmī, al-Manṣūr's client, and then the arcade with the gate known as Bāb al-Muḥawwal. From there, you reach the suburb of Ḥumayd b. Qaḥṭaba al-Ṭāʾī, which extends along the upper Ṣarāt. The mansion of Ḥumayd, his comrades, and some members of the family of Qaḥṭaba b. Shabīb was there. It was adjacent to the estate of the household attendants,[48] which was known as the Mansion of the Romans (Dār al-Rūmiyyīn) and opened onto the Karkhāyā canal. Then you return to the

45 Arabic *al-ṣaḥāba*: the descendants of the Companions of the Prophet, as by this date no one who had known the Prophet Muḥammad was still alive.

46 Anṣār (Helpers) refers mainly to the two tribes of Medina, the Aws and the Khazraj.

47 "and Yemen" has been added in the margin of the MS.

48 Text: *qaṭīʿat al-farrāshīn*.

main avenue—Bāb al-Muḥawwal Avenue, where there is a large market with all sorts of commodities. It is adjacent to the Old Pool (al-Ḥawḍ al-ʿAtīq), where the houses of the Persians, companions of the shah, were. The route continues toward the place known as the Kunāsa, where there are places for people to tie up their mounts and where dealers in riding animals are located. Then comes the old cemetery known as the Kunāsa, extending to the canal of ʿĪsā b. ʿAlī, which draws from the Euphrates, and the tanners' quarter. Across from the Romans' (Rūmiyya) estate, on the Karkhāyā canal, which is spanned by the bridge known as the Romans' (Bridge), is the mansion of Kaʿyūba the chief gardener, who planted the date palms in Baghdad. Then there are continuous gardens that Kaʿyūba al-Baṣrī planted as far as the place known as Barāthā.

Returning to the Old Bridge: before you cross the bridge, to the east lies the suburb of Abū l-Ward Kawthar b. al-Yamān, custodian of the treasury. There is a market with all sorts of goods there, extending to Bāb al-Karkh, known as Abū l-Ward's Little Market. Behind the estate of Abū l-Ward Kawthar b. al-Yamān is the estate of Ḥabīb b. Raghbān al-Ḥimṣī. The mosque of Ibn Raghbān
245 is there, | as is the mosque of the Anbārīs, who were secretaries in the ministry of the land tax. Before you cross the Old Bridge, coming from Bāb al-Kūfa on the Grand Avenue, is the estate of Sulaym, client of the Commander of the Faithful and chief of the ministry of the land tax; then the estate of Ayyūb b. ʿĪsā al-Sharawī; then the estate of Rabāwa al-Kirmānī and his comrades. Then you arrive at the city gate known as Bāb al-Baṣra, which overlooks the Ṣarāt and the Tigris. Opposite it is the New Bridge (al-Qanṭara al-Jadīda), so-called because it was the last of the bridges to be built. There is a large market on it with all sorts of shops extending adjacent to each other. Then comes the suburb of Waḍḍāḥ, the client of the Commander of the Faithful, known as the compound of Waḍḍāḥ the chief of the armory. There are markets there, and most of those occupying them at the present time are booksellers; it has over a hundred bookshops.

Next you come to the estate of ʿAmr b. Simʿān al-Ḥarrānī; the Ḥarrānī arcade is there. Then comes al-Sharqiyya. It was named al-Sharqiyya (Eastern) because it was intended as a city for al-Mahdī before (al-Manṣūr) decided that al-Mahdī's residence should be on the east bank of the Tigris, and so it was called al-Sharqiyya. The Great Mosque is there, where people used to congregate for the Friday prayer, and there was a pulpit in it. It was the mosque where the judge (*qāḍī*) of al-Sharqiyya used to hold court. Then the pulpit was removed from it.

Turning from al-Sharqiyya, you pass to the estate of Jaʿfar b. al-Manṣūr on the bank of the Tigris. The house of ʿĪsā b. Jaʿfar is there, and nearby is the house of Jaʿfar b. Jaʿfar b. al-Manṣūr. Then you leave the four roads we have mentioned

for the avenue of Bāb al-Karkh. First, at the Gate of the Slave Merchants,[49] there is the estate of Suwayd, al-Manṣūr's client. Suwayd Square is behind the slave market; next, shops extend along both sides of the avenue. You bear right from Bāb al-Karkh to the estate of al-Rabīʿ, client of the Commander of the Faithful, in which there are cloth merchants from Khurāsān who sell various types of material imported from Khurāsān and nothing else. | There is a canal there that 246
branches off from the Karkhāyā canal, along which are the residences of the merchants. It is called the Poultry Canal (Nahr al-Dajāj) because chickens used to be sold there at that time. Behind al-Rabīʿ's estate are the residences of the merchants and a variety of people from every country. Each lane is known by (the ethnic name of) its inhabitants, and each street by (the name of) someone who resided on it.

Karkh is the great market that extends in length from Waḍḍāḥ's Compound to the Tuesday Market (Sūq al-Thulathāʾ), a distance of two farsakhs, and in width from al-Rabīʿ's estate to the Tigris, a distance of one farsakh. There are particular streets for every type of merchant and trade. There are rows of shops and lots in these streets; one group of people and type of commerce never mixes with another, no type of goods is sold with another, and the practitioners of one occupation do not mix with other sorts of artisans. Each market is separate, and all the people are engaged only in their particular type of commerce. The people of each occupation are segregated from those of other groups.

Between these suburbs that we have mentioned and the estates that we have described were the residences of various people—Arabs, soldiers, *dihqāns*,[50] merchants, and other sorts of people for whom the lanes and streets were named. This was one quarter of Baghdad, and it was the large quarter. It was administered by al-Musayyab b. Zuhayr, al-Rabīʿ the client of the Commander of the Faithful, and ʿImrān b. al-Waḍḍāḥ the engineer. There was no quarter in Baghdad larger or grander than it.

∴

49 Bāb al-Nakhkhāsīn. This could also mean Gate of the Cattle Merchants, but according to Le Strange, *Baghdad*, 68, it was the slave market.

50 *Dihqān*, pl. *dahāqīn* (Middle Persian *dēhkān* or *dahigān*, pl. *dēhkānān*): "villager, landlord, a member of the local class of Persian landlords in Iraq who administered subdistricts." See the articles by Ann K. S. Lambton in *EI*², s.v. Dihḳān, and by Jürgen Paul in *EI*³, s.v. Dihqān; Morony, *Iraq after the Muslim Conquest*, 529.

From Bāb al-Kūfa to Bāb al-Shām was the suburb of Sulaymān b. Mujālid—he was the one who administered this quarter, and it was named after him. In it were: the estate of Wāḍiḥ; then the estate of ʿĀmir b. Ismāʿīl al-Muslī; then the suburb of al-Ḥasan b. Qaḥṭaba (his houses and those of his family fronted onto what was known as al-Ḥasan's Lane); then the suburb of the Khwārazmians, the companions of al-Ḥārith b. Ruqād al-Khwārazmī, and the estate of al-Ḥārith was on that lane; then the estate of ... the equerry,[51] client of the Commander of the Faithful, which was the mansion that later belonged to Isḥāq b ʿĪsā b. ʿAlī al-Hāshimī and then was bought by a secretary of Muḥammad b. ʿAbdallāh
247 b. Ṭāhir named Ṭāhir b. | al-Ḥārith; then the suburb of al-Khalīl b. Hāshim al-Bāwardī; then the suburb of al-Khaṭṭāb b. Nāfiʿ al-Ṭaḥāwī; then the estate of Hāshim b. Maʿrūf, which is in Cages Lane (Darb al-Aqfāṣ); and then the estate of al-Ḥasan b. Jaʿfarāt, which is also in Cages Lane and adjacent to Fullers' Lane (Darb al-Qaṣṣārīn).

From the Anbār Road, the first estate one comes to is the estate of Wāḍiḥ,[52] client of the Commander of the Faithful, and his children; then Ayyūb b. al-Mughīra al-Fazārī Lane [...][53] in Kufa, so the lane was known as Kufans' Lane (Darb al-Kūfiyyīn). Then comes the estate of Salāma b. Samʿān al-Bukhārī and his comrades—the Bukharans' Mosque and the Green Minaret are in it. Then comes the estate of al-Lajlāj the physician; then the estate of ʿAwf b. Nizār al-Yamāmī and the Yamāmiyya Lane, leading to the mansion of Sulaymān b. Mujālid; then the estate of al-Faḍl b. Jaʿwana al-Rāzī, which later belonged to Dāwūd b. Sulaymān, secretary to Umm Jaʿfar, known as Dāwūd al-Nabaṭī; then the Sīb (Canal)[54] and the mansion of Hubayra b. ʿAmr—also on the Sīb was the estate of Ṣāliḥ al-Baladī in Ṣabbāḥ Lane, which led to ʿAbd al-Wahhāb's Little Market. Then comes the estate of Qābūs b. Samaydaʿ. Across from it was the estate of Khālid b. al-Walīd, which later belonged to Abū Ṣāliḥ Yaḥyā b. ʿAbd al-Raḥmān the secretary, chief of the ministry of the land tax in the days of al-Rashīd, so that it became known as Abū Sāliḥ's Mansions.

Then comes the estate of Shuʿba b. Yazīd al-Kābulī; then the suburb of al-Quss, al-Manṣūr's client, after whom the garden of al-Quss is named; then the suburb of al-Haytham b. Muʿāwiya, known as al-Haytham's Shār-sūq,[55]

51 Text: *ṣāḥib al-rikāb*. The name has fallen out of the text.

52 See note 13 above.

53 Part of the text seems to be missing here.

54 The word is undotted, so the reading is uncertain. The Leiden editor read it as *al-Sīb* and treated it as a toponymn; however, the word may simply be another term for a kind of watercourse or canal.

55 An Arabized version of Persian *chahār-sū* (square or marketplace).

where a large extended market, residences, lanes, and streets, all named for al-Haytham's Shār-sūq, are found; then the estate of the Marwarrūdhiyya, the family of Abū Khālid al-Anbārī; then the suburb of Abū Yazīd al-Sharawī, client of Muḥammad b. ʿAlī, | and his comrades; then the estate of Mūsā b. Kaʿb al- 248
Tamīmī, who used to be the head of al-Manṣūr's police (*shurṭa*); then the estate of Bishr b. Maymūn and his residences; then the estate of Saʿīd b. Daʿlaj al-Tamīmī; then the estate of al-Shikhkhīr and Zakariyyāʾ b. al-Shikhkhīr; then the suburb of Abū Ayyūb Sulaymān b. Ayyūb, known as Abū Ayyūb al-Khūzī al-Mūriyānī—Mūriyān is a village in one of the rural districts of al-Ahwāz known as Manādhir. Then comes the estate of Raddād b. Zādhān, known as al-Raddādiyya; then al-Mamadd-dār.[56] Then comes the border of the Ḥarb suburb, before which is al-Ramaliyya (the Sandy Place). This is the quarter that was governed by Sulaymān b. Mujālid, Wāḍiḥ the client of the Commander of the Faithful, and the engineer ʿImrān b. al-Waḍḍāḥ.

∴

At the beginning of the Bāb al-Shām quarter is the estate of al-Faḍl b. Sulaymān al-Ṭūsī, and adjacent to it are the prison known as the Bāb al-Shām Prison and the shops known as the Sūq Bāb al-Shām. The latter is a great market in which there are all sorts of merchandise and goods for sale spread out to the right and to the left. It is densely populated and provided with avenues, lanes, and lots. It extends along a grand avenue off which are long lanes; each lane is named for a nationality that resides on both sides of it. It comprises everything as far as the suburb of Ḥarb b. ʿAbdallāh al-Balkhī. At the present time, there is no more spacious suburb in Baghdad, nor one greater, nor one with more lanes and markets. Its residents include people from Balkh, Marw, al-Khuttal, Bukhārā, Asbīshāb, Ishtākhanj, Kābul-shāh, and Khwārazm. Each ethnic group has a military and a civilian leader (*qāʾid wa-raʾīs*). Also there is the estate of al-Ḥakam b. Yūsuf al-Balkhī, *ṣāḥib al-ḥirāb*,[57] who used to be in charge of the police.

From Bāb al-Shām, along the great avenue which runs to the bridge over the Tigris, there is a market on the left and right. Then comes a suburb known as House of the Slaves (Dār al-Raqīq), which housed Abū Jaʿfar's slaves who had been purchased from distant lands and were entrusted to al-Rabīʿ, his client;

---

56 The reading and identification of the place are uncertain.

57 This title, not attested elsewhere, apparently refers to the commander of a specialized military unit; Hugh Kennedy, trans., *The History of al-Ṭabarī, XXIX*, 85, n. 235, suggests that *ḥirāb* were small throwing spears.

249 then the suburb | of the Kirmāniyya and (their) commander Būzān b. Khālid al-Kirmānī; then the estate of the Sogdians and the mansion of Kharfāsh al-Ṣughdī; then the estate of Māhān al-Ṣāmaghānī and his comrades; and then the estate of the Marzubān Abū Asad b. Marzubān al-Fāryābī and his comrades, (former) nomads (*aṣḥāb al-ʿumud*).[58] Then you reach the bridge. This is the quarter that was governed by Ḥarb b. ʿAbdallāh, client of the Commander of the Faithful, and the engineer al-Ḥajjāj b. Yūsuf.[59]

As for the quarter from Bāb Khurāsān to the bridge over the Tigris and beyond, facing (the river) is al-Khuld (Palace),[60] and the stables, the parade ground, and a palace fronting onto the Tigris were there. Abū Jaʿfar (al-Manṣūr) continued to reside there, and al-Mahdī used to live there before he moved to his palace in al-Ruṣāfa on the east bank of the Tigris. After you pass the approach to the bridge, the bridge itself, the police station, and a workshop for the bridge, the first of the estates is that of Sulaymān b. Abī Jaʿfar, on the grand avenue along the Tigris and in a lane known as Sulaymān's Lane. Next to Sulaymān's estate on the grand avenue is the estate of Ṣāliḥ, son of the Commander of the Faithful al-Manṣūr, who was (known as) Ṣāliḥ the Unfortunate, which extended to the mansion of Najīḥ, al-Manṣūr's client, which was later owned by ʿAbdallāh b. Ṭāhir. At the end of Ṣāliḥ's estate is the estate of ʿAbd al-Malik b. Yazīd al-Jurjānī, known as Abū ʿAwn, and his comrades from Jurjān. Then comes the estate of Tamīm al-Bādhghīsī, adjacent to the estate of Abū ʿAwn; then the estate of ʿAbbād al-Farghānī and his comrades from Farghāna; then the estate of ʿĪsā b. Najīḥ, known as Ibn Rawḍa, and the pages of the office of the chamberlain;[61] then the estate of the Afāriqa;[62] then the estate of Tammām al-Daylamī, which bordered the Bridge of the Straw-vendors (Qanṭarat al-Tabbānīn); then the

58 Marzubān al-Fāryābī would seem to be the "Marzubān b. Turksafī" mentioned by al-Iṣṭakhrī and Ibn Ḥawqal; see Matthew S. Gordon, *The Breaking of a Thousand Swords: A History of the Turkish Military of Samarra*, 33. The *aṣḥāb al-ʿumud* (possessors of tent poles, clubs, or maces) would presumably have been former Turkish nomads who followed him to join the caliph's army in Iraq.

59 See note 39 above.

60 On this palace built by al-Manṣūr on the west bank of the Tigris outside the walls of the Round City, see the article by C. E. Bosworth in *EI*², s.v. al-K͟huld, Ḳaṣr.

61 Arabic *ghilmān al-ḥijāba*.

62 *Afāriqa*: people from Ifrīqiya (North Africa).

estate of Ḥanbal b. Mālik; then the estate of the Baghayīn,[63] comrades of Ḥafṣ b. ʿUthmān, and the mansion of Ḥafṣ, which later belonged to Isḥāq b. Ibrāhīm; then the market along the Tigris | at the river harbor; and then an estate of 250
Jaʿfar, son of the Commander of the Faithful al-Manṣūr, which later belonged to Umm Jaʿfar, in the area of the Bāb Quṭrubbul, known as the estate of Umm Jaʿfar. On the *qibla* side were the estate of Marrār al-ʿIjlī and the estate of ʿAbd al-Jabbār b. ʿAbd al-Raḥmān al-Azdī. He was in charge of the security forces, but then was removed and made governor of Khurāsān; he revolted there, so (al-Manṣūr) dispatched al-Mahdī with armies against him, and the latter fought against ʿAbd al-Jabbār and defeated him. Al-Mahdī had ʿAbd al-Jabbār carried back to Abū Jaʿfar (al-Manṣūr), who had him beheaded and crucified.

In some of these suburbs and estates there are things we have not mentioned since many (ordinary) people built or inherited estates and other properties there.

∴

The lanes and streets were counted, and there were six thousand of them. There were thirty thousand mosques, apart from those constructed later. The public baths were counted and numbered ten thousand, not including those built later.

The aqueduct which comes from the Karkhāyā canal, which itself draws water from the Euphrates, carries (water) on strong vaults (mortared) with quick-lime on the bottom and baked bricks on top and with solidly constructed arches. It runs into the city and is distributed to most of the avenues of the suburbs, providing water in summer and winter, since it was engineered in such a way that its water does not cease at any time. Another aqueduct, similar to this one, comes from the Tigris and is named the Little Tigris (Dujayl). Water for the people of al-Karkh and its environs is drawn from a canal called the Poultry Canal (so named because chicken merchants used to conduct business there) and from a canal called Ṭābaq b. al-Ṣamīh's Canal. They also have the grand ʿĪsā Canal (Nahr ʿĪsā),[64] which draws from the main part of the Euphrates. Large boats coming from al-Raqqa can enter it, bringing flour and merchandise from Syria and Egypt. They arrive at a harbor where there are markets and

63 So vocalized in al-Ṭabarī, *Taʾrīkh*, 3:634, followed by Wiet, 32, and Lassner, 68. Le Strange, *Baghdad*, 108, prefers Baghîyîn.

64 The Nahr ʿĪsā, the southernmost of the major canals supplying Baghdad with water, connected the Euphrates, from which it drew its water, with the Tigris. See the description in Le Strange, *Baghdad*, 49 ff.

merchants' shops that are not interrupted at any time, since the water is never
251 cut off. They also have cisterns | which are filled with water from these canals; it is sweet water, and all the people drink from them. These canals were especially needed because of the populousness and extent of the country. Because the people are surrounded on all sides by the Tigris and the Euphrates, water is so plentiful that they planted date palms, which were imported from Basra; these have become more numerous in Baghdad than in Basra, Kufa, or the Sawād. The people planted trees that bear wonderful fruits. There were many gardens and orchards everywhere in the suburbs of Baghdad because of the abundance and sweetness of the water. Everything that was made in any country was made there, because the most skillful artisans moved there from every country. They have come there from every direction, emigrating from near and far. This then is the western part of Baghdad: the city proper, al-Karkh, and the suburbs. On every side of it there are cemeteries, contiguous villages, and cultivated lands extending out.

∴

The eastern part of Baghdad is where al-Mahdī b. al-Manṣūr resided when he was his father's heir-apparent. He began its construction in the year 143.[65] Al-Mahdī laid out his palace at al-Ruṣāfa, next to the congregational mosque there. He dug a canal drawing from the Nahrawān (Canal); it was called al-Mahdī's Canal and flowed along the eastern side. Al-Manṣūr gave land grants to his brothers and military officers after he had made grants to those on the western side. It was the side of his city. Land grants were distributed on this side, known as 'Askar al-Mahdī (al-Mahdī's Camp), just as they had been on the city side. People vied to reside near al-Mahdī because of their affection for him and his generosity towards them with money and gifts, and because there was a greater amount of land on that side, for people previously had gone to the western side, which was an island between the Tigris and the Euphrates, and built there and made shops and stores there. When construction began on the eastern side, it had become impossible for anyone who wanted to build expansively (to do so on the western side).

The first of the land grants, at the head of the bridge, belonged to Khu-
252 zayma b. Khāzim al-Tamīmī, who was chief of al-Mahdī's security force; | then came the estate of Ismā'īl b. 'Alī b. 'Abdallāh b. al-'Abbās b. 'Abd al-Muṭṭalib;

65 143 A.H. = April 22, 760 – April 11, 761.

then the estate of al-ʿAbbās b. Muḥammad b. ʿAlī b. ʿAbdallāh b. al-ʿAbbās b. ʿAbd al-Muṭṭalib, because he had made his estate on the western side into an orchard; then the estate of al-Sarī b. ʿAbdallāh b. al-Ḥārith b. al-ʿAbbās b. ʿAbd al-Muṭṭalib; then the estate of Qutham b. al-ʿAbbās b. ʿUbaydallāh b. al-ʿAbbās b. ʿAbd al-Muṭṭalib, who was Abū Jaʿfar's governor of al-Yamāma; then the estate of al-Rabīʿ, the client of the Commander of the Faithful, who, because he had made his estate on the Karkh side into markets and commercial ventures, received a land grant with al-Mahdī, where the palace of al-Faḍl b. al-Rabīʿ and the parade ground (*maydān*) are; then the estate of Jibrīl b. Yaḥyā al-Bajalī; then the estate of Asad b. ʿAbdallāh al-Khuzāʿī; then the estate of Mālik b. al-Haytham al-Khuzāʿī; then the estate of Salm b. Qutayba al-Bāhilī; then the estate of Sufyān b. Muʿāwiya al-Muhallabī; then the estate of Rawḥ b. Ḥātim; then the estate of Abān b. Ṣadaqa the secretary; then the estate of Ḥamūya al-Khādim,[66] al-Mahdī's client; then the estate of Nuṣayr al-Waṣīf,[67] al-Mahdī's client; then the estate of Salama al-Waṣīf, al-Mahdī's chief of the armory; then the estate of Badr al-Waṣīf, with the Thirst Market,[68] which is a large, spacious market; then the estate of al-ʿAlāʾ al-Khādim, al-Mahdī's client; then the estate of Yazīd b. Manṣūr al-Ḥimyarī; then the estate of Ziyād b. Manṣūr al-Ḥārithī; then the estate of Abū ʿUbayd Muʿāwiya b. Barmak al-Balkhī, on the Burdān[69] bridge; then the estate of ʿUmāra b. Ḥamza b. Maymūn; then the estate of Thābit b. Mūsā, the secretary of the land tax for Kufa and the region irrigated by the Euphrates; then the estate of ʿAbdallāh b. Ziyād b. Abī Laylā al-Khathʿamī, the secretary of the ministry for the Ḥijāz, Mosul, the Jazīra, Armenia, and Azerbaijan;[70] then the estate of the judge (*qāḍī*) ʿUbaydallāh b. Muḥammad b. Ṣafwān |; then the estate of the secretary Yaʿqūb b. Dāwūd al-Sulamī, who served 253
as secretary to al-Mahdī during his caliphate; then the estate of Manṣūr, al-Mahdī's client, which is the place known as the Tarred Gate (Bāb al-Muqayyar); then the estate of the general Abū Hurayra Muḥammad b. Farrūkh, in the place known as al-Mukharrim; then the estate of Muʿādh b. Muslim al-Rāzī,

66 *Khādim* (servant) often was a euphemism for eunuch.

67 *Waṣīf* (slave) was a general term; later it came to designate a black slave, but whether it had this meaning at this time is unclear. See Dozy, *Supplément*, 2:810.

68 Arabic *Sūq al-ʿAtash*. "The original intention of the Caliph Mahdî had been to have called it the Market of Satiety ... The name of Thirst Market, however, was given to it by the people in derision." (Le Strange, *Baghdad*, 222).

69 Wiet gives Baradān; the vocalization here follows Ibn al-Athīr, *Lubāb*, 1:135.

70 A ministry combining the Ḥijāz and these other areas does not seem very plausible; something may have dropped out of the text here.

grandfather of Isḥāq b. Yaḥyā b. Muʿādh; then the estate of the admiral[71] al-Ghamr b. al-ʿAbbās al-Khathʿamī; then the estate of Sallām, al-Mahdī's client (who was in charge of the *maẓālim* court[72]), in al-Mukharrim; then the estate of ʿUqba b. Salm al-Hunāʾī; then the estate of Saʿīd al-Ḥarashī, at the Ḥarashī Intersection; then the estate of Mubārak al-Turkī; then the estate of Sawwār, client of the Commander of the Faithful, and Sawwār Square (Raḥbat Sawwār); then the estate of Nāzī, client of the Commander of the Faithful, chief of the livery, and the Nāzī Stable; then the estate of Muḥammad b. al-Ashʿath al-Khuzāʿī; then the estate of ʿAbd al-Kabīr b. ʿAbd al-Ḥamīd b. ʿAbd al-Raḥmān b. Zayd b. al-Khaṭṭāb, brother of ʿUmar b. al-Khaṭṭāb; then the estate of Abū Ghassān, client of the Commander of the Faithful al-Mahdī.

Interspersed among the estates are the homes of the soldiers, wealthy residents, merchants, and other people in each quarter and suburb. The great market for this side, where various goods, wares, and crafts come together, is at the head of the bridge, running east from the head of the bridge, with goods and crafts displayed on both sides.

The roads of the eastern side—ʿAskar al-Mahdī—branch into five. One road goes straight to al-Ruṣāfa, where al-Mahdī's palace and the congregational mosque are; one road is in the market known as Khuḍayr Market, which is a source for luxury goods from China, and goes from it to the parade ground and the mansion of al-Faḍl b. al-Rabīʿ; one road goes left to Bāb al-Burdān, where the residences of Khālid b. Barmak and his children were; the Bridge Road (Ṭarīq
254 al-Jisr) goes from the mansion of Khuzayma to the market known as | Yaḥyā b. al-Walīd's Market and thence to the place known as al-Dūr and on to the Baghdad gate known as al-Shammāsiyya, by which one leaves for Samarra; and one road is near the first bridge, which one crosses in order to come from the western side, leading along the Tigris to the Tarred Gate and al-Mukharrim and its environs. This was the more spacious of the two sides due to the number of markets and shops on the western side as we have described.

Al-Mahdī resided there when he was heir-apparent and during his caliphate. Mūsā al-Hādī resided there, as did Hārūn al-Rashīd, al-Maʾmūn, and al-Muʿtaṣim. It had four thousand lanes and streets, fifteen thousand mosques, other than those people added later, and five thousand baths, apart from those

---

71 Arabic *ṣāḥib al-baḥr* (master of the sea), apparently refers to his having led naval campaigns in the Mediterranean; see al-Ṭabarī, *Taʾrīkh*, 3:477, 491 (trans. Kennedy, *The History of al-Ṭabarī*, XXIX, 188).

72 A special court set up to hear petitions against official and unofficial abuse of power—*maẓālim* means unjust or oppressive actions. On the development of the system, see the article by J. S. Nielsen in *EI*², s.v. Maẓālim.

people built later. The rent from the markets of Baghdad on both sides, including the Patrician's Mill and its environs, amounted each year to twelve million dirhams.

Seven caliphs resided in Baghdad: al-Manṣūr, al-Mahdī, Mūsā al-Hādī, Hārūn al-Rashīd, Muḥammad al-Amīn, ʿAbdallāh al-Maʾmūn, and al-Muʿtaṣim. Only one of them died there, Muḥammad al-Amīn b. Hārūn al-Rashīd, who was murdered outside Bāb al-Anbār near Ṭāhir's Garden.

We have described these estates, avenues, lanes, and streets as they were laid out in the days of al-Manṣūr and at the time of their inception. They have changed—the people who originally owned them died, and they were possessed by one group of people and another, generation after generation. Some places became more built up, and houses changed hands. The notables, grandees, military officers, and notable people moved with al-Muʿtaṣim to Samarra in the year 223.[73] They stayed there in the days of al-Wāthiq and al-Mutawakkil. However, Baghdad did not fall into ruin, and its markets were not diminished, since they could not be replaced; cultivated areas and houses went on continuously between Baghdad and Samarra on both the land and river sides, that is, along the Tigris and on both banks of the Tigris. | 255

Samarra[74]

We have given an account of Baghdad, its foundation, and the time when Abū Jaʿfar al-Manṣūr built it. We have described how it was designed, and how its suburbs, estates, markets, lanes, streets, and quarters—on the west side of the Tigris, which is the side of the (Round) City and al-Karkh, and on the east side, which is the side of al-Ruṣāfa, which is called ʿAskar al-Mahdī—were apportioned. Having said what we know about this, let us now give an account of Samarra. It is the second of the cities of the caliphs of the Banū Hāshim. Eight caliphs resided there, including al-Muʿtaṣim, who founded it and constructed it; al-Wāthiq, who was Hārūn b. al-Muʿtaṣim; al-Mutawakkil Jaʿfar

73 223 A.H. = December 3, 837 – November 23, 838.

74 On Samarra (Surra-man-raʾā as al-Yaʿqūbī gives it) and its community, see the article by A. Northedge in *EI*², s.v. Sāmarrāʾ. One may add to the bibliography mentioned there: Alastair Northedge, *Samarra: Residenz der ʿAbbāsidenkalifen 836–892 n. Chr., 221–279 Hiğri*; idem, *The Historical Topography of Samarra*; C. F. Robinson, ed., *A Medieval Islamic City Reconsidered: An Interdisciplinary Approach to Samarra*; and Matthew S. Gordon, *The Breaking of a Thousand Swords: A History of the Turkish Military of Samarra, A.H. 200–275/815–889 C.E.*

b. al-Muʿtaṣim; al-Muntaṣir Muḥammad b. al-Mutawakkil; al-Mustaʿīn Aḥmad b. Muḥammad b. al-Muʿtaṣim; al-Muʿtazz Abū ʿAbdallāh b. al-Mutawakkil; al-Muhtadī Muḥammad b. al-Wāthiq; and al-Muʿtamid Aḥmad b. al-Mutawakkil.

Aḥmad b. Abī Yaʿqūb[75] said: In olden times, Samarra was nothing but an open plain in the land of al-Ṭīrhān. There were no buildings there except for a Christian monastery at the site where the government palace known as the Dār al-ʿĀmma came to be; the monastery was taken over as the treasury. When al-Muʿtaṣim came to Baghdad, returning from Ṭarsūs in the year in which he was recognized as caliph, which was 218,[76] he resided at al-Maʾmūn's palace. Then he built a palace on the eastern side of Baghdad and moved there, staying there in the years 218, 219, 220, and 221. A group of Turks, who at the time spoke no Arabic,[77] were with him.

∴

Jaʿfar al-Khushshakī informed me, saying: In the days of al-Maʾmūn, al-Muʿtaṣim used to send me to Nūḥ b. Asad in Samarqand to purchase Turks.
256 I would bring him a group of them each year. | In the days of al-Maʾmūn about three thousand slaves were acquired for him. When he became caliph, he applied himself diligently to seeking them and even bought whatever slaves were in Baghdad from private citizens. Those he bought in Baghdad formed a large group. They included Ashnās,[78] who was a slave of Nuʿaym b. Khāzim, the father of Hārūn b. Nuʿaym; Ītākh, who was a slave of Sallām b. al-Abrash; Waṣīf, who was a slave armorer belonging to al-Nuʿmān's family; and Sīmā al-Dimashqī, who was a slave of Dhu l-Riʾāsatayn al-Faḍl b. Sahl.[79] When these barbarian Turks rode their horses, they would gallop about and crash into people left and right; so the rabble would pounce on them, killing some and beating up others. Their blood could be shed with impunity, with no one bothering the culprit. This weighed heavily on al-Muʿtaṣim, and he decided to leave Bagh-

75 That is, al-Yaʿqūbī, the author of the work.

76 Al-Yaʿqūbī, *Taʾrīkh*, 2:575, gives the date as 12 nights remaining (i.e., the 18th day) in Rajab, 218 (August 9, 833).

77 Arabic *wa-hum yawmaʾidhin ʿajam* (and they at that date were *ʿajam*): that is, they were speakers of an incomprehensible language, barbarians in the literal sense.

78 Ashnās is the usual reading of this name, but the etymology given by al-Ṭabarī, *Taʾrīkh*, 3:1017, suggests that the reading Ashinās may be more correct.

79 On this passage and on Ashnās, Ītākh, Waṣīf, and Sīmā, see Gordon, *Breaking of a Thousand Swords*, 17–18.

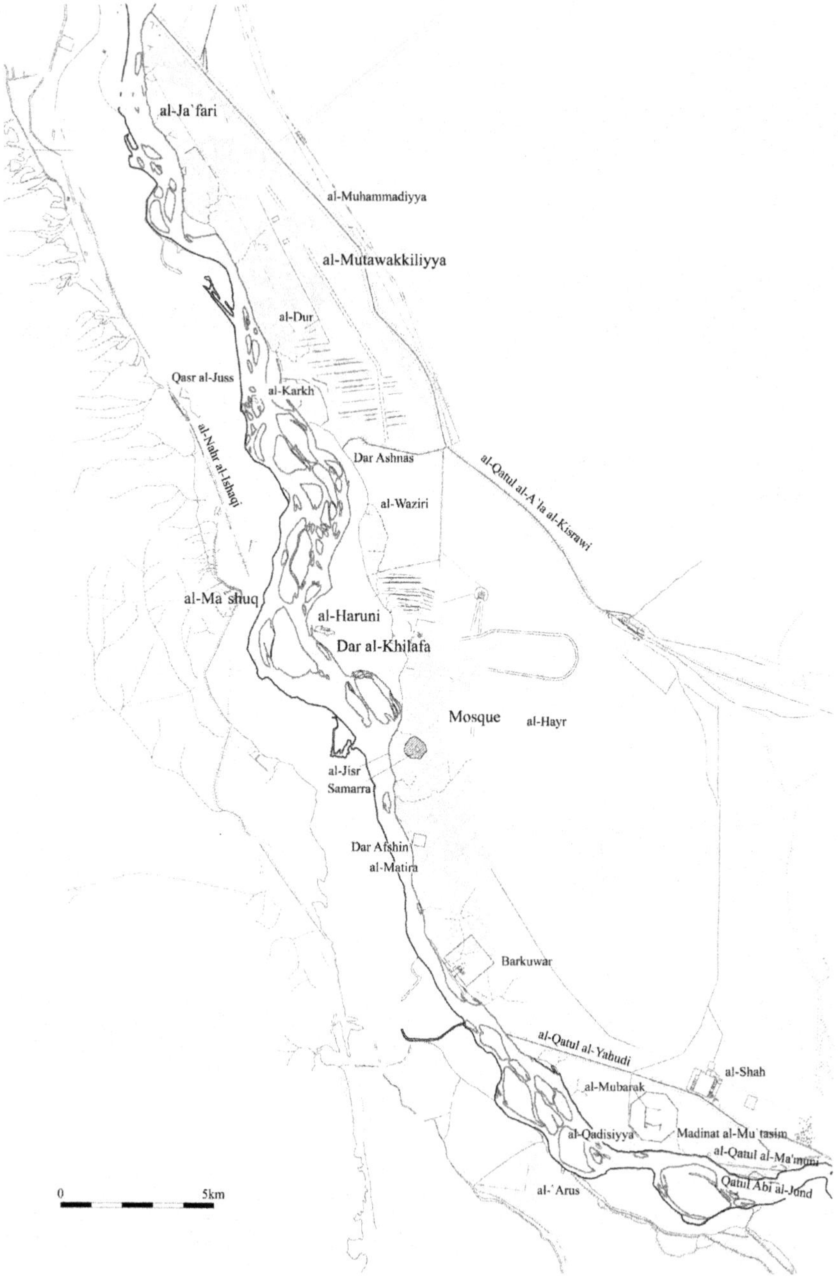

MAP 3 *Samarra*

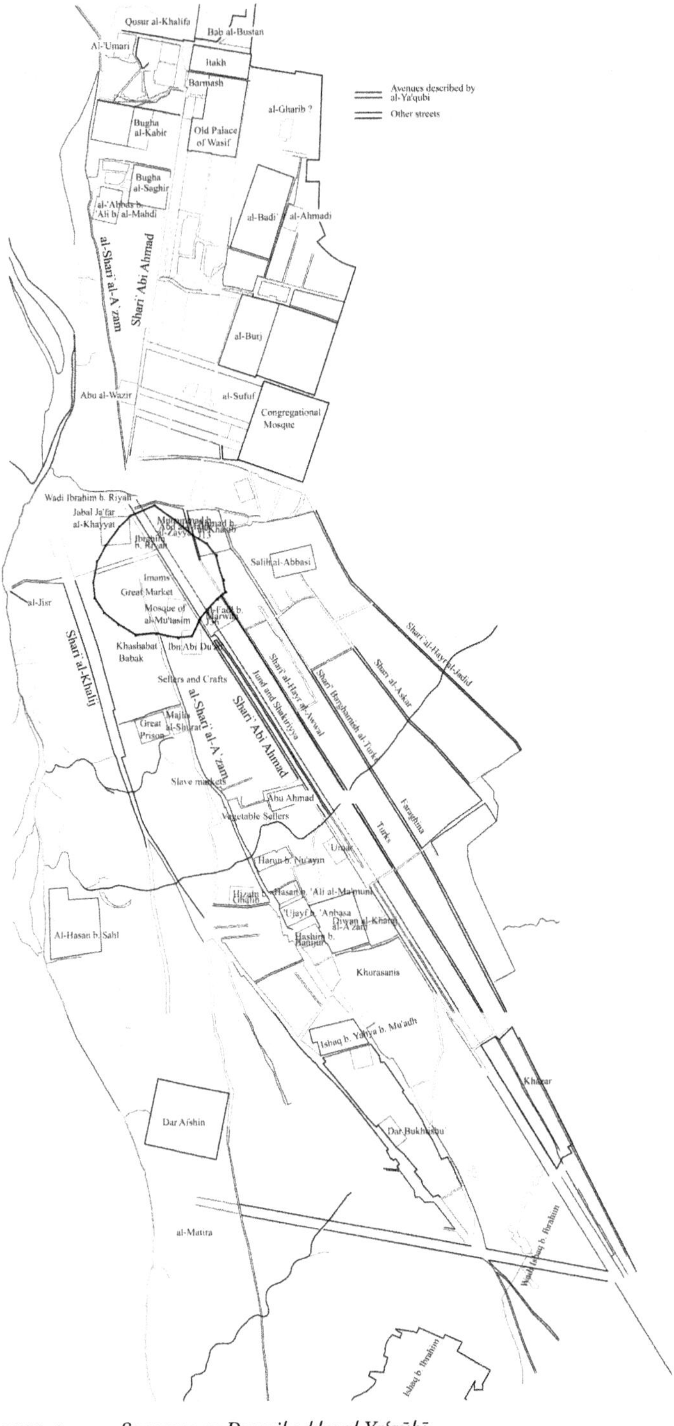

MAP 4 *Samarra as Described by al-Yaʿqūbī*

dad.[80] He went to al-Shammāsiyya, the place where al-Ma'mūn used to go to pass some days or months. He intended to build a city outside Baghdad at al-Shammāsiyya, but the land at that spot seemed too constricted to him, and he also disliked its proximity to Baghdad. So he went on to al-Burdān at the advice of al-Faḍl b. Marwān, who was vizier at the time. That was in the year 221.[81] He stayed at al-Burdān a few days and summoned the engineers, but that site did not please him either. Then he came to a place known as Bāḥamshā on the east bank of the Tigris. He surveyed there for a city on the Tigris and looked for a place where a canal could be dug, but he did not find one. He went on to the village known as al-Maṭīra and stayed there a while, and then continued to al-Qāṭūl. He said, "This is the most suitable place." He caused the canal known as the Qāṭūl to go through the center of the city and the buildings to be along both the Tigris and the Qāṭūl. He began construction and assigned land-grants to military officers, bureaucrats, and important people. | They built until the 257
buildings became tall and markets were laid out along the Qāṭūl and the Tigris. Al-Muʿtaṣim took up residence in one of the buildings that had been built for him, and some of the important people did likewise. Then he said that the land around the Qāṭūl was unsatisfactory; it was full of pebbles and stones, was very difficult to build on, and had insufficient space. Then he rode out hunting and went on his way until he came to a place that would please whoever saw it.[82] It was a desolate area in the land of al-Ṭīrhān where there were no buildings and no people, except for a Christian monastery. He stopped at the monastery and talked with the monks there. He asked, "What is the name of this place?" One of the monks replied: "We find in our ancient books that this place is named Surra-man-ra'ā;[83] that it was the city of Shem, son of Noah; and that it will be rebuilt in the fullness of time by a great, triumphant, and victorious king whose comrades have faces like birds of the wasteland. He will reside there, and his children will reside there." So al-Muʿtaṣim said: "By God! I will build it and reside there, and my children will reside there." Once, al-Rashīd had ordered that his children should go out hunting, so I went with Muḥammad, al-Ma'mūn, and al-Rashīd's

80 On this and related versions of the caliph's decision to leave Baghdad, see Gordon, ibid., 50–55.

81 221 A.H. = December 26, 835 – December 13, 836.

82 The name of Sāmarrā' (probably from an older toponym, cf. Syriac *Shūmaʿrā*) was popularly derived from the phrase *Surra Man Ra'ā* (He who Sees It Is Delighted), a folk etymology that became the new city's official name; al-Yaʿqūbī consistently spells the name in this way. See the article by A. Northedge in *EI*², s.v. Sāmarrā'. The Arabic therefore can also be translated, "He came to the site of Samarra."

83 See the previous note.

older children. Each one of us caught some game—I caught an owl. Then we went back and presented our game to him. The servants who were with us were saying, "This is so-and-so's catch, and that is so-and-so's catch," until my catch was presented to him. When he saw the owl, which the servants were reluctant to present lest he regard it as a bad omen or treat me badly me because of it, he said, "Who caught this?" They replied, "Abū Isḥāq."[84] He regarded it as auspicious and laughed and was happy. Then he said, "He will attain the caliphate; his soldiers, companions, and those who have influence with him will be people whose faces are like the face of this owl. He will rebuild an ancient city and reside there with those people; and his children after him will reside there." Al-Rashīd was not as happy that day with anything that had been caught as he was with my catching that owl.

∴

Thus al-Muʿtaṣim decided to reside at that place. He summoned Muḥammad
258 b. ʿAbd al-Malik al-Zayyāt, Ibn Abī Du'ād,[85] | ʿUmar b. Faraj, and Aḥmad b. Khālid, known as Abū l-Wazīr, and told them, "Buy this land from the owners of this monastery and pay them four thousand dinars as its price." They did so. Then he summoned the engineers and said, "Chose the most suitable of these sites." They selected a number of places for compounds. He assigned each of his comrades to construct a compound. He assigned Khāqān ʿUrṭūj Abū l-Fatḥ b. Khāqān to build al-Jawsaq[86] al-Khāqānī; ʿUmar b. Faraj to build the the compound known as al-ʿUmarī;[87] and Abū l-Wazīr to build the compound known as al-Wazīrī.

Then he drew the boundaries for the land-grants for the military officers, the bureaucrats, and the populace. He laid out the congregational mosque and demarcated the markets around this mosque. The boundaries of the markets were spacious; each type of trade was set up in a separate area, and each group of tradesmen was confined to that area, as the markets in Baghdad had been planned. He ordered the assembling of laborers, builders, and craftsmen such as blacksmiths, carpenters, and other trades, as well as the importing of teak and other types of wood and logs from Basra and its environs, from Baghdad

84 Abū Isḥāq was the *kunya* (familiar name) of Muḥammad b. Hārūn, the future caliph who took the regnal name of al-Muʿtaṣim.

85 Aḥmad b. Abī Du'ād al-Iyādī (d. 240/854) was chief judge under the ʿAbbāsids starting with al-Muʿtaṣim (r. 218–227/833–842) until the year 232/847, in the reign of al-Mutawakkil.

86 *Jawsaq* is the Arabic form of Persian *kūshk*, palace, villa.

87 The text has al-Ghumarī, presumably a typographical error.

and other parts of the Sawād, and from Antioch and other coastal towns of Syria. He brought in masons to cut and dress marble, and shops for working marble were set up in Latakia and elsewhere.

Al-Muʿtaṣim kept the land-grants for the Turks separate from those of all other people. He kept the Turks segregated from the others, so that they would not mix with any of the assimilated people[88] and only people from Farghāna would be their neighbors. He granted Ashnās and his comrades estates in the place known as al-Karkh and joined to him a number of Turkish military officers and men, ordering him to build mosques and markets. He granted estates to Khāqān ʿUrṭūj and his comrades adjacent to al-Jawsaq al-Khāqānī and ordered him to keep his comrades together and forbid them to mix with the populace. He granted estates to Waṣīf and his comrades adjacent to al-Ḥayr; he built an enclosure named Ḥāʾir al-Ḥayr around them. The land-grants for all the Turks and the non-Arabs from Farghāna were kept far from the markets and the crowds of the wide avenues and long lanes. There was not a single merchant or other ordinary person | interspersed among them in their estates and lanes. Al- 259
Muʿtaṣim bought them slave girls and had them take wives from among them. He forbade them to marry or to become related through marriage to any of the assimilated people; even when their children grew up, they too could marry only among themselves. Fixed stipends were established for the Turks' slave girls, and their names were registered in the administrative records. None of the Turks could divorce his wife or separate from her.

Having granted Ashnās the Turk an estate at the western end of the built-up area, and having granted his comrades estates with him and named the place al-Karkh, al-Muʿtaṣim ordered that no outside merchant and other person should be permitted to settle near them and forbade them to have any contact with the indigenous people. He also granted estates beyond al-Karkh to another group of people and named the place al-Dūr. He built mosques and baths for them among the mansions and estates. In each place, he established a small market in which were a number of shops for grocers,[89] butchers, and other essential tradesmen.

He granted al-Afshīn Khaydhar b. Kāwūs al-Usrūshanī an estate at the eastern end of the built-up area, about two farsakhs away, and named the place al-Maṭīra. He granted al-Afshīn's comrades from Usrūshana and others who

---

88 Arabic *bi-qawmin min al-muwalladīn*: the term *muwallad* refers to persons of mixed ancestry, Arab and non-Arab, and by extension to persons assimilated to Arabic culture.

89 Text: *al-fāmiyyīn*. Sources cited by Wiet indicate that these were merchants of wheat or other grains; however, Ibn al-Athīr, *Lubāb*, 2:410 says that the word designated grocers who sold dried fruits and vegetables.

had been attached to him estates around his mansion, and he ordered him to build a small market there with shops for essential trades, mosques, and baths.

Al-Ḥasan b. Sahl requested an estate between the furthest markets, at the end of which was the hill where the gibbet for Bābak[90] came to be erected, and al-Maṭīra, the site of Afshīn's estate. There were no buildings in the area at the time, but later it became so surrounded with buildings that al-Ḥasan b. Sahl's estate came to be in the middle of Samarra. People's buildings stretched out in every direction all the way to al-Maṭīra.

Avenues were laid out to the estates of the military officers of Khurāsān and their comrades in the army and the Shākiriyya.[91] To the right and left of
260 the avenues | were lanes and houses for the general populace. The avenue known as al-Sarīja, which was the principal avenue, stretched from al-Maṭīra to the watercourse known at that time as Wādī Isḥāq b. Ibrāhīm, because Isḥāq b. Ibrāhīm moved from his estate in the days of al-Mutawakkil and built extensively at the head of the watercourse.

Then came the estate of Isḥāq b. Yaḥyā b. Muʿādh; after it there were estates for people on the left and the right of that grand avenue and in lanes on both sides of the avenue, which led in one direction to an avenue named for Abū Aḥmad, who was Abū Aḥmad b. al-Rashīd, and in the other direction to the Tigris and vicinity. The estates continued to the principal ministry of the land tax, which was in that large avenue. In that avenue were the estates of the Khurāsānī military officers, among them the estate of Hāshim b. Bānījūr; the estate of ʿUjayf b. ʿAnbasa; the estate of al-Ḥasan b. ʿAlī al-Maʾmūnī; the estate of Hārūn b. Nuʿaym; and the estate of Ḥizām b. Ghālib. Behind Ḥizām's estate were the stables for the caliph's mounts, both the official and private ones; Ḥizām and his brother Yaʿqūb were in charge of them.

---

90 Bābak was the leader of a religious and social movement that rebelled against the caliphate during the reigns of al-Maʾmūn and al-Muʿtaṣim. Its followers received the name of Jāwīdāniyya from the leader of the Khurramiyya sect, Jāwīdhān b. Sahl, whose mantle Bābak inherited. The revolt was put down, and Bābak himself was taken to Baghdad and executed in 222/837. See the article by P. Crone in EI^{3}, s.v. Bābak, and the fuller account in Crone's *Nativist Prophets of Early Islamic Iran*, 46–76. On al-Badhdh, see Barthold, *Historical Geography*, 224, and the article by C. E. Bosworth in EI^{2}, s.v. al-Badhdh.

91 Shākiriyya (from Persian *čākir*, servant) probably refers to private militias fighting under the patronage of princes from the ruling dynasty or commanders belonging to the class of military nobility. The institution originated in the eastern provinces of the empire, but developed in the heartland of the caliphate under the ʿAbbāsids. See the article by Khalīl ʿAthāmina in EI^{2}, s.v. al-Shākiriyya.

Then came places for the date-sellers; the slave-market, at an intersection where a number of roads branched off, with chambers, upper rooms, and slave-shops; the police station and main prison; and private residences. There were markets to the left and right on this avenue with various wares and manufactured goods. That continued until Bābak's gibbet. After that came the grand market, where there were no houses—each trade was in a separate area, and each type of artisan was segregated from the others. Then came the Old Mosque (al-Jāmiʿ al-Qadīm), which continued to be used for Friday prayers down to the time of al-Mutawakkil; then it became too small for the people, so that it was torn down and a spacious congregational mosque was built next
to | al-Ḥayr. The congregational mosque and markets were on one side, and on 261
the other were estates, residences, and markets for lowly tradesmen such as sellers of beer (*fuqqāʿ*),[92] *harīsa*,[93] and wine.

Then came the estate of Rāshid al-Maghribī; the estate of Mubārak al-Maghribī; Mubārak's Little Market; Jaʿfar al-Khayyāṭ Hill, on which was Jaʿfar's estate; then the estate of Abū l-Wazīr; then the estate of al-ʿAbbās b. ʿAlī b. al-Mahdī; then the estate of ʿAbd al-Wahhāb b. ʿAlī b. al-Mahdī. The avenue continued on, with the estates of common people along it, to the mansion of Hārūn b. al-Muʿtaṣim—that is, al-Wāthiq—near the Dār al-ʿĀmma, which is the mansion where Yaḥyā b. Aktham resided in the days of al-Mutawakkil, after he had been appointed chief judge. Then came Bāb al-ʿĀmma and the caliphal palace, or Dār al-ʿĀmma, where the caliph held audience on Mondays and Thursdays; then the treasuries for the privy purse and the public treasury; then the estate of Masrūr Sammāna al-Khādim, who was in charge of the treasuries; then the estate of Qarqās al-Khādim, a native of Khurāsān; then the estate of Thābit al-Khādim; then the estate of Abū l-Jaʿfāʾ and other important court attendants.[94]

The second avenue was known by the name of Abū Aḥmad—that is, Abū Aḥmad b. al-Rashīd. In the east, this avenue began at the mansion of Bakhtīshūʿ the physician, which he built in the days of al-Mutawakkil. Then it bore right, southward in the direction of the *qibla*, alongside the estates of the Khurāsānī military officers and their forces composed of Arabs and men from Qumm, Isfahan, Qazwīn, al-Jabal, and Azerbaijan. This led to the great Sarīja Avenue.

---

92 *Fuqqāʿ* was a kind of nonalcoholic beer, a carbonated drink made from malted barley and flavored with salt, sugar, and aromatics. For recipes see Nawal Nasrallah, *Annals of the Caliphs' Kitchens*, 454–459, 551.

93 *Harīsa* was a porridge of cooked crushed grains. See Nasrallah, *Annals of the Caliphs' Kitchens*, 560.

94 Or the caliph's eunuchs (*al-khadam al-kibār*); see note 66 above.

To the north, opposite the *qibla*, it connected with Abū Aḥmad Avenue, the principal ministry of the land tax, ʿUmar's estate, and then an estate for the scribes and other people. The estate of Abū Aḥmad b. al-Rashīd was halfway
262 along the avenue; at its end, adjacent to the western watercourse, | which is called Wādī Ibrāhīm b. Riyāḥ, were the estates of Ibn Abī Du'ād, al-Faḍl b. Marwān, Muḥammad b. ʿAbd al-Malik al-Zayyāt, and Ibrāhīm b. Riyāḥ, all on the grand avenue. These estates were contiguous with each other all along this avenue and in the lanes on the right and left as far as the estate of Bughā the Younger; then the estate of Bughā the Elder; then the estate of Sīmā al-Dimashqī; then the estate of Barmash; then the old estate of Waṣīf; then the estate of Ītākh, which was adjacent to Bāb al-Bustān and the caliphal palaces.

The third avenue was the original al-Ḥayr Avenue, on which the mansion of Aḥmad b. al-Khaṣīb was built in the days of al-Mutawakkil. The start of this avenue was to the east and from the watercourse which joined the Wādī Isḥāq b. Ibrāhīm. On it were the estates of the troops, the Shākiriyya, and various other people. It extended to Wādī Ibrāhīm b. Riyāḥ.

The fourth avenue was known as Barghāmush al-Turkī Avenue. On it were the estates of the Turks and the people from Farghāna. The Turkish lanes were separate and the Farghānī lanes were separate. The Turks were in the lanes which were on the *qibla* side, and the Farghānīs were across from them in the lanes opposite the *qibla*. Each lane was across from another lane, and none of the assimilated people were intermixed with the Turks and Farghānīs. The last of the houses and estates for the Turks were the estates of the Khazars, in the eastern areas. This avenue began from al-Maṭīra, at the estates of al-Afshīn, which were taken over by Waṣīf and Waṣīf's comrades. Then the avenue extended to the watercourse which joined Wādī Ibrāhīm b. Riyāḥ.

The fifth avenue was known by the name of Ṣāliḥ al-ʿAbbāsī. It was al-Askar Avenue, in which there were estates of the Turks and the Farghānīs. The Turks again were in separate lanes and the Farghānīs in separate lanes. The avenue extended from al-Maṭīra to the palace of Ṣāliḥ al-ʿAbbāsī at the head of the watercourse. It adjoined the estates of the military officers, bureaucrats, notables, and ordinary people.

Then came an avenue beyond al-Askar Avenue which was called the New
263 al-Ḥayr Avenue (Shāriʿ al-Ḥayr al-Jadīd), in which there were a variety | of people consisting of military officers from the people of Farghāna, Usrūshana, Ishtākhanj, and other rural districts of Khurāsān. Whenever estates for a group of people were added to these avenues which came from al-Ḥayr, the enclosure wall would be torn down and another one built further back. Beyond the enclosure wall, wild animals such as gazelles, onagers, oryx, hares, and ostriches were kept in a spacious, pleasant plain surrounded by a fence.

The avenue along the Tigris was named Canal Avenue (Shāriʿ al-Khalīj). Docks and boats were there, with wares arriving from Baghdad, Wāsiṭ, Kaskar, and other places in the Sawād; from Basra, al-Ubulla, al-Ahwāz, and that area; and from Mosul, Baʿarbāyā, Diyār Rabīʿa, and that area. Most or all of the estates of the Maghāriba were there. The place known as al-Azlākh, which was where the Maghāriba[95] foot-soldiers lived, was one of the first parts of Samarra to be laid out.

Because people had more room for building in Samarra than they did in Baghdad, they built spacious homes. However, everyone's drinking water came from the Tigris and was carried in bags on mules and camels, since their wells had to be very deep, and were salty, unpalatable, and did not yield an abundance of water; but the Tigris was nearby and there were many water-carriers.

The profits and income from Samarra and its markets amounted to 10 million dirhams a year. Sources of supply for imports, such as Mosul, Baʿarbāyā, and other areas of Diyār Rabīʿa, were nearby, and the goods were transported on boats via the Tigris, so that prices were reasonable.

∴

When al-Muʿtaṣim had finished surveying and laying the foundations of the buildings on the east side of the Tigris, the Samarra side, he built a bridge to the west side of the Tigris. He established cultivated areas, orchards, and gardens there; he had canals dug from the Tigris, and each military officer was entrusted with the development of one locality. Date palms were imported from Baghdad and Basra and other areas of the Sawād, and plants were brought in from the Jazīra, Syria, al-Jabal, al-Rayy, Khurāsān, and other countries. Water was plentiful | for these cultivated areas on the west[96] side of Samarra. The 264
date palms flourished, the trees took root, the produce ripened, the fruits were excellent, and the herbs and vegetables were good. People planted various kinds of crops, herbs, vegetables, and succulent plants. Because the land had been fallow for thousands of years, whatever was planted in it flourished—so much so that the revenue from the cultivated areas on the canal known as the

95 *Maghāriba* (pl. of *Maghribī*) means "people from the Maghrib." The term *Maghrib* normally refers to North Africa, that is, the provinces west of Egypt. Brief references in ʿAbbāsid-era sources, however, indicate that the Magharriba were Arab tribesmen from the districts of al-Ḥawf in the Nile Delta conscripted late in the reign of al-Maʾmūn, c. 214–215/830–832; see Matthew S. Gordon, *The Breaking of a Thousand Swords*, 37–40.

96 Text: east, which must be a copyist's mistake.

Isḥāqī and alongside it, the Ītākhī Canal, the ʿUmarī Canal, the ʿAbd al-Malikī Canal, the Ibn Ḥammād Waterwheel, the Masrūrī Canal, the Sīf Canal, the five villages of al-ʿArabāt al-Muḥadditha, the seven lower villages, the orchards, and the gardens, plus the taxes (*kharāj*) on agricultural property amounted to 400,000 dinars a year.

From every country al-Muʿtaṣim summoned workers and craftsmen who were skilled at construction, farming, date cultivation, planting, channeling and measuring (the flow of) water, tapping water, and finding underground water. From Egypt, he brought those who knew how to make papyrus and other things; from Basra, those who knew how to make glass, pottery, and mats; from Kufa, those who could make ceramics and who could make oils; and from other countries, people of every profession and craft. He settled them with their families in these places, and they received land-grants there. He set up markets there for those who practiced their professions in the city. Al-Muʿtaṣim built palaces [in] the cultivated areas. In every orchard, he set a compound with reception rooms, pools, and courtyards. The cultivated areas became so beautiful that the notables were eager to have even a modest plot of land in them, and competed for them, and a *jarīb*[97] of land cost a great deal of money.

Al-Muʿtaṣim-biʾllāh died in the year 227,[98] and Hārūn al-Wāthiq b. al-Muʿtaṣim became caliph. Al-Wāthiq built the palace known as al-Hārūnī on the Tigris. He had it constructed with audience halls on eastern and western terraces.[99] He moved there, and the number of land-grants increased. He had some people settled near him and others settled further away, out of respect, not out of disfavor. He granted Waṣīf as land-grant the mansion of Afshīn in al-Maṭīra, so Waṣīf moved from his original mansion to Afshīn's mansion. He
265 continued | to reside there with his comrades and retainers around him.

He expanded the markets, and the docks where ships from Baghdad, Wāsiṭ, Basra, and Mosul arrived were enlarged. People resumed building and built more durably and elaborately when they realized that this had become a real city; before that they had just called it "the Camp."

Al-Wāthiq passed away in the year 232.[100] Jaʿfar al-Mutawakkil b. al-Muʿtaṣim became caliph and resided at al-Hārūnī, which he liked best of all al-Muʿtaṣim's

97 Originally, a *jarīb* was the amount of land on which one could sow a *jarīb* of seed (a bushel of a variety of sizes, depending on region), and so a *jarīb* of unirrigated land was larger than one of irrigated land. However, there was a tendency to fix the *jarīb* at 100 *qaṣabas* (approximately 1,600 square meters). See the article by C. E. Bosworth in *EI*^{2}, s.v. Misāḥa.

98 Al-Yaʿqūbī, *Taʾrīkh*, 2:584, gives a date of Thursday, 19 Rabīʿ I, 227 (January 6, 842).

99 Arabic *dakka*: presumably some kind of elevated room. See Lane, *Lexicon*, s.v.

100 Al-Yaʿqūbī, *Taʾrīkh*, 2:590, gives a date of Wednesday, 24 Dhū l-Ḥijja, 232 (August 11, 847).

palaces. He settled his son Muḥammad al-Muntaṣir in al-Muʿtaṣim's palace known as al-Jawsaq. He settled his son Ibrāhīm al-Muʾayyad in al-Maṭīra, and settled his son al-Muʿtazz to the east of al-Maṭīra at a place called Balkuwārā. Building became continuous from Balkuwārā to the end of the area known as al-Dūr, a distance of four farsakhs. He added al-Askar Avenue and New Avenue to the avenues of al-Ḥayr. He built the congregational mosque at the beginning of al-Ḥayr in a spacious place outside the inhabited area, so that it was not adjacent to any land-grant or market. He built it skillfully, spaciously, and sturdily. He made a fountain in it which ran water constantly. He made the roads leading to it to consist of three forums,[101] grand and wide, coming from the avenue which begins at Wadi Ibrāhīm b. Riyāḥ. In each forum there were shops with various kinds of wares, manufactured goods, and things for sale. The width of each forum was one hundred *dhirāʿ*s (in black *dhirāʿ*s), so that the caliph's access to the mosque would not be constricted if he attended Friday prayers at the mosque accompanied by his troops and retainers, his cavalry and infantry. There were lanes and streets from each forum to the next; the estates of a number of ordinary people were in them. The homes and mansions had ample room for their residents; and the merchants, | craftsmen, and artisans 266
had plenty of room in the shops and markets that were in the forums of the congregational mosque.

He granted Najāḥ b. Salama the secretary an estate at the end of the forums on the *qibla* side of the mosque; he also granted Aḥmad b. Isrāʾīl the secretary an estate near there. He granted estates to Muḥammad b. Mūsā the astronomer and his brothers, and a group of bureaucrats, military officers, members of the clan of Hāshim, and others.

Al-Mutawakkil decided to build himself a city in order to move there—one that would be named for him and for which he would be remembered. So he ordered Muḥammad b. Mūsā the astronomer and the engineers at his court to choose a site. Their choice fell on a place called al-Māḥūza.[102] Al-Mutawakkil was told that al-Muʿtaṣim had been about to build a city there and

---

101 Arabic *ṣufūf* (plural of *ṣaff*) originally meant *rows*. Northedge, *Topography*, 271, translates *rows*, but *forums* seems to fit the context here. Lane, *Lexicon*, s.v. *ṣaff*, notes that the plural *ṣufūf* can refer both to rows of men and to the *place* where men assemble in rows.

102 One is tempted to equate al-Māḥūza with al-Madāʾin, the old Sasanian capital about 26 miles (41.9 km) south of Baghdad. Indeed, one of the Aramaic names for that capital was Māḥōzē (the Cities), which translates into Arabic as al-Madāʾin. Against this, one notes that al-Yaʿqūbī elsewhere refers to the old Sasanian capital as al-Madāʾin, that Aramaic *māḥōzā* (city, settlement) was a generic term, and that the new foundation was close to Samarra; see Yāqūt, *Muʿjam al-buldān*, 2:86–89, s.v. al-Jaʿfarī.

to dig out a canal that had been there in antiquity. Al-Mutawakkil therefore decided to do this and began planning for it in the year 245.[103] He directed that the canal should be dug to run through the middle of the city. The expenditure for the canal was estimated at 1,500,000 dinars. That did not trouble the caliph, who agreed to it. The digging began, and great sums were spent for that canal. The site for the caliph's palaces and residences was marked out, and he made land-grants to his heirs-apparent and his other children, military officers, bureaucrats, soldiers, and ordinary people. The grand avenue extended from the mansion of Ashnās in al-Karkh—it was later owned by al-Fatḥ b. Khāqān—for a distance of three farsakhs to his palaces. He set three great, high gates outside his palaces; a horseman with his lance could enter through them. He granted estates to people to the right and left of the grand avenue, which he made two hundred *dhirā*'s wide. He proposed to dig canals on both sides of the avenue, for water to flow from the large canal that was being excavated. The palaces were built, the mansions were erected, and the construction rose up. The caliph would go around in person; whenever he saw someone building diligently, he rewarded him with gifts and presents, so people built in earnest. Al-Mutawakkil named this city al-Jaʿfariyya. Buildings ran continuously from al-Jaʿfariyya to the place known as al-Dūr, and thence to al-Karkh and Samarra,
267 extending to the place where | his son Abū ʿAbdallāh al-Muʿtazz had settled. There was no empty space anywhere between them, no gap, no place without buildings, for a distance of seven farsakhs.

The construction rose in the space of a year. The markets were set up in a separate area; there was a market at each intersection and in each neighborhood. The congregational mosque was built. Al-Mutawakkil moved to the palaces of this city on the first day of Muḥarram in the year 247.[104] When he held court, he bestowed splendid prizes on the people and rewarded them. He gave stipends to all the military officers, bureaucrats, and those who had undertaken any of the work. He was overjoyed and said, "Now I know that I am a king, for I have built myself a city in which I have taken up residence." The ministries were moved there: the ministry of the land tax, the ministry of country estates, the ministry of finances,[105] the ministry of the army and the Shākiriyya, the ministry of clients and pages, the ministry of the post, and all the (other) ministries. However, the canal was not finished; only a trickle of water was flowing in it,

---

103 245 A.H. = April 8, 859 – March 27, 860.

104 17 March 861. Cf. al-Yaʿqūbī, *Taʾrīkh*, 2:601, where the date of Muḥarram 246, one year earlier, is given.

105 Arabic *dīwān al-zimām*. Literally, "bureau of registry," a ministry that kept a record of revenues and expenses. See Dozy, *Supplément*, 1:601, and the article in *EI*², s.v. Zimām.

and it was not continuous or ready for use, although something like a million dinars had already been spent on it: digging it was extremely difficult because they were digging into gravel and stones where picks were ineffective.

Al-Mutawakkil remained in residence in his palaces at al-Jaʿfariyya for nine months and three days. He was murdered on 3 Shawwāl 247[106] at his Jaʿfarī palace, the most ill-omened of the palaces.

Muḥammad al-Muntaṣir, the son of al-Mutawakkil, became ruler. He moved to Samarra and ordered the people to move en masse from al-Māḥūza, to tear down the houses, and to haul the rubble to Samarra. So the people moved and hauled the rubble of the houses to Samarra. The Jaʿfarī palaces, houses, dwellings, and markets quickly went to ruin, and the place became deserted without a person or inhabitant in it—a wasteland, as if nothing had ever been built there and no one ever had lived there.

Al-Muntaṣir died at Samarra in Rabīʿ II 248.[107] Al-Mustaʿīn Aḥmad b. Muḥammad b. al-Muʿtaṣim became ruler. | He stayed in Samarra for two years 268
and eight months, until his circumstances became troubled; he went down to Baghdad in Muḥarram 251.[108] He stayed there, fighting against the supporters of al-Muʿtazz for an entire year, while al-Muʿtazz was in Samarra, backed by the Turks and other clients. Then al-Mustaʿīn was deposed, and al-Muʿtazz became ruler. He stayed (in Samarra) until he was murdered, three years and seven months after the deposition of al-Mustaʿīn. Muḥammad al-Muhtadī b. al-Wāthiq received the oath of allegiance as caliph in Rajab 255.[109] He resided for a whole year in al-Jawsaq Palace until he was murdered—may God have mercy on him. Aḥmad al-Muʿtamid b. al-Mutawakkil became ruler. He stayed at Samarra in al-Jawsaq and the caliphal palaces; then he moved to the eastern (*sic*) side of Samarra and built a beautiful palace, which he named al-Maʿshūq.[110] He took up residence there and stayed in it until upheaval set in, whereupon he moved to Baghdad, and thence to al-Madāʾin.

From the time Samarra was built and inhabited until we have written about it in this book of ours, fifty-five years have passed. Eight caliphs ruled there, and five died or were murdered there: al-Muʿtaṣim, al-Wāthiq, al-Muntaṣir, al-Muʿtazz, and al-Muhtadī. Two were killed in its environs, in areas adjacent to it or near it: al-Mutawakkil and al-Mustaʿīn. Its name in ancient books was Zawrāʾ

---

106 December 10, 861.

107 Al-Yaʿqūbī, *Taʾrīkh*, 2:603, gives a date of Saturday, 4 Rabiʿ II, 248 (June 7, 862).

108 February 865.

109 Al-Yaʿqūbī, *Taʾrīkh*, 2:617, gives a date of Tuesday, 27 Rajab, 255 (July 11, 869).

110 "The Beloved."

Banī l-ʿAbbās.[111] This is justified because the *qibla*s of its mosques were all off-axis. Although not a single one was accurate, not one has been torn down or forgotten.

∴

We have now described Baghdad and Samarra. We began with them because they are the two royal cities and seats of the caliphate, and we have described the foundation of each of them. Let us now give an account of the other countries and the distances between one country and another and one city and another, in four parts, according to the four regions of the world: east; west; south, the direction of the *qibla*, which is where Canopus, which the astronomers call al-Tayman, rises; and north, which is the abode of the Bear,[112]
269 which the astronomers call Polaris.[113] | We shall describe each country according to the quarter in which it is located and what is adjacent to it. May God grant success.

The First Quarter: The East

From Baghdad to al-Jabal, Azerbaijan, Qazwīn, Zanjān, Qumm, Isfahan, al-Rayy, Ṭabaristān, Jurjān, Sijistān, and Khurāsān and the parts of Tibet and Turkistan that border on it.

The Rural Districts (KUWAR) *of al-Jabal*[114]

If one wishes to proceed eastward from Baghdad, one begins from the part of it on the east bank of the Tigris and then heads east to the place known as Three Gates, which is the easternmost part of Baghdad. Next one travels straight on to the bridge at al-Nahrawān.[115] Nahrawān is a venerable old town beside a canal that branches off from a canal called the Tāmarrā that comes from al-Jabal

---

111 "The Oblique of the ʿAbbāsids."

112 The Arabic *banāt al-naʿsh* does not specify whether Ursa Minor (*al-ṣughrā*) or Ursa Major (*al-kubrā*) is meant.

113 Arabic "Al-Jady," which usually means Capricorn, also can mean Polaris, which is clearly intended here.

114 On the province known as al-Jabal, see note 24 above.

115 On the town of al-Nahrawān and the canal system, see the article by M. Morony in *EI*^{2}, s.v. al-Nahrawān.

and then goes on to irrigate some of the counties of the Sawād and which is navigable by large boats and big ships. After one crosses the Nahrawān bridge, the various routes to al-Jabal branch out.

If one wishes to go to the rural districts of Māsabadhān,[116] Mihrijānqadhaq,[117] and al-Ṣaymara,[118] one bears right upon crossing the Nahrawān bridge. After six stages, one reaches the county-seat of Māsabadhān, a city known as al-Sīrawān,[119] which is important, large, and spread out between mountains and valleys. It is the city which most resembles Mecca. It has springs from which water gushes out and flows through the town to large streams which irrigate the fields, villages, country estates, and gardens along their banks for a distance of three stages. These springs are hot in winter and cold in summer. The city has a mixed population of Arabs and non-Arabs.

Al-Ṣaymara

From the city of al-Sīrawān to the city of al-Ṣaymara, which is the main city of the rural district known as Mihrijānqadhaq, is a distance of two stages. The city of al-Ṣaymara is situated in a vast meadow dotted with springs and streams | 270
that water the villages and fields. The population is a mixture of Arabs and of non-Arabs who are Persians and Kurds. Māsabadhān and al-Ṣaymara were conquered during the caliphate of ʿUmar b. al-Khaṭṭāb. The land tax from this area amounts to 2.5 million dirhams. The people speak Persian.

∴

If one wishes to go from Baghdad to Ḥulwān,[120] one bears left after crossing the Nahrawān bridge, going to Daskarat al-Malik,[121] where there are wonderfully constructed, beautiful palaces of the Persian kings. From Daskarat al-Malik one goes to Ṭarāristān,[122] where there are more wonderful remains of buildings

116 Le Strange, *Lands of the Eastern Caliphate*, 202.

117 Ibid.; also vocalized as Mihrijānqudhaq (Yāqūt, *Muʿjam al-buldān*, 4:698).

118 Barthold, *Historical Geography*, 207; article by C. E. Bosworth in EI^2, s.v. Ṣaymara.

119 Barthold, *Historical Geography*, 207.

120 On Ḥulwān see the article by L. Lockhart in EI^2, s.v. Ḥulwān; Barthold, *Historical Geography*, 198–199.

121 Daskarat al-Malik (King's Daskara) was located on the Khurāsān Road, about 16 farsakhs (88 kilometers) from Baghdad. See the article by A. A. Duri in EI^2, s.v. Daskara.

122 The reading of the text and identification are uncertain. The printed edition reads *Ṭarāri-*

attributed to the Persian kings. There are also aqueducts constructed of gypsum and bricks, some built in channels on top of each other. Some come from the Qāṭūl canals, and others from the Nahrawān canal. From Ṭarāristān one goes to the battlefield of Jalūlā',[123] the first part of al-Jabal. This is where the battle with the Persians took place in the days of 'Umar b. al-Khaṭṭāb, when Sa'd b. Abī Waqqāṣ overtook them. God scattered the Persian forces and put them to flight. This was in the year 19 A.H.[124] From Jalūlā' one goes to Khāniqīn,[125] a particularly attractive and important village. From Khāniqīn one goes to Qaṣr Shīrīn.[126] Shīrīn was the wife of Kisrā and spent her summers in this castle. Many antiquities of the Persian kings are found in this area. From Qaṣr Shīrīn one goes to Ḥulwān.

Ḥulwān

The city of Ḥulwān is large and beautiful. Its inhabitants are a mixture of Arabs and of non-Arabs who are Persians and Kurds. It was conquered in the days of 'Umar b. al-Khaṭṭāb. Although Ḥulwān is one of the rural districts of al-Jabal, its land tax is included as part of the revenue from the counties of the Sawād. From Ḥulwān one proceeds to the meadow known as Marj al-Qal'a,[127] where the caliph's mounts are put to pasture. From Marj al-Qal'a one goes to al-Zubaydiyya, and thence to the city of Qarmāsīn. Qarmāsīn is an important, populous place. Most of the people are non-Arabs: Persians and Kurds. From the town of Qarmāsīn to al-Dīnawar is three stages.

Al-Dīnawar

271 Al-Dīnawar[128] is an important city with a mixed population of Arabs and non-Arabs. It was conquered in the days of 'Umar. It is called Māh al-Kūfa[129] because its revenue was used to pay the stipends of the people of Kufa. A number of

---

stān, with a note that a second hand has corrected it in the margin of the MS to Ṭabaristān, which is geographically impossible. Perhaps one should read *Ṭazāristan*, and identify the place as Ṭazar of al-Muqaddasī, 393, and Yāqūt, 3:537; see Barthold, *Historical Geography*, 198 n. 20; Wiet, 67.

123 For accounts of the Arab victory over the Persians at Jalūlā', see al-Ya'qūbī, *Ta'rīkh*, 2:173; al-Ṭabarī, *Ta'rīkh*, 1:2456 ff.; and the article by M. Streck in *EI*², s.v. Djalūlā'.

124 That is, 640 C.E.; al-Ṭabarī dates the battle to the end of the year 16 (late 637 or early 638).

125 See the article by P. Schwarz in *EI*², s.v. Khāniḳīn; Barthold, *Historical Geography*, 199.

126 See the article by M. Streck and J. Lassner in *EI*², s.v. Ḳaṣr-i Shīrīn; Barthold, *Historical Geography*, 199.

127 Le Strange, *Lands of the Eastern Caliphate*, 192.

128 See the article by L. Lockhart in *EI*², s.v. Dīnawar; Barthold, *Historical Geography*, 207–208.

129 Arabic and Persian writers explain *Māh* as coming from a Persian word variously glossed as

districts and cantons[130] are included among its dependencies. The revenue from its land tax, not counting the crown estates, amounts to 5.7 million dirhams.

Qazwīn and Zanjān

Whoever wants to go from al-Dīnawar to Qazwīn and Zanjān[131] proceeds from al-Dīnawar to the town of Abhar, where the roads diverge. If one is heading for Zanjān, one bears left from Abhar to Zanjān; then one goes on to the city of Qazwīn. Qazwīn is off the main road, at the foot of a mountain which borders al-Daylam. There are two riverbeds there, one called al-Wādī al-Kabīr and the other Wādī Sīram. Water flows in them during the winter, but dries up in the summer. The population is a mixture of Arabs and non-Arabs. Some Persian antiquities are found there, including fire temples. Its land tax, along with that of Zanjān, is 1.5 million dirhams. Roads fan out from it to Hamadhān, al-Dīnawar, Shahrazūr, Isfahan, and al-Rayy, as well as the road from it to Azerbaijan.

Azerbaijan

Whoever wants to go to Azerbaijan[132] travels four stages from Zanjān to the city of Ardabīl,[133] the first town in Azerbaijan that one reaches. From Ardabīl to Barzand,[134] one of the rural districts of Azerbaijan, is a three-day journey. From Barzand one goes to the city of Warthān,[135] in another rural district of Azerbai-

town, capital, province, or kingdom. A more likely explanation is that *Māh* reflects *Māda*, the old word for Media, the land of the Medes, where the city was located. See L. Lockhart's article in *EI*², s.v. Dīnawar.

130 Arabic *aqālīm wa rasātīq*. For *iqlīm*/*aqālīm*, see note 10 above. The *rustāq* (plural *rasātīq*) was an administrative unit that in al-Ya'qūbī's usage seems to be a division of a *kūra*, without any sizable town, and often located in a hilly or mountainous area. It is translated by convention here as "canton."

131 See the article by C. E. Bosworth in *EI*², s.v. Zandjān; Barthold, *Historical Geography*, 208–211.

132 See the article by V. Minorsky in *EI*², s.v. Ādharbaydjān; Barthold, *Historical Geography*, 214–225.

133 See the articles by R. N. Frye in *EI*², s.v Ardabīl, and by Kishwar Rizvi in *EI*³, s.v. Ardabil; Barthold, *Historical Geography*, 215–217.

134 See the article by R. N. Frye in *EI*², s.v. Barzand; Barthold, *Historical Geography*, 224 gives the distance from Ardabīl to Barzand as 14 farsakhs (c. 91 km on modern maps).

135 Modern Altan; see V. Minorsky in *EI*², s.v. Ādharbaydjān; Le Strange, *Lands of the Eastern Caliphate*, 230.

jan; from Warthān to al-Baylaqān;[136] and from al-Baylaqān to al-Marāgha,[137]
the main city of Upper Azerbaijan. The rural districts of Azerbaijan are Arda-
272 bīl, Barzand, Warthān, Bardha'a,[138] al-Shīz,[139] Sarāt,[140] Marand,[141] Tabrīz,[142] |
al-Mayānij,[143] Urmiya,[144] Khuwayy,[145] and Salmās.[146] The inhabitants of the towns and rural districts of Azerbaijan are a mixture of Ādharī Persians and the ancient Jāwīdāniyya, lords of the city of al-Badhdh where Bābak was.[147] The Arabs settled in Azerbaijan when it was conquered in the year 22 by al-Mughīra b. Shu'ba al-Thaqafī during the caliphate of 'Uthmān b. 'Affān.[148] The revenue from its land tax is 4 million dirhams, more in one year and less in another.

Hamadhān

Whoever wants to go from al-Dīnawar to the city of Hamadhān[149] proceeds two stages from the town of al-Dīnawar to a place called Muḥammadābādh.[150] From Muḥammadābādh to Hamadhān is another two stages. Hamadhān is a

---

136 The site has been identified as modern Ören Kal'e in Azerbaijan. See the articles by D. M. Dunlop in *EI*^{2}, s.v. Baylaḳān, and by J. M. Rogers, s.v. Ören Kal'e; Barthold, *Historical Geography*, 228, locates the town near the confluence of the Araxes and Kur rivers.

137 See the article by V. Minorsky in *EI*^{2}, s.v. Marāgha; Barthold, *Historical Geography*, 214. The situation of al-Marāgha at an elevation of 5,500 feet explains why al-Ya'qūbī calls it the main city of Upper Azerbaijan (*Adharbayjān al-'Ulyā*).

138 On Bardha'a (modern Barda), see the article by D. M. Dunlop in *EI*^{2}, s.v. Bardha'a; Barthold, *Historical Geography*, 227–228.

139 Described in many sources as a major Zoroastrian religious site, now known as Takht-e Sulaymān: See the article by J. Ruska and C. E. Bosworth in *EI*^{2}, s.v. Shīz; Barthold, *Historical Geography*, 208, 214.

140 On Sarāt (usually given as Sarāv), see Le Strange, *Lands of the Eastern Caliphate*, 163, 168, 230.

141 On Marand, see the article by V. Minorsky and C. E. Bosworth in *EI*^{2}, s.v. Marand.

142 On Tabrīz, see the article by V. Minorsky, C. E. Bosworth, and Sheila S. Blair in *EI*^{2}, s.v. Tabrīz; Barthold, *Historical Geography*, 217 ff.

143 Al-Mayānij is probably the same as the town listed by Yāqūt, *Mu'jam al-buldān*, 4:710, s.v. Miyāna, located midway between between Marāgha and Tabrīz.

144 On the lake and the city of Urmiya, see the article by V. Minorsky and C. E. Bosworth in *EI*^{2}, s.v. Urmiya.

145 So in the text; modern Khōī. See the article by R. M. Savory in *EI*^{2}, s.v. Khōī, Khūy.

146 On Salmās, see the article by C. E. Bosworth in *EI*^{2}, s.v. Salmās.

147 On Bābak, see note 90 above.

148 22 A.H. = November 30, 642 – November 18, 643; cf. al-Ya'qūbī, *Ta'rīkh*, 2:180.

149 On Hamadhān (modern Hamadān), see the article by R. N. Frye in *EI*^{2}, s.v. Hamadhān; Barthold, *Historical Geography*, 128–132.

150 Not to be confused with a place of the same name in Khurāsān.

large, important country to which many regions and rural districts are attached. It was conquered in the year 23.[151] Its land tax amounts to six million dirhams. It is called Māh al-Baṣra because its land tax used to be taken for the stipends of the people of Basra.[152] The people's drinking water comes from springs and streams that flow both in winter and in summer. One of them flows to al-Sūs,[153] a rural district of al-Ahwāz, and then passes via the Dujayl,[154] the river of al-Ahwāz, to the city of al-Ahwāz.[155]

Nihāwand

From Hamadhān to Nihāwand[156] is two stages. Nihāwand is a splendid city, where the Persians assembled when al-Nuʿmān b. Muqarrin al-Muzanī attacked them in the year 21.[157] It has several dependent districts inhabited by a mixture of Arabs and non-Arabs. Its land tax, apart from the crown estates, is one million dirhams.

Al-Karaj

From Nihāwand to the city of al-Karaj[158] is two stages. Al-Karaj is the residence of ʿĪsā b. | Idrīs b. Maʿqil b. Shaykh b. ʿUmayr al-ʿIjlī, Abū Dulaf.[159] Not a famous 273
city in the days of the Persians, it counted only as one of the large villages in a canton known as Fā'iq[160] in the rural district of Isfahan. It is sixty farsakhs from it to the city of Isfahan. The ʿIjlī tribesmen settled there, building fortresses and compounds. The compounds were named for Abū Dulaf, his brothers, and his

---

151 23 A.H. = November 19, 643 – November 6, 644; cf. al-Yaʿqūbī, *Taʾrīkh*, 2:180.

152 On the name, see the article by M. Morony in *EI*², s.v Māh al-Baṣra.

153 On al-Sūs (modern Persian Shūsh), see the article by M. Streck and C. E. Bosworth in *EI*², s.v. al-Sūs.

154 That is, the Kārūn River, which the Arabs called the Dujayl al-Ahwāz; see Le Strange, *Lands*, 232.

155 On al-Ahwāz, the main town of Khūzistān, see the article by Mathieu Tillier, in *EI*³, s.v. al-Ahwāz; Barthold, *Historical Geography*, 190 ff.

156 On this town in the Zagros Mountains, see the article by V. Minorsky in *EI*², s.v. Nihāwand.

157 21 A.H. = December 10, 641 – November 29, 642. Cf. the account in al-Yaʿqūbi, *Taʾrīkh*, 2:179; also the bibliography in Minorsky's article mentioned in the previous note.

158 Not the modern town of Karaj; the exact location is uncertain, but this al-Karaj was about halfway between modern Golpāyegān and Hamadān. Barthold, *Historical Geography*, 180; Le Strange, *Lands*, 197; Ibn Ḥawqal, 262, *Ḥudūd*, 132, 201; *EI*², s.v. (al-)Karadj.

159 On this politically active family that played a role in the initial ʿAbbāsid movement, the civil war between al-Amīn and al-Maʾmūn, and the campaign against Bābak, see the article by J. E. Bencheikh in *EI*², s.v. al-Ḳāsim b. ʿĪsā b. Idrīs, Abū Dulaf.

160 The MS reading is ambiguous. Other sources give both Fā'iq and Fātik.

kinsmen. Four cantons are attached to (al-Karaj): the two Fāʾiqs, Jābalq,[161] and Barqrūdh.[162] Al-Karaj is situated amid four mountains covered with estates, fields, villages, perennial rivers, and flowing springs. The inhabitants are non-Arabs, except for the family of ʿĪsā b. Idrīs al-ʿIjlī and other Arabs who have joined them. The land tax from al-Karaj was 3.4 million dirhams. This included one million dirhams from the cantons and a 400,000 dirham tax on beverages. This decreased in the days of al-Wāthiq to 3.3 million dirhams.

Qumm and Its Dependencies

Whoever wants to go to Qumm[163] proceeds east from the city of Hamadhān through its cantons. It is five stages from the city of Hamadhān to the city of Qumm. The largest urban area[164] of Qumm is called Manījān.[165] It is an important place, said to contain a thousand lanes. There is an old Persian fortress inside the city. Adjacent to it is an urban area called Kumundān.[166] There is a watercourse with a stream that flows between the two urban areas.
274 There are some arched stone bridges across it | by which one crosses from Manījān to Kumundān. Most of the population belong to the tribe of Madhḥij, specifically to the Ashʿarīs.[167] There are also people of non-Arab ancestry as well as a group of clients who report that they were freedmen of ʿAbdallāh b. al-ʿAbbās b. ʿAbd al-Muṭṭalib. Qumm has two canals: one, in the upper part of the city, is known as Raʾs al-Mūr, and the other, in the lower city, is called Fūrūz. Both have water from springs made to flow through excavated channels. Qumm is situated in a broad plain that stretches about ten farsakhs to the mountains. Among them is a mountain known as Rustāq Sardāb and a mountain known

---

161 Cf. Yāqūt, *Muʿjam al-buldān*, 2:2–3, s.v. Jābalq.

162 Barqrūdh is also attested as Barq al-Rūdh.

163 On the city of Qumm (Modern Persian Qom) see the article by J. Calmard in *EI*², s.v. Ḳum.

164 Text: *madīnat Qumm al-kubrā*. Al-Yaʿqūbī treats Qumm as a single municipality with multiple components; indeed, the sources speak of Qumm as consisting of many villages, seven of which were surrounded by a defensive wall. *Madīna* therefore has been translated in this case as "urban area" ("village" might be another possibility) to avoid confusing repetitions of the term "city."

165 Manījān, the principal settlement, was one of the seven original villages. See the article by J. Calmard cited in note 163.

166 Also vocalized as Kumandān.

167 As the Ashʿarīs (members of the South Arabian tribe of al-Ashʿar b. Udad) were a sister tribe to the Madhḥij (descended from Mālik b. Udad), the text, which normally would mean, "belong to the tribe of Madhḥij, specifically to the subgroup group of Ashʿar," should be taken in an extended sense: "belong to the tribe of Madhḥij, specifically to the related group of Ashʿar." See Wüstenfeld, *Genealogische Tabellen*, 7.

as al-Mallāḥa. Qumm has twelve cantons: Sitāra, Karizmān, al-Farāhān, Warah, Ṭīras,[168] Kūrdur, Wardirāh, Sardāb, Barāwistān, Sirāḥa,[169] Qāriṣ, and Hindijān. During summer, the people of the city drink mostly from wells. Roads fan out from Qumm to al-Rayy, Isfahan, al-Karaj, and Hamadhān. Its land tax is 4.5 million dirhams.

Isfahan (Iṣbahān)

From Qumm to Isfahan[170] is sixty farsakhs, which equals six stages. Isfahan comprises two urban areas, one of which is called Jayy and the other al-Yahūdiyya. The population is mixed: a few are Arabs, but most are Persians (descended from) aristocratic *dihqāns*. There are Arabs there who immigrated from Kufa and Basra, of the tribes of Thaqīf, Tamīm, Banū Ḍabba, Khuzāʿa, Banū Ḥanīfa, Banū ʿAbd al-Qays, and others. It is said that Salmān al-Fārisī[171]—may God's mercy be upon him—was a native of Isfahan from a village called Jayyān—this is what the people of Isfahan have handed down among themselves. The inhabitants of Isfahan have plenty of water from streams and springs that flow towards al-Ahwāz from Isfahan via Tustar, Manādhir al-Kubrā, and then to the city of al-Ahwāz. Isfahan was conquered | in the year 23.[172] Its land tax amounts 275
to ten million dirhams. It has the following cantons: Jayy, where the city is located; Baraʾān, inhabited exclusively by *dihqāns*; Burkhār, where a group of *dihqāns* also live; Ruwaydasht, which is the border between Isfahan and a district of Fārs known as Yazd; al-Barān; Mīrabin; al-Qāmidān, which is inhabited by Kurds and a mixture of non-Arabs who are not of noble descent like the others and out of which came the Khurramiyya,[173] and which is the border between the provinces of Iṣbahān and al-Ahwāz; Fahmān, also inhabited by

168 Possibly to be read Ṭabrīsh.

169 The reading is uncertain; restored by the editor on the basis of Ibn al-Faqīh al-Hamadhānī, *Kitāb al-Buldān*, 265.

170 On Isfahan, see the article by A. K. S. Lambton and J. Sourdel-Thomine in *EI*², s.v. Iṣfahān.

171 On Salmān al-Fārisī ("Salmān the Persian," also known as Salmān Pāk, "Salmān the Pure"), a Companion of the Prophet, often regarded as the first Persian convert to Islam, see the article by G. Levi Della Vida in *EI*², s.v. Salmān al-Fārisī.

172 23 A.H. = November 19, 643 – November 6, 644; cf. al-Yaʿqūbī, *Taʾrīkh*, 2:180.

173 The Arabic historians use Khuramiyya to designate a variety of sects with roots in the doctrines of the late 5th-century Iranian religious figure Mazdak. By ʿAbbāsid times, there were a variety of such groups, anti-Arab and anti-Islamic in orientation, said to believe in dualism, transmigration, and continued prophecy. They were frequently accused of believing in free love and community of property. See the article by W. Madelung in *EI*², s.v. Khurramiyya, and the extensive treatment in P. Crone, *The Nativist Prophets of Early Islamic Iran*.

Kurds and Khurramiyya; Farīdīn, inhabited by lower-class non-Arabs whom the noble Persians of Isfahan call the Luyabah;[174] al-Rādmīla;[175] the twin districts of Sardqāsān and Jarmqāsān, inhabited by noble *dihqāns* and some Arabs from Yemen of the tribe of Hamdān, which form the border between the province of Isfahan and Qumm; Ardistān, inhabited by the grandest of the *dihqāns* and which is said to have been the place where Kisrā Anūshirawān[176] was born; and al-Taymarā, which consists of two cantons inhabited by Arabs of the Banū Hilāl and various divisions of the Qays and which forms the boundary between the province of Isfahan and al-Karaj.

Al-Rayy

If one's destination is al-Rayy,[177] one leaves the city of al-Dīnawar for Qazwīn, and then one travels three stages from Qazwīn along the main highway—al-Rayy is located on the Khurāsān highway. The city of al-Rayy is named al-Muḥammadiyya. It was given that name because al-Mahdī[178] stayed there during the caliphate of al-Manṣūr, when he was sent to Khurāsān to fight 'Abd al-Jabbār b. 'Abd al-Raḥmān al-Azdī, and built up the city. Al-Rashīd was born
276 there, | for al-Mahdī spent several years there and constructed a marvelous building there. The wives of notables among its people nursed al-Rashīd. The people of al-Rayy are a mixture of Persians and a few Arabs. It was conquered by Qaraẓa b. Ka'b al-Anṣārī, during the caliphate of 'Umar b. al-Khaṭṭāb, in the year 23.[179] The people obtain water from numerous springs and large watercourses. One large watercourse comes from the country of al-Daylam and is called the Nahr Mūsā. Because of the country's abundant water, its fruits, gardens, and trees are numerous. It has several cantons and districts. The country estates of Isḥāq b. Yaḥyā b. Mu'ādh and Abū 'Abbād Thābit b. Yaḥyā, al-Ma'mūn's secretary, are there; both were natives of Rayy. Its land tax amounts to ten million dirhams.

---

174 The vocalization and meaning of the word, apparently Persian, are unknown.

175 The correct reading and vocalization are unknown.

176 The Sasanian ruler Kisrā Anūshirawān (Khusraw Anūshirwān) ruled from 591 to 628 C.E.

177 On the city of al-Rayy, whose ruins are located about 5 miles south-southeast of modern Tehran, see the article by V. Minorsky in *EI*², s.v. al-Rayy; Barthold, *Historical Geography*, 121 ff.

178 The future third 'Abbāsid caliph, whose given name was Muḥammad. He was made governor of al-Rayy in 141/758–759.

179 23 A.H. = November 19, 643 – November 6, 644; cf. al-Ya'qūbī, *Ta'rīkh*, 2:180.

Qūmis

From al-Rayy to Qūmis[180] via the main highway and great road is twelve stages, some in inhabited areas and some in the desert. Qūmis is a large, important country. The name of the main town is al-Dāmaghān,[181] which is the first of the towns of Khurāsān. It was conquered by ʿAbdallāh b. ʿĀmir b. Kurayz during the caliphate of ʿUthmān b. ʿAffān, in the year 30.[182] The people are Persians, and they are the most skillful of people in knowing how to make the fine woolen apparel known as Qūmisiyya. Its land tax, amounting to 1.5 million dirhams, is included as part of the revenue of Khurāsān. As for the territory which borders the Caspian Sea (Baḥr al-Daylam) in Khurāsān, (it extends) from al-Rayy to Ṭabaristān.[183] The main city of Ṭabaristān is Sāriya,[184] which is seven stages from al-Rayy.

Ṭabaristān

(From Sāriya) to the second city of Ṭabaristān, which is called Āmul,[185] is two stages. The city of Āmul is on the Caspian Sea (Baḥr al-Daylam). Ṭabaristān is a separate country with an important kingdom. Its king is still known as the Ispahbadh.[186] It is the country of al-Māzyār,[187] who used to write to | the caliphs 277
al-Maʾmūn and al-Muʿtaṣim: "From the Jīl-Jīlān, Ispahbadh of Khurāsān, al-Māzyār Muḥammad b. Qārin, the supporter (*muwālī*) of the Commander of the Faithful"—he did not say "client (*mawlā*) of the Commander of the Faithful." Ṭabaristān is a country with many fortresses and protected by ravines. The

---

180 On Qūmis, see the article by E. E. Bosworth in *EI*², s.v. Ḳūmis; Barthold, *Historical Geography*, 112–120.

181 On Dāmaghān (modern Dāmghān), some 344 km east of Tehran, see the article by D. N. Wilber in *EI*², s.v. Dāmg͟hān.

182 30 A.H. = September 4, 650 – August 23, 651; cf. al-Yaʿqūbī, *Taʾrīkh*, 2:192.

183 Modern Māzandarān; article in *EI*², s.v. Ṭabaristān; Barthold, *Historical Geography*, 230–242.

184 Modern Sārī; see the article by C. E. Bosworth in *EI*², s.v. Sārī; Barthold, *Historical Geography*, 238.

185 Āmul grew in importance after it became the province's administrative center under Arab rule; see the article by L. Lockhart in *EI*², s.v. Āmul; Barthold, *Historical Geography*, 238 f.

186 Written in Arabic as *iṣbahbadh*. The title ("chief of the army") and had roots as far back as Achaemenid Iran. The rulers of Ṭabarisān maintained the title down to the Mongol invasions. See the article by C. E. Bosworth in *EI*², s.v. Ispahbadh.

187 On the career of Māzyār b. Qārin, who maintained his quasi-autonomous power in Ṭabaristān by converting to Islam, whereupon he received the name of Muḥammad b. Qārin, but revolted and was flogged to death during the caliphate of al-Muʿtaṣim, see the article by M. Rekaya in *EI*², s.v. Māzyār; cf. al-Yaʿqūbī, *Taʾrīkh*, 2:582–583; al-Ṭabarī, *Taʾrīkh*, 3:1268 ff.

inhabitants are noble Persians, descendants of their kings, and they are most handsome people. It is said that Kisrā Yazdajird left his slave girls there, and the people of Ṭabaristān, being descended from them, inherited their good looks. The land tax of the country is four million dirhams. The textiles and apparel known as *al-ṭabariyya* are made there.

Jurjān

From al-Rayy to Jurjān[188] is seven stages. The city of Jurjān is located on the River of al-Daylam.[189] Saʿīd b. ʿUthmān conquered the country of Jurjān during the reign of Muʿāwiya. Then it revolted, and the people apostatized from Islam until Yazīd b. al-Muhallab conquered it again during the reign of Sulaymān b. ʿAbd al-Malik b. Marwān. The land tax from the country is ten million dirhams. The inhabitants work rare woods such as khalanj[190] and other kinds, as well as various kinds of silk garments. Large Bactrian[191] camels are found there. There are many date palms in the land of Jurjān.

Ṭūs

Adjoining these countries bordering the Caspian Sea, and among the rural districts of Nīshāpūr and its dependencies, is Ṭūs,[192] which is two stages from Nīshāpūr. There are Arabs from Ṭayyiʾ and other tribes in Ṭūs, but most of the people are Persians. The tomb of the Commander of the Faithful al-Rashīd is there. It was also there that al-Riḍā ʿAlī b. Mūsā b. Jaʿfar b. Muḥammad b. ʿAlī b. al-Ḥusayn[193] passed away (peace be upon them). The main urban area of Ṭūs is called Nūqān. The land tax of the country is included with that of Nīshāpūr.[194]

---

188 On the province of Jurjān (Persian Gurgān), at the southeastern corner of the Caspian Sea, see the article by R. Hartmann in *EI*², s.v. Gurgān; Barthold, *Historical Geography*, 115–117.

189 Also known as the Jurjān (Gurgān) River.

190 A scented wood, variously identified; see V. Mozaffarian, *A Dictionary of Iranian Plant Names*, 210.

191 Text: *bakhātī*, probably to be understood as a plural of *bukhtī*, the normal word for the Bactrian camel. See Dozy, *Supplément*, 1:54.

192 On Ṭūs, see the article by V. Minorsky and C. E. Bosworth in *EI*², s.v. Ṭūs; Barthold, *Historical Geography*, 102–105.

193 ʿAlī b. Mūsā, surnamed al-Riḍā, was the eighth Imam of the Twelver Shīʿa. In 201/816, the caliph al-Maʾmūn named him heir to the caliphate, but the move caused a revolt in Baghdad. In 203/818, ʿAlī al-Riḍā died in Ṭūs after a brief illness. The Shīʿite version of the story says that he was poisoned (cf. al-Yaʿqūbī, *Taʾrīkh*, 2:551). See the article by Tamima Bayhom-Daou in *EI*³, s.v. ʿAlī al-Riḍā.

194 Al-Yaʿqūbī uses the Arabic spelling Naysābūr throughout. The translation uses the more common Persian form of the name.

From Ṭūs to Nasā,[195] another rural district of Nīshāpūr, is two stages. | From Nasā to Bāward[196] is two stages. From Nasā to Khwārazm[197] is eight stages in an easterly direction. Khwārazm is at the end of the Oxus River (Nahr Balkh) at a place where the waters of the Oxus empty into the Caspian Sea (Baḥr al-Daylam).[198] It is a vast territory that Salm b. Ziyād b. Abīhi[199] conquered in the time of Yazīd b. Muʿāwiya. Furs and all sorts of pelts are processed there: sable, fox, ermine, lynx, and squirrel. These rural districts on this side of the Oxus form part of Khurāsān. The Oxus rises from springs amid a mountain range; it is ten stages from its mouth to the city of Balkh. 278

Nīshāpūr

From Qūmis to the city of Nīshāpūr[200] via the Great Highway is nine stages. Nīshāpūr is a vast country with many rural districts, among them: al-Ṭabasayn,[201] Qūhistān, Nasā, Bīward,[202] Abrashahr, Jām, Bākharz, Ṭūs (the main urban area of which is called Nūqān[203]), Zūzan,[204] and Isfarā'īn[205] (on the highway to Jurjān). ʿAbdallāh b. ʿĀmir b. Kurayz conquered the country during the caliphate of ʿUthmān in the year 30.[206] Its inhabitants are a mixture of Arabs

195 On Nasā, see the article by V. Minorsky and C. E. Bosworth in EI², s.v. Nasā, Nisā; Barthold, *Historical Geography*, 89.

196 Abīward in other sources; see the article by V. Minorsky in EI², s.v. Abīward; Barthold, *Historical Geography*, 89.

197 On Khwārazm, see the article by C. E. Bosworth in EI², s.v. Khʷārazm.

198 Here, Nahr Balkh must mean the Oxus, and this seems to be the name al-Yaʿqūbī consistently uses for this river. According to Barthold, *Historical Geography*, 11, the actual "river of Balkh," the Balkh Āb (Baktros) apparently connected with the Oxus (Āmū Daryā) in classical times but not in the time of the Arab geographers, when Balkh was separated from the Oxus by a journey of two days (ibid., 12). This passage implies that in al-Yaʿqūbī's time the Oxus emptied into the Caspian, rather than into the Aral Sea, as it does today. There is abundant evidence for shifts in the channel of the Oxus, but the chronology remains unclear. See the article by B. Spuler in EI², s.v. Āmū Daryā.

199 Cf. al-Yaʿqūbī, *Taʾrīkh*, 2:300.

200 Nīshāpūr, together with Marw, Herat, and Balkh, were the four great cities of Khurāsān. See the article by E. Honigmann and C. E. Bosworth in EI², s.v. Nīshāpūr; Barthold, *Historical Geography*, 95–103; *Ḥudūd*, 102.

201 *Ḥudūd*, 103.

202 Or Bāward/Bāvard; *Ḥudūd*, 103.

203 Or Nawqān; *Ḥudūd*, 103.

204 One of the districts on the border of Nīshāpūr mentioned by *Ḥudūd*, 103.

205 Or Isfarāyīn; see the article by C. E. Bosworth in EI², s.v. Isfarāyīn; Barthold, *Historical Geography*, 114; *Ḥudūd*, 102: Siparāyin.

206 30 A.H. = September 4, 650 – August 23, 651; cf. al-Yaʿqūbī, *Taʾrīkh*, 2:192.

and Persians. Its water comes from springs and streams. Its land tax amounts to four million dirhams, which is included as part of the land tax of Khurāsān. They manufacture [cotton and silk textiles in all the districts[207]]. ʿAbdallāh b. Ṭāhir resided in the city of Nīshāpūr and did not leave it for Marw as the governors had formerly done.[208] He built a marvelous structure there, the Shādhiyākh;[209] then he built the Tower.[210] A member of the Ṭāhirid family told me that it is ten stages from Nīshāpūr to Marw; ten stages from Nīshāpūr to Herat;
279 ten stages from Nīshāpūr to Jurjān; ten stages from Nīshāpūr to al-Dāmaghān; | and six stages from Nīshāpūr to Sarakhs via the main highway and great road. The first stage is Qaṣr al-Rīḥ, called Dizbād in Persian,[211] then Khāksār, and then Mazdūrān, where the Ṭīn Pass is.[212] Sarakhs[213] is an important region. Its main city, which is very large, is situated in a sand desert; it has a mixed population. ʿAbdallāh b. Khāzim al-Sulamī, at the time under the command of ʿAbdallāh b. ʿĀmir b. Kurayz, conquered it during the caliphate of ʿUthmān. The inhabitants drink well water; there is no stream or spring. It has a group of people from […].[214] Its land tax amounts to one million dirhams, which is included with the land tax of Khurāsān.

Marw

From Sarakhs to Marw[215] via the main road is six stages, the first of which is Ushturmaghāk; then Talastāna; then al-Dandānqān; then Kanūkird, where the clan of ʿAlī b. Hishām b. Farrakhusraw[216] has estates. These stations are situated in the open desert, and each of them has a fortress in which the people take refuge from the Turks, who sometimes attack some of these places.

---

207 Added in the editor's notes on the basis of a parallel text in Iṣṭakhrī, 255.

208 ʿAbdallāh b. Ṭāhir was governor of Khurāsān in 213–230/828–845; see the article by C. Edmond Bosworth in EI^3, s.v. ʿAbdallāh b. Ṭāhir.

209 On the suburb named for this monument, see Barthold, *Historical Geography*, 99.

210 Arabic *manār* ("lighthouse" or "minaret"), probably a minaret for the principal mosque; see Barthold, *Historical Geography*, 98.

211 Both the Persian and Arabic mean "Castle of the Wind."

212 Arabic *ʿAqabat Ṭīn* (Clay Pass).

213 On Sarakhs, see the article by C. E. Bosworth in EI^2, s.v. Sarakhs.

214 There is a lacuna in the MS.

215 On Marw (Merv; Mary), see the article by C. E. Bosworth in EI^2, s.v. Marw al-Rūdh; Barthold, *Historical Geography*, 35–46.

216 This appears to be ʿAlī b. Hishām al-Marwazī, who was governor of Baghdad during the reign of al-Maʾmūn, but was executed in 217/832; cf. al-Ṭabarī, *Taʾrīkh*, 3:1108 ff.

Then one comes to Marw, the most important district in Khurāsān. Ḥātim b. al-Nuʿmān al-Bāhilī, who was under the command of ʿAbdallāh b. ʿĀmir, conquered it during the caliphate of ʿUthmān. It is said that al-Aḥnāf b. Qays participated in its conquest, and that was in the year 31.[217] Its inhabitants are nobles (descended) from the Persian *dihqāns*. It also has some Arab tribesmen from the Azd, Tamīm, and other tribes. It used to be the residence of the governors of Khurāsān. The first who resided there was al-Maʾmūn, and then whoever governed Khurāsān subsequently, until ʿAbdallāh b. Ṭāhir took up residence in Nīshāpūr. The inhabitants of Marw get water from flowing springs and streams. Its land tax is included with that of Khurāsān. The famous fine apparel known as Khurāsān clothing is made there. | Among its rural districts 280
are Zarq,[218] Aram Kaylabaq, Sawsaqān,[219] and Jarāra. From Marw to Āmul[220] is six stages, the first of which is Kushmāhan,[221] whence come Kushmāhanī raisins. All the stages are in the desert and are fortified posts. These are the rural districts of Khurāsān along the main road. The inhabitants of Āmul drink well water, except in areas near the Oxus (Jayḥūn), which is (also known as) the Balkh River (Nahr Balkh). As for the areas to the right of the main road, in the direction of the Indian Ocean, they extend for ten stages in an easterly direction from Nīshāpūr to Herat. Herat is one of the most prosperous regions of Khurāsān and has the most handsome people. Al-Aḥnaf b. Qays conquered it during the caliphate of ʿUthmān. Its inhabitants are Persian nobles and some Arabs. Its water comes from springs and streams. Its land tax is included in the land tax of Khurāsān.

Būshanj

From Herat to Būshanj is one stage.[222] Būshanj is the homeland of Ṭāhir b. al-Ḥusayn b. Muṣʿab.[223] Aws b. Thaʿlaba al-Taymī and al-Aḥnāf b. Qays, both of

217 31 A.H. = August 24, 651 – August 11, 652; cf. al-Yaʿqūbī, *Taʾrīkh*, 2:193–194.

218 Barthold, *Historical Geography*, 41; *Ḥudūd*, 105.

219 Sūsanaqān in *Ḥudūd*, 105.

220 A town near an important ford across the Oxus (now known as Āmūyā or Charjūy), not to be confused with the city in Ṭabaristān mentioned earlier: see al-Maqdisī, 291–292; Yāqūt, *Muʿjam al-buldān*, 1:69; and the article by L. Lockhart, M. Streck, and A. Bennigsen in *EI*², s.v Āmul.

221 Cf. *Ḥudūd*, 105.

222 On the town of Būshanj, about a day's journey from Herat, see the article by W. Barthold and B. Spuler in *EI*², s.v. Būshandj; Barthold, *Historical Geography*, 60.

223 Ṭāhir b. al-Ḥusayn was the general who in 198/813 took Baghdad for al-Maʾmūn in the civil war between al-Amīn and al-Maʾmūn. Al-Maʾmūn afterward appointed him to various

whom were under the command of ʿAbdallāh b. ʿĀmir, conquered it during the caliphate of ʿUthmān.[224] Its inhabitants are a mix of non-Arabs;[225] there are only a few Arabs there.

Bādghīs

From Būshanj to Bādghīs[226] is three stages. Bādghīs was conquered by ʿAbd al-Raḥmān b. Samura in the days of Muʿāwiya b. Abī Sufyān.[227]

Sijistān

281 From Būshanj to Sijistān[228] is five, some say seven, stages | by the desert route.[229] Sijistān is an important country. The chief city is Bust,[230] where Maʿn b. Zāʾida al-Shaybānī[231] resided during the caliphate of Abū Jaʿfar al-Manṣūr. Its inhabitants are Persians, but most of them say that they are descended from the Ḥimyarites of Yemen. It has about the same number of rural districts as Khurāsān, or more, but they are isolated and adjacent to the countries of Sind and Hind. It used to be comparable to Khurāsān and was its peer. Among its rural districts are Bust; Juwayn;[232] Rukhkhaj;[233] Khushshak; Bālis;[234]

---

governorships and ultimately to the governorship of Khurāsān, where he died in 207/822. His descendants, the Ṭāhirids, continued to rule the province until 259/873. See the article by C. E. Bosworth in *EI*², s.v. Ṭāhir b. al-Ḥusayn.

224 Cf. al-Yaʿqūbī, *Taʾrīkh*, 2:192–193.

225 Arabic *akhlāṭ min al-ʿajam*, perhaps to distinguish them from the "noble Persians" mentioned in other cities.

226 A mountainous rural area north of Herat between the Harī Rūd and Kūshk rivers. See W. Barthold, *Historical Geography*, 47–49, and the article by Jürgen Paul in *EI*³, s.v. Bādghīs.

227 Cf. al-Yaʿqūbī, *Taʾrīkh*, 2:192, 258.

228 Usually known by the later Persian form of the name, Sīstān. See the article by C. E. Bosworth in *EI*², s.v. Sīstān; Barthold, *Historical Geography*, 64–72; *Ḥudūd*, 110, 344–346.

229 Arabic *majāba*. See Dozy, *Supplément*, 1:230.

230 See the articles by J. Sourdel-Thomine in *EI*², s.v. Bust, and by Martina Rugiadi in *EI*³, s.v. Bust; Barthold, *Historical Geography*, 70–73; *Ḥudūd*, 110, 344.

231 Maʿn b. Zāʾida was a military commander who served the last Umayyads, but was pardoned by the ʿAbbāsids and later sent to suppress a rebellion in Sīstān. He was killed at Bust in 152/769–770. See the article by H. Kennedy in *EI*², s.v. Maʿn b. Zāʾida.

232 On the crossroads town of Juwayn in Sijistān (there are at least two other towns with the same name), see the article by R. Hartmann in *EI*², s.v Dj̲uwayn.

233 An area of southeastern Afghanistan around the later city of Qandahār. See the article by C. E. Bosworth in *EI*², s.v al-Rukh̲kh̲adj̲; Barthold, *Historical Geography*, 73–74; *Ḥudūd*, 111.

234 MS *?-l-m-r*, corrected to Bālis by Wiet on the basis of Marquart, *Eranshahr*, 255; Bālis was an area in Baluchistan around Isfanjāy and Sībī; see Barthold, *Historical Geography*, 75; *Ḥudūd*, 111.

Khwāsh;[235] Great Zaranj,[236] the capital of King Rutbīl,[237] four farsakhs in circumference, surrounded by a trench, with five gates, and with a river called al-Hindmand[238] flowing through the middle of it, the place to which the Tubbaʿ of Yemen fled and stayed;[239] Zāliq; and Sanārūdh. Sijistān has the river known as al-Hindmand, which comes from lofty mountains and flows through no country but desert before reaching Sijistān. It[240] borders on Makrān, toward the countries of Sind and al-Qandahār. Al-Rabīʿ b. Ziyād al-Ḥārithī was the first to conquer it,[241] crossing 75 farsakhs of desert to reach Zaranj, the capital where the kings resided, during the caliphate of ʿUthmān. He did not go beyond the place known as al-Qarnīn. Then ʿAbd al-Raḥmān b. Samura b. Ḥabīb b. ʿAbd Shams came there. Sijistān was in revolt until the caliphate of Muʿāwiya; then ʿAbd al-Raḥmān b. Samura was appointed governor; he conquered the area and advanced to Kirmān and conquered it. Then he returned to Sijistān and reached a settlement with its people. Then the province revolted again, until al-Rabīʿ b. Ziyād al-Ḥārithī went there. Then it revolted yet again, until ʿUbaydallāh b. Abī Bakra became governor. | 282

The Governors of Sijistān

Al-Rabīʿ b. Ziyād al-Ḥārithī, on behalf of ʿAbdallāh b. ʿĀmir b. Kurayz, during the caliphate of ʿUthmān.

Ribʿī b. Kās al-ʿAnbarī al-Kūfī, on behalf of ʿAbdallāh b. ʿAbbās, during the caliphate of the Commander of the Faithful ʿAlī b. Abī Ṭālib—God's blessings be upon him.

---

235 *Ḥudūd*, 110 (Khuvāsh).

236 On Zaranj (Persian Zarang), one of the main towns of Sijistān, see the article by C. E. Bosworth in *EI*², s.v. Zarang; *Ḥudūd*, 110.

237 Rutbīl (perhaps to be read as Zunbīl) was apparently a title held by a line of native rulers who opposed Islamic penetration into the region. See the article by C. E. Bosworth in *EI*², s.v Zunbīl.

238 Sic, for Hilmand, the river which with its tributaries drains southwest Afghanistan; on Zaranj (Zarang) and this river, see Barthold, *Historical Geography*, 70; and the article by M. E. Yapp in *EI*², s.v. Hilmand (Helmand).

239 The reference is to a legend about one of the pre-Islamic kings of Yemen, rather than to any identifiable historical event.

240 The feminine pronoun (*hiya*) could refer to the desert (*mafāza*) or to Sijistān, both of which are feminine in Arabic, but not to the river, which is masculine in Arabic. The language is abbreviated and hard to parse. Wiet's translation ("cette rivière est limitrophe du Mékran du côté du Sind et de Kandahar") violates the grammar of the Arabic and the geography of the area.

241 See *Tārīkh-e Sīstān*, trans. Gold, 63–66, on the exploits of al-Rabīʿ.

ʿAbd al-Raḥmān b. Samura, again[242] during the time of Muʿāwiya, and he died there.

Al-Rabīʿ b. Ziyād al-Ḥārithī again, on behalf of Ziyād, in the time of Muʿāwiya.

ʿUbaydallāh b. Abī Bakra, on behalf of Ziyād, in the time of Muʿāwiya.

ʿAbbād b. Ziyād, who governed Sijistān on behalf of Muʿāwiya after the death of Ziyād.

Yazīd b. Ziyād, on behalf of Yazīd b. Muʿāwiya.

Ṭalḥa b. ʿAbdallāh b. Khalaf al-Khuzāʿī, on behalf of Salm b. Ziyād—Ṭalḥa b. ʿAbdallāh died in Sijistān.

ʿAbd al-ʿAzīz b. ʿAbdallāh b. ʿĀmir, on behalf of al-Qubāʿ, i.e., al-Ḥārith b. ʿAbdallāh al-Makhzūmī, Ibn al-Zubayr's governor of Basra; when Muṣʿab b. al-Zubayr came to Iraq as governor on behalf of his brother, he confirmed ʿAbd al-ʿAzīz over Sijistān, as he was a brave horseman.

ʿAbdallāh b. ʿAdī b. Ḥāritha b. Rabīʿa b. ʿAbd al-ʿAzīz b. ʿAbd Shams, on behalf of ʿAbd al-Malik b. Marwān.

Umayya b. ʿAbdallāh b. Khālid b. Asīd b. Abī l-ʿĪṣ b. Umayya, on behalf of ʿAbd al-Malik b. Marwān.

Then ʿAbdallāh b. Umayya b. ʿAbdallāh b. Khālid b. Asīd, on behalf of his father.

ʿUbaydallāh b. Abī Bakra, on behalf of al-Ḥajjāj in the time of ʿAbd al-Malik b. Marwān; ʿUbaydallāh b. Abī Bakra died in Sijistān, and when he was near death he appointed his son Abū Bardhaʿa to succeed him.

Then al-Ḥajjāj wrote to al-Muhallab b. Abī Ṣufra to assume the governorship of Sijistān along with Khurāsān, and al-Muhallab appointed Wakīʿ b. Bakr b. Wāʾil al-Azdī over Sijistān.

283 Then al-Ḥajjāj appointed | ʿAbd al-Raḥmān b. Muḥammad b. al-Ashʿath al-Kindī—people advised him not to do so, but he refused to accept their advice. ʿAbd al-Raḥmān was disobedient. He revolted against al-Ḥajjāj, marched against him, and waged war on him, but he returned to Sijistān in defeat. Al-Ḥajjāj wrote to Rutbīl, king of Sijistān, to seize ʿAbd al-Raḥmān and send him back to him; Rutbīl captured him, fettered him, and sent him along with al-Ḥajjāj's envoys. ʿAbd al-Raḥmān, however, threw himself from a roof on which he was, broke his neck, and died in Rukhkhaj. A peace was concluded between al-Ḥajjāj and Rutbīl, the King of Sijistān.

Al-Ḥajjāj appointed ʿUmāra b. Tamīm al-Lakhmī, but Rutbīl disliked him, so al-Ḥajjāj deposed him.

---

242 "Again" (*ayḍan*) refers to ʿAbd al-Raḥmān b. Samura's having conquered territory in Sijistān during the caliphate of ʿUthmān; cf. al-Yaʿqūbī, *Taʾrīkh*, 2:192, 258.

Al-Ḥajjāj appointed ʿAbd al-Raḥmān b. Sulaym al-Kinānī, but deposed him after a year; then he appointed Mismaʿ b. Mālik b. Mismaʿ al-Shaybānī, who died in Sijistān after deputizing his nephew, Muḥammad b. Shaybān b. Mālik.

Al-Ḥajjāj appointed al-Ashhab b. Bishr al-Kalbī, one of the people of Khurāsān.

Then al-Ḥajjāj joined Sijistān to Khurāsān under Qutayba b. Muslim al-Bāhilī, who dispatched his brother ʿAmr b. Muslim; but al-Ḥajjāj then wrote him to go to Sijistān in person, so he went in the year 92,[243] in the days of al-Walīd b. ʿAbd al-Malik.

Qutayba left Sijistān and deputized ʿAbd Rabbihi b. ʿAbdallāh b. ʿUmayr al-Laythī over it; but after ʿAbd Rabbihi had been there for a while, Qutayba heard something about ʿAbd Rabbihi that displeased him. He therefore sent Manīʿ b. Muʿāwiya b. Farwa al-Minqarī to take his place and ordered him to torture ʿAbd Rabbihi until he gave up what he had acquired; but Manīʿ did not do so, and Qutayba therefore deposed Manīʿ b. Farwa and appointed al-Nuʿmān b. ʿAwf al-Yashkurī, who tortured ʿAbd Rabbihi b. ʿAbdallāh so severely that he died.

Sulaymān b. ʿAbd al-Malik made Yazīd b. al-Muhallab b. Abī Ṣufra governor of Iraq, and Yazīd appointed his brother Mudrik b. al-Muhallab over Sijistān; however, Rutbīl would not give him anything (in tribute), so Yazīd b. al-Muhallab deposed Mudrik his brother and made his son Muʿāwiya | b. Yazīd 284
b. al-Muhallab governor.

Then ʿUmar b. ʿAbd al-ʿAzīz became ruler and appointed ʿAdī b. Arṭāt al-Fazārī governor of Iraq. ʿAdī appointed al-Jarrāḥ b. ʿAbdallāh al-Ḥakamī governor of Khurāsān, joining Sijistān to it; then he deposed him and appointed ʿAbd al-Raḥmān b. Nuʿaym al-Ghāmidī—al-Sarī b. ʿAbdallāh b. ʿĀṣim b. Mismaʿ was in charge of Sijistān at the time, and ʿUmar b. ʿAbd al-ʿAzīz confirmed him.

Then Yazīd b. ʿAbd al-Malik b. Marwān became ruler. He made Ibn Hubayra al-Fazārī governor of Iraq, and Ibn Hubayra appointed al-Qaʿqāʿ b. Suwayd b. ʿAbd al-Raḥmān b. Uways b. Bujayr b. Uways al-Minqarī of Kufa over Sijistān.

Then Ibn Hubayra deposed al-Qaʿqāʿ and appointed al-Sayyāl b. al-Mundhir b. al-Nuʿmān al-Shaybānī. During all these years Rutbīl was resisting them.

Hishām b. ʿAbd al-Malik b. Marwān became ruler and made Khālid b. ʿAbdallāh al-Qasrī governor of Iraq. Khālid appointed Yazīd b. al-Ghurayf al-Hamdānī of Jordan over Sijistān, but Rutbīl resisted him. Then Khālid b. ʿAbdallāh al-Qasrī deposed Yazīd b. al-Ghurayf and appointed al-Aṣfaḥ b. ʿAbdallāh al-Kalbī over Sijistān; he remained in Sijistān until Khālid deposed him and appointed ʿAbdallāh b. Abī Burda b. Abī Mūsā al-Ashʿarī. The latter remained

243 92 A.H. = October 29, 710 – October 18, 711.

governor until Khālid b. ʿAbdallāh was deposed and Yūsuf b. ʿUmar al-Thaqafī was appointed (governor of Iraq).

When Yūsuf b. ʿUmar became governor of Iraq for Hishām b. ʿAbd al-Malik, he appointed Ibrāhīm b. ʿĀṣim al-ʿUqaylī over Sijistān. He went to Sijistān and sent ʿAbdallāh b. Abī Burda back in chains to Yūsuf.

Then Yazīd b. al-Walīd b. ʿAbd al-Malik became ruler and made Manṣūr b. Jumhūr governor of Iraq, and Manṣūr appointed Yazīd b. ʿIzzān al-Kalbī over Sijistān.

Then ʿAbdallāh b. ʿUmar b. ʿAbd al-ʿAzīz became governor of Iraq and appointed Ḥarb b. Qaṭan b. al-Mukhāriq al-Hilālī over Sijistān.

285 Then ʿAbdallāh | b. ʿUmar b. ʿAbd al-ʿAzīz dispatched Ibn Saʿīd b. ʿUmar b. Yaḥyā b. al-ʿĀṣ al-Aʿwar, but the people of Sijistān expelled him from the country. Bujayr b. al-Salhab of the Bakr b. Wāʾil had forged a document in the name of ʿAbdallāh b. ʿUmar b. ʿAbd al-ʿAzīz that stirred up animosity between the tribes of Bakr and Tamīm.

Yazīd b. ʿUmar b. Hubayra al-Fazārī became governor of Iraq and dispatched ʿĀmir b. Ḍubāra al-Murrī to Sijistān, but he never arrived there. The dynasty of the Banū Hāshim[244] was established, and Abū Muslim sent Mālik b. al-Haytham al-Khuzāʿī to Sijistān. He said, "People of Sijistān, there will be war between you and us until you turn over to us the Syrians who are with you." They said, "We will pay ransom for them," and they ransomed them for a million dirhams. The Syrians expelled (Mālik) from Sijistān.[245]

Then Abū Muslim sent ʿUmar b. al-ʿAbbās b. ʿUmayr b. ʿUṭārid b. Ḥājib b. Zurāra, whom he held in high esteem, to rule Sijistān. The people of Sijistān killed his brother Ibrāhīm b. al-ʿAbbās, and war broke out between them. Abū Muslim dispatched Abū l-Najm ʿImrān b. Ismāʿīl b. ʿImrān to ʿUmar, telling him, "Join ʿUmar b. al-ʿAbbās; if he has been killed, then you take over as commander of the country."

Then Abū Jaʿfar al-Manṣūr made Ibrāhīm b. Ḥumayd al-Marwarrūdhī governor. Next, al-Manṣūr deposed him and made Maʿn b. Zāʾida b. Maṭar b. Sharīk al-Shaybānī governor. He stayed at Bust and fought the rebels. Maʿn governed badly. The people suffered all sorts of tribulations from him, so some of them concealed their swords inside bundles of reeds, jumped on him, and killed him.

---

244 That is, the ʿAbbāsid dynasty, which traced its descent from the Prophet's uncle, al-ʿAbbās b. ʿAbd al-Muṭṭalib b. Hāshim.

245 *Taʾrīkh-i Sīstān*, trans. Gold, 107, gives the ransom as a million dirhams and adds that the Syrian commander, al-Haytham b. ʿAbdallāh, and a thousand of his horsemen were then given safe passage out of the province.

The one who killed him was a man from Ṭāq, one of the cantons of Zaranj. This was in the year 156.[246]

Yazīd b. Mazyad b. Zā'ida continued to fight the dissidents, and Abū Ja'far dispatched Tamīm b. 'Amr of the Banū Taymallāh b. Tha'laba to assist Yazīd b. Mazyad. He went to the country and sent back some of the dissidents to Abū Ja'far. Yazīd b. Mazyad returned to Iraq. Then Abū Ja'far deposed Tamīm b. 'Amr and made 'Ubaydallāh b. al-'Alā' of the tribe of Bakr b. Wā'il | governor of 286
Sijistān. Abū Ja'far died while he was governor. Sijistān was then annexed to the governors of Khurāsān, who appointed men to govern it on their behalf. This was because the Khārijite rebels,[247] who had become numerous, had gained control of it. The land tax of Sijistān amounted to ten million dirhams, which was spent on its army, the security forces, and the border posts.

Kirmān

Kirmān[248] is to the right[249] of Sijistān, opposite to al-Jūzjān.[250] The main city of Kirmān is al-Sīrajān,[251] a well-fortified, important city whose people are brave and heroic. It has several towns and fortresses: Bīmand, Khannāb, Kūhistān, Karistān, Maghūn,[252] Ṭamaskān, Sarwistān, and the fortresses of Bamm,[253] Manūjān, and Narmāshīr.[254] The country is vast and grand, but has little water. There are many palm trees there in a city called Jīrubt.[255] There is a route to Sind from Jīrubt via al-Rataq, al-Dihqān, and thence to al-Bul and al-Fahraj,[256] which the natives call Fahrah. It is the last town in the province of Kirmān, and the ruler of Makrān claims that it is one of his dependencies. From there one

---

246 156 A.H. = December 2, 772 – November 20, 773.

247 Arabic *shurāt*, (literally, "sellers") a term applied to the Khārijites, who claimed to have "sold" their lives to God in exchange for Paradise, although the rebellions in Sīstān at this time involved many other groups as well; see *Ta'rīkh-e Sīstān*, trans. Gold, 113, 118.

248 See the article by A. K. S. Lambton in *EI*², s.v. Kirmān; Barthold, *Historical Geography*, 133–147.

249 That is, if one is traveling east toward Sijistān, one turns right (south) to reach Kirmān, which lies southwest of Sijistān.

250 That is, on the side of Sijistān that lies opposite to al-Jūzjān, which lies to the north of Sijistān.

251 Or Sīrjān; see the article by C. E. Bosworth in *EI*², s.v. al-Sīradjān; Barthold, *Historical Geography*, 137–138; *Ḥudūd*, 124, 374.

252 The reading is uncertain; possibly Māhān.

253 Or Bam; Barthold, *Historical Geography*, 139; *Ḥudūd*, 125.

254 Barthold, *Historical Geography*, 137.

255 Or Jīruft; Barthold, *Historical Geography*, 140–142.

256 See Aurel Stein, *Archaeological Tour in Gedrosia*; P. M. Sykes, *Ten Thousand Miles*.

goes to Khurūj, which is the first town in Makrān, and thence to Fannazbūr, the capital of Makrān. ʿAbd al-Raḥmān b. Samura b. Ḥabīb b. ʿAbd Shams conquered Kirmān, making a treaty with its king for two million dirhams and two thousand slaves in tribute. This was during the caliphate of ʿUthmān.

As for the countries that lie between Sarakhs and the Indian Ocean:

Al-Ṭālaqān

287 From the city of Sarakhs to al-Ṭālaqān[257] is four stages. Al-Ṭālaqān is situated between two great mountains. Because of its size, it has two congregational mosques where Friday prayers are held. It is where the felts called *ṭālaqāniyya* are made. From al-Ṭālaqān to al-Fāryāb[258] is four stages. Al-Fāryāb is the old city; the other urban area, called Yahūdān, is where the tax collector (*ʿāmil*) of al-Fāryāb resides.[259]

Al-Jūzjān

From al-Fāryāb to al-Jūzjān[260] is five stages. It has four towns: the capital of al-Jūzjān, called Anbār,[261] where the governors reside; the second is called Asān[262] or Ṣamʿākan; the third, which is where the king of al-Jūzjān used to reside, is called Kundarm or Qurzuman;[263] and the fourth is called Shubūrqān,[264] which

---

257 Not to be confused with a town of the same name near Qazvīn; see the article by C. E. Bosworth and J. L. Lee in *EI*², s.v. Ṭālaḳān; Barthold, *Historical Geography*, 35–37; *Ḥudūd*, 107.

258 The spelling of the name varies: al-Yaʿqūbī's spelling implies the reading al-Fāryāb or al-Fāriyāb; other versions include Faryāb and Paryāb. See the article by R. N. Frye in *EI*², s.v. Faryāb; *Ḥudūd*, 107 (Pāryāb).

259 Barthold, *Historical Geography*, 33 interprets this to mean there was a large Jewish colony in this town and that Yahūdān (or al-Yahūdiyya) was where the "ruler" of Fāryāb lived. *Ḥudūd*, 107, mentions Jahūdhān as the residence of the "*malik* of Gūzgānān" (which was actually in a military camp outside the town).

260 Persian, Gūzgān. See the article by R. Hartmann in *EI*², s.v. Djūzdjān; Barthold, *Historical Geography*, 32; *Ḥudūd*, 105–106, 328–337.

261 Barthold, *Historical Geography*, 32; *Ḥudūd*, 107 (Anbīr), 335; Ghirshman, *Chionites*, 26.

262 Perhaps the Sān mentioned in *Ḥudūd*, 107.

263 Usually Arabized as al-Jurzuwān from the Persian Gurzivān; see Le Strange, *Lands*, 424. According to the *Ḥudūd*, 107, Gurzivān was the former residence of the kings of Gūzgān, and K.nd.rm (vocalization uncertain) was a separate borough. Barthold, *Historical Geography*, 32, describes Kundarm as a village in Gurziwān and the residence of the local ruler.

264 Probably the Ushbūrqān of *Ḥudūd*, 107; the modern town of Shibargān preserves the name.

was also a principality in ancient times. Al-Jūzjān is opposite Kirmān on the frontier of India.

Balkh

For one going east, it is four stages from al-Jūzjān to Balkh.[265] Balkh has several rural districts and towns. ʿAbd al-Raḥman b. Samura conquered it in the days of Muʿāwiya b. Abī Sufyān. The city of Balkh is the greatest city of Khurāsān. King Ṭarkhān, the ruler of Khurāsān, used to reside there. It is a powerful city surrounded by two concentric walls; in olden days, it used to have three. It has twelve gates. Balkh is said to be the center of Khurāsān: Farghāna is thirty stages from it to the east; Rayy is thirty stages from it to the west; Sijistān is thirty stages from it in the direction of the *qibla*; Kābul and Qandahār are thirty stages from it; Kirmān is thirty stages from it; Qashmīr is thirty stages
from it; Khwārazm is thirty stages from it; | and al-Multān is thirty stages from 288
it.[266] The villages, estates, and farms in the environs of Balkh were enclosed by a great wall. From one gate of the wall enclosing the fields and villages to the gate on the opposite side is twelve farsakhs. Beyond this wall, there is no cultivation, estate, or village; there is nothing outside it but sand. This great wall surrounding Balkh has twelve gates. A second wall, which surrounds the suburb of the city, has four gates.[267] From the great wall to the second wall is five farsakhs. Then there is a city wall which is one farsakh inside the wall around the suburb. Al-Nawbahār,[268] which was the residence of the Barmakids,[269] is in the suburb. From one gate of the city wall to the one

265 On Balkh, the main city of ancient Bactria, now located in northern Afghanistan, see the article by Jürgen Paul in *EI*³, s.v. Balkh; Barthold, *Historical Geography*, 11–15; *Ḥudūd*, 108, 337.

266 As noted by Barthold, *Historical Geography*, this attempt to make Balkh equidistant from all these cities is contrived and not quite accurate.

267 Barthold, *Historical Geography*, 13, notes that other geographers gave the inner wall seven gates.

268 On this important Buddhist sanctuary, see the article in *EI*², s.v. Naw Bahār, as well as Bulliet, *Patricians of Nishapur*. Barthold, *Historical Geography*, 14–15, summarizes the information that can be gleaned from descriptions by the Chinese Buddhist pilgrim Hsüan-tsang and by Arabic geographers.

269 The family that served the ʿAbbāsid caliphs as viziers from the time of al-Ṣaffāḥ until their fall under al-Rashīd. The family name (Barmakī, pl. Barāmika) comes from the title of the hereditary head of the Nawbahār temple, derived from Sanskrit *parmak* (superior, chief). See the article by Kevin van Bladel in *EI*³, s.v. Barmakids.

opposite it is one farsakh. The city measures three miles by three miles.[270] Balkh has forty-seven pulpits (*minbar*s) in its less important towns, including the ones called Khulm,[271] Siminjān,[272] Baghlān,[273] Sakalkand,[274] Walwālij,[275] Hūẓa, Ārhan,[276] Rāwan, Ṭārakān, Nawdiz,[277] Badhakhshān,[278] and Jurm,[279] which is the easternmost city among the dependencies of Balkh in the direction of Tibet. The first of the cities situated to the right of someone traveling east is
289 Andarāb;[280] then come Khast, Banjahār,[281] Barwān, and Ghūrawand,[282] | which al-Faḍl b. Yaḥyā b. Khālid b. Barmak conquered in the days of al-Rashīd. It was well protected and was one of the dependencies of the Kābul-Shāh. These towns are located between the city proper of Balkh and al-Bāmiyān.

Then one comes to the town of al-Bāmiyān,[283] which is a town located on a mountain. There was a *dihqān* there named Asad, which is Shēr in Persian.[284] He was converted to Islam by Muzāḥim b. Bisṭām in the days of al-Manṣūr. Muzāḥim b. Bisṭām married Shēr's daughter to his son Muḥammad

270 That is, Arab miles (*mīl*, pl. *amyāl*), consisting of 1000 *bāʿ* (fathoms), each of 4 canonical ells (*al-dhirāʿ al-sharʿiyya*), each of 49.875 cm. = 1.995 km (1.240 English miles).

271 An agricultural area located in a plain at the foot of a mountain between Balkh and Ṭukhāristān and watered by a river according to *Ḥudūd*, 108 (modern Tāsh Qurghān according to Minorsky's note, 337).

272 Identified by Barthold, *Historical Geography*, 22 with the fortress of Haybak in the Khulm valley; description in *Ḥudūd*, 108–109, 338 (Simingān). Al-Yaʿqūbī is apparently unfamiliar with the antiquities located in this region.

273 Derived from a Bactrian word meaning sanctuary or temple; site of the ruins of the Surkh Kutal temple complex. See Barthold, *Historical Geography*, 22 n. 62; *Ḥudūd*, 109.

274 *Ḥudūd*, 109, 338.

275 Also spelled Warwalīz or Walwalīz; located by Barthold, *Historical Geography*, 24, in the Aq Saray valley in the area of Qunduz; *Ḥudūd*, 109, 340.

276 Perhaps the site of a ford across the Oxus mentioned by Barthold, *Turkestan*, 69–70, and n. 7.

277 The reading is uncertain; Wiet, 102, corrected it to Nawdiz (citing Iṣṭakhrī, 298); the editor suggested Barwāz (after al-Maqdisī, 296), but the orthography makes this unlikely.

278 Barthold, *Historical Geography*, 24–26.

279 Wiet gives Jirm; Barthold, *Historical Geography*, 24 has Jurm (a town which still exists).

280 Barthold, *Historical Geography*, 23; *Ḥudūd*, 109, 341.

281 Perhaps Banjhīr (Panjshīr); see Barthold, *Historical Geography*, 23.

282 Or Ghūrband/Ghōrband; see Barthold, *Historical Geography*, 23; also the article by M. Jamil Hanifi in *Encyclopaedia Iranica*, s.v. Ḡōrband.

283 On Bāmiyān, see the article by Pierre Centlivres in *EI*^{3}, s.v. Bāmiyān; Barthold, *Historical Geography*, 23; *Ḥudūd*, 109, 341.

284 Al-Yaʿqūbī equates the Arabic name Asad (Lion) with the Persian word for lion, *shēr*, but

b. Muzāḥim, whose *kunyā* was Abū Ḥarb. When al-Faḍl b. Yaḥyā came to Khurāsān, he dispatched one of (Muḥammad's) sons, named al-Ḥasan, to Ghūrawand, and he and some other military officers conquered it. He gave him control of al-Bāmiyān and gave him the title[285] "Shēr-Bāmiyān" after that of his grandfather. Al-Bāmiyān is one of the nearest of the towns of Ṭukhāristān.

Several springs of water arise from the mountain of al-Bāmiyān. From them a river valley runs to al-Qandahār, the distance of a month's march. One river passes through another gorge and runs to Sijistān, the distance of a month's march. Another river goes to Marw, a journey of about thirty days. Another river goes to Balkh, a journey of twelve days. Another river goes to Khwārazm, a journey of forty days. All these rivers come from the mountain of al-Bāmiyān, owing to its elevation. It has mines of copper, lead, and mercury.

Among the cities to the left of one headed east are those called al-Tirmidh,[286] Sarmankān,[287] Dārazankā,[288] al-Ṣaghāniyān (the largest of the towns to the left of one headed east from Balkh),[289] Kharūn, Māsand, Bāsārān,[290] Kabarsarāʿ,[291] Qubādhiyān, Yūz (which is the land of Ḥātim b. Dāwūd), Wakhsh,[292] Halāward,[293] Kārbank,[294] | Andīshārāʿ, Rūstābīk[295] (which is the principality of 290
al-Ḥārith b. Asad b. Bīk, after whom the horses called Bīkiyya are named), Hulbuk,[296] Munk[297] (which is the boundary of the land of the Turks, which continues on to the place known as Rāsht), Kumād, and Bāmir.[298]

---

the word in this case is actually a title meaning shah or king, rather than lion; see Wiet, 103, n. 1.

285 Literally "name."

286 On Tirmidh, see the article by W. Barthold in EI^2, s.v. Tirmidh; Barthold, *Turkestan*, 71–76.

287 Sarmakān in the MS, corrected by the editor; Barthold, *Turkestan*, 73 gives Ṣarmanjān, Ṣarmanjīn, or Charmangān; his note says that Samʿānī gives Jarmankān as Persian form of the name.

288 Or Dārzangī; see Barthold, *Turkestan*, 74.

289 Barthold, *Turkestan*, 73.

290 Barthold, *Turkestan*, 70 n. 1.

291 The reading is uncertain; the Leiden editor suggests that it may be Kabarshārāgh.

292 Barthold, *Turkestan*, 69.

293 Barthold, *Turkestan*, 69.

294 Barthold, *Turkestan*, 70 (Kārbang).

295 That is, "the Canton of Bīk"; see Barthold, *Turkestan*, 69.

296 Barthold, *Turkestan*, 68–69.

297 Barthold, *Turkestan*, 69.

298 Or, in Arabic, Fāmir; in Persian Pāmīr; see Barthold, *Turkestan*, 70 n. 2.

The towns of Balkh lying to the north are Daryāhanīn (meaning Iron Gate),[299] Kishsh, Nakhshab, and Ṣughd, from which one goes to the principality of Samarqand.

As for the lands which are south of the Balkh River (Oxus), in the direction of the *qibla*, from Balkh one goes in the direction of the *qibla* toward Tukhāristān,[300] toward Andarāb, and toward al-Bāmiyān, which is the first of the principalities of lower (or) western Ṭukhāristān. It is situated on a large mountain and has a strong fortress. From there one goes to Badhakhshān and to the city of the Kābul-Shāh, a strongly fortified, impregnable city called Ḥrr?d?n.[301] It is difficult to reach because before it there are rugged mountains, rough paths, difficult valleys, and strong forts. There is one road to it from Kirmān and another from Sijistān. It has a powerful king who rarely pays obeissance to anyone. However, al-Faḍl b. Yaḥyā b. Khālid b. Barmak, when he became governor of Khurāsān for al-Rashīd, dispatched an army headed by Ibrāhīm b. Jibrīl to the land of the Kābul-Shāh in the year 176,[302] and sent with them the rulers of the principalities of Ṭukhāristān and the *dihqān*s. Among the rulers was al-Ḥasan Shēr, king of Bāmiyān. They invaded the region and conquered the city of al-Ghūrawand, the Gorge of Ghūrawand, Sārḥūd, Yandil-
291 Ustān, | and Shāh Bahār,[303] where the idol the people worshipped was kept; it was broken up and burned. Some of the princes of the lands of the Kābul-Shāh sought a safe-conduct from al-Faḍl b. Yaḥyā—the people of the town of Kāwsān with their ruler ______k.s[304] and the people of the towns of al-Māzarān and M____[305] with their rulers. He granted them safe conduct, and they sent hostages. The capital of Kābul, which is called Jurwas,[306] was conquered by ʿAbd al-Raḥmān b. Samura during the caliphate of ʿUthmān b. ʿAffān. At the

299 Arabic Bāb al-Ḥadīd, translating the Persian place name, which could be transcribed more accurately as Dar-i Āhanīn.

300 Sic ed. Leiden. Wiet, 105, emends to Badhakhshān.

301 This place is not mentioned by any other source; the orthography and vocalization are uncertain; on Kābul, see the article by C. E. Bosworth in *EI*², s.v. Kābul.

302 176 A.H. = April 28, 792 – April 17, 793 C.E.

303 Sārḥūd, Yandil-Ustān, and Shāh Bahār: the letters in the MS are completely undotted, and therefore the readings are conjectural. Wiet, 106, interprets the names as Shārajwadh, Yandil-Istān, and Shāh-Bahār.

304 The only letters of this six-letter word that are unambiguous are the final k and s.

305 Only the initial m of this six-letter word is unambiguous.

306 Amended without explanation by the editor from MS *ḥrws* (?); another name known only from al-Yaʿqūbī and of doubtful orthography and vocalization.

present time, it is in rebellion, although merchants can enter it and export from it the very large myrobalan[307] known as Kābulī.

Marwarrūdh

As for the countries from the city of Marw to the city of Balkh: From the city of Marw to Marwarrūdh[308] is five stages. Marwarrūdh was conquered by al-Aḥnaf b. Qays on behalf of ʿAbdallāh b. ʿĀmir b. Kurayz during the caliphate of ʿUthmān in the year 31.[309] One goes from Marwarrūdh to Balkh via Zamm,[310] which is on the Oxus River (Nahr Balkh), and Āmul, which is also on the Oxus. It is six stages between the latter and Marw. These are the towns (*buldān*) of the rural districts of Khurāsān in the direction of the Indian Ocean.

As for the towns on the right bank of the Oxus, there is al-Tirmidh. It is an important city on the east bank of the Oxus, while Balkh is on the west bank. It is a very populous, spacious city. On the same side as al-Tirmidh, also on the Oxus, is the city of al-Quwādhiyān,[311] similar to al-Tirmidh. From there one goes to the principality of Hāshim b. Bānījūr, which consists of Wakhsh and Halāward,[312] two important, well-fortified cities. Then one goes to the city of Shūmān,[313] which is adjacent to the principality of Hāshim b. Bānījūr and Hāshim's family. From there one goes to al-Aḥd?lī,[314] which is the city of Dāwūd b. Abī Dāwūd; and thence to Wāshjird,[315] a major frontier city | and extensive 292
territory containing seven hundred strong forts. This is because they raid the Turks, and it is four farsakhs between them and the land of Turkistan. From al-Tirmidh to al-Ṣaghāniyān is four stages. Al-Ṣaghāniyān[316] is a large, important country incorporating rural districts and a number of towns, including the

307 Arabic *ihlīlaj*, the plum-like fruit of the *Terminalia chebula* tree, used in various medicines. See the article by Al Dietrich, in *EI*², s.v. Halīladj̲.

308 Marwarrūdh (or Marw al-Rūdh), on the Murghāb River, was five stages upriver from Marw al-Shāhijān (here called simply "Marw"). See the article by C. E. Bosworth in *EI*², s.v. Marw al-Rūd̲h̲.

309 31 AH = August 24, 651 – August 11, 652.

310 Now Kerki, according to Barthold, *Historical Geography*, 19.

311 On this town and district, also written as Qubādhiyān, see the article by C. E. Bosworth in *EI*², s.v. Ḳubād̲h̲iyān; Barthold, *Turkestan*, 71–72.

312 Barthold, *Turkestan*, 69.

313 See the article by C. E. Bosworth in *EI*², s.v. S̲h̲ūmān; Barthold, *Turkestan*, 74.

314 The reading is conjectural; perhaps to be read as Afdiyān.

315 Barthold, *Turkestan*, 71.

316 Persian, Chaghāniyān; see the article by B. Spuler in *EI*², s.v. Čag̲h̲āniyān; Barthold, *Turkestan*, 72–74.

rural districts of Ḥardan, Bahārān,[317] and Kāsak. From al-Ṣaghāniyān to the principality of al-Khuttal[318] is three stages. The capital city of al-Khuttal is Wāshjird. It is the one we mentioned as having seven hundred forts and as being on the Turkish frontier.

Khuttal

From al-Khuttal one goes to upper Tukhāristān [sic] and the principality of Ḥumār Beg,[319] the king of Shiqinān[320] and Badhakhshān. The large river comes from there to Shiqinān. All of this is the principality of upper Ṭukhāristān.

As for what lies beyond the Oxus River on the main road, the first town is Farabr,[321] which is the frontier post for the people of Marw—that is, when the Turks advance towards this city, the people of Marw and its environs rush to it. From Farabr to Bākand is one stage. Bākand is an important city with a mixed population. From Bākand to Bukhārā is two stages.

Bukhārā

Bukhārā[322] is a spacious country with a mixed population of Arabs and non-Arabs. It has always been strongly defended. Sa'īd b. 'Uthmān b. 'Affān conquered Bukhārā in the days of Mu'āwiya. Then he left it to go to Samarqand, and its people rebelled. It remained in rebellion until Salm b. Ziyād conquered
293 it in the days of Yazīd b. Mu'āwiya. Then it revolted and resisted | until Qutayba b. Muslim al-Bāhilī arrived there in the days of al-Walīd b. 'Abd al-Malik and conquered it. The land tax of the country—the country of Bukhārā—amounts to one million dirhams. Their dirhams are nearly copper.[323]

---

317 Probable reading: the first letter is defective in the text.

318 On the region of Khuttal on the upper Oxus River, see the article by C. E. Bosworth in *EI*², s.v. Khuttalān or Khuttal.

319 The letters are unpointed; the reading is based on Barthold, *Turkestan*, 65.

320 Better known as Shughnān.

321 Also vocalized as Firabr. The town was on the opposite side of the Oxus from Āmul; see the article by B. Spuler in *EI*², s.v. Firabr; Le Strange, *Lands*, 404, 443.

322 On Bukhārā, see the article by W. Barthold and R. N. Frye in *EI*², s.v. Bukhārā.

323 Arabic *darāhimuhum shabīh bi-l-nuḥās*: As the dirham was normally struck of silver, this may refer to a debased coinage or to coins struck of bronze (sometimes referred to by the related word *shabah* or *shibh*, see Lane, *Lexicon*, 4:1500, s.v. *shabah*). Wiet, 110, renders: "Ses dirhems ressemblent à des monnaies de cuivre."

Sogdia (*al-Ṣughd*)

From Bukhārā to the country of Sogdia, for one who turns toward the *qibla*,[324] is seven stages. The country of Sogdia is spacious and has important, strong, well-fortified towns including Dabūsiyya,[325] Kushāniyya,[326] Kishsh,[327] and Nasaf (which is Nakhshab).[328] These rural districts—the rural districts of Sogdia—were conquered by Qutayba b. Muslim al-Bāhilī in the days of al-Walīd b. ʿAbd al-Malik.

Samarqand

From Kishsh to the capital city of Sogdia is four stages. Samarqand[329] is one of the most important, grandest, best defended, and most populous of cities, and its men are the strongest, bravest, and most persevering in warfare. It is in close proximity to the Turks. Samarqand revolted several times after it had been conquered, owing to its fortifications, the courage of its men, and the degree of their bravery. Qutayba b. Muslim al-Bāhilī conquered it in the days of al-Walīd b. ʿAbd al-Malik and made a peace settlement with its *dihqān*s and princes. It had a great defensive wall, which was torn down, but the Commander of the Faithful al-Rashīd rebuilt it. It has a large river which comes from the land of the Turks; it resembles the Euphrates and is called ?āsif.[330] It flows through the land of Samarqand to the country of Sogdia and thence to Usrūshana,[331] going through Ishtākhanj, Usrūshana, and Shāsh. From Samarqand to Usrūshana, the principality of Afshīn,[332] is five stages in an easterly direction. The principality of Usrūshana is vast | and important; it is said to have four hundred forts 294

---

324 That is, south; however, the towns mentioned lie either directly east or southeast of Bukhārā.

325 See the article by C. E. Bosworth in EI^2, s.v. Dabūsiyya; *Ḥudūd*, 113 (Dabūsī); Barthold, *Turkestan*, 96 n., 97.

326 *Ḥudūd*, 113 (Kushānī, "the most prosperous town of Sughd"); Barthold, *Turkestan*, 95–96.

327 Or Kish; see the article by C. E. Bosworth in EI^2, s.v. Kish; *Ḥudūd*, 113; Barthold, *Turkestan*, 134–135 (now Shahr-e Sabz).

328 Also called Ḳarshi; see the articles by B. Spuler in EI^2, s.v. Ḳarshi, by V. Minorsky, s.v. Nakhshab; *Ḥudūd*, 114 (Nakhshab); Barthold, *Turkestan*, 136–142.

329 On Samarqand, see the article by H. H. Schaeder and Yolande Crowe in EI^2, s.v. Samarḳand.

330 The river is the Zarafshān; see the article by C. E. Bosworth in EI^2, s.v. Zarafshān. Barthold, *Turkestan*, 82 n. 2, suggests a reading of Nāmiq.

331 See the article by J. H. Kramers in EI^2, s.v. Usrūshana; *Ḥudūd*, 115, 354 (where the name is given in an alternate form as Surūshana).

332 Arabic *mamlakat Afshīn*. On Afshīn as the title of the princes of Usrūshana, see the article by W. Barthold, H. A. R. Gibb, and Matthew S. Gordon in EI^3, s.v. Afshīn.

and a number of large towns, among them Arsmanda,[333] Zāmin,[334] Mānk,[335] and Ḥiṣnak. It has a large river, which is a tributary of the ?āsif, the river of Samarqand. Nuggets of gold are found in this river and in no other place in Khurāsān, according to what I have heard. In all the cities of Khurāsān there are Arabs from the tribes of Muḍar, Rabīʿa, and all the divisions of Yemen, except in Usrūshana, where the people resisted letting the Arabs live with them, until a man of the Banū Shaybān came to them, settled there, and married one of them. From the city of Usrūshana to Farghāna is two stages.

Farghāna

The town in Farghāna[336] where the king resides is called Kāsān.[337] It is an important and powerful town. All these towns are dependencies of Samarqand.

Ishtākhanj

Ishtākhanj[338] is an important city with forts and cantons. It used to be a separate principality, but al-Muʿtaṣim turned over the principality of Ishtākhanj to ʿUjayf.[339] From it to Samarqand is two stages. From Farghāna to al-Shāsh[340] is five stages. Al-Shāsh is an important town and one of the dependencies of Samarqand. Whoever travels from Samarqand to al-Shāsh travels seven stages to Khujanda,[341] which is one of the towns of Samarqand, then four stages from Khujanda to al-Shāsh.

---

333 Marsmanda according to *Ḥudūd*, 115; Barthold, *Turkestan*, 168.

334 *Ḥudūd*, 115; Barthold, *Turkestan*, 94.

335 In other sources Mīnk; see Barthold, *Turkestan*, 168.

336 On the Farghāna Valley, see the articles by W. Barthold in *EI*², s.v. Farghāna, and by Scott C. Levi in *EI*³, s.v. Farghana Valley; *Ḥudūd*, 115–116.

337 Barthold, *Turkestan*, 162–163.

338 In other sources, Ishtīkhān; the article by C. E. Bosworth in *EI*², s.v. Ishtīkhān; Barthold, *Turkestan*, 95.

339 On the army commander ʿUjayf b. ʿAnbasa, who served al-Maʾmūn and al-Muʿtaṣim, see the article by C. E. Bosworth in *EI*², s.v. ʿUdjayf b. ʿAnbasa. He is mentioned by al-Yaʿqūbī in the *Taʾrīkh*, 2:570, 571, 574, 576, 582, and 584.

340 Al-Shāsh is the Arabic transcription of the native name (Čāč) of the city later known as Tashkent; see the article by W. Barthold in *EI*², s.v. Tashkent; *Ḥudūd*, 118 (Chāch).

341 On Khujand(a), see the article by C. E. Bosworth in *EI*², s.v. Khudjand(a); Barthold, *Turkestan*, 164–165 (Khojend).

Al-Shāsh

From al-Shāsh to the major frontier town of Asbīshāb[342] is two stages. It is the town from which campaigns against the Turks are launched. It is the furthest of the dependencies of Samarqand. 295

These are the towns of Ṭukhāristān, Sogdia, Samarqand, al-Shāsh, and Farghāna that lie beyond the (Oxus) river on the main road. Beyond that are the countries of the polytheists. The countries of the Turks which surround Khurāsān and Sijistān are collectively known as Turkistan. The Turks comprise a number of nationalities and a number of principalities, among them the Kharlukhiyya, the Tughuz-Ughuz, the Turkash, the Kaymāk, and the Ghuzz.[343] Each nationality of the Turks has a separate principality, and they fight each other. They have no permanent dwellings or forts; rather, they stay in Turkish ribbed dome-tents, whose supports are strips of leather of hides of horses or cattle and whose coverings are felt. They are the most skillful of people at working felt, because it is their clothing. There are no crops in Turkistan except for millet (*dukhn*), which is *jāwars*.[344] Their food is mare's milk, and they also eat horse meat, but they mostly eat game. Iron is scarce among them, so they tip their arrows with bone. Nevertheless, they surround the land of Khurāsān and attack from every direction and carry out raids. There is no country in Khurāsān where the people do not have to fight the Turks or where Turks of every nationality do not attack.

These are the towns and rural districts of Khurāsān and Sijistān, the distances between all the cities, and their circumstances. Let us now mention its governors from the conquest to the present time, as well as the amount of its land tax.

The Governors of Khurāsān

The first to enter Khurāsān was ʿAbdallāh b. ʿĀmir b. Kurayz b. Rabīʿa b. Ḥabīb b. ʿAbd Shams. ʿUthmān b. ʿAffān wrote to him in the year 30,[345] when he was in charge of Basra, and wrote to Saʿīd b. al-ʿĀṣ b. Umayya b. ʿAbd Shams, who was his governor in Kufa, commanding the two of them to invade Khurāsān. | He 296

342 Isfījāb (Ispījāb) in most accounts: see the article by C. E. Bosworth in *EI*², s.v. Isfīdjāb; *Ḥudūd*, 118; Barthold, *Turkestan*, 175–178.

343 On early Turkish ethnography, see the article by Edith Ambros, et. al., in *EI*², s.v. Turks, and the article by Cl. Cahen, G. Deverdun, and P. M. Holt in *EI*², s.v. Ghuzz. Al-Yaʿqūbī's Tughuz-Ughuz, more properly Toquz-Oghuz (Nine Clans), refers to a confederation of Turkish tribes formed at the beginning of the 7th century C.E.

344 That is, *gāwars*, the Persian word for millet. See the article by A. Dietrich in *EI*², s.v. Djāwars.

345 30 A.H. = September 4, 650 – August 23, 651; cf. al-Yaʿqūbī, *Taʾrīkh*, 2:192–193.

said that whichever of them got to Khurāsān first would be commander over it. ʿAbdallāh b. ʿĀmir received a letter from the king of Ṭūs, saying, "I will get you there first, provided that you make me ruler of Nīshāpūr." So he got ʿAbdallāh there first, and the latter wrote him a document that remains in the possession of his descendants to the present day. ʿAbdallāh b. ʿĀmir conquered several rural districts in Khurāsān in the year 31.[346] His vanguard was commanded by ʿAbdallāh b. Khāzim al-Sulamī, and he was accompanied by al-Aḥnaf b. Qays al-Tamīmī.

Then ʿAbdallāh b. ʿĀmir left, putting Qays b. al-Haytham b. Asmāʾ b. al-Ṣalt al-Sulamī in charge of Khurāsān. He left al-Aḥnaf b. Qays with him.

Then ʿAbdallāh appointed Ḥātim b. al-Nuʿmān al-Bāhilī, who stayed in Khurāsān conquering and raiding until ʿUthmān was killed in the year 35.[347]

The Commander of the Faithful ʿAlī b. Abī Ṭālib—peace be upon him—appointed Jaʿda b. Hubayra b. Abī Wahb b. ʿAmr b. ʿĀʾidh al-Makhzūmī governor of Khurāsān.[348] Māhawayh, the *marzubān* of Marw, had approached ʿAlī—peace be upon him—while he was in Basra; ʿAlī granted him terms of capitulation and wrote him a document which is preserved in Marw to this day.

After ʿAlī—peace be upon him—was assassinated, Muʿāwiya appointed ʿAbdallāh b. ʿĀmir over Khurāsān. Ibn ʿĀmir dispatched ʿAbdallāh b. Khāzim al-Sulamī and ʿAbd al-Raḥmān b. Samura there. The two of them went together and besieged Balkh until they conquered it.[349]

Then ʿAbd al-Raḥmān b. Samura left and turned over Khurāsān to ʿAbdallāh b. Khāzim al-Sulamī.

Then Muʿāwiya appointed Ziyād b. Abī Sufyān over Basra, Khurāsān, and Sijistān. Ziyād dispatched al-Ḥakam b. ʿAmr al-Ghifārī, a Companion of the Prophet—God's blessing be upon him—to Khurāsān as commander. He left for
297 Khurāsān in the year 44.[350] He was a well-behaved, pious man. | After he had conquered some of the rural districts of Khurāsān, Ziyād wrote to him, "The Commander of the Faithful Muʿāwiya has written to me that I should reserve the white and the yellow for him,[351] so do not distribute any silver or gold." Disregarding the letter, al-Ḥakam paid the fifth, but distributed the remainder among the troops, and wrote to Ziyād: "I have found the Book of God to take

346 31 A.H. = August 24, 651 – August 11, 652.

347 ʿUthmān died on 18 Dhū l-Ḥijja 35 (June 17, 656); see al-Yaʿqūbī, *Taʾrīkh*, 2:204.

348 Cf. al-Yaʿqūbī, *Taʾrīkh*, 2:213–214; Gardīzī, *Zayn al-Akhbār*, 103.

349 Cf. al-Yaʿqūbī, *Taʾrīkh*, 2:258.

350 44 A.H. = April 4, 664 – March 24, 665; cf. al-Yaʿqūbī, *Taʾrīkh*, 2:264.

351 I.e., that all the silver and gold ("the white and the yellow") taken as spoils should be sent to Muʿāwiya, not just the customary fifth (the *khums*), as mandated by Qurʾān 8:41.

precedence over the letter of the Commander of the Faithful Muʿāwiya. Even if the heavens and the earth were closed up over a believer, if he feared God, God would give him a way of deliverance from them.[352] Peace." Al-Muhallab b. Abī Ṣufra was one of al-Ḥakam b. ʿAmr's men. Al-Ḥakam died in Khurāsān.

Then Ziyād dispatched al-Rabīʿ b. Ziyād b. Anas b. al-Dayyān b. Qaṭan b. Ziyād al-Ḥārithī as commander over Khurāsān. Al-Ḥasan al-Baṣrī was his secretary. Muʿāwiya appointed Khālid b. Muʿammar al-Sadūsī governor of Khurāsān. He set out to go there, but Ziyād had him poisoned, and he died and never reached Khurāsān. Ziyād appointed ʿAbdallāh b. al-Rabīʿ b. Ziyād to replace his father. Then he deposed him and appointed ʿAbd al-Raḥmān b. Samura b. Ḥabīb.

Then Ziyad died, and Muʿāwiya confirmed ʿAbd al-Raḥmān over Sijistān and appointed ʿUbaydallāh b. Ziyād as governor of Khurāsān. He dispatched him with troops and ordered him to cross the river of the country of Ṭukhāristān. He went out with a large force and raided the country of Ṭukhāristān. Al-Muhallab b. Abī Ṣufra was the tactical commander and in charge of the campaign. ʿUbaydallāh b. Ziyād remained in Khurāsān for two years; then he returned to Muʿāwiya, making Aslam b. Zurʿa b. ʿAmr b. al-Ṣaʿiq al-Kilābī his deputy over Khurāsān.

Muʿāwiya appointed ʿUbaydallāh governor of Basra and his brother ʿAbdallāh b. Ziyād over Khurāsān. He was there for four months, but Muʿāwiya heard of his weakness and shameful behavior and deposed him.[353]

After ʿAbdallāh b. Ziyād, Muʿāwiya appointed ʿAbd al-Raḥmān b. Ziyād[354] governor of Khurāsān, but he did not approve of him and so deposed him.

Then Muʿāwiya appointed Saʿīd b. ʿUthmān—Saʿīd b. ʿUthmān had previously refused and had spoken insultingly to him. Saʿīd made his way to Khurāsān and raided Samarqand—he is said to have been the first who crossed beyond the Oxus.[355] He raided Ṭukhāristān, | Bukhārā, and Samarqand. Aslam 298
b. Zurʿa al-Kilābī was in charge of the land tax in Khurāsān. Saʿīd b. ʿUthmān asked him for the funds, but he would not give them to him and instead had them sent to ʿUbaydallāh b. Ziyād, the governor of Basra. Aslam b. Zurʿa then fled from Khurāsān and wrote to Muʿāwiya to inform him that he had done so, and that Saʿīd b. ʿUthmān wanted to take the money. So Muʿāwiya deposed Saʿīd b. ʿUthmān and appointed Aslam b. Zurʿa over Khurāsān. Aslam set out for Khurāsān and reached Marw al-Shāhijān, where Saʿīd b. ʿUthmān was. Aslam

352 Cf. Qurʾān, 21:30, 65:2.

353 Cf. al-Yaʿqūbī, *Taʾrīkh*, 2:281–282.

354 Cf. al-Yaʿqūbī, *Taʾrīkh*, 2:281; Gardīzī, *Zayn*, 107.

355 Cf. al-Yaʿqūbī, *Taʾrīkh*, 2:282.

was in command of a sizable troop. One of his officers thrust a lance into Saʿīd b. ʿUthmān's tent and killed one of his slave girls. Saʿīd wrote to Muʿāwiya, and Muʿāwiya wrote back to him and to Aslam, summoning both of them before him. Qutham b. al-ʿAbbās b. ʿAbd al-Muṭallib had gone to Saʿīd b. ʿUthmān, but he died in Marw. The poet Mālik b. al-Rayb was also with Saʿīd b. ʿUthmān, along with Yazīd b. Rabīʿa b. Mufarrigh al-Ḥimyarī. Saʿīd b. ʿUthmān then departed from Khurāsān.

ʿUbaydallāh b. Ziyād made his brother ʿAbbād b. Ziyād governor of Khurāsān. He went there and asked Yazīd b. Mufarrigh to become his comrade. Ibn Mufarrigh left Saʿīd and joined him, but the association turned out badly and that is why he satirized it and mocked Ziyād's family.[356]

Then ʿAbd al-Raḥmān b. Ziyād became governor of Khurāsān, but he left it and designated Qays b. al-Haytham al-Sulamī as his deputy.

Then Yazīd b. Muʿāwiya made Salm b. Ziyād[357] governor of Khurāsān. There was strong hostility between him and his brother ʿUbaydallāh b. Ziyād. He was accompanied by al-Muhallab b. Abī Ṣufra, ʿAbdallāh b. Khāzim, Talḥa b. ʿAbdallāh b. Khalaf al-Khuzāʿī—known as "the Ṭalḥa of Ṭalḥas" (*Ṭalḥat al-Ṭalḥāt*)—ʿAmr b. ʿUbaydallāh b. Muʿammar al-Taymī, ʿAbbād b. Ḥuṣayn al-Ḥabaṭī, ʿImrān b. Faṣīl al-Burjumī, and other notables of Basra. ʿUbaydallāh b. Ziyād tore down the houses of all those who had set out with his brother. However, Yazīd b. Muʿāwiya wrote to him that he should rebuild them with
299 gypsum, | baked brick, and teak at his own expense, so he rebuilt them. Salm raided Khwārazm and conquered the cities of Kandākīn and Bukhārā.

Yazīd b. Muʿāwiya died, and the insurrection of Ibn al-Zubayr broke out; so Salm went back, appointing ʿArfaja b. al-Ward al-Saʿdī as his deputy. ʿAbdallāh b. Khāzim al-Sulamī[358] went with Salm to follow him, but he sent him back and wrote out his investiture over Khurāsān. When he went back, ʿArfaja refused to yield power to him. They fought with arrows, and an arrow struck ʿArfaja, who died.

ʿAbdallāh b. Khāzim remained in Khurāsān, raiding and conquering. He was loyal to Ibn Zubayr until ʿAbd al-Malik b. Marwān killed Muṣʿab b. al-Zubayr and sent his head to ʿAbdallāh b. Khāzim, writing to invite him to submit.[359] But the latter took Muṣʿab's head, washed it, embalmed it, put it in a shroud,

---

356 On Ibn Mufarrigh and his invectives against the family of Ziyād, see the article by Ch. Pellat in *EI*², s.v. Ibn Mufarrigh.

357 Cf. al-Yaʿqūbī, *Taʾrīkh*, 2:300–301; Gardīzī, *Zayn*, 107.

358 Gardīzī, *Zayn*, 108.

359 Cf. al-Yaʿqūbī, *Taʾrīkh*, 2:323–324.

and buried it. He replied insolently to ʿAbd al-Malik and refused to accept what ʿAbd al-Malik b. Marwān wanted him to do, and so the troops (*ahl*) of Khurāsān fell upon him and murdered him. The one who killed him was Wakīʿ b. al-Dawriqiyya,[360] who swore allegiance to ʿAbd al-Malik b. Marwān, to whom they sent ʿAbdallāh's head.

When affairs became settled for ʿAbd al-Malik b. Marwān, he appointed Umayya b. ʿAbdallāh b. Khālid b. Asīd b. Abī l-ʿĪṣ b. Umayya b. ʿAbd Shams[361] governor of Khurāsān. Umayya crossed into the territory beyond the Oxus and reached Bukhārā. Then Bukayr b. Wishāḥ[362] revolted against him, so he returned.

Umayya remained in charge of Khurāsān until al-Ḥajjāj was appointed governor of Iraq.[363] When al-Hajjāj became governor, he wrote to ʿAbd al-Malik, informing him that there were disturbances in Khurāsān, and authority over it was returned to him. He made al-Muhallab b. Abī Ṣufra governor of Khurāsān and ʿUbaydallāh b. Abī Bakra governor of Sijistān. When al-Muhallab reached Khurāsān, he stayed there a while and then went on to Ṭukhāristan and then to Kishsh, the capital of Sogdia. Then al-Muhallab fell ill and returned to Marwarrūdh suffering from gangrene in his leg. Al-Muhallab died in Khurāsān after having delegated authority to his son | Yazīd b. al-Muhallab, who governed it for 300
a while.[364]

Then al-Ḥajjāj deposed Yazīd b. al-Muhallab and made al-Mufaḍḍal b. al-Muhallab governor of Khurāsān.[365] He remained in Khurāsān until al-Ḥajjāj seized Yazīd b. al-Muhallab and imprisoned him. After al-Ḥajjāj had seized Yazīd b. al-Muhallab, he wrote to Qutayba b. Muslim al-Bāhilī,[366] who was his agent (*ʿāmil*) in Rayy, to become governor of Khurāsān, ordering him to arrest al-Mufaḍḍal and the rest of the Muhallabid family and send them to him in fetters. He did this: Qutayba b. Muslim went to Khurāsān and sent the Muhallabids to al-Ḥajjāj. He went to Bukhārā and conquered it; then he went to al-Ṭālaqān, where Bādhām had revolted, and fought him until he defeated him

---

360 Cf. al-Yaʿqūbī, *Taʾrīkh*, 2:324, where he is called Wakīʿ b. ʿUmayr, after his father—b. al-Dawriqiyya means "the son of the Dawriqī woman." Cf. Gardīzī, *Zayn*, 108.

361 Cf. al-Yaʿqūbī, *Taʾrīkh*, 2:324; Gardīzī, *Zayn*, 109.

362 So in the MS, but the Leiden editor of the corresponding passage of the *Taʾrīkh* (2:324) prefers the reading Wassāj.

363 The appointment took place in 75/694; cf. Gardīzī, *Zayn*, 109.

364 Cf. al-Yaʿqūbī, *Taʾrīkh*, 2:330.

365 Cf. al-Yaʿqūbī, *Taʾrīkh*, 2:341–342.

366 Gardīzī, *Zayn*, 111.

and killed him. Qutayba was still in Khurāsān when al-Walīd b. ʿAbd al-Malik became ruler. His authority and power over the country had become great: he killed Nīzak Ṭarkhān and went to Khwārazm; then he went to Samarqand and conquered it and concluded a peace treaty with Ghūzak the Ikhshīd of Samarqand.

A few months after al-Ḥajjāj died, Sulaymān b. ʿAbd al-Malik became ruler.[367] He made Yazīd b. al-Muhallab governor of Iraq and ordered him to hunt down the partisans of al-Ḥajjāj. When Qutayba b. Muslim heard about that, he decided to revolt, but Wakīʿ b. Abī Sūd al-Tamīmī seized him and killed him.[368] Wakīʿ remained in Khurāsān, confident that Sulaymān would appoint him governor. However, he did not do so; instead, Sulaymān made Yazīd b. al-Muhallab[369] governor of Khurāsān as well as Iraq.

Yazīd b. al-Muhallab went to Khurāsān in person to pursue Qutayba's partisans; he arrested Wakīʿ b. Abī Sūd and treated him brutally. The rural districts of Khurāsān revolted against Yazīd b. al-Muhallab, so he dispersed his brothers and sons as officials over the rural districts of Khurāsān and put them in charge of tax collection. ʿUmar b. ʿAbd al-ʿAzīz b. Marwān became ruler. When Yazīd heard about his accession, he left Khurāsān, designating his son Mukhallad as his deputy there and taking all his money with him. Some people advised him against doing this, but he did not listen and went to Basra.[370]

Meanwhile, ʿUmar b. ʿAbd al-ʿAzīz had deposed Yazīd and had appointed ʿAdī b. Arṭāt al-Fazārī. ʿAdī convinced Yazīd to go to ʿUmar; so he went, but
301 ʿUmar imprisoned him. ʿUmar b. ʿAbd al-ʿAzīz made | al-Jarrāḥ b. ʿAbdallāh al-Ḥakamī[371] governor of Khurāsān and ordered him to detain Mukhallad b. Yazīd b. al-Muhallab and make sure he could not get away; which he did. A delegation from Tibet came to him, asking him to send them someone to enlighten them about the religion of Islam.

Then ʿUmar b. ʿAbd al-ʿAzīz deposed al-Jarrāḥ b. ʿAbdallāh and appointed ʿAbd al-Raḥmān b. Nuʿaym al-Ghāmidī.[372] He instructed him to move the female dependents and children of the Muslims from the territory beyond the Oxus to Marw, but they would not comply and stayed there.

---

367 Al-Ḥajjāj died in Ramaḍān 95/June 714, and according to al-Yaʿqūbī, *Taʾrīkh*, 2:351, Sulaymān became caliph on 15 Jumādā I 96 (January 26, 715).

368 Cf. al-Yaʿqūbī, *Taʾrīkh*, 2:354–356; Gardīzī, *Zayn*, 112, gives the name as Wakīʿ b. Abī Aswad.

369 Gardīzī, *Zayn*, 112.

370 Cf. al-Yaʿqūbī, *Taʾrīkh*, 2:362.

371 Cf. al-Yaʿqūbī, *Taʾrīkh*, 2:362; Gardīzī, *Zayn*, 113.

372 Cf. al-Yaʿqūbī, *Taʾrīkh*, 2:362–363; Gardīzī, *Zayn*, 113.

Yazīd b. ʿAbd al-Malik b. Marwān became ruler[373] and made Maslama b. ʿAbd al-Malik governor of Iraq and Khurāsān. Maslama appointed Saʿīd b. ʿAbd al-ʿAzīz b. al-Ḥārith b. al-Ḥakam b. Abī l-ʿĀṣ[374] over Khurāsān. He made war on the kingdom of Farghāna and besieged Khujanda in the country of Sogdia and killed and took prisoners.

Then Maslama deposed him and appointed Saʿīd b. ʿAmr al-Ḥarashī, a Syrian. Then Khurāsān and Iraq were united under ʿUmar b. Hubayra al-Fazārī,[375] who made Muslim b. Saʿīd b. Aslam b. Zurʿa al-Kilābī governor of Khurāsān. He went to Khurāsān and started raiding, but accomplished nothing; the people of Farghāna fought him until they defeated him.

Hishām b. ʿAbd al-Malik became ruler,[376] and by then the propagandists in Khurāsān on behalf of the Banū Hāshim had appeared.[377] He made Khālid b. ʿAbdallāh b. Yazīd b. Asad b. Kurz al-Qasrī[378] governor of Iraq and Khurāsān and ordered him to send someone he could trust to Khurāsān. Khālid sent his brother Asad b. ʿAbdallāh. When news reached him about the ʿAbbāsid propagandists, Asad arrested a number of people he suspected and had their hands and feet cut off.[379]

News of the unrest in Khurāsān reached Hishām, who then appointed as his own representative Ashras b. ʿAbdallāh al-Sulamī.[380] Then he deposed him and appointed al-Junayd b. ʿAbd al-Raḥmān b. ʿAmr b. al-Ḥārith b. Khārija b. Sinān al-Murrī,[381] whom he then deposed and replaced with ʿĀṣim b. ʿAbdallāh b. Yazīd al-Hilālī.[382]

Then news reached Hishām that civil strife had broken out in Khurāsān, so he reattached it to Khālid | b. ʿAbdallāh al-Qasrī.[383] The latter dispatched 302

373 Yazīd b. ʿAbd al-Malik became caliph in Rajab 101 (January–February 720); cf. al-Yaʿqūbī, *Taʾrīkh*, 2:371.

374 Cf. al-Yaʿqūbī, *Taʾrīkh*, 2:373; Gardīzī, *Zayn*, 114.

375 Cf. al-Yaʿqūbī, *Taʾrīkh*, 2:374; Gardīzī, *Zayn*, 114.

376 Hishām b. ʿAbd al-Malik became caliph on the death of Yazīd b. ʿAbd al-Malik in Shaʿbān 105 (January 724). Curiously, al-Yaʿqūbī, *Taʾrīkh*, 2:379, says that Hishām reached Damascus in Ramaḍān 105, which he identifies as "Kānūn of the non-Arabs" (December or January), which would apply to Shaʿbān, but not to Ramaḍān 105, which fell in February 724.

377 Cf. al-Yaʿqūbī, *Taʾrīkh*, 2:383, on the beginnings of the ʿAbbāsid propaganda.

378 Cf. al-Yaʿqūbī, *Taʾrīkh*, 2:379; Gardīzī, *Zayn*, 114.

379 Cf. al-Yaʿqūbī, *Taʾrīkh*, 2:383.

380 Gardīzī, *Zayn*, 115.

381 Ibid.

382 Ibid.

383 That is, placed the province again under the authority of the governor of Iraq.

his brother Asad b. ʿAbdallāh. Asad b. ʿAbdallāh died in Khurāsān, having designated Jaʿfar b. Ḥanẓala al-Bahrānī, a Syrian, as his deputy over it.

Hishām deposed Khālid b. ʿAbdallāh from Iraq, made Yūsuf b. ʿUmar al-Thaqafī governor, and ordered him to send him a man who knew about Khurāsān. He sent ʿAbd al-Karīm b. Salīṭ b. ʿAṭīya al-Ḥanafī to him, and Hishām questioned him about Khurāsān and its conditions and its notables. He discussed the matter with him and finally recommended Naṣr b. Sayyār al-Laythī.[384] So Hishām wrote out his investiture as governor of Khurāsān—he had previously been in charge of one of the rural districts of Khurāsān. He deposed Jaʿfar b. Ḥanẓala and took over the administration of the province. He arrested Yaḥyā b. Zayd b. al-Ḥusayn in Balkh and imprisoned him in the citadel. He wrote to Hishām, but Hishām had already died when the letter arrived.

Al-Walīd b. Yazīd b. ʿAbd al-Malik became ruler.[385] Yaḥyā b. Zayd managed to escape from prison and made his way to the district of Nīshāpūr. Naṣr b. Sayyār dispatched Salm b. Aḥwaz al-Hilālī, who overtook Yaḥyā b. Zayd in al-Jūzjān. They fought, and Yaḥyā b. Zayd was struck by a stray arrow and killed. Salm b. Aḥwaz crucified the body over the gate of al-Jūzjān. Yaḥyā b. Zayd remained crucified there until Abū Muslim was victorious and took him down, shrouded him and buried him, and killed everyone who had approved of his murder.

The propagandists of the Banū Hāshim in Khurāsān became numerous in the year [1]26.[386] Naṣr b. Sayyār fought with Judayʿ b. ʿAlī al-Kirmānī al-Azdī.

Then al-Walīd was murdered, and Yazīd b. al-Walīd b. ʿAbd al-Malik became ruler.[387] Khurāsān was in a state of unrest, the Hāshimite propagandists had become numerous, and the tribes of Rabīʿa and Yemen had both dissociated themselves from Naṣr b. Sayyār.

When Marwān b. Muḥammad b. Marwān b. al-Ḥakam became ruler,[388] the activity of Abū Muslim in Khurāsān had come out into the open. Naṣr b. Sayyār was powerless against him, so he sought a truce and cessation of hostilities. Then Abū Muslim killed Naṣr b. Sayyār and took control of Khurāsān in the year 130.[389] He sent out his agents and troops, and he dispatched Qaḥṭaba

384 Cf. al-Yaʿqūbī, *Taʾrīkh*, 2:392; Gardīzī, *Zayn*, 116.

385 According to al-Yaʿqūbī, *Taʾrīkh*, 2:397, he became caliph on 20 Rabīʿ I 125 (January 21, 743).

386 126 A.H. = October 25, 743 – October 12, 744.

387 According to al-Yaʿqūbī, *Taʾrīkh*, 2:401, he became caliph on 1 Rajab 126 (April 19, 744).

388 According to al-Yaʿqūbī, *Taʾrīkh*, 2:404, he became caliph in Ṣafar 127 (November–December, 744).

389 130 A.H. = September 11, 747 – August 30, 748.

and others to Iraq. | Abū l-ʿAbbās ʿAbdallāh b. Muḥammad the Commander of the Faithful became the ruler, and the blessed Hāshimite dynasty was established.[390] 303

Abū Muslim stayed in Khurāsān until the year 136.[391] Then he asked the Commander of the Faithful Abū l-ʿAbbās for permission to perform the pilgrimage. Having received permission, he came to Iraq, leaving Abū Dāwūd Khālid b. Ibrāhīm al-Dhuhlī[392] as his deputy over Khurāsān. Then the Commander of the Faithful Abū l-ʿAbbās died, and Abū Jaʿfar al-Manṣūr became ruler.[393] Abū Dāwūd Khālid b. Ibrāhīm was still Abū Muslim's deputy in Khurāsān. Then Abū Muslim was murdered,[394] and Sunfādh[395] revolted in Khurāsān, seeking revenge for Abū Muslim. Al-Manṣūr dispatched Jahwar b. Marrār al-ʿIjlī against him; he defeated him, killed him, and dispersed his followers.

Abū Jaʿfar al-Manṣūr made ʿAbd al-Jabbār b. ʿAbd al-Raḥmān al-Azdī[396] governor of Khurāsān in the year 148,[397] and he went there. He had been in charge of al-Manṣūr's police (*shurṭa*). When he had amassed a lot of money and supplies in Khurāsān, he rebelled openly and made no secret of his opposition. Al-Manṣūr dispatched al-Mahdī against him. He fought him, captured him, and sent him to Abū Jaʿfar, who had him killed and crucified at Qaṣr Ibn Hubayra in the year 149.[398] Al-Mahdī resided at al-Rayy. When Qārin the Iṣbahbadh of Ṭabaristān revolted, al-Mahdī dispatched Khāzim b. Khuzayma al-Tamīmī and Rawḥ b. Ḥātim al-Muhallabī against him. Ṭabaristān was conquered, and Qārin was captured.

Al-Mahdī made Asīd b. ʿAbdallāh al-Khuzāʿī[399] governor of Khurāsān—Asīd died there. Then he appointed Ḥumayd b. Qaḥṭaba al-Ṭāʾī over it; he stayed

---

390 Arabic *al-dawla al-Hāshimiyya al-mubāraka*. According to al-Yaʿqūbī, *Taʾrīkh*, 2:418, Abū l-ʿAbbās ʿAbdallāh b. Muḥammad (al-Saffāḥ) became caliph on 13 Rabīʿ I 132 (November 26, 749).

391 136 A.H. = July 7, 753 – June 26, 754; the pilgrimage would have taken place in the last month of the year.

392 Gardīzī, *Zayn*, 123.

393 According to al-Yaʿqūbī, *Taʾrīkh*, 2:436, he became caliph on 12 Dhū l-Ḥijja 136 (June 8, 754).

394 According to al-Ṭabarī, *Taʾrīkh*, 3:115, Abū Muslim died on 24 Shaʿbān 137 (February 12, 755).

395 Called Sunbādh in al-Yaʿqūbī, *Taʾrīkh*, 2:442; cf. al-Ṭabarī, *Taʾrīkh*, 3:119–120.

396 Gardīzī, *Zayn*, 123.

397 148 A.H. = February 27, 765 – February 15, 766; but this is a mistake for 140 (May 25, 757 – May 13, 758); see al-Ṭabarī, *Taʾrīkh*, 3:128; Wiet, 127 n. 1.

398 Al-Ṭabarī, *Taʾrīkh*, 3:134–135, places the revolt and death of ʿAbd al-Jabbār in 141 (May 14, 758 – May 3, 759).

399 Gardīzī, *Zayn*, 125 (reverses the order with Abū ʿAwn).

there for a while, but then al-Manṣūr deposed him and appointed Abū ʿAwn ʿAbd al-Malik b. Yazīd.[400] Then ʿAbd al-Malik b. Yazīd was deposed.

Having become caliph,[401] al-Mahdī sent back Ḥumayd b. Qaḥṭaba,[402] who stayed there until he died.

Then al-Mahdī made Muʿādh b. Muslim al-Rāzī,[403] a client of the Rabīʿa, governor of Khurāsān. Meanwhile, Yūsuf al-Barm the Khārijite[404] (*al-Ḥarūrī*)
304 had revolted, and al-Mahdī dispatched | Yazīd b. Mazyad b. Zāʾida al-Shaybānī to fight Yūsuf al-Barm. He fought him until he captured him and sent him to al-Mahdī, who cut off his hands and feet. Yūsuf al-Barm's revolt was followed immediately by that of Ḥakīm al-Aʿwar, known as al-Muqannaʿ,[405] while Muʿādh b. Muslim was still governor of Khurāsān. With him were ʿUqba b. Salm al-Hunāʾī, Jibrīl b. Yaḥyā al-Bajalī, and al-Layth, client of the Commander of the Faithful. But al-Mahdī designated Saʿīd al-Ḥarashī to fight al-Muqannaʿ; he repeatedly defeated him until al-Muqannaʿ went to Sogdia and barricaded himself in a fortress at Kishsh. Hard pressed by the siege, he and his partisans drank poison; they all died together, and the fortress was conquered.

Al-Mahdī deposed Muʿādh b. Muslim from Khurāsān and made al-Musayyab b. Zuhayr al-Ḍabbī[406] governor. Towards the end of his caliphate, al-Mahdī deposed al-Musayyab and made al-Faḍl b. Sulaymān al-Ṭūsī[407] governor of Khurāsān, who remained there until al-Mahdī died and in the caliphate of Mūsā al-Hādī.[408]

---

400 Gardīzī, *Zayn*, 124.

401 According to al-Yaʿqūbī, *Taʾrīkh*, 2:468, 472, al-Mahdī became caliph on the day of his father's death, 3 Dhū l-Ḥijja 158 (October 4, 775).

402 Gardīzī, *Zayn*, 125 (after ʿAbda b. Qudayd).

403 Gardīzī, *Zayn*, 127.

404 On the revolt of Yūsuf al-Barm in eastern Khurāsān, see the article by C. E. Bosworth in EI^2, s.v. Yūsuf al-Barm; al-Yaʿqūbī, *Taʾrīkh*, 2:478–479; Gardīzī, *Zayn*, 126–127. Although al-Yaʿqūbī labels the revolt's leader a Khārijite in allusion to the groups that "seceded" (*kharaja*) from the army of the caliph ʿAlī, rejecting his acceptance of human mediation between himself and Muʿāwiya—their assembling at a place called al-Ḥarūrāʾ earned them the name of Ḥarūrīyya—there is little evidence that the revolt was a continuation of the Khārijite movement.

405 On the revolt of al-Muqannaʿ ("the Masked One"—he is said to have hidden his face behind a veil of silk or a mask of gold and to have claimed to be divine), see the article in EI^2, s.v al-Muḳannaʿ, and Patricia Crone, *Nativist Prophets*, 106–143. Curiously, al-Yaʿqūbī does not mention this revolt in the *Taʾrīkh*.

406 Gardīzī, *Zayn*, 127.

407 Gardīzī, *Zayn*, 114 (Abū l-ʿAbbās ...)

408 Mūsā al-Hādī ruled from Muḥarram 169/August 785 to Rabi I 170/September 786. The

Hārūn al-Rashīd made Jaʿfar b. Muḥammmad b. al-Ashʿath al-Khuzāʿī[409] governor of Khurāsān, but he suffered a stroke and died. Then he made the latter's son, al-ʿAbbās b. Jaʿfar b. Muḥammad b. al-Ashʿath,[410] governor in his father's place; then he deposed him and made al-Ghiṭrīf b. ʿAṭāʾ,[411] who was al-Rashīd's maternal uncle, governor. He could not control Khurāsān, and so he deposed him and appointed Ḥamza b. Mālik b. al-Haytham al-Khuzāʿī. Then he deposed him, and appointed al-Faḍl b. Yaḥya b. Khālid b. Barmak[412] governor of Khurāsān. The latter went to Balkh and conquered a number of rural districts of Ṭukhāristān, Kābul-Shāh, and Shiqinān.

Then al-Rashīd deposed al-Faḍl b. Yaḥyā b. Khālid and appointed ʿAlī b. ʿĪsā b. Māhān[413] governor. He had been in charge of al-Rashīd's security forces (*shurṭa*). ʿAlī b. ʿĪsā came to Khurāsān. Abū ʿAmr the Khārijite had revolted, so he fought him until he killed him. Then Ḥamza the Khārijite revolted against ʿAlī b. ʿĪsā b. Māhān in Bādhghīs. | ʿAlī b. ʿĪsā hastened to oppose him, defeating 305
him and pursuing him to Kābul, where he fought him until he killed him. After Ḥamza, Abū l-Khaṣīb revolted against him at Bāward, so he fought him and killed him. ʿAlī b. ʿĪsā acquired an impressive amount of wealth. ʿAlī had dispatched Rāfiʿ b. al-Layth b. Naṣr b. Sayyār b. Rāfiʿ al-Laythī to Samarqand; Rāfiʿ revolted, and his might increased and his movement gained momentum.

---

text of the Leiden edition at this point is problematic. The editor decided to suppress an instance of the word *wa-* (and) that he deemed a copyist's error. As printed, the text translates: "Towards the end of his caliphate, al-Mahdī deposed al-Musayyab and made al-Faḍl b. Sulaymān al-Ṭūsī governor of Khurāsān, who remained there until al-Mahdī died, and in the caliphate of Mūsā al-Hādī [*and*, suppressed by the editor] Hārūn al-Rashīd made Jaʿfar b. Muḥammad … governor of Khurāsān." This implies the unlikely scenario that Hārūn, who was out of favor during al-Hādī's reign, appointed the governor of Khurāsān. Furthermore, al-Ṭabarī, *Taʾrīkh*, 3:605, 609, places Jaʿfar b. Muḥammad's appointment after the death of al-Hādī and attributes the appointment of al-ʿAbbās b. Jaʿfar and al-Ghiṭrīf b. ʿAṭāʾ to al-Rashīd. One solution is to assume that the editor has wrongly emended the MS and mispunctuated the text. The translation here reverts to the MS reading. However, there is still the problem that al-Yaʿqūbī, *Taʾrīkh*, 2:488, locates al-Ghiṭrīf's disastrous governorship in the reign of al-Hādī and makes no mention of him during the reign of al-Rashīd.

409 Gardīzī, *Zayn*, 129.

410 Gardīzī, *Zayn*, 129.

411 Cf. al-Yaʿqūbī, *Taʾrīkh*, 2:488; Gardīzī, *Zayn*, 129.

412 Gardīzī, *Zayn*, 130.

413 Gardīzī, *Zayn*, 131 (after Manṣūr b. Yazīd).

Hārūn heard that this had happened with the collaboration of ʿAlī b. ʿĪsā;[414] he therefore dispatched Harthama b. Aʿyan, who seized ʿAlī b. ʿĪsā and took him to al-Rashīd in irons. His wealth was also seized and confiscated. Harthama b. Aʿyan al-Balkhī was made governor of Khurāsān in the year 191.[415]

Then al-Rashīd went to Khurāsān, leaving his son Muḥammad al-Amīn as his deputy in Baghdad. He took al-Maʾmūn with him to Khurāsān, and the army accompanied him. When he reached Ṭūs he fell ill. The illness became severe, so he sent al-Maʾmūn, along with Harthama and the military officers, to Marw. Al-Rashīd died in Ṭūs in Jumādā II of the year 193,[416] and he was buried there.

Al-Maʾmūn stayed in Marw as governor of Khurāsān, its rural districts, and its other dependencies. He dispatched Harthama b. Aʿyan to Samarqand for the war against Rāfiʿ b. al-Layth b. Naṣr b. Sayyār al-Laythī; he fought him until he conquered Samarqand. Rāfiʿ surrendered under safe-conduct, and Harthama sent him to al-Maʾmūn, who sent him on to Muḥammad (al-Amīn), informing him of the victory. Al-Maʾmūn remained in Marw for the remainder of the year 193 and 194.[417] Then Muḥammad summoned him to Baghdad, dispatching for that purpose al-ʿAbbās b. Mūsā b. ʿĪsā, Muḥammad b. ʿĪsā b. Nahīk, and Ṣāliḥ the *ṣāḥib al-muṣallā*.[418] Al-Maʾmūn refused to go back, saying this was in violation of the agreement. (Al-Amīn) therefore sent ʿIṣma b. Abī ʿIṣma al-Sabīʿī against
306 him with an army, | but ʿIṣma stayed in al-Rayy and did not leave. Then (al-Amīn) dispatched ʿAlī b. ʿĪsā b. Māhān, whom he had released from prison,[419] to Khurāsān. When al-Maʾmūn heard of that, he sent Ṭāhir b. al-Ḥusayn b. Muṣʿab al-Būshanjī from Marw with four thousand troops. He encountered ʿAlī b. ʿĪsā at al-Rayy and killed him. Then al-Maʾmūn also dispatched Harthama b. Aʿyan to

---

414 Cf. al-Yaʿqūbī, *Taʾrīkh*, 2:515.

415 191 A.H. = November 17, 806 – November 5, 807; cf. Gardīzī, *Zayn*, 132.

416 March 809; the parallel passage in al-Yaʿqūbī, *Taʾrīkh*, 2:521, dates the death of al-Rashīd to the preceding month, Jumādā I (February 809); al-Ṭabarī, *Taʾrīkh*, 3:739–740, reports both dates.

417 That is, the remainder of 809 until October 810.

418 "Keeper of the Caliph's Prayer Rug"; on the ceremonial functions of this court official see al-Ṭabarī, *Taʾrīkh*, 3:778, 795 (trans. M. Fishbein, *The History of al-Ṭabarī*, XXXI, 25, n. 122, and 45), and 3:979, 1016 (trans. C. E. Bosworth, *The History of al-Ṭabarī*, XXXII, 17, n. 38, and 66). Al-Yaʿqūbī's narrative of the falling out of the two brothers and their eventual war begins at *Taʾrīkh*, 2:529.

419 As has been mentioned, Hārūn al-Rashīd had dismissed ʿAlī b. ʿĪsā as governor of Khurāsān, confiscated his wealth, and had him placed under house arrest in Baghdad (cf. al-Ṭabarī, *Taʾrīkh*, 3:732). After Hārūn's death, al-Amīn released ʿAlī and put him in charge of the campaign against al-Maʾmūn in Khurāsān.

Iraq. Al-Ma'mūn remained in Marw until Muḥammad (al-Amīn) was killed at the end of Muḥarram 198,[420] and he was given the oath of allegiance as caliph.

Al-Ma'mūn remained in Khurāsān for the years 199 and 200, sending officials to Iraq. He sent successively Ḥumayd b. ʿAbd al-Ḥamīd b. Ribʿī al-Ṭāʾī al-Ṭūsī; ʿAlī b. Hishām b. Khusraw al-Marwarrūdhī; Dhū l-ʿAlamayn ʿAlī b. Abī Saʿīd, son of al-Faḍl b. Sahl's maternal aunt, as chief of the land tax in Iraq; and al-Ḥasan b. Sahl, as plenipotentiary.[421] Harthama b. Aʿyan left Iraq in anger and went to al-Ma'mūn; al-Ma'mūn arrested him, and he died after three days in prison in Marw in the year 200.[422] Then, in 202,[423] al-Ma'mūn swore an oath of allegiance in Marw to al-Riḍā ʿAlī b. Mūsā b. Jaʿfar b. Muḥammad b. ʿAlī b. al-Ḥusayn b. ʿAlī b. Abī Ṭālib—upon whom be peace—as heir apparent. He left Marw that same year, journeying at a leisurely pace until he came to Sarakhs. He stayed there, and al-Faḍl b. Sahl, his vizier, was killed in the bath in Sarakhs.[424] Al-Ma'mūn executed a number of others in connection with him. Al-Ma'mūn traveled on to Ṭūs, and when he reached Ṭūs he stayed there. That was in the year 203.[425] Al-Riḍā—upon whom be peace—died in Ṭūs.[426] Al-Ma'mūn had written all the princes | of Khurāsān to pacify them until things became calm. 307

Al-Ma'mūn made Rajā' b. Abī l-Ḍaḥḥāk, the husband of al-Faḍl b. Sahl's sister, governor of all Khurāsān. Al-Ma'mūn arrived in Baghdad on 15 Ṣafar 204.[427] All of Khurāsān deteriorated under Rajā' b. Abī l-Ḍaḥḥāk; al-Ma'mūn therefore appointed Ghassān b. ʿAbbād[428] governor. He set things right and restored order. Al-Ma'mūn found him praiseworthy, and he stayed in office for the rest of 204 and several months of 205.

Then Ṭāhir b. al-Ḥusayn b. Muṣʿab al-Būshanjī[429] maneuvered al-Ma'mūn into appointing him governor of Khurāsān and investing him over it. He went

---

420 30 Muḥarram 198 = September 30, 813. Cf. al-Yaʿqūbī, *Ta'rīkh*, 2:536–537.

421 Arabic *ʿalā jamīʿ al-umūr*, literally "over all matters."

422 200 A.H. = August 11, 815 – July 29, 816. According to al-Ṭabarī, *Ta'rīkh*, 3:996 ff. Harthama did indeed die in 200; but cf. al-Yaʿqūbī, *Ta'rīkh*, 2:546, where the date of his death is given as 201.

423 202 A.H. = July 20, 817 – July 8, 818; but cf. al-Yaʿqūbī, *Ta'rīkh*, 2:545, where the date of this event is given as 7 Ramaḍān 201 (March 29, 817); al-Ṭabarī, *Ta'rīkh*, 3:1013, gives it as 2 Ramaḍān 201 (March 24, 817).

424 Cf. al-Yaʿqūbī, *Ta'rīkh*, 2:548; al-Ṭabarī, *Ta'rīkh*, 3:1027, gives a date of 2 Shaʿbān 202 (February 13, 818) for the murder.

425 203 A.H. = July 9, 818 – June 27, 819.

426 Cf. al-Yaʿqūbī, *Ta'rīkh*, 2:550–551.

427 August 11, 819; but al-Yaʿqūbī, *Ta'rīkh*, 2:551, gives the date as the following month, Rabīʿ I.

428 Cf. al-Yaʿqūbī, *Ta'rīkh*, 2:550; Gardīzī, *Zayn*, 134.

429 Gardīzī, *Zayn*, 135–136.

there in the year 205.[430] When he heard that al-Ma'mūn had an unfavorable opinion of him, he encouraged signs of rebellion but did nothing openly himself. Al-Ma'mūn heard about it, and it is said that Ṭāhir was guilefully given a (poisoned) drink. Ṭāhir died in the year 207.[431]

Al-Ma'mūn appointed Ṭāhir's son, Ṭalḥa b. Ṭāhir b. al-Ḥusayn,[432] to replace him. He remained in firm control as commander of Khurāsān for seven years. Ṭalḥa b. Ṭāhir died in the year 215.[433]

Al-Ma'mūn had appointed ʿAbdallāh b. Ṭāhir[434] governor of the rural districts of al-Jabal and Azerbaijan; he went there, but fell ill in al-Dīnawar. Then al-Ma'mūn named him governor of Khurāsān in place of his brother Ṭalḥa b. Ṭāhir, sending the document of investiture to him via Isḥāq b. Ibrāhīm and Yaḥyā b. Aktham, the Chief Qadi. ʿAbdallāh b. Ṭāhir went to Khurāsān and resided at Nīshāpūr, which he made his home; no other governor of Khurāsān before him had resided there. ʿAbdallāh b. Ṭāhir remained in charge of Khurāsān and its districts for fourteen years, with firm authority, governing powerfully, and the entire province was in good order. He died at Nīshāpūr in the year 230,[435] at the age of forty-eight.

Al-Wāthiq appointed ʿAbdallāh b. Ṭāhir's son, Ṭāhir b. ʿAbdallāh b. Ṭāhir,[436] governor of Khurāsān. He remained in Khurāsān during the caliphates of al-Wāthiq, al-Mutawakkil, and al-Muntaṣir and for part of the caliphate of al-Mustaʿīn. He governed it firmly for eighteen years. He died at Nīshāpūr in Rajab 248,[437] at the age of forty-four.

308 Al-Mustaʿīn appointed Ṭāhir b. ʿAbdallāh's son, Muḥammad b. Ṭāhir b. | ʿAbdallāh b. Ṭāhir,[438] governor of Khurāsān. He remained its governor from the year 248 to the year 259. Affairs were disturbed by the revolt of al-Ḥasan b. Zayd al-Ṭālibī in Ṭabaristān and elsewhere, as well as by the revolt of Yaʿqūb b. al-Layth al-Ṣaffār in Sijistān,[439] which spread to the rural districts of Khurāsān. Yaʿqūb b. al-Layth al-Ṣaffār advanced to Nīshāpūr in Shawwāl 259[440] and cap-

430 205 A.H. = June 17, 820 – June 5, 821.
431 207 A.H. = May 27, 822 – May 15, 823; cf. al-Yaʿqūbī, *Taʾrīkh*, 2:556–557.
432 Gardīzī, *Zayn*, 135.
433 215 A.H. = February 28, 830 – February 17, 831.
434 Gardīzī, *Zayn*, 135.
435 230 A.H. = September 18, 844 – September 6, 845.
436 Gardīzī, *Zayn*, 137.
437 September 862.
438 Gardīzī, *Zayn*, 138.
439 Gardīzī, *Zayn*, 138.
440 August 873.

tured Muḥammad b. Ṭāhir. He made certain that he and the members of his family could not escape, confiscated their property and what was in their residences, and carried them in fetters to a fortress in Kirmān called the fortress of Bamm. They remained in that state until al-Ṣaffār died. Khurāsān came to be without them,[441] and ʿAmr b. al-Layth,[442] al-Ṣaffār's brother, took control of it. Five commanders of the Ṭāhirid family were governors of Khurāsān, ruling for fifty-five years. With the fall of dynasties, affairs pass away, circumstances alter, weakness befalls, and inadequacy becomes visible.

The land tax of Khurāsān, from all the districts, amounted every year to forty million dirhams, apart from the fifths (of spoils) paid from the frontier regions. The Ṭāhirid family spent all of it as they saw fit. In addition, they received thirteen million from Iraq, apart from gifts.

Such is the Eastern Quarter. We have mentioned every report about it we have received and every account we have learned, and we have described its circumstances. Let us now mention the Southern Quarter[443] and what is in it. In God lies success.

The Southern Quarter

For anyone who wishes to travel from Baghdad to Kufa and to the road leading to the Ḥijāz, Medina, Mecca, and al-Ṭāʾif, it is 30 farsakhs, three stages, from Baghdad to Kufa. The first stage ends at Qaṣr Ibn Hubayra, 12 farsakhs from Baghdad. Yazīd b. ʿUmar b. Hubayra al-Fazārī had it built in the days of Marwān b. Muḥammad b. Marwān.[444] | At that time, Ibn Hubayra was Marwān's 309
governor of Iraq and wanted to distance himself from Kufa. Qaṣr Ibn Hubayra is a great and prosperous city in which officials and governors reside. Its populace is a mixture of peoples. It is on a canal called al-Ṣarāt that feeds from the Euphrates. From Qaṣr Ibn Hubayra it is a distance of two Arab miles to the main part of the Euphrates, at a bridge over the main part of the Euphrates called the Sūrā Bridge.[445] From Qaṣr Ibn Hubayra one travels to a place named Sūq Asad

441 That is, without a Ṭāhirid ruler.

442 Gardīzī, *Zayn*, 142.

443 Arabic *al-Rubʿ al-Qiblī*, the quarter that lies toward the *qibla*, the direction toward Mecca faced by Muslims in prayer: in Iraq, this would be south-southwest, but al-Yaʿqūbī uses the expression more generally to designate the Southern Quarter.

444 Marwān II, the last Umayyad caliph, reigned 127–132/744–750.

445 On Qaṣr Ibn Hubayra and the Sūrā Bridge, see the article by J. Lassner in *EI*², s.v. Ḳaṣr ibn Hubayra, and G. Le Strange, *Lands of the Eastern Caliphate*, 70–71. As Le Strange notes, by

on the west bank of the Euphrates in the county (*ṭassūj*) called al-Fallūja. Then one travels from Sūq Asad to Kufa. The stretches from Baghdad to Kufa are in populous areas and large, prosperous villages, one after another, with a mixed population of non-Arabs and Arabs.

Kufa is the chief city of Iraq, the largest garrison city,[446] the Dome of Islam,[447] and the Abode of Emigration (*Dār al-Hijra*) of the Muslims. It is the first city that the Muslims laid out in Iraq, in the year 14.[448] In it are the tribal land allotments (*khiṭaṭ*) of the Arabs. It is located on the main part of the Euphrates, from which its people obtain water. It is one of the finest of towns, one of the most spacious, salubrious, and extensive.

Its land tax revenues (*kharāj*) are included within the land tax revenues of the counties of the Ṣawād. The counties of the Ṣawād associated with Kufa are the county of al-Jubba; the county of al-Budāt; Furāt Bādaqlā; al-Sāliḥīn; and Nahr Yūsuf. Al-Ḥīra is three Arab miles from it.

Al-Ḥīra is above al-Najaf.[449] Al-Najaf was on the shore of Baḥr al-Milḥ, which in ancient times used to reach up to al-Ḥīra. Al-Ḥīra is the residence of the clan of Buqayla and others. It used to be the residence of the kings of the Banū Naṣr

---

"main part" of the Euphrates (*muʿẓam al-furāt*), al-Yaʿqūbī refers to the western branch of the Euphrates after the river bifurcated around the latitude of Karbalāʾ, *not* the present-day main channel (cf. his placement of Kufa on the "main part" of the Euphrates, below). The eastern branch was also known to ʿAbbāsid-era writers as the Sūrā River. *Pace* al-Yaʿqūbī, the Sūrā Bridge spanned this eastern (Sūrā) branch, *not* the "main part" or western branch.

446 Arabic *al-miṣr al-aʿẓam*: The term *miṣr* (pl. *amṣār*) in early Islam applied to the settlements that developed out of armed encampments established by the Arabs in conquered territories. It applied especially to Basra and Kufa in Iraq, and to Fusṭāṭ in Egypt. Later usage extended the word to any large urban area. Al-Yaʿqūbī appears to intend both senses here, as he mentions both the size of Kufa and its history. See the articles by C. E. Bosworth in *EI*², s.v. Miṣr (section B), and by Hichem Djaït in *EI*², s.v. al-Kūfa.

447 Arabic *Qubbat al-Islām*: the dictionaries mention this epithet for Kufa (e.g., Lane, *Lexicon*, 2536, s.v. *qubba*). Al-Zamakhsharī, *Asās al-balāgha*, s.v., notes a related idiom, *huwa qabb qawmihi*, which he glosses as "he is the head (*qabb*) of his people." The epithet may be connected with another expression, *qubbat al-arḍ*, the "dome of the earth," that is, its geographical center; see the article by Ch. Pellat in in *EI*², s.v. al-Ḳubba.

448 14 A.H. = February 25, 635 – February 13, 636.

449 Al-Najaf (the Embankment) is here the name not just of the town near Kufa, the location of the tomb of the first Shīʿi Imam, ʿAlī b. Abī Ṭālib, but also the surrounding site more generally, a slightly raised plateau which did indeed hem in the marshy lake known as Baḥr al-Milḥ (the Salty Sea). This lake is now, as in al-Yaʿqūbī's time, limited to the area further north around Karbalāʾ and is also known today as Buḥayrat al-Razāza. See the article by E. Honigmann and C. E. Bosworth in *EI*², s.v. al-Nad̲j̲af.

of Lakhm, who were of the clan of al-Nuʿmān b. al-Mundhir.[450] The notables of the populace of al-Ḥīra are Christians. Among them, from the Arab tribes who follow the Christian religion, are, from the Banū Tamīm, the clan of the poet ʿAdī b. Zayd al-ʿIbādī,[451] others from Sulaym, others from Ṭayyiʾ, and still others. Al-Khawarnaq is nearby to the east, three Arab miles from al-Ḥīra. Al-Sadīr is in the steppe nearby.[452]

The Tribal Land Allotments (Khiṭaṭ) *of Kufa*

ʿUmar b. al-Khaṭṭāb[453] wrote to Saʿd b. Abī Waqqāṣ[454] when he conquered 310
Iraq, ordering him to settle at Kufa and ordering the troops to divide it into allotments. Every tribe with its leader marked out its allotment, and ʿUmar granted plots to the Companions of the Messenger of God—God's blessings and peace be upon him. Thus, ʿAbs was settled alongside the mosque, although a group of them later moved to the outskirts of Kufa. Salmān b. Rabīʿa al-Bāhilī, al-Musayyab b. Najaba al-Fazārī, and some people from Qays claimed an allotment opposite the house of Ibn Masʿūd. ʿAbdallāh b. Masʿūd, Ṭalḥa b. ʿUbaydallāh, and ʿAmr b. Ḥurayth claimed the houses around the mosque. ʿUmar granted a plot to Jubayr b. Muṭʿim, who built a house and then sold it to Mūsā b. Ṭalḥa. He granted a plot to Saʿd b. Qays near the house of Salmān b. Rabīʿa, with a street running between the two plots. Saʿd b. Abī Waqqāṣ claimed as a plot for himself the house that is known as the house of ʿUmar b. Saʿd. (ʿUmar) granted plots to Khālid b. ʿUrfuṭa, Khabbāb b. al-Aratt, ʿAmr b. al-Ḥārith b. Abī Ḍirār, and ʿUmāra b. Ruwayba al-Tamīmī. He granted a plot to Abū Masʿūd ʿUqba b. ʿAmr al-Anṣārī, and another plot next to that of Juhayna to the Banū Shamkh b. Fazāra. He granted the Square of Khunays[455] as a plot to Hāshim b. ʿUtba b. Abī Waqqāṣ, and granted a plot to Shurayḥ b. al-Ḥārith al-Ṭāʾī. ʿUmar granted Usāma b. Zayd what lay between the mosque and the house of ʿAmr b. al-Ḥārith b. Abī Ḍirār for a house. He granted to Abū Mūsā al-Ashʿarī half of al-Ārī (the Stables), which was an open space by the mosque. He granted

450 On the pre-Islamic city of al-Ḥīra, the Christian Arab clan of the Lakhmids, and their famous king al-Nuʿmān, see the article by A. F. L. Beeston and I. Shahid in *EI²*, s.v. al-Ḥīra.

451 ʿAdī b. Zayd (d. c. 600 C.E.) was a member of a family of Christian Arab bureaucrats that served the Sasanians. See the article by Tilman Seidensticker in *EI³*, s.v. ʿAdī b. Zayd.

452 Al-Khawarnaq and al-Sadīr were famous palaces in the vicinity of Kufa attributed to the Lakhmids. See the article by L. Massignon in *EI²*, s.v. al-Khawarnaḳ.

453 The second caliph, ruled 13–23/634–644.

454 One of the commanders who led the early Islamic conquest of Iraq, and its first governor.

455 Reading Persian *chahār-sū* for al-Yaʿqūbī's Shihār Sūj, and Khunays for Khunaysh, on the basis of al-Ṭabarī, *Taʾrīkh*, 2:745.

to Ḥudhayfa b. al-Yamān with a group of ʿAbs (the other) half of al-Ārī, which was an open space where the horses of the Muslims were kept. He granted to ʿAmr b. Maymūn al-Awdī the plaza that is named after ʿAlī b. Abī Ṭālib—upon him be peace.[456] He granted a plot to Abū Jabīra al-Anṣārī, who was in charge of the military register (*dīwān al-jund*). He granted to ʿAdī b. Ḥātim and the rest of Ṭayyi' the area of Bishr's Pasture.[457] He granted a plot to al-Zubayr b. al-ʿAwwām, and he granted a large, extensive plot to Jarīr b. ʿAbdallāh al-Bajalī
311 and the rest of Bajīla. He granted | a plot to al-Ashʿath b. Qays al-Kindī and Kinda from the area of Juhayna up to (the plot of) the Banū Awd. A group from Azd came and found an open space between Bajīla and Kinda, and so they settled there. Hamdān were scattered throughout al-Kūfa. Tamīm, Bakr, and Asad came and settled on the outskirts. When (ʿUmar) granted Abū ʿAbdallāh al-Jadalī a plot among Bajīla, Jarīr b. ʿAbdallāh said, "Why did this man, who is not one of us, settle among us?" ʿUmar said to him, "Move to wherever you think best." So he moved to Basra, but most of Aḥmas left Jarīr b. ʿAbdallāh and moved to the pasture-lands.[458] Since then, the tribal allotments have changed and have become known by (the name of) the group that bought them and built upon them.

To every tribe belonged a pasture (*jabbāna*) named after them and their notables: among them were the ʿArzam pasture, the Bishr pasture, the Azd pasture, the Sālim pasture, the Murād pasture, the Kinda pasture, the pasture

---

456 ʿAlī (d. Ramaḍān 40/January 661), the Prophet Muḥammad's cousin, was the fourth caliph and the first Shīʿi Imam.

457 Arabic *Jabbānat Bishr* (Bishr's Jabbāna). The original sense of *jabbāna* was "high, level pasturage" (Lane, *Lexicon*, 2:377, s.v.). In the layout of the new Arab garrison cities, the term designated "a piece of unbuilt land serving, *inter alia*, as a meeting place and a cemetery" (P. Crone in *EI*², s.v. Khiṭṭa). Thus one might translate, "Bishr's Pasture/Open Space/Cemetery." Similarly, al-Yaʿqūbī will refer shortly to *Jabbānat ʿArzam*, and so on for each *jabbāna* (pasture/open space/cemetery).

458 Aḥmas b. al-Ghawth b. Bajīla was a subtribe of Bajīla. See Wüstenfeld, *Genealogische Tabellen*, 9:14. Arabic *intaqalat Aḥmas ... ilā l-jabbāna*: again, in accordance with Arabic usage, the definite article on *al-jabbāna* may indicate that the word is being used generically, to indicate the *kind* of land to which the clan of Aḥmas moved, or that they moved to *the* Jabbāna (pasture/cemetery) later known by their name. What is being described is a situation where ʿUmar granted lands to an interloper, al-Jadalī, from the vast allotment previously granted to the tribe of Bajīla described earlier. This annoyed the leader of Bajīla, Jarīr b. ʿAbdallāh, a warlord active in the conquest of Iraq who might have expected better treatment, and so he decamped to the other new garrison town of al-Baṣra. However, the Aḥmas segment of his tribe refused to go with him and instead moved to other unclaimed pasture lands, presumably on the outskirts of Kūfa.

of the Ṣā'idīs, the green space (*ṣaḥrā'*) of Uthayr, the green space of the Banū Yashkur, and the green space of the Banū ʿĀmir.

ʿUmar b. al-Khaṭṭāb wrote to Saʿd, ordering him to make the streets of Kufa 50 black cubits wide. The marketplace was placed in the area extending from the palace and the mosque to the house of al-Walīd, to al-Qallā'ūn, and to the houses of Thaqīf and Ashjaʿ. There were rush mat awnings over it until the days of Khālid b. ʿAbdallāh al-Qasrī,[459] who rebuilt the markets, created a booth and an arched portico for sellers of each sort of merchandise, and assigned its rental income to the army—10,000 soldiers used to reside in Kufa.

The Stages from Kufa to Medina and Mecca

Whoever wishes to travel from Kufa to the Ḥijāz leaves by the southern road, amid thriving stopping places and watering stations where there stand palaces belonging to the caliphs of the Banū Hāshim.[460] The first stage is al-Qādisiyya; then comes al-Mughītha, then al-Qarʿā', then Wāqiṣa, then al-ʿAqaba; then al-Qāʿ, then Zubāla, then al-Shuqūq, then Biṭān, which is Qabr al-ʿIbādī—the four latter places are dwelling places of the Banū Asad—and al-Thaʿlabiyya, which is a walled compound (*madīna*), Zarūd |, and al-Ajfur—encampments of the 312
Ṭayyi'. Next comes the compound of Fayd, which is the compound in which the agents responsible for the Mecca road reside. Its people are Ṭayyi' and it is at the foot of their mountain known as Salmā. Then comes Tūz, which is also a Ṭayyi' area, then Samīrā' and al-Ḥājir—the people of the latter two places are Qays, mostly from the Banū ʿAbs. Then come al-Naqira and the mines of al-Naqira, whose people are a mixture of Qays and others. From there, whoever wants to go to Medina, the City of the Messenger of God—God's blessings and peace be upon him—turns off toward Baṭn Nakhla; whoever is bound for Mecca turns toward Mughīthat al-Māwān, which is the territory of the Banū Muḥārib; then comes al-Rabadha, then al-Salīla, then al-ʿUmaq, then the mines of the Banū Sulaym, then Ufayʿiya, then al-Mislaḥ, then Ghamra, from which one commences the pilgrimage.[461] Then comes Dhāt ʿIrq, then Bustān Ibn ʿĀmir, then Mecca.

---

459 The Umayyad governor of Iraq from 105/723 to 120/738. See the article by G. R. Hawting in *EI*², s.v. Khālid b. ʿAbd Allāh al-Ḳasrī.

460 That is, belonging to the ʿAbbāsid family.

461 The *ḥajj*: the pilgrimage to Mecca that every Muslim is enjoined to undertake at least once in his or her lifetime. In fact, Dhāt ʿIrq, the next place mentioned by al-Yaʿqūbī (about 94 km north-east of Mecca), is the place where pilgrims from Iraq traditionally enter the consecrated state known as *iḥrām*, donning the garments of a pilgrim and beginning to observe the obligatory prohibitions. See the article by A. J. Wensinck in *EI*², s.v. Iḥrām.

The City of the Messenger of God—God's Blessings and Peace be upon Him

Whoever is bound for the City of the Messenger of God—God's blessing and peace be upon him—heads from the stopping place called the mines of al-Naqira to Baṭn Nakhl, then to al-ʿUsayla, then Ṭarafa, then to Medina. Medina, or Ṭayba,[462] as the Messenger of God—God's blessing and peace be upon him—named it, is situated on level land: green and open, yet having two hills, one of them Uḥud, the other ʿAyr. Its populace are the Emigrants (*Muhājirūn*), the Supporters (*Anṣār*), and the Successors (*Tābiʿūn*).[463] Also in it are Arab tribes from (the confederation of) Qays b. ʿAylān—from Muzayna, Juhayna, Kināna, and others.

Medina has four streambeds whose waters come in the season of rains and spring torrents from hills at a place called Ḥarrat Banī Sulaym at a distance of 10 farsakhs from the city. These streambeds are Wādī Buṭḥān, Greater ʿAqīq, Lesser ʿAqīq, and Wādī Qanāt. The water of these streams comes at the time of spring torrents, and it all collects at a place called al-Ghāba and issues forth
313 into a streambed called | Wādī Iḍam. Then the Greater and Lesser ʿAqīq pour into certain wells, among them Biʾr Rūma, which is Ḥafīr Banī Māzin, and Biʾr ʿUrwa.[464] During the rest of the year, the people of Medina drink from these two wells and from other wells not as well known as these two. There are also wells that water the palm groves and fields, whose water is drawn by *nāḍiḥa*s, which are camels that work (drawing water) at irrigation wells.[465] At Medina there are also springs flowing and running with water, among them ʿAyn al-Ṣawrayn, ʿAyn Thaniyyat Marwān, ʿAyn al-Khāniqayn, ʿAyn Abī Ziyād, Khayf al-Qāḍī, ʿAyn Barad, and the Spring of the Wives of the Prophet—God's blessing and peace be upon him. Most of the holdings of the populace are palm groves from which they derive their living and their food. The city's revenues come from the tithes on the dates and the alms-tax.

---

462 Ṭayba (Sweet Smelling) is one of the nicknames of Medina.

463 The Emigrants (*Muhājirūn*) were the Meccan converts to Islam who followed the Prophet from Mecca to his new headquarters at Medina in the year 1/622 or shortly thereafter. The Supporters (*Anṣār*) were the members of Medinan tribes (primarily Aws and Khazraj) who became Muslims. The Successors (*Tābiʿūn*) were those of the second generation of early Muslims.

464 Arabic *biʾr* = well; *Ḥafīr Banī Māzin* = the Excavation (that is, Well) of the Banū Māzin.

465 Arabic *zarānīq* (pl. of *zurnūq*). For a description of these devices, see Lane, *Lexicon*, 3:1229, s.v. *zurnūq*.

The Great Sea is three days from Medina; its seaport is a place called al-Jār,[466] where merchant ships and ships carrying food from Egypt anchor.

It is six Arab miles from Medina to Qubāʾ, where the halting places of al-Aws and al-Khazraj used to be before Islam, and where the Messenger of God—God's blessing and peace be upon him—halted before traveling on to Medina itself. It was at Qubāʾ that he stayed—God's blessing and peace be upon him—at the home of Kulthūm b. al-Hidm, but then Kulthūm died, so he stayed with Saʿd b. Khaythama al-Anṣārī. The house of Saʿd b. Khaythama is next to the mosque of Qubāʾ. Then the Prophet moved to Medina, where he settled its feuds.[467] The people laid out the allotments (*khiṭaṭ*)—before that, they had lived dispersed in separate areas—and the built-up areas became connected, so that they became a city.

It is ten stages from Medina to Mecca, and the route is heavily populated and prosperous. The first stage ends four Arab miles from Medina, at Dhū l-Ḥulayfa, where pilgrims leaving Medina enter into a state of consecration.[468] From there one goes to al-Ḥufayra, where are the settlements of the Banū Fihr of Quraysh, then to Malal, which at this time is the settlement of a group of descendants of Jaʿfar b. Abī Ṭālib.[469] Then one proceeds to al-Sayāla, where there is | a group of descendants of al-Ḥasan b. ʿAlī b. Abī Ṭālib[470]—God's peace 314
be upon him—and where there was a group of Quraysh and others. Then one proceeds to al-Rawḥāʾ, which is the settlement of Muzayna, and then to al-Ruwaytha, where there is a group of descendants of ʿUthmān b. ʿAffān and other Arabs.[471] Then one proceeds to al-ʿArj, which is another settlement of Muzayna, and then to Suqyā Banī Ghifār, which is the settlement of the Banū Kināna. Then one proceeds to al-Abwāʾ, which is the settlement of Aslam, and then to

---

466 The old Red Sea port for Medina, south of modern Yanbuʿ; see the article by A. Dietrich in *EI*², s.v. al-Djār.

467 Arabic *kataba maʿāqilaha* (he wrote its blood-moneys). See al-Ṭabarī, *Taʾrīkh, Glossarium*, ccclxxi–ccclxxii, s.v. ʿ-Q-L. The document referred to is the so-called Constitution of Medina; on which see Michael Lecker, *The "Constitution of Medina": Muḥammad's First Legal Document.*

468 As part of the pilgrimage rituals, pilgrims enter a state of consecration symbolized by donning a special seamless wrap worn as a pilgrimage garment called the *iḥrām*. While in this state, pilgrims are also subject to certain restrictions: they may not shave, trim their nails, hunt, uproot plants, etc.

469 Jaʿfar b. Abī Ṭālib, the brother of ʿAlī b. Abī Ṭālib and cousin of the Prophet, died in a military expedition against the Byzantines at Muʾta in southern Jordan in the year 8/629.

470 Al-Ḥasan was the son of ʿAlī and the second Shīʿi Imam. Al-Yaʿqūbī, *Taʾrīkh*, 2:266, dates his death to Rabīʿ I 49 (April/May 669).

471 ʿUthmān, the third caliph, reigned 23/644 to 35/656.

al-Juḥfa, where there is a group of the Banū Sulaym. Ghadīr Khumm is two Arab miles off the road from al-Juḥfa.[472] Then one proceeds to Qudayd, where there is the settlement of Khuzāʿa, then to ʿUsfān, and then to Marr al-Ẓahrān, which is the settlement of Kināna. From there one proceeds to Mecca.

Mecca and Its Dependencies

It is 225 Arab miles from Medina to Mecca. The pilgrims halt at these stations and other watering-places, one group tarrying, another cutting their stay short, according to their pace on the road, quick or slow. The people enter Mecca from Dhū Ṭuwā, which is the lower part of Mecca, and by ʿAqabat al-Madaniyyīn, which is the upper part of Mecca and from which the Messenger of God—God's blessing and peace be upon him—entered.[473]

Mecca is situated amid great mountains, and it contains streambeds that come from ravines.[474] The mountains surrounding the city are: Abū Qubays, the high mountain from which the sun rises upon the Sacred Mosque;[475] Quʿayqiʿān; Fāḍiḥ; al-Muḥaṣṣab; Thawr, near al-Ṣafā; Ḥirāʾ; Thabīr; Tuffāḥa; al-Maṭābikh; al-Falaq; al-Ḥajūn; and Saqar.

Mecca's ravines are as follows: al-Ḥajūn Ravine, Dār Māl Allāh Ravine, al-
315 Baṭṭāṭīn Ravine, Falaq Ibn al-Zubayr Ravine, Ibn ʿĀmir | Ravine, al-Jawf Ravine, al-Khūz Ravine, Adhākhir Ravine, Khaṭṭ al-Ḥizāmīya Ravine, al-Ṣafā Ravine, al-Razzāzīn Ravine, al-Jubayriyyīn Ravine, al-Jawf Ravine,[476] al-Jazzārīn Ravine, Zuqāq al-Nār Ravine, Jabal Tuffāḥa Ravine, al-Ḥajjāj Ravine, al-ʿAṭṭārīn Ravine, Great Jiyād Ravine, Little Jiyād Ravine, al-Nafar Ravine, the Ravine of Thawr and Khiyām ʿUnqūd, Yarranī Ravine, the Ravine of ʿAlī, Thaniyyat al-Madaniyyīn Ravine, and al-Ḥamām Ravine.

---

472 Ghadīr Khumm is a pool near Mecca at which the Prophet stopped in the year 10/632 as he returned from his Farewell Pilgrimage. According to tradition (reported by al-Yaʿqūbī, *Taʾrīkh*, 2:125), he is said to have spoken words indicating his closeness to ʿAlī. As a result, Shīʿites have taken the Prophet's speech at Ghadīr Khumm as proof of ʿAlī's status as Imam and rightful leader of the Muslim community. The event is commemorated by many Shīʿite groups. See the article by L. Veccia Valieri in *EI*², s.v. Ghadīr Khumm.

473 That is, at the time of the conquest of Mecca in 8/630.

474 Arabic *wa-hiya awdiyatun dhātu shiʿāb*, literally, "and it is streambeds possessing ravines." The idea is that these streambeds (dry, except during the infrequent rains, when they can turn into torrents) pass through the basin in which the city is built, but originate back toward the mountains in deep ravines, gorges, or canyons (*shiʿāb*, pl. of *shiʿb*, which appears as an element in the following toponyms).

475 That is, the mosque surrounding the Kaʿba.

476 This ravine is repeated in the MS, as noted by De Goeje.

The Sacred Mosque stands between Jiyād and Quʿayqiʿān. The last person to restore the Sacred Mosque, adding to it and enlarging it so that the Kaʿba stood in the center of it, was al-Mahdī in the year 164.[477] The Sacred Mosque covers an area of 120,000 square cubits. The length of the Mosque from the Banū Jumaḥ Door to the Banū Hāshim Door, which is near the green marker,[478] is 404 cubits; its width from the al-Nadwa Door to the al-Ṣafā Door is 304 cubits. It boasts 484 marble columns, each pillar ten cubits in height, 498 arches, and 23 doors.

The Commander of the Faithful al-Mahdī built the two green markers that stand between al-Ṣafā and al-Marwa. There are 112 cubits between the two markers; there are 754 cubits between al-Ṣafā and al-Marwa.

The height of | the Kaʿba is 28 cubits. From the corner of the Black Stone to 316
the Syrian corner is 25 cubits; from the western corner in al-Ḥijr to the Syrian corner, 22 cubits; from the western corner to the Yamānī corner, 25 cubits; from the Yamānī corner to the corner in which lies the Black Stone, 21 cubits.

The people of Mecca obtain drinking water from brackish wells and from the *qanāt*s that Umm Jaʿfar, the daughter of Jaʿfar the son of the Commander of the Faithful al-Manṣūr, built during the caliphate of the Commander of the Faithful al-Rashīd.[479] She had them flow from the place called al-Mushāsh in lead channels 12 Arab miles apart. The people of Mecca and the pilgrims thus obtain water from the cistern of Umm Jaʿfar.

Al-Ṭāʾif is two stages from Mecca. Al-Ṭāʾif is the settlement of the tribe of Thaqīf; it is a dependency of Mecca subject to Mecca's governor.

Mecca's dependencies are: Ruʿaylāʾ al-Hawdha; Ruʿaylāʾ al-Bayāḍ, where lie the mines of Sulaym, Hilāl, and ʿUqayl of Qays; Tabāla, the people of which are of Khathʿam; Najrān, which belongs to the Banū l-Ḥārith b. Kaʿb, and which was their settlement in the Time of Ignorance;[480] al-Sarāt, the people of which

---

477 The ʿAbbāsid caliph al-Mahdī reigned 158/775 to 169/785. On his reconstruction of the Meccan sanctuary, see al-Yaʿqūbī, *Taʾrīkh*, 2:476–477. 164 A.H. = September 7, 780 – August 25, 781.

478 This and the following lines about markers refer to the green pillars placed between the hills of al-Ṣafā and al-Marwa. These two places figure in the pilgrimage ritual of *saʿy* (running), in which (according to the most common understanding) pilgrims re-enact Hagar's desperate search for water by running seven times between these two hills. The green markers indicate places where pilgrims should begin and end their running.

479 A *qanāt* is an underground water-channel. The one described here was built by the caliph Hārūn al-Rashīd's wife Zubayda (Umm Jaʿfar). For an account of her philanthropic work in improving the water supply of Mecca, initiated in 193/808, see the article by Renate Jacobi in *EI*², s.v. Zubayda bt. D̲jaʿfar b. Abī D̲jaʿfar al-Manṣūr.

480 *Al-Jāhiliyya*, that is, the period before the preaching of Islam by the Prophet Muḥammad.

are of al-Azd; ʿAsham, which is a gold mine; Baysh; al-Sirrayn; al-Ḥasaba; ʿAthr; Jedda, which is the sea-port; Ruhāṭ; Nakhla; Dhāt ʿIrq; Qarn; ʿUsfān; Marr al-Ẓahrān; and al-Juḥfa.

Of the Arab tribes around Mecca, there are, from Qays: Banū ʿUqayl, Banū Hilāl, Banū Numayr, and Banū Naṣr; from Kināna: Ghifār, Daws, Banū Layth, Khuzāʿa, Khathʿam, Ḥakam, and al-Azd.

Mecca has many springs where the productive lands of the people lie, at
317 Marr al-Ẓahrān; ʿArafa; Ruhāṭ; Tathlīth, where there is a gold mine at ʿAsham; |
Dhū ʿAlaq; and ʿUkāẓ.

Its revenues come from the tithes and alms-taxes. Provisions are transported to it from Egypt, to its port, which is Jedda.

From Mecca to Yemen

From Mecca to Ṣanʿāʾ there are 21 stages: the first is al-Malakān; then Yalamlam, where pilgrims from Yemen enter the state of ritual purity; then al-Līth; then ʿUlyab; then Qurbā; then Qanawnā; then Yaba; then al-Maʿqir; then Ḍankān; then Zanīf; then Rīm; then Baysh; then al-ʿUrsh of Jāzān; then al-Sharja; then al-Salʿ; then Balḥa; then al-Mahjam; then al-ʿĀra; then al-Marwa; then Sawadān; and then Ṣanʿāʾ, the largest city, in which the governors and notables of the Arabs reside.

Yemen is comprised of 84 *mikhlāf*s, which are like the (administrative divisions known as) *kūra*s and *madīna*s (in other provinces).[481] Their names are:
al-Yaḥṣibayn; Yaklā; Dhimār; Ṭamuʾ; ʿIyān; Ṭamām; Hamal; Qudam; Khaywān;
318 Sinḥān; Rayḥān |; Jurash; Ṣaʿda; al-Akhrūj; Majnaḥ; Ḥarāz; Hawzan; Qufāʿa; al-
Wazīra; al-Ḥujr; al-Maʿāfir; ʿUnna; al-Shawāfī; Jublān; Waṣāb; al-Sakūn; Sharʿab;
al-Janad; Maswar; al-Thujja; al-Mazraʿ; Ḥayrān; Maʾrib; Haḍūr; ʿUlqān; Rayshān;
Jayshān; al-Nihm; Baysh; Ḍankān; Qanawnā; Yaba; Zanīf; al-ʿUrsh of Jāzān;
al-Khaṣūf; al-Sāʿid; Balḥa, which is (also called) Mawr; al-Mahjam; al-Kadrāʾ,
which is (also called) Sahām; al-Maʿqir, which is (also called) Dhuwāl; Zabīd;
319 Rimaʿ |; al-Rakb; Banī Majīd; Laḥj; Abyan; Bayn al-Wādiyayn; Alhān; Ḥaḍra-
mawt; Muqrā; Ḥays; Ḥaraḍ; al-Ḥaqlayn; ʿAns; Banī ʿĀmir; Maʾdhin; Ḥumlān; Dhī
Jura; Khawlān; al-Sarw; al-Dathīna; Kubayba; and Tabāla.

481 *Mikhlāf* (pl. *makhālīf*) is a geographic term used specifically in Yemen. It apparently is related to the Sabaic (Old South Arabian) term *kh.l.f*, meaning "vicinity of a town." See the article by C. E. Bosworth in *EI*², s.v. Mikhlāf. Al-Yaʿqūbī gives a similar list, with minor variants, in the *Taʾrīkh*, 1:227–228. Neither here nor in the parallel passage in the *Taʾrīkh* do these names add up to 84.

The Islands of Yemen

Zaylaʿ, which is off al-Mandab; Dahlak, which is off Ghalāfiqa and is the island of the Negus;[482] Raḥsū, which is off al-Dahlak; and Bāḍiʿ, which is off ʿAthr, the port for Baysh, and is the territory of the tribe of Kināna.[483]

Its Ports

Aden, the port of Ṣanʿāʾ, where ships from China dock; Salāhiṭ; al-Mandab; Ghalāfiqa; al-Ḥirda; al-Sharja, which is Sharjat al-Qarīṣ; ʿAthr; al-Ḥasaba; al-Sirrayn; and Jedda |. 320

A List of the Arab Tribes Inhabiting Each Region of Yemen

Baysh: its populace is of al-Azd, and there is also a group from the Banū Kināna. Al-Khaṣūf and al-Sāʿid: its populace is of Ḥā and Ḥakam. Al-Kadrāʾ and al-Mahjam: its populace is of ʿAkk. Al-Ḥuṣayb: its populace is of Zubayd and of Ashʿar. Ḥays is the main center (*madīna*) for al-Rakb and the Banū Majīd. Ḥaraḍ is the main center for al-Maʿāfir. Al-Janad is the main center for Sharʿab. The city of Jayshān belongs to Ḥimyar; Tabāla, to Khathʿam; Najrān, to the Banū l-Ḥārith b. Kaʿb; Ṣaʿda, to Khawlān; and Sharʿab, Qufāʿa, and al-Ḥujr are Kinda territory.

The Third or Polar Quarter Which is the Northern Quarter

Having mentioned (the Quarter of) Canopus, which is the Southern Quarter, let us now mention the Quarter of Polaris, which is the Northern Quarter, and the cities and rural districts that lie in it.[484]

---

482 The King of Abyssinia. The Dahlak archipelago was often held as an Abyssinian dependency.

483 It is difficult to identify these islands. Zaylaʿ, according to Yāqūt, *Muʿjam al-Buldān*, 2:966–967, s.v., is the name of an African people and their land on the coast opposite Yemen. The only *island* that fits our author's description is Mayyun, directly off Bāb al-Mandab between Yemen and Djibouti. Dahlak is the well-known archipelago off the coast of Eritrea (presumably the island of Great Dahlak is what our author is identifying here). Rahsū (or perhaps Rahsuwa) may perhaps be identified with Saso Island just opposite Jīzān in Saudi Arabia. Bāḍiʿ is almost certainly Bodhi Island, just where it should be off the coast north of Baysh.

484 On al-Yaʿqūbī's division of the world into quarters, see above, ed. Leiden, 268–269, where he explains his use of the star Canopus (al-Tayman) to designate the Southern Quarter.

Whoever wishes to travel from Baghdad to al-Madāʾin and the cities and counties (*ṭasāsīj*) that adjoin it along the banks of the Tigris, and to Wāsiṭ, Basra, al-Ubulla, al-Yamāma, Bahrain, Oman, Sind, and India, leaves Baghdad and travels along whichever bank of the Tigris he wishes, either the east or the west. He goes through large towns inhabited by Persians, until he reaches
321 al-Madāʾin, seven | farsakhs from Baghdad. Al-Madāʾin was the residence of the kings of the Persians, and the first to settle there was Anūshirwān.[485] Al-Madāʾin is composed of a number of cities on both banks of the Tigris. On the east bank lies the city called al-ʿAtīqa (the Ancient), in which is the old White Palace—no one knows who built it.[486] The Congregational Mosque, which the Muslims built when the city was conquered, is in al-ʿAtīqa. Also on the east bank is the city called Asbānbur, in which is the great Audience Hall of Chosroës.[487] The Persians have nothing else like it: its roof is 80 cubits high. Between these two cities is a distance of one Arab mile. It was in this city that Salmān al-Fārisī and Ḥudhayfa b. al-Yamān used to live;[488] their tombs are located there. Adjoining these two cities is a city called al-Rūmiyya. It is said that the Romans built it when they were victorious over the kingdom of Persia. It was there that the Commander of the Faithful al-Manṣūr was staying when he killed Abū Muslim.[489] The distance between these three cities is approximately two or three Arab miles.

There he also describes his use of the star Polaris (al-Jady) to designate the Northern Quarter. *Al-Jady* is thus the reading to be favored over the Leiden edition's *al-jarbī* in this section. De Goeje adds the following note here (translated here from Latin): "From what follows, it is clear that there has been an error in placement (of this section-title), for the description of eastern Iraq, eastern Arabia and India belongs to the southern quarter. Therefore the title, with the introductory remarks, should properly be located in the lost part of the manuscript before the description of Armenia, etc."

485 The Sasanian king, Chosroës (Persian *Khusraw*, Arabic *Kisrā*) I Anūshirvān, ruled 531–579 C.E. On al-Madāʾin, see the article by M. Streck in *EI*², s.v. al-Madāʾin.

486 Al-ʿAtīqa (the Ancient) is Ctesiphon; the White Palace was the old royal residence.

487 Asbānpur (Persian, Aspānbur) is the site of the Audience Hall of Chosroës (Arabic *Īwān Kisrā*), an imposing brick ruin, the only surviving structure from the Sasanian capital, and one of the largest vaults ever constructed in antiquity.

488 Salmān al-Fārisī was a Companion of the Prophet, reputed to have been the first Persian convert to Islam. The site of his tomb in Iraq is now called Salmān Pāk. Ḥudhayfa b. al-Yamān al-ʿAbsī, also a Companion of the Prophet, was an important commander during the Muslim conquest of Iraq.

489 In 136/753, the ʿAbbāsid caliph al-Manṣūr had his powerful—and possibly treacherous—general Abū Muslim killed in his presence at al-Rūmiyya. For an account of the event, see al-Yaʿqūbī, *Taʾrīkh*, 2:438–441.

On the west bank of the Tigris is a city called Bahurasīr and one called Sābāṭ al-Madā'in, one farsakh from Bahurasīr. The towns on the east bank of the Tigris draw their water from the Tigris and those on the west bank from the Euphrates by means of a canal called the King's Canal, which feeds from the Euphrates. All these cities were conquered in the year 14 by Sa'd b. Abī Waqqāṣ.[490]

From al-Madā'in to Wāsiṭ is five stages. The first of them is Dayr al-'Āqūl, which is the main city of the Middle Nahrawān and in which reside a group of leading non-Arab landowners (*dahāqīn ashrāf*). Next comes Jarjarāyā, which is the main city of the Lower Nahrawān and the residence of some Persian nobles; from it came Rajā' b. Abī l-Ḍaḥḥāk and Aḥmad b. al-Khaṣīb.[491] Next comes al-Nu'māniyya, which is the main city of the Upper Zāb; near it are the residences of the Nawbakht family.[492] In the city of al-Nu'māniyya is Dayr Hizqil, in which the mentally ill are treated.[493] Next comes Jabbul, which is a prosperous, ancient city. Next comes Mādarāyā |, which is an ancient residence of non- 322
Arab nobles. Next comes al-Mubārak, an ancient canal. After al-Nu'māniyya, on the west bank of the Tigris, lies the town known as Nu'mābādh, which is a river port from which provisions are transferred from the Tigris to the Nīl Canal. Next comes Nahr Sābus, which is on the west bank and lies across the river from the city of al-Mubārak, on the east bank. From there, one travels by road to the counties of Bādarāyā and Bākusāyā, and then to the Bridges of Khayzurān, traveling along the east bank. Next comes Fam al-Ṣilḥ, where the residences of al-Ḥasan b. Sahl are located. It was to this place that al-Ma'mūn traveled when he visited al-Ḥasan b. Sahl and consummated his marriage to al-Ḥasan's daughter Būrān.[494]

Next comes Wāsiṭ, which is composed of two cities on either bank of the Tigris: the old city is on the east bank of the Tigris, and al-Ḥajjāj had a (new) city built on the west bank and built a bridge of boats between them.[495] In

---

490 14 A.H. = February 25, 635 – February 13, 636.

491 Rajā' b. Abī l-Ḍaḥḥāk was an 'Abbāsid financial administrator and secretary under the caliph al-Ma'mūn (r. 198–218/813–833). Aḥmad b. al-Khaṣīb was vizier under the caliph al-Muntaṣir (r. 247–248/861–862).

492 On this family of courtiers, astrologers, theologians, and littérateurs of 'Abbāsid times, see the article by L. Massignon in *EI*², s.v. Nawbakht.

493 The asylum was well known. A report of a visit to it by the littérateur al-Mubarrad during the caliphate of al-Mutawakkil can be found in al-Mas'ūdī, *Murūj*, 5:9–10 (§ 2883–2884).

494 On this wedding in Ramaḍān 210 (December 825 – January 826), which became famous for its opulent 17-day-long celebration, see the article by Katherine H. Lang in *EI*³, s.v. Būrān. Al-Ya'qūbī gives an account of it in *Ta'rīkh*, 2:559.

495 Al-Ḥajjāj b. Yūsuf was the Umayyad governor of Iraq and later of the East more generally, from 75/694 to 95/713. On the city of Wāsiṭ, see the article in *EI*², s.v. Wāsiṭ.

this western city, al-Ḥajjāj built his palace and the Green Dome, which is called the Green (Dome) of Wāsiṭ,[496] and the Congregational Mosque. It has city walls around it. The governors after al-Ḥajjāj resided there. Yazīd b. ʿUmar b. Hubayra al-Fazārī was there when he was routed by the troops of Qaḥṭaba, and he fortified himself there until he was given safe-conduct.[497] The residents of these two cities are a mixture of Arabs and non-Arabs. Those who are of the (non-Arab) landholding class (*dahāqīn*) reside in the eastern city, which is the city of Kaskar. The land tax of Wāsiṭ is included in the land tax of the counties of the Sawād. The reason it was named Wāsiṭ (Equidistant) is that from it to Basra is 50 farsakhs, to Kufa 50, to al-Ahwāz 50, and to Baghdad 50; therefore it was called Wāsiṭ. Adjacent to it is Nahrabān, where the raw fiber from which Armenian cloth is made is produced. From there it is carried to Armenia, and there it is spun and woven.

Next one reaches ʿAbdāsī, and then al-Madhār, which is the main city of Maysān. The city of al-Madhār is on the Tigris also. Adjoining al-Madhār is the
323 rural district (*kūra*) of Abazqubādh |—the main city is called Fasā. From Wāsiṭ to Basra the route runs through the Baṭā'iḥ Marshes. They are called Baṭā'iḥ[498] because a number of watercourses come together there. One travels from the Baṭā'iḥ via the One-Eyed Tigris (Dijla al-ʿAwrā'),[499] and then one arrives at Basra and anchors on the banks of the Canal of Ibn ʿUmar.

Basra

Basra was the chief city of the world, the storehouse of its commodities and goods. It is an oblong city, its area being two farsakhs by one farsakh according to the original plan that was used to lay it out at the time of its conquest in the reign of ʿUmar b. al-Khaṭṭāb in the year 17.[500] The inner part of the city, which is the part that faces north, runs along two canals. The first is a canal known as the Canal of Ibn ʿUmar, which is the canal ....[501]

---

496 To distinguish it from *the* Green Dome, the palace of the Umayyads in Damascus.

497 Yazīd b. ʿUmar was the last Umayyad governor of Iraq, until early 132/749, when he was forced by ʿAbbāsid troops under the command of the general Qaḥṭaba to fortify himself in Wāsiṭ, only to surrender later that year. See al-Yaʿqūbī, *Taʾrīkh*, 2:411–412.

498 *Baṭāʾiḥ* (pl. of *baṭḥāʾ*) means a broad, low-lying watercourse.

499 In al-Yaʿqūbī's time, both the Tigris and the Euphrates flowed into the swamps (al-Baṭā'iḥ) about 60 miles below Wāsiṭ. The swamps, in turn, drained into the Persian Gulf by the single waterway called Dijla al-ʿAwra' (One-eyed Tigris). See the article by R. Hartmann in *EI*², s.v. Di<u>dj</u>la.

500 17 A.H. = January 23, 638 – January 11, 639.

501 Here there is a long gap in the text. The Leiden editor added the following footnote

∴

[The Western Quarter]

... and Kharshana 500 horsemen, Salūqiya 500 horsemen, Tarāqiya 5,000 horsemen, Maqadūniya 3,000 horsemen.[502] Thus the entire army of the land of the Romans[503]—troops stationed in the rural districts (*rasātīq*) and towns—is 40,000 horsemen. Of these men not a single soldier is paid a regular salary; rather, they station men in every area who go to battle with their *patricius* (*biṭrīq*) in time of war.

We have already mentioned some accounts of the land of the Romans, its manpower, cities, fortresses, ports, mountains, valleys, watercourses, lakes, and places for launching attacks upon it in another book.[504] Here now are the routes to the frontier regions (*al-thughūr*) and that which is adjacent to them.

Whoever wishes to travel from Aleppo by the main road to the west leaves Aleppo for the city of Qinnasrīn, and then to a place called Tall Mannas, which is the first dependency (*ʿamal*) of the military district of Ḥimṣ.[505]

(translated here from Latin): "Ten folia following in the MS are missing, so that the seventh quire is now gone. The part we lack contained the end of the description of Basra, the description of eastern Arabia, Khuzistan, Persia, and India, then the whole northern quarter [cf. note 484 above], and finally the beginning of the western quarter." Parts of the lost section will be found in the "Fragments" section, below.

502 One can infer that the missing section dealt with the Byzantine-Muslim frontier, including the military district (*jund*) of Qinnasrīn and the two frontier regions of al-Thughūr and al-ʿAwāṣim. It also appears to have given details about Byzantine military arrangements, including, as these figures suggest, troop deployments in Anatolia. These may reflect the Byzantine system of military themes (districts). "Kharshana" is the Charsianon theme, "Salūqiya" is the Seleucia theme, "Tarāqiya" apparently stands for the Thracesion theme—these lying in Anatolia—while "Maqadūniya" stands for Macedonia. Some other excerpts from this missing section appear in the "Fragments" section, below.

503 Arabic *al-Rūm*. Most historians writing in English would call them *Byzantines*; Arabic, however, maintains the self-designation of the rulers of the Eastern Roman Empire, who continued to call themselves *Romans* long after the administrative language had become Greek. Translators often render *al-Rūm* as 'Greeks,' mistakenly implying that these areas were populated by ethnic Greeks. In the text, *al-Rūm* will be rendered 'Roman(s).' In the footnotes, either 'Roman' or 'Byzantine' will be used according to context and convenience.

504 The other book to which al-Yaʿqūbī refers apparently is not his *History*, but a separate monograph on Byzantium. It has not survived.

505 A *jund* was one of the five military districts into which the province of al-Shām (Syria)

324

The Military District (Jund) *of Ḥimṣ*

Thence one travels to the city of Hama,[506] an old city on a river called the Orontes.[507] The populace of this city is a group from the tribal faction of Yemen, and the majority are from Bahrāʾ and Tanūkh. From the city of Hama one proceeds to the city of al-Rastan, then to the city of Ḥimṣ.

The city of Ḥimṣ is one of the most spacious cities of Syria, and it has a great river from which the people obtain their water.[508] The people of of Ḥimṣ are entirely from the tribal faction of Yemen: from Ṭayyiʾ, Kinda, Ḥimyar, Kalb, Hamdān, and other tribes of Yemen. Abū ʿUbayda b. al-Jarrāḥ[509] conquered the city by treaty in the year 16,[510] but the city rebelled after the conquest, so he made a treaty with its people a second time.

The subdistricts (*āqālīm*) of Ḥimṣ include: Al-Tamah,[511] whose people are from Kalb; al-Rastan; Hama, which is a city on a great river and whose people are from Bahrāʾ and Tanūkh; Ṣawwarān, where there is a group from Iyād; Salamiyya, a city in the hinterland built by ʿAbdallāh b. Ṣāliḥ b. ʿAlī b. ʿAbdallāh b. ʿAbbās b. ʿAbd al-Muṭṭalib,[512] who dug a canal to it and irrigated the soil in order to cultivate saffron and whose populace consists of descendants of ʿAbdallāh b. Ṣāliḥ al-Hāshimī, their clients (*mawālī*), and a mixture of people who are merchants and farmers; Tadmur (Palmyra), an old city of marvelous construction, said to have been built by Sulaymān b. Dāwūd the prophet—God's peace be upon him—because of its many wonderful monuments and

---

was divided. See the article by D. Sourdel in *EI*², s.v. Djund. Al-Yaʿqūbī's original text also included a description of the *jund* of Qinnasrīn in the north, but that section is missing. Some passages from this lost Qinnasrīn section have been included in the "Fragments" section, below.

506 Arabic Ḥamāt or Ḥamāh; see the article by D. Sourdel in in *EI*², s.v. Ḥamāt.

507 Al-Yaʿqūbī gives the name of the Orontes river in a form (*al-Urunṭ*) taken directly from Greek. The more common name of the river in Arabic is al-ʿĀṣī. See the article by R. Hartmann in *EI*², s.v. al-ʿĀṣī.

508 On Ḥimṣ (ancient Emessa, modern Homs), see the article by N. Elisséeff in *EI*², s.v. Ḥimṣ. The river is the Orontes.

509 Abū ʿUbayda was an early Companion of the Prophet and one of the principal commanders of the Muslim conquest of Syria and Palestine. See the article by Khalil Athamina in *EI*³, s.v. Abū ʿUbayda ʿĀmir b. al-Jarrāḥ.

510 16 A.H. = February 2, 637 – January 22, 638.

511 De Goeje notes that the reading of this name is uncertain. In his note on the relevant passage in Ibn Khurdādhbih, he suggests an alternate reading: al-Bamah. See Ibn Khurdādhbih, *Kitāb al-Masālik waʾl-mamālik*, 76.

512 ʿAbdallāh b. Ṣāliḥ was a prominent member of a branch of the ʿAbbāsid ruling family noted especially for their ties to Syria.

whose people are from Kalb; Tall Mannas, a settlement of Iyād, built as a residence by Ibn Abī Du'ād;[513] Ma'arrat al-Nu'mān, an old city in ruins, whose people are from Tanūkh; al-Bāra, whose people are from Bahrā'; Fāmiya,[514] an old Greek city in ruins on a large lake, its people being from 'Udhra and Bahrā'; the city of Shayzar, whose people are a group from Kinda; the city of Kafarṭāb; and al-Aṭmīm, which is an old city whose people are a group from the tribal faction of Yemen, from all the tribes, but mostly from Kinda.

There are four cities on the seacoast of the military district of Ḥimṣ: Latakia, whose people are a group from | Yemen, from the tribes of Salīḥ, Zubayd, 325
Hamdān, Yaḥṣub, and others; Jabala, whose people are from Hamdān, but which also includes groups from Qays and from Iyād; Bulunyās, with a mixed population; and Anṭarṭūs,[515] whose people are a group from Kinda. The usual official land tax from Ḥimṣ, excluding royal estates, is 220,000 dinars.

The Military District of Damascus

From Ḥimṣ to the city of Damascus is four stages. The first stage is Jūsiya, which is in (the military district of) Ḥimṣ. The second is Qārā, which is the first dependency (*'amal*) of the military district of Damascus. The third is al-Quṭayyifa, where there are residences that belonged to Hishām b. 'Abd al-Malik b. Marwān.[516] From there one continues to the city of Damascus.

Whoever travels from Ḥimṣ along the Post Road (Ṭarīq al-Barīd) takes it from Jūsiya to al-Biqā', then to the city of Baalbek, which is one of the most majestic cities of Syria. In it there is a wondrous building of stone and a wondrous spring from which issues a great river. Inside the city are gardens and orchards. From the city of Baalbek one proceeds to 'Aqabat al-Rummān (Pomegranate Pass), then to the city of Damascus.

The city of Damascus is an old, majestic city.[517] It was the main city of Syria in the Days of Ignorance (*al-Jāhiliyya*) as well as the Days of Islam. It has no peer in all the military districts of Syria in the number of its waterways and buildings. Its main river is called the Baradā. The city of Damascus was conquered in the caliphate of 'Umar b. al-Khaṭṭāb in the year 14 by Abū 'Ubayda b. al-Jarrāḥ, who

---

513 Aḥmad b. Abī Du'ād (d. 240/854) was chief judge under the 'Abbāsids, first under al-Mu'taṣim (r. 218/833–227/842) and continuing until the year 232/846, in the reign of al-Mutawakkil.

514 Classical Apamea.

515 De Goeje notes that the MS clearly marks this toponym as "Anẓarẓūs" instead of its more common name.

516 Umayyad caliph, reigned 105/724–125/743.

517 On the city of Damascus, see the article by N. Elisséeff in *EI*², s.v. Dimashq.

entered it by one of its gates, called the Jābiya Gate, under a peace agreement (*ṣulḥ*) after a year's siege.[518] Khālid b. al-Walīd entered from another of its gates, called the Eastern Gate, without a peace agreement, but Abū ʿUbayda extended the treaty status to the entire city. They wrote to ʿUmar b. al-Khaṭṭāb and he
326 confirmed what Abū | ʿUbayda had done.[519]

Damascus was a residence of the kings of Ghassān, and the city contains the remains of buildings that once belonged to the family of Jafna.[520] The majority of the people of the city of Damascus belong to the tribal grouping of Yemen. There is also a group from Qays and the residences of the Banū Umayya. Their palaces make up most of the residences. There is also the Green (Dome) of Muʿāwiya, which is the Governor's Residence,[521] and its mosque. None more beautiful than it exists in Islam in terms of its marble and gilded decoration. Al-Walīd b. ʿAbd al-Malik b. Marwān built it during his caliphate.[522]

The military district of Damascus has the following rural districts (*kuwar*): Al-Ghūṭa, whose people are from Ghassān and from the tribal faction of Qays, but who also include a group from Rabīʿa; Ḥawrān, whose main city is Buṣrā[523] and whose people are a group from the Banū Murra of Qays, except for al-Suwaydā, where there is a group from Kalb; al-Bathaniyya, whose main city is Adhriʿāt and whose people are a group from the tribal faction of Yemen and a group from Qays; al-Ẓāhir, whose main city is Amman; and al-Ghawr, whose main city is Jericho.[524] These last two cities comprise the territory of al-Balqāʾ.

---

518 Accordding to al-Ṭabarī, *Taʾrīkh*, 2:2146, Damascus fell in Rajab of the year 14 (August–September 635).

519 Al-Yaʿqūbī's point is to affirm that Damascus's status under Islamic law was that of property taken by treaty, not by conquest. This was something of a dilemma as, according to traditional accounts of the conquest of the city (which al-Yaʿqūbī follows), half of the city was conquered by force by Khālid b. al-Walīd, while the other half simultaneously surrendered peaceably to Abū ʿUbayda.

520 The clan of Jafna (Arabic *Āl Jafna*) was one of the ruling clans of the Ghassānids. The Ghassānids were Christian Arabs who functioned as auxiliaries for the Byzantine empire on its Syrian frontier, just as the Lakhmids in Iraq functioned for the Sasanians. See the article by Irfan Shahîd in *EI*^{2}, s.v. Ghassān.

521 Muʿāwiya b. Abī Sufyān (r. 41/661–60/680) was governor of Syria and founder and first caliph of the Umayyad dynasty. His primary residence, and that of his descendants, was Damascus, where his green-domed palace was a prominent landmark.

522 That is, al-Walīd I, ruled 86/705–96/715.

523 On the history of Buṣrā (ancient Bostra), see the article by A. Abel in *EI*^{2}, s.v. Boṣrā.

524 Arabic Rīḥā, corrected by another hand in the MS to Arīḥā, the longer form of the name. See the article by E. Honigmann in *EI*^{2}, s.v. Rīḥā.

Its people are a group from Qays, and there is also a group from Quraysh. Then there is Jibāl,[525] whose its main city is ʿArandal and whose people are a group from Ghassān, Balqayn, and others. Then there are Maʾāb and Zughar, which have a mixed population. Near them is a village called Muʾta, where Jaʿfar b. Abī Ṭālib, Zayd b. Ḥāritha, and ʿAbdallāh b. Rawāḥa were killed.[526] Then there is al-Sharāt, whose main city is Adhruḥ and whose people are clients of the Banū Hāshim. In it lies al-Ḥumayma, the residence of ʿAlī b. ʿAbdallāh b. al-ʿAbbās b. ʿAbd al-Muṭṭalib and his descendants.[527] Then there is al-Jawlān,[528] whose main city is Bāniyās and whose people are a group from Qays, most of them Banū Murra, but also a small group from the tribal faction of Yemen. Then there is Jabal Sanīr, whose people are from Banū Ḍabba, | but where there is also 327
a group from Kalb. Then there is Baalbek, whose people are a group of Persians, and in whose outskirts are a group from the tribal faction of Yemen. Then there is Jabal al-Jalīl, whose people are a group from ʿĀmila. Then there is Lebanon, (whose main city is) Sidon, where there are groups from Quraysh and from the tribal grouping of Yemen.[529]

The military district of Damascus has the following rural districts (*kuwar*) along the seacoast: the rural district of ʿIrqa, which has an old city, where there are a group of Persians who had been transferred there and also a group from the Banū Ḥanīfa tribe of Rabīʿa; the city of Tripoli, whose people are a group of Persians that Muʿāwiya b. Abī Sufyān moved there—they have a wonderful port that can harbor a thousand ships; Jubayl, Sidon, and Beirut—the people

525 More frequently al-Jibāl (with the article), an area southeast of the Dead Sea (not to be confused with Jibāl province in northwestern Iran); see the article by J. Sourdel-Thomine in *EI*², s.v. al-Djibāl.

526 The Battle of Muʾta, in southern Jordan, took place in Jumādā I of the year 8 (August–September 629) and was the first Muslim military encounter with the Byzantines. The Muslims were defeated, and three of the commanders whom the Prophet sent to lead the expedition were killed, including his cousin Jaʿfar and the poet Ibn Rawāḥa. Al-Yaʿqūbī gives an account of the expedition in *Taʾrīkh*, 2:66–67.

527 ʿAlī b. ʿAbdallāh al-Hāshimī was the grandfather of the first two ʿAbbāsid caliphs, al-Saffāḥ and al-Manṣūr. The Umayyad caliph al-Walīd I exiled him to his estate at al-Ḥumayma for plotting against the Umayyads, and he died there in 117/735 or 118/736. The estate subsequently became a hub of activity for the ʿAbbāsid cause under his son, Muḥammad.

528 The Golan in southwestern Syria; see the article by D. Sourdel in *EI*², s.v. al-Djawlān.

529 The Leiden text reads: *wa-Lubnān Ṣaydā wa-bihā qawm min Quraysh wa-min al-Yaman*. Given the repetitive structuring of the sentences in this section, one can assume that the phrase *wa-madīnatuhā* (and its city is) has been dropped out between the toponyms "Lubnān" and "Ṣaydā."

of all these rural districts are a group of Persians that Muʿāwiya b. Abī Sufyān moved there.

Abū ʿUbayda b. al-Jarrāḥ conquered all the rural districts (*kuwar*) of Damascus in the caliphate of ʿUmar b. al-Khaṭṭāb in the year 14.[530] The land tax of (the military district of) Damascus, excluding royal estates, amounts to 300,000 dinars.

The Military District of Jordan[531]

From the city of Damascus to the military district of Jordan is four stages. The first is Jāsim, a dependency (*ʿamal*) of Damascus; then Khisfīn, also a dependency of Damascus; then Fīq, with its well-known pass. One goes from there to the city of Tiberias,[532] which is the main city of (the military district of) Jordan. It is at the foot of a mountain on a majestic lake from which flows the famous river Jordan. In the city of Tiberias there are hot springs that flow summer and winter without interruption, so that hot water flows into their bath-houses without their needing fuel for this purpose. The people of the city of Tiberias are tribesmen from the Ashʿar, who are the majority there.

The military district of Jordan has the following rural districts (*kuwar*): Tyre, which is the main city of the coast. The arsenal (*dār al-ṣināʿa*) from which the warships of the regime (*sulṭān*) sail to raid the Greeks is located there. The city is fortified and majestic and is inhabited by a mixture of peoples. The city of Acre is also on the coast. Qadas is one of the most majestic of rural districts. Then come Baysān, Faḥl, Jarash, and al-Sawād: the people of these rural districts are
328 a mixture of | Arabs and non-Arabs.

The rural districts of Jordan were conquered in the caliphate of ʿUmar b. al-Khaṭṭāb by Abū ʿUbayda b. al-Jarrāḥ, except for the city of Tiberias, whose people sued for a treaty of peace. Other rural districts of the military district of Jordan were conquered by Khālid b. al-Walīd and ʿAmr b. al-ʿĀṣ[533] under the authority of Abū ʿUbayda b. al-Jarrāḥ in the year 14.[534] The land tax of the military district of Jordan, excluding royal estates, amounts to 100,000 dinars.

---

530 14 A.H. = February 25, 635 – February 13, 636.

531 For an overall account of the Islamic administrative area of Jordan (al-Urdunn), which was only partly coterminous with the modern state of Jordan, see the article by F. Buhl, C. E. Bosworth, P. M. Cobb, C. E. Bosworth, and Mary C. Wilson in EI^2, s.v. al-Urdunn.

532 Arabic Ṭabariyya; see the article by M. Lavergne in EI^2, s.v. Ṭabariyya.

533 ʿAmr b. al-ʿĀṣ (d. c. 42/663) was an early Muslim commander best known as the conqueror and first governor of Egypt. For an overview of his life, see the article by Khaled M. G. Keshk in EI^3, s.v. ʿAmr b. al-ʿĀṣ.

534 14 A.H. = February 25, 635 – February 13, 636.

The Military District of Palestine[535]

From the military district of Jordan to the military district of Palestine is three stages. The old main city of Palestine was a city called Ludd. However, when Sulaymān b. ʿAbd al-Malik became caliph,[536] he had the city of al-Ramla built; he destroyed the city of Ludd and transferred the people of Ludd to al-Ramla.[537]

Al-Ramla is the main city of Palestine. It has a small river, from which its people obtain drinking water, and the Abū Fuṭrus river is about 12 Arab miles from the city. The people of al-Ramla drink water from wells and from cisterns into which the rainwater flows. The people of the city are a mixture of Arabs and non-Arabs, and its non-Muslims[538] are Samaritans.

Palestine has the following districts (*kuwar*): Īliyā, which is Jerusalem,[539] in which are the monuments[540] of the prophets—God's peace be upon them; Ludd,[541] whose main city is still standing in its original state, but in ruins; ʿAmwās;[542] Nablus, an old city, site of the two holy mountains,[543] under which lies a city carved in the rock, | its people being a mixture of Arabs, non-Arabs, 329
and Samaritans; Sebastia,[544] which is a dependency of Nablus; Caesarea,[545] a

---

535 On the history of Islamic Palestine (Filasṭīn), see the article by D. Sourdel in EI^2, s.v. Filasṭīn.

536 The Umayyad caliph Sulaymān b. ʿAbd al-Malik ruled from 96–99 (February 715 to September 717).

537 As noted also in al-Yaʿqūbī, *Taʾrīkh*, 2:351. Ludd is ancient Lydda (modern Lod). On al-Ramla, see the article by E. Honigmann in EI^2, s.v. al-Ramla.

538 Arabic *dhimmatuhā*, (its *dhimmīs*), that is, its non-Muslims monotheists granted a promise (*dhimma*) of protection against the payment of a poll tax. See the article by Yohanan Friedman in EI^3, s.v. Dhimma.

539 The Arabic name used here, *Bayt al-Maqdis* (House of the Sanctuary), echoes the Aramaic *Bēt Maqdšā* and the Hebrew *Bayt ha-Miqdāsh*, both designations of the Temple. A shorter form of the same name is al-Quds, the usual name for Jerusalem in older and modern Arabic. Jerusalem was also called Īliyā, from its Roman name Aelia. See the article by S. D. Goitein and O. Grabar in EI^2, s.v. al-Ḳuds.

540 Arabic *āthār al-anbiyāʾ*, literally, "the vestiges, or relics, of the prophets."

541 Arabic Ludd corresponds to ancient Lydda (Hebrew Lod); see the article by M. Sharon in EI^2, s.v. Ludd.

542 On ʿAmwās (or ʿAmawās, ancient Emmaus), see the article by J. Sourdel-Thomine in EI^2, s.v. ʿAmwās.

543 That is, Mount Gerizim in the south and Mount Ebal in the north. On the role of these two mountains among the Jews and Samaritans, see Deuteronomy 27; on Nablus, see the article by F. Buhl in EI^2, s.v. Nābulus.

544 Arabic Sabasṭiyya; also known as Samaria.

545 Arabic Qayṣāriyya; see the article by M. Sharon in EI^2, s.v. Ḳayṣariyya, Ḳayṣāriyya.

city on the coast, one of the most impregnable cities of Palestine, and the last of the region's cities to be conquered, namely by Muʿāwiya b. Abī Sufyān in the caliphate of ʿUmar b. al-Khaṭṭāb; and Yubnā,[546] which is an old city on a hill. It is this city of which it is related that Usāma b. Zayd said: "When the Messenger of God—God's blessing and peace be upon him—sent me (to Syria on campaign), he gave me an order, saying: 'Go to Yubnā early in the morning, and burn it down.'"[547] The people of this city are a group of Samaritans. Then there are: Jaffa on the coast, which the people of al-Ramla use as a port; Bayt Jibrīn, an old city whose people are a group from Judhām and near which is the Dead Sea, from which is extracted *ḥumara*, which is bitumen (*mūmiyā*); ʿAsqalān[548] on the coast; Gaza[549] on the coast, it being the first part of the third clime and containing the tomb of Hāshim b. ʿAbd Manāf.[550] The populace of the military district of Palestine is a mixture of Arabs from Lakhm, Judhām, ʿĀmila, Kinda, Qays, and Kināna.

The land of Palestine was conquered in the year 16 after a lengthy siege that lasted until ʿUmar b. al-Khaṭṭāb went out (from Medina) and granted a treaty to the populace of the district (*kūra*) of Īliyā, which is Bayt al-Maqdis (Jerusalem).[551] They had said: "We will not agree to a treaty except with the caliph himself." So he went to them and granted them a treaty. Most of the rural districts of Palestine were conquered, except for Caesarea; Abū ʿUbayda b. al-Jarrāḥ made Muʿāwiya b. Abī Sufyān his deputy over them, and he conquered

---

546 Ancient Iamnia, Hebrew Yavneh.

547 In the last year of his life, Muḥammad sent Usāma b. Zayd in an expedition against the Byzantines to avenge the defeat the Muslims had suffered at Mut'a, where Usāma b. Zayd's father had been killed. Because of Muḥammad's sudden illness and death, the expedition did not leave until after Abū Bakr had become caliph. Accounts may be found in al-Ṭabarī, *Taʾrīkh*, 1:1794–1797, 1845–1851, and al-Wāqidī, *Maghāzī*, 3:1117–1127. In neither account is the place to be attacked and burned called Yubnā. In al-Ṭabarī it is called Ābil, and in al-Wāqidī it is called Ubnā, and is located near Mu'ta, where Zayd's father had been killed. De Goeje's note in the Leiden edition of the *Geography* discusses how an original reading of Ābil may have been transformed into Yubnā.

548 On ʿAsqalān (modern Ashkelon), see the article by Amalia Levanoni in *EI*[3], s.v. ʿAsqalān.

549 On Gaza (Arabic, Ghazza), see the article by D. Sourdel in *EI*[2], s.v. G͟hazza.

550 Great-grandfather of the Prophet Muḥammad. He is said to have died in Gaza while engaged in trade there.

551 According to al-Ṭabarī, *Taʾrīkh*, 1:2408, Jerusalem and its region were conquered in Rabīʿ II of the year 16 (May 637).

Caesarea in the year 18.[552] The total land tax of the military district of Palestine in addition to that accruing from the (royal) estates amounts to 300,000 dinars.

Whoever wishes to travel by road from Syria via Palestine to Mecca passes
through rugged, | rough mountainous terrain until he reaches Ayla[553] and then 330
Madyan.[554] Then he continues along the road with the people from Egypt and the Maghrib.

Egypt and Its Rural Districts[555]

Whoever leaves Palestine heading west, bound for Egypt, leaves al-Ramla for the city of Yubnā and then to the city of ʿAsqalān on the coast. Then he continues to the city of Gaza, also on the coast, and to Rafaḥ, which is the last of the dependencies (*aʿmāl*) of Syria (*al-Shaʾm*).[556]

Then he continues to a place called al-Shajaratān,[557] which marks the border of Egypt, and then to al-ʿArīsh,[558] which is the first of the outposts (*masāliḥ*) and dependencies (*aʿmāl*) of Egypt. Al-ʿArīsh is inhabited by tribesmen from Judhām and other tribes and is a coastal town. One continues from al-ʿArīsh to a town called al-Baqqāra, and from there to a town called al-Warrāda amid hills of sand.

Then one continues to al-Faramā, which is the first city of Egypt. It has a mixed population. It is three Arab miles between the city and the Green Sea.[559] From al-Faramā to a town called Jurjīr is one stage, and from it to a town called

---

552 As al-Ṭabarī, *Taʾrīkh*, 1:2579, notes, the dates for the conquest of Caesarea are given variously as 16, 19, and 20 (he does not mention 18, and places the narrative of the conquest under the year 15). 18 A.H. = January 12, 639 – January 1, 640. The length of the siege may have been responsible for the variation in dates. The article by M. Sharon in *EI*², s.v. Ḳayṣariyya, Ḳayṣāriyya, gives Shawwāl 19 (September–October 640) as the date.

553 On Ayla (Biblical Elath, modern Eilat), see the article by Michael Lecker in *EI*³, s.v. Ayla.

554 On the town of Madyan in northwestern Arabia, see the article by F. Buhl and C. E. Bosworth in in *EI*², s.v. Madyan Shuʿayb.

555 The material on Egypt in the Fragments indicates that this section may originally have been longer.

556 On Rafaḥ, see the article by M. A. Bakhit in *EI*², s.v. Rafaḥ. By "last of the dependencies of Syria," al-Yaʿqūbī means that Rafaḥ was close to the border between Egypt and the four military districts into which Greater Syria (al-Shaʾm) was divided, one of which was the military district (*jund*) of Palestine, to which Rafaḥ belonged.

557 The name means Two Trees; no precise location is known.

558 On al-ʿArīsh, see the article by F. Buhl in *EI*², s.v. al-ʿArīsh.

559 That is, the Mediterranean.

Fāqūs is one stage. From Fāqūs one goes to a town called Ghayfa, and then to al-Fusṭāṭ.[560]

Al-Fusṭāṭ used to be known as Babylon,[561] and it is the place now known as al-Qaṣr (the Palace).[562] When ʿAmr b. al-ʿĀṣ conquered Babylon in the caliphate of ʿUmar b. al-Khaṭṭāb in the year 20,[563] the Arab tribes marked out allotments around the tent (*fusṭāṭ*) of ʿAmr b. al-ʿĀṣ, and for that reason it was named al-Fusṭāṭ. Then they spread out over the land and marked out allotments along the Nile—each Arab tribe marked out its allotment in the place assigned to it. ʿAmr b. al-ʿĀṣ built the congregational mosque and the governor's residence, known
331 as Dār al-Raml (Sand House), | and set the markets around the congregational mosque on the east bank of the Nile. He established a guard post (*maḥras*) and a commandant (*ʿarīf*) for every tribe. He built the fortress of Giza on the west bank of the Nile, made it a garrison for the Muslims, and settled tribesmen there. He wrote announcing this to ʿUmar b. al-Khaṭṭāb, who wrote back saying, "Do not put any body of water between me and the Muslims." ʿAmr conquered the districts (*kuwar*) of Egypt by treaty, except for Alexandria. He continued fighting the people of that city for three years, conquering it in the year 23,[564] for there was no other city like it in the country in impregnability, size, and materiel.

The rural districts (*kuwar*) of Egypt are named for their main cities, since every district has a main city noted for some particular feature. Among the cities and rural districts of Upper Egypt are: the city of Memphis, standing, but in ruins (the people of Egypt say that it is the city in which Pharaoh lived); the city of Būṣīr Kūrīdis; the city of Dilāṣ, after which Dilāṣī bridles are named; the city of al-Fayyūm (in earlier times people used to say "Egypt and al-Fayyūm," due to the importance of al-Fayyūm and its extensive agriculture—it produces

---

560 On al-Fusṭāṭ, just south of modern Cairo and the first city to be founded in Egypt by its Muslim conquerors, see the article by J. Jomier in *EI*^{2}, s.v. al-Fusṭāṭ.

561 Arabic, Bābalyūn (as emended by the Leiden editor): the MS reads Bāb al-Nūn, as if the copyist understood it to mean "Gate of the Fish." Babylon was the old Roman fortress at the head of the Delta, now located in Old Cairo. The name probably goes back to ancient Egyptian Pi-Hapi-n-On, which the Greeks identified with the name of the Mesopotamian city of Babylon. See the article by C. H. Becker in *EI*^{2}, s.v. Bābalyūn.

562 This may refer to the palace built by Aḥmad b. Ṭūlūn in his new capital, al-Qaṭāʾiʿ, north of al-Fusṭāṭ. The palace was demolished after the fall of the Ṭūlūnids in 292/905, but the mosque, completed in 265/879, still stands. See the article by J. Jomier in *EI*^{2}, s.v. al-Fusṭāṭ.

563 The fortress of Babylon fell to the Arabs on 21 Rabīʿ II 20 (April 9, 641).

564 23 A.H. = November 18, 643 – November 6, 644; however, various dates are given, mostly earlier, in 21 or 22; see al-Ṭabarī, *Taʾrīkh*, 2:2580–2581. The confusion may have to do with the fact that Alexandria revolted after its conquest and had to be reconquered.

excellent wheat, and flax-cloth[565] is made there); the city of al-Qays (Qaysī robes and fine wool garments are made there); the city of al-Bahnasā (Bahnasī curtains are made there); the city of Ahnās (garments are made there and there are lebbek trees there);[566] the city of Ṭaḥā (it produces excellent wheat and the earthenware jugs [*kīzān*] that the people of Egypt call *bawāqīl*); Anṣinā, an old city on the east bank of the Nile (Pharaoh's magicians are said to have come from there and some magic is said to remain there); the city of al-Ushmūnayn, one of Egypt's largest cities (the swiftest horses, mules, and beasts of burden are there); the city of Asyut, one of Upper Egypt's largest cities (scarlet textiles are made there that resemble Armenian cloth); Qahqāwa, near which are an old | city called Būtīj and a city called Bushmūr, which produces variegated 332
Yūsufī wheat;[567] the city of Akhmīm[568] with a riverfront on the east bank of the Nile (*qaṭūʿ* textiles[569] and Akhmīmī hides are made there, and also there is the monastery known as Dayr Bū Shanūda, which is said to contain the tomb of two of Christ's disciples); and the city of Abshāya, also called al-Bulyanā.[570]

---

565 Arabic *khaysh*, a course flax cloth; in modern Egyptian Arabic the word means burlap.

566 Arabic *shajar al-labkh*, would seem to refer specifically the lebbek tree, Albizia lebbek, a large member of the mimosa family with showy seed-pods, but other identifications are possible.

567 Arabic *al-qamḥ al-yūsufī al-mujazzaʿ*. The nature of this variety of wheat is unknown. *Yūsufī* means that its origin was ascribed to Joseph, presumably when he served as Pharaoh's minister as described in the Qurʾān and the Bible. *Mujazzaʿ* normally means "opalescent" or "variegated." The same variety is mentioned in al-Masʿūdī, *Kitāb al-Tanbīh wa-l-ishrāf*, 22 ("Yusūfi wheat, which is the wheat with the largest grains, longest shape, and heaviest weight"), though without mention of the town of Bushmūr. In fact, de Goeje's textual apparatus calls the reading *Bushmūr* suspect (the word is undotted in the MS). Al-Masʿūdī, who does not mention Bushmūr, implies that Yusūfī wheat was produced in the Delta, and Yāqūt, *Buldān*, 1:634, locates al-Bushmūr (sic) near Dumyāṭ. S. Timm, *Das christlich-koptische Ägypten in arabischer Zeit*, 1:354–356, discusses the the location of the town, which Timm would place in the Delta, al-Yaʿqūbī's testimony notwithstanding. Yāqūt, *Buldān*, 1:755, lists Būtīj as a small town (*bulayda*) on the west bank of the Nile in the nearer part of Upper Egypt, another reason to suspect the reading *Bushmūr*. All that can be said, therefore, is that this variety of wheat may have been grown both in the Delta (according to al-Masʿūdī) and in Upper Egypt (according to al-Yaʿqūbī).

568 On Akhmīm (or Ikhmīm), see the article by Petra M. Sijpesteijn in *EI*³, s.v., Akhmīm.

569 Arabic *al-farsh* (or, *al-furush*) *al-quṭūʿ*: some sort of textile for use in carpeting or blankets; the exact meaning cannot be determined.

570 On al-Bulyanā, see Timm, *Ägypten*, 1:312–314. Al-Yaʿqūbī may be confused about the other place-name, Abshāya. Timm, *Ägypten*, 3:1140–1147 locates an Ibṣāy/Ibshāy at nearby al-Mansha, Coptic Psoi, Greek Ptolemais Hermiou, just upstream from Akhmīm.

From Abshāya, you travel to the oases through desert wastes and rugged mountains for six stages. Then you proceed to the Outer Oasis.[571] It is a country with forts, cultivated fields, bubbling springs, flowing waters, date palms, different varieties of trees, vines, rice fields, and more; then to the Inner Oasis.[572] It has a city called al-Farfarūn with a mixed population of Egyptians and others. [If you do not travel to the oases, you continue] from the city of Abshāya, which is called the city of al-Bulyanā, to the city of Hū. The city of Hū is an old city that used to have four rural districts (*kuwar*): Hū and Dandara on the west
333 bank of the Nile, Fāw and Qinā on the east | bank. The city fell into ruins and its population declined due to the large number of bedouins, rebels, and bandits of the region who went out to it. The people moved away from it to more prosperous places.

It is two stages from the city of Hū to the city of Qifṭ on the east bank.[573] It contains monuments of the kings of the Ancients and a temple. From Qifṭ you travel to the emerald mines. It is a mine called Kharibat al-Malik (the King's Ruin), eight stages from the city of Qifṭ. There are two mountains there: one called al-ʿArūs (the Bridegroom), the other al-Khaṣūm (the Quarreler). Both contain emerald mines. There is a place there called Kawm al-Ṣābūnī, (as well as) Kawm Muhrān, Makābir, and Safsīd. All these places contain mines in which gemstones are found—the pits from which the gems are extracted are called *shiyam*, or, in the singular, *shīma*. There used to be an old mine there called Bīrūmīṭ.[574] It was in use in pre-Islamic days, as was the mine of Makābir. From the mine called Kharibat al-Malik to Jabal Ṣāʿid, which is a gold mine, is one stage. Then one travels to a place called al-Kalbī, a place called al-Shukrī, a place called al-ʿIjlī, a place called al-ʿAllāqī al-Adnā,[575] and a place called al-Rīfa, which is the port of Kharibat al-Malik. All these places are gold mines. From Kharibat (al-Malik) to a gold mine called Raḥam is three stages. At Raḥam there are tribesmen from Balī, Juhayna, and a mixture of other people who are visited for the purpose of conducting trade. These are the mines of precious stones and the gold mines that are in close proximity to them.

---

571 Arabic *al-Wāḥ al-Khārija*, that is, Kharga Oasis. See the article by Ayman F. Sayyid in *EI*², s.v. al-Wāḥāt.

572 Arabic *al-Wāḥ al-Dākhila*, that is, Dakhla Oasis.

573 On Qifṭ, ancient Coptos, see the article by J.-C. Garcin in *EI*², s.v. Ḳifṭ.

574 Reading uncertain.

575 I.e., "Nearer al-ʿAllāqī", to distinguish it from the better-known al-ʿAllāqī (*tout court*), located some distance to the south.

From the city of Qifṭ (one continues) to the city of Luxor.[576] It is a city that has fallen into ruin, and the city | of Qūṣ on the east bank of the Nile has taken 334
its place.[577] The rural district (*kūra*) and city of Isnā are on the west bank of the Nile.[578] It is said that its people are (called) al-Marīs; Marīsī donkeys come from here.[579] Then the rural district (*kūra*) of Edfu,[580] on the west bank of the Nile; the rural district (*kūra*) of Binbān, on the west bank; then the great city of Aswan.[581] Merchants from the mines are there, and it is on the east bank of the Nile. It has many date palms and cultivated fields and merchandise brought from the lands of the Nubians and of the Buja.[582] The last city of the lands of Islam in this direction is a city on an island in the middle of the Nile called Philae,[583] which is enclosed by stone walls. Then comes the frontier with the lands of Nubia at a place called al-Qaṣr at a distance of one mile from Philae.

The Gold Mines

Whoever wishes to travel to the mines—the gold mines—leaves Aswan for a place called al-Ḍayqa, between two mountains, then to al-Buwayb, then to al-Bayḍiyya, then to Bayt Ibn Ziyād, then to ʿUdhayfir, then to Jabal al-Aḥmar, then to Jabal al-Bayāḍ, then to Qabr Abī Masʿūd, then to [...],[584] then to Wādī l-ʿAllāqī.[585] All these places are gold mines to which prospectors flock. Wādī l-ʿAllāqī is like a large city with a large number of people and a mixture of Arab and non-Arab prospectors. It also has markets and commodities for sale. They obtain their water from wells dug in the Wādī l-ʿAllāqī. Most of the people at al-ʿAllāqī are tribesmen from the Rabīʿa from the Banū Ḥanīfa, people originally

576 Arabic *al-Aqṣur* or *al-Uqṣur* (the Palaces), named for its monumental ruins of Pharaonic temples; see the article by U. Haarmann in *EI*², s.v. al-Uḳṣur.

577 Qūṣ, in fact, is some 30 km north of Luxor; see the article by J.-Cl. Garcin in *EI*², s.v. Ḳūṣ.

578 On Isnā (modern Esna), see the article by H. Ritter in *EI*², s.v. Isna.

579 Here al-Yaʿqūbī seems to be confused, for the term al-Marīs (from Coptic MA-PHC, denoting the southern lands of Egypt), designates the northernmost Nubian kingdom, beginning south of Aswan. See the article by S. Munro-Hay in in *EI*², s.v. Marīs. See also, Timm, *Ägypten*, 4:1590–1592, who suggests that a settlement by this name was located south of al-Ashmunein.

580 Arabic *Atfū*; on Edfu, see the article by G. Wiet in *EI*², s.v. Adfū.

581 On Aswan (ancient Syene, Arabic Aswān or Uswān) see the articles by J. Cl. Garcin in *EI*², s.v. Uswān, and by Johanna Pink in *EI*³, s.v. Aswan.

582 Al-Yaʿqūbī will soon devote a full section to the Buja (also known as Bija or Beja).

583 Arabic *Bilāq*, derived from Coptic *Pilāk*.

584 The undotted letters are too ambiguous to read.

585 Wādī l-ʿAllāqī in Lower Nubia extends to the east of Lake Nasser, starting about 100 km (62 miles) south of Aswan; see the article by G. Wiet in *EI*², s.v. al-ʿAllāḳī.

from al-Yamāma who moved there with their women and children. Wādī l-ʿAllāqī and its environs are mines for gold. The people work in every nearby spot. Each group of merchants and others has black slaves working in the pits. They bring out the gold in a form like yellow arsenic, and then it is smelted.

335 From al-ʿAllāqī to a place called | Wādī l-[...][586] is one stage. Then (the traveler continues) to a place called [...],[587] then to a place called [...],[588] where people gather in search of gold. There are Rabīʿa tribesmen from al-Yamāma there. From al-ʿAllāqī to a mine called Baṭn Wāḥ is one stage. From al-ʿAllāqī to a place called Iʿmād is two stages. To a mine called Māʾ al-Ṣakhra is one stage. To a mine called al-Akhshāb is two stages. To a mine called Mīzāb, where tribesmen of Balī and Juhayna have settled, is four stages. To a mine called [...][589] is two stages.

From al-ʿAllāqī to ʿAydhāb is four stages.[590] ʿAydhāb is a Salt Sea port from which people set sail to Mecca, the Ḥijāz, and Yemen. Merchants travel to it and carry away gold, ivory, and other things in their ships. From al-ʿAllāqī to [...],[591] which is the last of the gold mines to which Muslims travel, is thirty stages. From al-ʿAllāqī to a place called [...],[592] where tribesmen from the Banū Sulaym and others from Muḍar have settled, is ten stages. From al-ʿAllāqī to a mine called al-Sanṭa, where there are tribesmen from Muḍar and others, is ten stages. From al-ʿAllāqī to a mine called al-Rafaq is ten stages. From al-ʿAllāqī to a mine called Sakhtīt is ten stages. These are the mines to which the Muslims travel and to which they go in search of gold.

[*The Land of the Nubians*]

Whoever wishes to travel from al-ʿAllāqī to the land of the Nubians, who are called the ʿAlwa, travels thirty stages—first to Kabāw, then to a place called al-Abwāb, and then to the largest city of the ʿAlwa, which is called Sōba.[593] The

586 The undotted letters are too ambiguous to read.

587 The undotted letters are too ambiguous to read.

588 The undotted letters are too ambiguous to read.

589 The undotted letters are too ambiguous to read.

590 On the Red Sea port of ʿAydhab, see the article by Donald Whitcomb in *EI*^{3}, s.v. ʿAydhab.

591 The undotted letters are too ambiguous to read.

592 The undotted letters are too ambiguous to read.

593 On the geography and peoples of Nubia, see the article by S. Hillelson, V. Christides, C. E. Bosworth, A. S. Kaye, and Ahmed al-Shahi in *EI*^{2}, s.v. Nūba. Al-Yaʿqūbī lumps together several distinct kingdoms: Marīs, Muqurra, and ʿAlwa, proceeding from north to south. See the articles by S. Munro-Hay in *EI*^{2}, s.v. al-Mukurra, by S. M. Stern in *EI*^{2}, s.v. ʿAlwa, and by J. Spaulding in *EI*^{2}, s.v. Sōba.

king of the ʿAlwa resides there, | and Muslims frequently go there. From (this city) comes an account of the source of the Nile: It is said that the peninsula of ʿAlwa is connected to the peninsula of Sind, and that the Nile flows from beyond ʿAlwa to the land of Sind in a river called Mihrān, just as it flows in the Nile of Egypt, and there it floods at the same time as it floods in Egypt. In the peninsula of ʿAlwa there are animals like those in the lands of Sind: elephants, rhinoceroses, and the like. In the Mihrān River there are crocodiles just as in Egypt.[594] 336

From Aswan one can travel to the nearest part of the land of the Nubians, who are known as Muqurrā. It is a place called Māwā. It was there that Zakariyyāʾ b. Qirqī lived, who succeeded his father Qirqī as king of the Nubians. It is thirty stages from Māwā to the largest city of the Nubians, where the king of the Nubians resides. That city is Dongola.[595]

[*The Land of the Buja*]

From al-ʿAllāqī to the land of the Buja,[596] who are named al-Ḥadāriba and the [...][597] is 25 stages. The city of the king of the Ḥadāriba Buja is called Hajar. Muslims visit it for its trade goods. The Buja live in tents made of hides, pluck their beards, and remove the nipples from boys' breasts, lest their breasts resemble those of women. They eat sorghum[598] and similar things. They ride camels and fight in combat on them just as one fights on horseback, and they throw javelins without missing.

From al-ʿAllāqī to the land of the Buja people called al-Zanāfija is 25 stages. The city in which the king of the Zanāfija resides is called Baqlīn. Muslims travel | to it on occasion for trade. Their way of life is like that of the Ḥadāriba. 337

594 In early Islamic cartography, the Horn of Africa was often depicted as stretching far to the East, forming the southern shore of the Indian Ocean. Thus, al-Yaʿqūbī's claim that the Nile might, in unknown lands south of Nubia, "continue" flowing on to Sind (roughly modern Pakistan), where it is known as Mihrān (a name for the Indus), would not have seemed as far-fetched then as it does now. Zoologically his argument is flawless.

595 De Goeje, 336, notes that the text is corrupt here, including an illegible toponym alongside that of Dongola. The English translation slightly rephrases the Arabic.

596 Arabic geographers usually specify the vocalization as "Buja," but Bija is also given and is closer to the normal English form, Beja. On the ethnography of these nomadic peoples living between the Nile and the Red Sea, see the article by P. M. Holt in *EI*^{2}, s.v. Bedja.

597 The tribal name is illegible; presumably it is al-Zanāfija, as below; cf. also al-Yaʿqūbī, *Taʾrīkh*, 1:218, although the reading there is also conjectural.

598 Arabic *dhura*, usually is sorghum, but also can mean millet.

They have no religious law, and in times past they worshipped only an idol that they called Ḥaḥākhuwā.[599]

[*Lower Egypt*]

As for the cities of Lower Egypt, the first of them is Atrīb, which has an expansive hinterland. Nearby is the village known as Banhā, which produces a renowned variety of honey.[600] Then comes the city of ʿAyn Shams.[601] It is an ancient city said to contain residences that belonged to Pharaoh. Nearby are some wondrous ruins, where there are two massive, tall obelisks of hard stone inscribed with writing in the ancient tongue. Water drips from the top of one of them—no one knows its cause. Then come the cities of Natū, Basṭa, Ṭarābiya, Qurbayṭ, Ṣān, and Iblīl. These nine cities are called the rural districts (*kuwar*) of al-Ḥawf.[602]

Then come the cities of Banā, an ancient and majestic city; Būṣīr, which is comparable to Banā in size and majesty;[603] Samannūd;[604] Nawasā; al-Awsiya, which is the city of Damīra; and al-Bujūm. These six cities on the east bank of the Nile are called the rural districts (*kuwar*) of Baṭn al-Rīf.[605]

(Then come) the cities of Sakhā, Tīda, al-Afrāḥūn, Ṭuwwah, and the city of Manūf al-Suflā.[606] These seven cities and subdistricts are in an "island" in the Nile between the Dimyāṭ Branch and the al-Gharb Branch.[607]

---

599 The vocalization of the word is uncertain. More detail about Beja religion can be found in al-Yaʿqūbī, *Taʾrīkh*, 1:218. The Beja name for Satan given there (*Ṣaḥā Ḥarāqa*) and *Ḥaḥākhuwā* look like copyists' attempts to make sense of the same foreign word.

600 On Banhā and its famous honey, some of which is said to have been sent by the ruler of Egypt as a gift to the prophet Muḥammad, see the article by G. Wiet in *EI*², s.v. Banhā.

601 On ʿAyn Shams and its obelisks, see the article by C. H. Becker in *EI*², s.v. ʿAyn Shams.

602 See the article by G. Wiet and H. Halm in *EI*², s.v. al-Sharḳiyya. Basṭa, Ṭarābiya, and Qurbayṭ (thus ed. Leiden, but undotted in the MS and better read as Furbayṭ) correspond to three Byzantine pagarchies: Bubaste, Arabia, and Pharbaithos. On Ṣān (Byzantine Tanis) and Iblīl, see the article by G. Wiet in *EI*¹, s.v. Ṣān.

603 On the twin settlements of Būṣīr and Banā, see the article by G. Wiet in *EI*², s.v. Būṣīr or Abūṣīr.

604 On Sammanūd, see the article by Ayman F. Sayyid in *EI*², s.v. Sammanūd.

605 On the term Baṭn al-Rīf, see the article by G. Wiet and H. Halm in *EI*², s.v. al-Sharḳiyya.

606 On Lower and Upper Manūf (Manūf al-Suflā and Manūf al-ʿUlyā, respectively), see the article by H. Halm in *EI*², s.v. Manūf.

607 In fact, al-Yaʿqūbī has listed only five cities. By "island," al-Yaʿqūbī means the Nile Delta, the wedge of land between these two branches, not a real island in the course of the Nile. The al-Gharb (West) Branch is the modern Rashīd (Rosetta) Branch of the Nile.

As for the cities that are on the coast of the Salt Sea, the first of them is al-Faramā, which is the ancient city from which you enter Egypt. Then comes the city of Tinnīs, which is surrounded by the Great Salt Sea and by a lake that is fed by the Nile.[608] It is an ancient city in which are manufactured fine garments, densely woven and soft, of Dabīqī cloth, fine linen (*qaṣab*), | striped 338
cloth, velvet, embroidered cloth, and other sorts of garments. It has a harbor for ships arriving from Syria and the Maghrib. Then comes the city of Shaṭā, which is on the seacoast and is where the Shaṭawī *shurūb* garments are made.[609] Then comes the city of Damietta, which is on the seacoast.[610] The Nile extends up to Damietta, then branches off: some of it flows into Lake Tinnīs, which is navigable by great boats and ships, and the rest of it flows into the Salt Sea. At Damietta, densely-woven Dabīqī garments, *shurūb* garments, and fine linen (*qaṣab*) are made. Then comes Būra, a fortress on the seacoast, a dependency of Damietta. Garments and papyrus are made there. Then comes the fortress of Naqīza on the seacoast. Then comes the city of al-Barallus,[611] which is on the coast of the Salt Sea and is the site of the *ribāṭ*.[612] Then comes the city of Rosetta, which is a prosperous, populous city.[613] It has a harbor through which the waters of the Nile flow into the Salt Sea. Ships from the sea enter it in order to sail up the Nile. Then come the cities of Ikhnū on the seacoast and Wasīma, where papyrus is made.

Then comes the great and glorious city of Alexandria, whose size, magnificence, and numerous antiquities are beyond description.[614] One of the wonders of the ancient ruins there is the lighthouse on the seacoast at the mouth of the Great Harbor. It is a strong and artfully constructed lighthouse 175 cubits tall. Atop it are hearths in which fires are lit whenever the watchmen see ships

608 The city of Tinnīs is situated on an island in Lake Manzala. See the article by J.-M. Mouton in *EI*², s.v. Tinnīs.

609 On Shaṭā, a few miles from Damietta, on the western shore of Lake Tinnīs, see the article by G. Wiet and H. Halm in *EI*², s.v. Shaṭā. *Shurūb* cloth apparently was a variety of fine and precious linen; see Dozy, *Supplément*, s.v. SH-R-B.

610 On the town of Damietta (Arabic, Dimyāṭ), see the article by P. M. Holt in *EI*², s.v. Dimyāṭ.

611 So vocalized by the Leiden editor in a form closer to the Coptic and the original Greek name (Paralos). The modern form is Burullus. See the article by G. Wiet in *EI*², s.v. Burullus (Borollos).

612 A *ribāṭ* usually is a frontier fortress (often, as here, a coastal frontier) garrisoned by volunteers who hope to gain spiritual merit in prosecuting *jihād* against infidels. The exact sense here is problematic. See the article by J. Chabbi in *EI*², s.v. Ribāṭ.

613 On the city of Rosetta (Arabic, Rashīd), see the article by A. S. Atiya and H. Halm in *EI*², s.v. Rashīd.

614 On Alexandria, see the article by S. Labib in *EI*², s.v. al-Iskandariyya.

far out at sea. In Alexandria there are two obelisks of variegated stone resting on (bases of) copper (in the form of) crayfish;[615] they are both inscribed with ancient writing. The city's ancient ruins and wonders are many. The city has a canal that brings sweet water from the Nile and then empties into the Salt Sea.

339 Alexandria has the following rural districts (*kuwar*) | that are not on the coast of the Salt Sea, but along the banks of the Nile canals: the rural districts of al-Buḥayra, Maṣīl, al-Malīdas—these are the rural districts along the Alexandria Branch, which enters the city. Then come the rural districts of Tarnūṭ, Qarṭasā, Khirabtā—these also lie along that branch. Then there are the rural districts of Ṣā, Shabās, al-Ḥayyiz, al-Badaqūn, and al-Sharāk—these lie along a Nile branch called al-Nastarū. Alexandria has the following other rural districts: Maryūṭ, a prosperous district with vineyards and orchards, famous for its fruit; Lūbiya; and Marāqiya—the latter two are on the coast of the Salt Sea. Tribesmen from the Banū Mudlij division of Kināna inhabit the nearest villages of these of these districts, and Berber tribesmen inhabit most of the others. There are villages and fortresses in them.

All the rural districts of Egypt were conquered in the caliphate of ʿUmar b. al-Khaṭṭāb; the commander was ʿAmr b. al-ʿĀṣ b. Wāʾil al-Sahmī. The revenues of Egypt from the poll tax under ʿAmr in the caliphate of ʿUmar in the first year totalled 14,000,000 dinars. When ʿAmr collected only 10,000,000 in the second year, ʿUmar sent him a message saying, "O traitor!" In the caliphate of ʿUthmān b. ʿAffān, (the governor) ʿAbdallāh b. Saʿd b. Abī Sarḥ collected 12,000,000 dinars. Then the people converted to Islam, so that in the reign of Muʿāwiya the revenues from the land tax with the poll tax totalled (only) 5,000,000 dinars. In the reign of Hārūn al-Rashīd, they totalled 4,000,000 dinars, and then the revenues of Egypt fell to 3,000,000 dinars.

Egypt and all its villages obtain their water from the Nile summer and winter, with it rising in the summer. It comes from the land of the ʿAlwa,[616] emanating from springs and increasing from the rains that come in the summer, so that
340 it spreads over the face of the earth until it covers the whole | land. Then it begins to recede in one of the Coptic months called Bāba, which is Tishrīn al-Awwal,[617] and the people begin cultivating and planting crops, for the land of Egypt receives little rain, except for the part along the coasts. All of Egypt's non-

615 That is, bases of copper or copper-faced stone in the form of crayfish or decorated with crayfish. By crayfish, al-Yaʿqūbī is probably describing a scarab beetle.

616 That is, Nubia.

617 That is, October.

Arabs are Copts: those of Upper Egypt are called al-Marīs[618] and those of Lower Egypt are called al-Biyamā.

The Road to Mecca from Egypt

For anyone who wishes to go on pilgrimage to Mecca from Egypt, the first stage is called Jubb ʿAmīra, where all the pilgrims gather on the day of their departure. Then comes a stage called al-Qarqara in a waterless desert; then a stage called ʿAjarūd, where there is an ancient deep-shafted well of bitter water. Then one comes to Jisr al-Qulzum.[619] Whoever wishes to do so may enter the city of Qulzum, which is a large city on the seacoast, where there are merchants who prepare the supplies to be sent from Egypt to the Ḥijāz and to Yemen. There is also a harbor for ships. It has a mixed population, and its merchants are men of means. From Qulzum, the people camp in steppe and desert terrain for six stages until they reach Ayla—they supply themselves with water for these six stages. The city of Ayla is an important city on the coast of the Salt Sea. It is where the pilgrims from Syria meet the pilgrims from Egypt and the Maghrib,[620] and there are many | commodities available. It has a mixed 341
population, and there is a group of people who claim to be clients of ʿUthmān b. ʿAffān.[621] At Ayla there is also a striped mantle said to be the mantle of the Messenger of God—God's blessing and peace be upon him. He is said to have given it to Ru'ba b. Yuḥanna when he traveled to Tabūk.[622]

From Ayla one proceeds to Sharaf al-Baʿl, and from Sharaf al-Baʿl to Madyan, which is a prosperous ancient city with many springs, continuously flowing streams of sweet water, orchards, gardens, and date groves. It has a mixed population.

Whoever wishes to leave Madyan for Mecca proceeds along the coast of the Salt Sea to a place called ʿAynūnā, where there is some cultivation and date

---

618 The term also designates the northernmost Nubian kingdom, extending south from Aswan to the northern border of al-Muqurra. See the article by S. Munro-Hay in *EI*², s.v. al-Marīs.

619 Jisr al-Qulzum (al-Qulzum Bridge) was a bridge over an ancient canal leading from Qulzum (ancient Klysma), a mile from modern Suez on the Red Sea, to the Nile near Fusṭāṭ. By al-Yaʿqūbī's time, the canal was no longer navigable, but the bridge remained a landmark. See the article by E. Honigmann and R. Y. Ebied in *EI*², s.v. al-Ḳulzum.

620 That is, from North Africa.

621 Probably to be interpreted, "who claim to be *descendants of* clients (*mawālī*) of ʿUthmān b. ʿAffān."

622 Ru'ba b. Yuḥanna was the Aylī notable (possibly a bishop) with whom the Prophet is said to have negotiated the city's surrender, along with that of Tabūk, in the year 9/630. See al-Yaʿqūbī, *Ta'rīkh*, 2:70.

groves and where there are mining sites where people prospect for gold. Then one proceeds to al-ʿAwnīd, which is similar, then to al-Ṣalā, then to al-Nabk, then to al-Quṣayba, then to al-Buḥra, then to al-Mughaytha, which is Tubʿal, then to Ẓuba, then to al-Wajh, and then to Munkhūs. In Munkhūs there are divers who harvest pearls. Then one proceeds to al-Ḥawrāʾ, then to al-Jār, then to al-Juḥfa, then to Qudayd, then to ʿUsfān, and then to Baṭn Marr.

Whoever wishes to travel the road that goes to the City of the Messenger[623]—God's blessing and peace be upon him—proceeds from Madyan to a stop called Aghrāʾ then to Qālas, then to Shaghb, then to Baddā, then to al-Suqyā, then to Dhū l-Marwa, then to Dhū Khushub, then to Medina. These are the stages from Egypt to Mecca and Medina.

342 ### *Al-Maghrib*[624]

Whoever wishes to travel by road from Egypt to Barqa and the furthermost parts of the Maghrib passes from al-Fusṭāṭ onto the west bank of the Nile until he reaches Tarnūṭ.[625] Then he continues to a station known as al-Minā, which has been deserted by its people. Then he comes to the large monastery known as Bū Mīnā, in which stands the famous church of wondrous construction abounding in marble decoration.[626] Then he comes to the station known as Dhāt al-Ḥumām, where there is a congregational mosque.[627] It a dependency (*ʿamal*) of the rural district (*kūra*) of Alexandria. Then he continues amid stations in the territory of the Banū Mudlij in the steppe, some along the coast, some set back from the coast. Among them are the stations known as al-Ṭāḥūna, al-Kanāʾis, and as Jubb al-ʿAwsaj.

Then the traveler continues into the dependency (*ʿamal*) of Lūbiya (Libya), which is a rural district (*kūra*) after the fashion of the rural districts of Alexandria. Among its stations are the station known as Manzil Maʿn, then the station known as Qaṣr al-Shammās, then Khirbat al-Qawm, then al-Rammāda, which is

---

623 That is, Medina.

624 "The West," that is, North Africa, excluding Egypt. For an overview of geographical and historical details, see the article by G. Yver in in *EI*², s.v. al-Maghrib.

625 Tarnūṭ (ancient Terenouthis, near modern al-Ṭarrāna) lay about 70 km north of Cairo on the western branch of the Nile. See the article in Yāqūt, *Muʿjam al-buldān*, 1:845, s.v. Tarnūṭ.

626 The monastery, better known as Dayr Abū Mīnā, was dedicated to St. Minas. Its ruins lie about 45 km south of Alexandria.

627 A town Dhāt al-Ḥammām (apparently a variant of Dhāt al-Ḥumām), is mentioned by Yāqūt, *Muʿjam al-buldān*, s.v. (2:330), as lying between Alexandria and Ifrīqiya; that is, to the west of Alexandria.

the first station of the Berbers. It is inhabited by Mazāta[628] tribesmen and other indigenous non-Arabs. There are also Arab tribesmen from the Balī, Juhayna, Banū Mudlij, and others of mixed descent.

Then the traveler continues to al-ʿAqaba (The Pass), which is on the coast of the Salt Sea, difficult to traverse, rough, rugged, and dangerous. Upon reaching the top of the pass, one continues to the station known as al-Qaṣr al-Abyaḍ, then Maghāyir Raqīm, then Quṣūr al-Rūm, then Jubb al-Raml. These are territories of the Berbers from the tribes of Māṣala b. Luwāta and a mixture of peoples. Then the traveler reaches Wādī Makhīl, which is a station like a city. It has a congregational mosque, cisterns, permanent markets, and a redoubtable fortress. It has a mixed population, most of them Berbers from Māṣala, Zanāra, Maṣʿūba, Marāwa, and Faṭīṭa. From Wādī Makhīl to the city of | Barqa is three 343
stages through Berber territory belonging to the Marāwa, Mafraṭa, Maṣʿūba, Zakūda, and other Lawāta tribes.

Barqa[629]

The city of Barqa stands in a wide plain on intensely red soil. It is a city surrounded by walls, with iron portals and a moat. Al-Mutawakkil ʿalā Allāh[630] ordered the walls to be built. The people drink rainwater that comes from the mountains in watercourses that lead to great cisterns that the caliphs and governors made to supply drinking water for the people of the city of Barqa. Surrounding the city are suburbs in which the troops and others live. The city's houses and suburbs have a mixed population, with most of the people being veteran soldiers who have children and grandchildren. The city of Barqa is six Arab miles from the coast of the Salt Sea.

On the seacoast is a city called Ajiya, which has markets, guardposts, a congregational mosque, gardens, cultivated fields, and plentiful fruit. Another port city is called Ṭulmaytha,[631] where ships anchor from time to time. Barqa has two mountains: one of them, called al-Sharqī (Eastern), is home to Arab tribesmen from al-Azd, Lakhm, Judhām, Ṣadif, and other Yemenis; the other mountain, called al-Gharbī (Western), is home to tribesmen from Ghassān, and tribesmen from Judhām, al-Azd, Tujīb and other Arab tribes, as well as villages of Luwāta Berber clans from Zakūda, Mafraṭa, and Zanāra. On these two mountains there are flowing springs, trees, fruit, fortresses and ancient cisterns built by the Romans.

---

628 On the Mazāta, a powerful Berber grouping, see the article by T. Lewicki, in *EI*², s.v. Mazāta.

629 On the town of Barqa in the region known as Cyrenaïca, see the article by J. Despois in *EI*², s.v. Barḳa.

630 The ʿAbbasid caliph al-Mutawakkil reigned 232/847–247/861.

631 Ancient Ptolemais; see the article by T. Lewicki in *EI*², s.v. Mazāta.

Barqa has many regions (*aqālīm*) that are inhabited by the aforementioned Berber tribes. One of the cities included among them is Barnīq,[632] a city on the coast of the Salt Sea. It has a harbor, wondrous in convenience and excellence, where ships can take refuge. It is inhabited by people descended from the ancient Romans, who in olden times formed the city's population, and Berber
344 tribesmen from Taḥlāla, Sawa, Masūsa, Maghāgha, Wāhila, and Jadāna. | Barnīq is two stages from the city of Barqa, and it also has regions (*aqālīm*) under its control.

(The other city) is Ajdābiya.[633] It is a city with an overlooking citadel and with a congregational mosque and permanent markets. From Barnīq to it is two stages, and from Barqa to it is four stages. It is inhabited by Berber tribesmen from Zanāra, Wāhila, Masūsa, Suwa, Taḥlāla, and others, as well as by Jadāna, who are predominant there. It has regions (*aqālīm*) and a port on the Salt Sea six Arab miles away where ships can anchor. It is the last of the cities in Luwāta territory.

The Luwāta tribes say that they are descended from Luwāta b. Barr b. Qays ʿAylān. Some of them say that they are a group from Lakhm, the first of whom came from Syria and were transferred to these territories, while still others say that they are descended from the Romans.[634]

Surt[635]

From the city of Ajdābiya to the city of Surt on the coast of the Salt Sea is five stages. One stage belongs to the territory of the Luwāta, but among them are tribesmen from the Mazāta, and it is they who are dominant in it. Among these stages are al-Fārūj, Qaṣr al-ʿAṭish, al-Yahūdiya, Qaṣr al-ʿIbādī; then the city of Surt. The people of these stations and the people of the city of Surt are from the Mindāsa, Maḥanḥā, Wanṭās, and other tribes.[636] Their last settlement is two

632 Ancient Berenike, now the site of modern Benghazi; see the article by J. Despois in *EI*², s.v. Benghāzī.

633 On Ajdābiya, now a small village between Benghazi and Surt, see the article by H. H. Abdul-Wahab in *EI*², s.v. Adjdābiya.

634 That is, the Berber Luwāta (also vocalized Lawāta) claimed an Arab or Roman (or Greek, as Arabic *al-Rūm* can refer to either) lineage. Al-Yaʿqūbī gives a more detailed account of the Berber tribes in *Taʾrīkh*, 1:215–216. See also the article by T. Lewicki in *EI*², s.v. Lawāta.

635 On the history of the medieval city of Surt, 55 km east of modern Sirt, see the article by A. Hamdani in *EI*², s.v. Surt.

636 The rendering of the names is uncertain. For Maḥanḥā, de Goeje notes that Ibn Khaldūn read Majīja, and Wanṭās (or Wūnṭās) is Goeje's emendation of MS Finṭās (or Qinṭās, the first letter being undotted).

stages from the city of Surt at a place called Tawargha,[637] which is the furthest limit of Barqa. All the Mazāta are Ibāḍīs,[638] but they neither are versed in sacred law nor do they practice religion.

The land tax of Barqa is (based on) an established financial regulation. (The caliph) al-Rashīd sent out a client of his named Bashshār, who apportioned the land tax (*kharāj*) of 24,000 dinars so that each estate (*ḍayʿa*) would owe a specified amount—this was apart from the tithes (*aʿshār*), alms taxes (*ṣadaqāt*), and poll tax (*jawālī*).[639] The total amount from the tithes, alms-tax and poll tax is 15,000 dinars, sometimes more and sometimes less. The tithes are levied from areas that | have neither olive groves, trees, nor well-watered villages. Barqa has 345
a dependency (*ʿamal*) called Awjala, which is in a desert region lying to the west. Whoever wishes to go out to it turns off to the south, proceeding to two cities, one of which is called Jālaw, the other Waddān. Each has date palms, dried dates and *qasb*, of which there is no better.[640] Of the two, Waddān is the more pleasant.

Waddān[641]

Waddān, which is a region approached through a desert, was formerly a dependency of Barqa; now it is attached to the district (*ʿamal*) of Surt. Waddān is five stages south of the city of Surt. Some Muslims live there who claim to be Arabs from the tribal faction of Yemen, but most of the people are from (the Berber tribe of) Mazāta, and it is they who dominate the place. Dates, of which there are several varieties, are the main export. It is governed by a local resident, and no land tax is collected from it.

Zawīla

Beyond and to the south lies the land of Zawīla.[642] The people are Muslims all of whom are Ibāḍīs who perform the pilgrimage to the Sacred House.[643]

637 Tawargha (modern Tawergha) is approximately 172 km west of Surt and 38 km south of Miṣrāta.

638 That is, members of the Khārijite sect known as Ibāḍīs. On the origin and history of this sect that persists to this day in Oman, East Africa, Tripolitana, and southern Algeria, see the article by T. Lewicki in *EI*², s.v. al-ʿIbāḍiyya.

639 On *jawālī* as a synonym for *jizya* (poll tax), see the article by Cl. Cahen in *EI*², s.v. Djawālī.

640 *Qasb* is a particularly tough variety of dried date.

641 Waddān is one of three oases in the al-Jufra depression of the Libyan desert about 238 km southwest of Surt. See the article by J. Despois in *EI*², s.v. al-Djufra.

642 On the geography and history of Zawīla, see the article by K. S. Vikør in *EI*², s.v. Zawīla.

643 This implies that although they belong to the same Khārijite sect as the Mazāta, who have

Most of them are of [...].[644] They bring out black slaves from the Mīriyyūn, the Zaghāwiyyūn, the Marwiyyūn, and other black peoples, as they are near them and take them captive. I have also heard that the kings of the black peoples simply sell blacks for no reason without there being any war.

From Zawīla come Zawīlī hides. It is a land of date palms, sorghum fields, and other things. It has a mixed population of people from Khurāsān, Basra, and Kufa. Fifteen stages beyond Zawīla is a city called Kuwwār, where there are Muslims from a variety of tribes. Most of the people, however, are Berbers, and they import blacks (as slaves). Between Zawīla and the city of Kuwwār and those dependencies of Zawīla on the road to Awjala and Ajdābiya is a group of people called Lamṭa, who closely resemble the Berbers. They are the source of white Lamṭī shields.[645]

Fazzān

The people known as Fazzān are a mixture of peoples who have a chief whom
346 they all obey. | It is a vast region and a large city. There is unending war between these people and the Mazāta.

∴

Barqa is also called Anṭābulus, which is its ancient name.[646] ʿAmr b. al-ʿĀṣ conquered it by treaty in the year 23.[647] From the last dependency (*ʿamal*) of Barqa, the place called Tawargha, to Tripoli[648] is six stages. From Tawargha,

---

just been described as not practicing religion, the people of Zawīla perform the pilgrimage to Mecca like other Muslims.

644 The undotted letters are too ambiguous to read.

645 On the Lamṭa tribe see the article by G. S. Colin in *EI*², s.v. Lamṭa. The shields were covered with the skin of the *lamṭ* antelope, a kind of oryx, hardened by soaking in milk. See the article by F. Viré in *EI*², s.v. Lamṭ.

646 The name Anṭābulus (i.e., Anṭāpolis) probably comes from the Greek for Antaeus' City (Ἀνταίου πόλις), as Libya was the birthplace of this mythical giant and the scene of Heracles' combat with him. One reads in Isaac Newton's work "The Chronology of antient Kingdoms amended" (*Opera*, v, London, 1785), p. 172: "Antæus reigned over all Afric to the Atlantic Ocean, and built Tingis or Tangieres. Pindar tells us, that he reigned at Irasa, a town of Libya, where Cyrene [i.e., Barqa] was afterwards built. He invaded Egypt and Thebais; for he was beaten by Hercules and the Egyptians near Antæa or Antæopolis, a town of Thebais; and Diodorus tells us, that 'this town had its name from Antæus, whom Hercules slew in the days of Osiris.'"

647 23 A.H. = November 19, 643 – November 7, 644.

648 The usual Arabic form is Ṭarābulus; al-Yaʿqūbī uses the form Aṭrābulus.

one leaves Mazāta territory and reaches the territory of the Hawwāra,[649] which begins at Wardāsa; then comes Labda, which is a fortress like a city on the seacoast. The Hawwāra claim to be descended from the indigenous Berbers, and that the Mazāta and the Luwāta were part of them, but cut themselves off from them and left their territories and moved to the region of Barqa and other places. The Hawwāra also claim to be a group of people from Yemen who became ignorant of their genealogies. The tribes of Hawwāra keep track of genealogies just as the Arabs do. Among their tribes are the Banū l-Luhān, Malīla, and Warsaṭifa. The subtribes of al-Luhān are the Banū [...],[650] the Banū [...], the Banū Warfala, and the Banū Masrāta. The encampments of the Hawwāra stretch from the last dependency (*ʿamal*) of Surt as far as Tripoli.

Tripoli

Tripoli is a majestic ancient city on the coast, prosperous and populous, with a mixed population. ʿAmr b. al-ʿĀṣ conquered it in the year 23[651] in the caliphate of ʿUmar b. al-Khaṭṭāb; it was the last place in the Maghrib to be conquered in ʿUmar's caliphate.[652]

From Tripoli (the traveler continues) to the land of the Nafūsa.[653] They are a group whose language is not Arabic—Ibāḍīs all of them. They have a leader called Alyās,[654] from whose command they do not deviate. Their residences in the mountains of Tripoli include estates, villages, fields, and many tracts of cultivated land. They pay no land tax to any government, nor do they give obedience to anyone except a leader of theirs in Tāhart, who is the leader of the Ibāḍīya, called ʿAbd al-Wahhāb b. ʿAbd al-Raḥmān b. Rustam, a Persian.[655] The territory of the Nafūsa stretches from the limits of (the district of) Tripoli south to the vicinity of al-Qayrawān. They have many tribes and various clans.

649 On the Hawwāra, see the article by T. Lewicki and P. M. Holt in *EI*², s.v. Hawwāra.

650 The undotted letters of this and the following tribal name are too ambiguous to read.

651 23 A.H. = November 19, 643 – November 7, 644.

652 On the Islamic history of Tripoli (Arabic, Ṭarābulus), see the article by G. Oman, V. Christides, and C. E. Bosworth in *EI*², s.v. Ṭarābulus.

653 See the article by F. Béguinot in *EI*², s.v. al-Nafūsa.

654 Thus vocalized in ed. Leiden, but almost certainly to be identified as Abū Manṣūr Ilyās al-Nafūsī, governor of the Nafūsa mountains and the Tripoli region for its Rustamid ruler during al-Yaʿqūbī's lifetime. See the article by T. Lewicki in in *EI*², s.v. Abū Manṣūr Ilyās al-Nafūsī.

655 Founder of the Ibāḍī Rustamid dynasty, which ruled from Tāhart in what is now Algeria 161/778–296/909. On its history, see the articles by M. Talbi in *EI*², s.v. Rustamids or Rustumids, and by Virginie Prevost in *EI*³, s.v. ʿAbd al-Raḥmān b. Rustam.

From Tripoli (the traveler continues) along the main road to a large city
347 called Qābis[656] on the coast of the Salt Sea, prosperous, with | many trees, fruit, and bubbling springs. Its people are a mixture of Arabs, non-Arabs, and Berbers. Residing there is a governor appointed by Ibn al-Aghlab, the ruler of Ifrīqiya.[657] From Tripoli to Qābis is a five-stage journey through prosperous lands inhabited by Berber groups from the Zanāta, the Luwāta and the indigenous Africans. The first of these stages is [...],[658] the first stage from Tripoli; then comes Ṣabra, a stop where there are ancient stone idols; then Qaṣr Banī [...]; then [...]; then al-Fāṣilāt; and then Qābis.

Al-Qayrawān[659]

From Qābis to the city of al-Qayrawān is four stages. The first is ʿAyn al-Zaytūna, which is not populous, then Lalas,[660] a castle in which there is some habitation, then Ghadīr al-Aʿrābī, and then Qalshāna, which is the halting-place for those coming and going from al-Qayrawān. Then one reaches the great city of al-Qayrawān, which was laid out by ʿUqba b. Nāfiʿ al-Fihrī in the year 60[661] in the caliphate of Muʿāwiya. It was ʿUqba who conquered most of the Maghrib, although the first to enter the territory of Ifrīqiya and conquer it was ʿAbdallāh b. Saʿd b. Abī Sarḥ in the caliphate of ʿUthmān b. ʿAffān in the year 36.[662]

Al-Qayrawān is a city that used to have walls of mud and unbaked bricks. But Ziyādat Allāh b. Ibrāhīm b. al-Aghlab pulled them down when ʿImrān b.

---

656 Modern Gabès in Tunisia; see the article by M. Talbi in *EI*^{2}, s.v. Ḳābis.

657 On the Aghlabid dynasty of rulers of Ifrīqiya, see the article by G. Marçais and J. Schacht in *EI*^{2}, s.v. Aghlabids.

658 The undotted letters of this and the two following toponyms are too ambiguous to read.

659 On the city of al-Qayrawān, located in modern Tunisia, see the article by M. Talbi in *EI*^{2}, s.v. al-Ḳayrawān.

660 Reading uncertain.

661 60 A.H. = October 13, 679 – September 30, 680. De Goeje adds the following note to the Leiden edition (translated here from Latin): "In fact, it happened in the year 50 [January 29, 670 – January 17, 671]. The fault is the copyist's, not the author's, as is evident from comparing *History* [*Taʾrīkh*] 2:272. What soon follows about the first expedition's having been in the years 36 and 37 (p. 349, l. 20), instead of 26 and 27, must also be attributed to the copyist's fault, as demonstrated by *History* 2:191. One may therefore conclude that in the autograph the number was written not in words but in figures."

662 36 A.H. = June 30, 656 – June 18, 657. See, however, the previous note, which concludes that one should read 26 (October 17, 646 – October 6, 647) on the basis of al-Yaʿqūbī, *Taʾrīkh* 2:191. The correction to 26 is all the more necessary as ʿUthmān was assassinated at the end of 35/656.

Mujālid, ʿAbd al-Salām b. al-Mufarraj, and Manṣūr al-Ṭanbadhī revolted against him.[663] They revolted against him at al-Qayrawān—they were (descendants) of the old soldiers (*jund*) who had arrived with Ibn al-Ashʿath.[664]

Their source of drinking water is rainwater. During the winter, when the rains and | torrents come, the rainwater from the streams goes into great cisterns 348
called *mawājil*,[665] from which the water carriers obtain their water. They also have a watercourse called Wādī al-Sarāwīl south of the city; it carries salty water because it lies in swampy ground, but the people use it for their various needs.

The residences of the Banū l-Aghlab are two Arab miles from the city of al-Qayrawān in palaces around which numerous walls have been built. These remained as their residences until Ibrāhīm b. Aḥmad moved out of them; he settled in a place called al-Raqqāda, eight Arab miles from the city of al-Qayrawān, and built a palace there.[666]

The city of al-Qayrawān has a mixed population of people from Quraysh and from all the other Arab lineages: Muḍar, Rabīʿa, and Qaḥṭān. There are also groups of non-Arabs from among the Khurāsānī troops and from whatever other troops came with the governors of the Banū Hāshim.[667] There are also non-Arabs from the indigenous non-Arab population: Berbers, Romans, and the like.

---

663 In his note to the Leiden edition, De Goeje notes that ʿImrān b. Mujālid was killed in 200 (August 11, 815 – July 29, 816), while the revolt of Abd al-Salām and Manṣūr took place in 209 (May 4, 824 – April 23, 825). He therefore suggests reading ʿĀmir b. Nāfiʿ instead of ʿImrān b. Mujālid, referring to the note in his 1860 edition of this section of al-Yaʿqūbī under the title *Descriptio al-Maghribi*. For a synopsis of the political turmoil of these years in al-Qayrawān, see the article by G. Marçais and J. Schacht in *EI*², s.v. Aghlabids or Banu'l-Aghlab.

664 This refers not to the famous ʿAbd al-Raḥmān b. Muḥammad b. al-Ashʿath, who led a revolt against the Umayyads the days of al-Ḥajjāj in 80/699, but to Muḥammad b. al-Ashʿath al-Khuzāʿī who was sent to Ifriqiyā for the first time by the caliph al-Saffāḥ in 133 (August 9, 750 – July 29, 751; see al-Ṭabarī, *Taʾrīkh*, 3:74) and who took Qayrawān from the ʿIbāḍiyya in 144/761. In 148/765, he was succeeded as governor by the founder of the Aghlabid dynasty, al-Aghlab b. Salīm, during the reign of whose grandson, Ziyādat Allāh (r. 201/817 to 223/838), these revolts took place.

665 So vocalized by Dozy, *Supplément*, 1:11; De Goeje vocalizes the word in accordance with its etymology as *maʾājil*.

666 Ibrāhīm b. Aḥmad ruled from 261/875 to 289/902. His new residence at al-Raqqāda was built in 264/878. See the article by G. Marçais and J. Schacht in *EI*², s.v. Aghlabids or Banu'l-Aghlab.

667 That is, the ʿAbbāsids.

It is one stage from al-Qayrawān to Sūsa, which is on the coast of the Salt Sea.[668] It has an arsenal in which naval ships are built, and other ships come to it. Sūsa has a mixed population.

From al-Qayrawān it is one stage to a place called al-Jazīra. This is Jazīrat Abī Sharīk, which protrudes into the sea and is surrounded by its waters.[669] It is commercially very busy. In it is a group of kinsmen of ʿUmar b. al-Khaṭṭāb, and other Arab and non-Arab lineages. This place has numerous cities of no great size in which the population is dispersed. Its governor resides in a city called al-Nawātiya[670] near Iqlībiya, from which one can sail to Sicily.

From al-Qayrawān it is two easy stages to the city of Saṭfūra. This is a large city that has people from Quraysh, Quḍāʿa, and other tribes.

From al-Qayrawān (one can also travel) to the city of Tunis, which is on the seacoast and has an arsenal.[671] It is a great city. From it came Ḥammād al-Barbarī, the client of Hārūn al-Rashīd and governor of Yemen. Around the city
349 of Tunis were walls made of mud and unbaked brick; the walls of the areas | adjacent to the sea were of stone. Then the people of Tunis opposed Ziyādat Allāh b. al-Aghlab—among them were Manṣūr al-Ṭanbadhī, Ḥuṣayn al-Tujībī, and al-Qurayʿ al-Balawī—and Ziyādat Allāh therefore fought them. When he defeated them, having killed a great many people, he pulled down the walls of the city. From the coast of Tunis, one can cross to the peninsula of al-Andalus: we have already mentioned the peninsula of al-Andalus and its circumstances when we mentioned Tāhart.[672]

From al-Qayrawān it is three stages to the city of Bāja.[673] Bāja is a large city with ancient stone walls. In contains people descended from the old troops of the Banū Hāshim, as well as non-Arabs. Near the city of Bāja there are Berber tribesmen called Wazdāja. They are recalcitrant and offer no obedience to Ibn al-Aghlab.

From al-Qayrawān it is two stages to the city of al-Urbus,[674] which is a large, prosperous city with a mixed population.

---

668 On Sūsa (modern Sousse), see the article by Mohamed Jedidi in *EI*², s.v. Sūsa.

669 On the peninsula of Jazīrat Sharīk, see the article by Hussain Monés in *EI*², s.v. Djazīrat Sharīk.

670 The reading is uncertain.

671 On the city of Tunis (Arabic, Tūnis), see the article by P. Sebag in *EI*², s.v. Tūnis.

672 In fact, the section on al-Andalus occurs below, on pages 353–355 of the Leiden edition, which suggests that al-Yaʿqūbī did not compile the *Buldān* sequentially.

673 On Bāja (modern Béja), about 100 km west of Tunis, see the article by Élise Voguet in *EI*³, s.v. Bāja.

674 Modern Laribus or Lorbeus in Kef Province of Tunisia.

From al-Qayrawān it is four stages to a city called Majjāna.[675] At this city there are mines of silver, antimony, iron, litharge, and lead among the mountains and canyons. Its people are tribesmen called al-Sanājira. It is said that the first of them was from Sinjār, in the region of Diyār Rabīʿa.[676] They are troops for the government. There are also groups of non-Arabs there: Berbers and others.

South from al-Qayrawān one travels to the land of Qamūda, which is a vast region with cities and fortresses. The city in which the governor resides at this time is Madhkūra.[677] The old chief city is called Subayṭila;[678] it is the city that was conquered in the reign of ʿUthmān b. ʿAffān. ʿAbdallāh b. ʿUmar b. al-Khaṭṭāb, ʿAbdallāh b. al-Zubayr, and the army commander ʿAbdallāh b. Saʿd b. Abī Sarḥ besieged it in the year 37.[679] From the region of Qamūda (one can travel) to the city of Qafṣa,[680] which is a fortified city with stone walls and springs located inside the city. It is paved with stones. Around the city are many cultivated lands and famous varieties of fruit.

From Qafṣa (one travels) to the cities | of Qasṭīliya: four cities in an extensive 350
region of date palms and olive trees.[681] The chief city is called Tawzar; the local officials reside there. The second is called al-Ḥāmma, the third Taqiyūs, and the fourth, Nafṭa. Around these cities lie four salt flats.[682] The people of these cities are non-Arabs: indigenous Romans, Africans, and Berbers.

From the cities of Qasṭīliya it is three stages to the cities of Nafzāwa. Nafzāwa comprises a number of cities. The chief city, in which the local officials reside, is called Bishshara. Its people are indigenous Africans and Berbers. The cities to the south are surrounded by sand.

---

675 Modern Medjana in Algeria, about 85 km southwest of Béjaïa in Algeria.

676 Sinjār is a city in northwestern Iraq. It is uncertain that the populace of Majjāna in North Africa hailed from this Iraqi town. More likely, al-Yaʿqūbī is relaying a folk etymology for the group's name, which was also a way for them to claim Arab ancestry.

677 De Goeje was unable to identify this town, though it is attested elsewhere. It may be a misreading for Mazūna, modern Mezzouna, a small town not far from Subayṭila (Sbeïtla).

678 On Subayṭila (modern Sbeïtla) in south-central Tunisia, see the article by Fethi Béjaoui in *EI*^{2}, s.v. Subayṭila.

679 37 A.H. = June 19, 657 – June 8, 658. But see note 661 above. The correction to 27 (October 7, 647 – September 24, 648) is all the more necessary as ʿUthmān was assassinated at the end of 35/656.

680 Modern Gafsa; see the article by M. Talbi in *EI*^{2}, s.v. Ḳafsa.

681 On the city and its dependencies, see the article by M. Talbi in *EI*^{2}, s.v. Ḳasṭīliya.

682 Arabic *sibākh* (pl. of *sabkha*). These are the so-called shotts (French spelling, chotts; from Arabic *shaṭṭ*): marshy depressions that are covered by a salt crust in the dry summer season, but fill with water to become shallow, temporary lakes in the winter rainy season. See the articles by Y. Callot in *EI*^{2}, s.v. S͟haṭṭ, and by G. Yver in *EI*^{2}, s.v. Sabk͟ha.

South of al-Qayrawān is a region called al-Sāḥil (the Coast), but it is not the coast of a sea. It has much arable land for olive trees, fruit trees, and vineyards, and comprises numerous villages, each leading to the next. This region has two cities, one of them called [...],[683] the other, Qabīsha. From the al-Sāḥil region it is two stages from [...] and Qabīsha to the city called Sfax.[684] Sfax is on the seacoast and the Salt Sea breaks against its city walls. It is the furthest limit of al-Sāḥil. From Sfax to a place called Bizerte[685] is an eight days' journey. At every halting-place there are fortresses, each close to the other, in which the pious and the people of the *ribāṭ*s live.

From al-Qayrawān it is ten stages to the lands of the Zāb.[686] The chief city of the Zāb is Ṭubna, which is where the governors reside.[687] It has a mixed population of Quraysh, Arabs, the garrison, non-Arabs, Africans, Romans, and Berbers. The Zāb is a large region. Located in it is an ancient city called Bāghāya, where there are Arab tribes from the garrison, non-Arabs from the Khurāsānī troops, and non-Arabs from the local non-Arab population of descendants of the Romans. Around it there are Berber tribesmen from the Hawwāra on a mighty mountain called Aurès,[688] on which snow falls. (Also located in it is) a
351 city called Tījis, | which is a dependency of Bāghāya. Around it there are Berber tribesmen: non-Arabs called Nafza. (Also located in it is) a large and majestic city called Mīla; it is prosperous and fortified, but has never been controlled by a governor. It has a fortress surrounding another fortress in which there is a man from the Banū Sulaym called Mūsā b. al-ʿAbbās b. ʿAbd al-Ṣamad, who represents Ibn al-Aghlab.[689] The seacoast is close to this city. It has a port called Jījal,[690] one called Qalʿat Khaṭṭāb, one called Iskīda,[691] one called

683 The unpointed letters here and in the next sentence are too ambiguous to read. De Goeje's conjectural reading is Ṭarnāsa.

684 Al-Yaʿqūbī spells it Asfāqus; the more common Arabic spelling (e.g., in Yāqūt, *Muʿjam al-buldān*) is Safāqus. The conventional spelling Sfax reflects the modern pronunciation of the name of this city located about 233 km south of Tunis.

685 Arabic, Banzart; the conventional spelling Bizerte reflects the modern pronunciation of the name of this Tunisian city, located on the coast about 60 km northwest of Tunis and about 290 km overland from Sfax. See the article by G. Marçais in *EI*^{2}, s.v. Banzart.

686 On this region of northern Algeria, centering on the city of Biskra in the southern foothills of the Atlas and Aurès Mountains, see the article by M. Côte in *EI*^{2}, s.v. Zāb.

687 On Ṭubna, now a ruined site between Barika and Bitham in Algeria, see the article by M. Côte in *EI*^{2}, s.v. Ṭubna.

688 Arabic, Awrās.

689 That is, it is tributary, but not subject, to the Aghlabids.

690 Modern Jijel.

691 Probably corresponding to modern Skīkda.

[...],[692] and one called Marsā Danhāja. The entire region is cultivated, with many trees and fruits amid mountains and springs. (Also located in it is) a city called Saṭīf,[693] where there are tribesmen from the Banū Asad b. Khuzayma acting as agents on behalf of Ibn al-Aghlab. (Also located in it is) a city called Bilizma, whose people are tribesmen from the Banū Tamīm and clients (*mawālī*) of the Banū Tamīm. They are in revolt against Ibn al-Aghlab at the present time. (Also located in it is) a city called Niqāwus,[694] with many cultivated areas, trees, and fruit and with men from the garrison. Around it there are Berbers from the Miknāna, a clan of the Zanāta, and around them a group called the Awraba. Ṭubna is the chief city of the Zāb; it is located in the middle of the Zāb, and the governors reside there. (Then there is) the city called Maqqara; it has many fortresses, but the chief city is Maqqara. Its people are tribesmen from the Banū Ḍabba, but there is also a group of non-Arabs. Around it there are Berber tribesmen called the Banū Zandāj, along with a group called [...] and a group called [...].[695] From there (one continues) to fortresses called [...], Ṭalma, and [...].[696] In (these places) there are tribesmen from the Banū Saʿd of the Banū Tamīm called the Banū l-Ṣamṣāma. They rose up against Ibn al-Aghlab, but Ibn al-Aghlab defeated some of them and imprisoned them. The city of [...][697] is in the mountains. Its people rose up against Ibn al-Aghlab—those who did so were tribesmen from the Hawwāra called the Banū Saghmār,[698] the Banū Warjīl, and others. The city of Arba is | 352
the last city of the Zāb toward the west, the last dependency (*ʿamal*) of the Banū l-Aghlab. The ʿAbbāsid revolutionary army (*al-musawwida*) never went beyond it.[699]

If the traveler travels west from the district of the Zāb, he comes to a group called the Banū Barzāl. They are a division of the Banū Dammar of the Zanāta, and they are all Khārijites (*shurāt*).

We have already mentioned the conquest of Ifrīqiya and the accounts of it in a separate book that we devoted to the subject.

---

692 The unpointed consonants are too ambiguous to read.

693 Modern Sétif.

694 Niqāwus is modern Ngaus, about 60 km southeast of Sétif.

695 The unpointed letters of both tribal names are too ambiguous to read.

696 The unpointed letters of both toponyms are too ambiguous to read.

697 The unpointed letters of the toponym are too ambiguous to read.

698 Reading as suggested by De Goeje in his note; the MS reads Banū Simʿān.

699 Al-Yaʿqūbī uses the term *musawwida* here for the ʿAbbāsid revolutionary army—the term literally means "those who wear black," from the black garments and banners that became the symbol of the movement that put the dynasty in power.

From this place onward is the region that was taken over by al-Ḥasan b. Sulaymān b. Sulaymān b. al-Ḥusayn b. ʿAlī b. al-Ḥusayn b. ʿAlī b. Abī Ṭālib—God's blessing and peace be upon him.[700] The first city under his control is a city called Hāz, whose residents are a group of indigenous Berbers called the Banū Yarniyān, who belong to the Zanāta also. Beyond that there are some cities whose residents are Ṣanhāja and Zawāwa, who are known as al-Barānis. They own cultivated lands, fields, and livestock. The whole region is named after Hāz. Between it and the district (*ʿamal*) of Adna is a journey of three days. Then (one reaches) a group called the Banū Dammar of Zanāta in a vast region. All of them are Khārijites (*shurāt*). Over them rules a chief from among them, called Muṣādif b. Jārtīl. (They dwell) in a region of fields and livestock, one stage away from Hāz. (One continues) from there to a fortress called Ḥiṣn Ibn Kirām. Its people are not Khārijites (*shurāt*), but mainstream Muslims.[701] Their land is arable. Then one arrives at a region called Mattīja, which was taken over by descendants of al-Ḥasan b. ʿAlī b. Abī Ṭālib—God's peace be upon him—called the Banū Muḥammad b. Jaʿfar.[702] It is a vast region with a number of cities and fortresses, a land of fields and cultivation. Between this region and the fortress of Muṣādif b. Jartīl is a three-day journey along the sea-coast. Then comes the city of Madkara, where there are descendants of Muḥammad b. Sulaymān b. ʿAbdallāh b. al-Ḥasan b. al-Ḥasan b. ʿAlī b. Abī Ṭālib—God's peace
353 be upon him.[703] Then comes the city of al-Khaḍrāʾ, | to which many cities, fortresses, villages, and arable lands are connected. This region is controlled by the descendants of Muḥammad b. Sulaymān b. ʿAbdallāh b. al-Ḥasan b. al-Ḥasan b. ʿAlī b. Abī Ṭālib—God's peace be upon him. Every one of these men lives in and fortifies himself in a different city or district. There are so many of them that the region is known by them and named after them. The farthest city under their control is a city near the seacoast called Sūq Ibrāhīm, which is the renowned city where a man named ʿĪsā b. Ibrāhīm b. Muḥammad b. Sulaymān b. ʿAbdallāh b. al-Ḥasan b. al-Ḥasan lives.

---

700 This al-Ḥasan was a descendant of the caliph ʿAlī and of the Ḥusaynid line of Shīʿite Imams.

701 Al-Yaʿqūbī uses the term *jamāʿiyya* to describe these Muslims, which we might translate as "the Consensus-Minded," a shorthand for the label *ahl al-sunna wa-l-jamāʿa*, "the people of (the Prophet's) example and consensus," adopted by adherents of what is now known as Sunni Islam.

702 That is, like the Banū l-Ḥasan b. Sulaymān above, they are descendants of the caliph ʿAlī. However, the Banū Muḥammad b. Jaʿfar are related instead to the Ḥasanid line of Shīʿite Imams.

703 Another descendant of ʿAlī from the Ḥasanid line.

From these places one continues to Tāhart.[704] The chief city is the city of Tāhart, immense and greatly reputed, nicknamed "the Iraq of the Maghrib." It has a mixed population. It is controlled by a group of Persians called the Banū Muḥammad b. Aflaḥ b. ʿAbd al-Wahhāb b. ʿAbd al-Raḥmān b. Rustam al-Fārisī.[705] ʿAbd al-Raḥmān b. Rustam had served as governor of Ifrīqiya, and his descendants moved to Tāhart. They became Ibāḍīs and came to lead the Ibāḍī movement. They are (now) the leaders of the Ibāḍīs of the Maghrib. Adjoining the city of Tāhart is a large area ruled from Tāhart under the authority of Muḥammad b. Aflaḥ b. ʿAbd al-Wahhāb b. ʿAbd al-Raḥmān b. Rustam. The fortress on the seacoast at which the ships of Tāhart anchor is called Marsā Farūkh.

The Peninsula of al-Andalus and Its Cities

Whoever wishes to travel to the peninsula of al-Andalus goes overland from al-Qayrawān to Tunis, as we have mentioned. Tunis is on the coast of the Salt Sea. Then he sails the Salt Sea, hugging the coast for ten days and not going far out to sea, until he is across from the peninsula of al-Andalus at a place called Tanas,[706] which is a four days' journey from Tāhert. Or he can travel (overland) to (the region of) Tāhert and proceed from there to the peninsula—the peninsula of al-Andalus. The traveler crosses the main channel in a day | 354
and a night and arrives in the region of Tudmīr,[707] a large and prosperous region with two cities, one called al-ʿAskar, the other, Lūrqa,[708] each of which possesses a *minbar*.[709] Then he leaves that region for the city where the one holding power from the Umayyad dynasty resides, a city called Córdoba.[710] The journey takes six days from this place, through densely spaced villages, cultivated lands, meadows, valleys, rivers, springs, and cultivated fields. Before reaching the city of Córdoba from Tudmīr, the traveler arrives at a city called Elvira,[711] which was settled by Arabs who had come to the area from the military

704 On this town in western Algeria (Modern Tagdemt or Tīhert), see the article by Mohamed Talbi in *EI*², s.v. Tāhart.

705 That is, the Rustamid dynasty. See note 655 above.

706 Modern Ténès, about midway between Algiers and Oran on the Mediterranean coast.

707 Tudmīr, the older name for the region of Murcia, is derived from the name of the last Visigothic governor of the area, Theodemir, who surrendered his territory to the Arabs in 94/713. See the article by L. Molina in *EI*², s.v. Tudmīr.

708 Spanish, Lorca.

709 Literally, "a pulpit," that is, has a congregational mosque.

710 Arabic, Qurṭuba; see the article by C. F. Seybold and M. Ocaña Jiménez in *EI*², s.v. Ḳurṭuba.

711 Arabic, Ilbīra; see the article by J. F. P. Hopkins in *EI*², s.v. Ilbīra.

district (*jund*) of Damascus. They are from the tribal faction of Muḍar—the bulk of them from Qays—with small contingents from other Arab tribes. It is a two days' journey from Córdoba. To the west (of Córdoba) is a city called Reyyo,[712] which was settled by (men from) the military district (*jund*) of Jordan, who are all from various clans of (the tribal faction of) Yemen. West of Reyyo is a city called Sidonia,[713] which was settled by (men from) the military district (*jund*) of Ḥimṣ. Most of them belong to (the tribal faction of) Yemen, but there are a few who belong to Nizār. West of Sidonia is a city called Algeciras,[714] which was settled by Berbers, with a few Arabs of mixed origins. West of the city of Algeciras is a city called Seville.[715] It is on a large river which is also the river of Córdoba.[716] In the year 229,[717] the pagans (*majūs*) who are called al-Rūs entered the city, took prisoners, looted, burned, and killed.[718] West of Seville is a city called Niebla,[719] which was settled by the Arabs who first entered the area with Ṭāriq, the client (*mawlā*) of Mūsā b. Nuṣayr al-Lakhmī.[720] West of it is a city called Beja,[721] which was also settled by the Arabs who accompanied Ṭāriq. West of it, on the Atlantic Ocean,[722] is a city called Lisbon,[723] and also to

712 Arabic, Rayya (probably to be read as Rayyu). See the article by E. Lévi-Provençal and J.-P. Molénat in *EI*², s.v. Rayya.

713 Arabic, Shadūna; see the article by F. Roldan Castro in *EI*², s.v. S̲h̲adūna.

714 Arabic, al-Jazīra, short for al-Jazīra al-Khaḍrā' (the Green Island, or Isla Verde); see the article by H. Huici Miranda in *EI*², s.v. al-D̲j̲azīra al-K̲h̲aḍrā'.

715 Arabic, Ishbīliya; see the article by J. Bosch-Vilá and H. Terrasse in *EI*², s.v. Is̲h̲bīliya.

716 The river is the Guadalquivir (from Arabic, al-Wādī al-Kabīr, the Great River); see the article by R. Pinilla-Melguizo in in *EI*², s.v. al-Wādī 'l-Kabīr.

717 229 A.H. = September 30, 843 – September 17, 844.

718 Majūs in this context refers not to the Zoroastrians of Iran, but to the Vikings, as does the term Rūs. Al-Ya'qūbī is referring to the attack on Seville by Norse Vikings. After appearing in the estuary of the Tagus in August 844, the Viking fleet of 54 longboats sailed south and then up the Guadaquivir, arriving at Seville in October 844 and subjecting the city to seven days of mayhem. It was not until the following month that Abd al-Raḥmān II inflicted a defeat on them, forcing the survivors to flee. See the article by A. Melvinger, in *EI*², s.v. al-Mad̲j̲ūs.

719 Arabic, Labla, which is close to the city's ancient name, Ilipla. See the article by J. Bosch-Vilá in *EI*², s.v. Labla.

720 That is, Ṭāriq b. Ziyād, the first Muslim conqueror of Andalusia.

721 Arabic, Bāja, the city Beja in southern Portugal, about 127 km northwest of Niebla; see the article by María Luisa Ávila in *EI*³, s.v. Beja.

722 Arabic *al-Baḥr al-Māliḥ al-Muḥīṭ*: literally, "the Surrounding Salt Sea."

723 Arabic, al-Ushbūna; lying about 135 km northwest of Beja; see the article by Amin Tibi in *EI*², s.v. al-Us̲h̲būna.

the west on the sea is a city called Ocsonoba.[724] Such is western al-Andalus, the part that abuts the sea, which leads to the Khazar Sea.[725] East of this city[726] is a city called Mérida,[727] situated on a large river, four days west[728] of Córdoba. Mérida lies opposite the land of the infidels.[729] One race of them is called the Galicians (*al-jalāliqa*) and they | (dwell within) the peninsula (itself). 355

Leaving Córdoba, one travels east to a city called Jaén.[730] Former members of the *jund* of Qinnasrīn and al-ʿAwāṣim live there—a mixture of Arabs from Maʿadd and Yemen. From Jaén one goes north to the city of Toledo.[731] Toledo is a majestic and well-protected city—there is no better-protected city in the peninsula. Its people, who are a mixture of Arabs, Berbers, and non-Arab clients, are opposed to the Banū Umayya. It has a great river called the Duero.[732] From Toledo, heading east,[733] one arrives at a city called Guadalajara,[734] which used to be governed by a Berber called [...][735] b. Faraj al-Ṣanhājī, a supporter of the Banū Umayya. His descendants and offspring live in this region to this day. From there, one travels east to Zaragoza.[736] It is one of the largest of the frontier-towns of al-Andalus, on a river called the Ebro.[737] North of Zaragoza is a city called Tudela,[738] opposite the land of the infidels who are called Basques

---

724 Arabic, Uḥsūnuba (more commonly Ukshūnuba): the province of Algarve and its main city of Faro on the southern coast of Portugal. See the article by Ch. Picard in *EI*^{2}, s.v. Ukshūnuba.

725 Like many other geographers of his time, al-Yaʿqūbī believed that the Ocean (the Atlantic) encircled the Afro-Eurasian land-mass. The Khazar (Caspian) Sea was held to be merely a northern branch of these same waters.

726 More accurately, northeast of Ocsonoba (Faro) and inland.

727 Arabic, Mārida, in Spain, about 265 km northeast of Faro; see the article by E. Lévi-Provençal in *EI*^{2}, s.v. Mārida.

728 More accurately, about 180 km northwest.

729 Referring to the persistence of Christian rule in the north and northwestern parts of the peninsula.

730 Arabic, Jayyān; see the article by A. Huici-Miranda in *EI*^{2}, s.v. Djayyān.

731 Arabic, Ṭulayṭula; see the article by E. Lévi-Provençal and J. P. Molénat in *EI*^{2}, s.v. Ṭulayṭula.

732 Arabic, Duwayr. Al-Yaʿqūbī or his source has confused the Tagus (Arabic, Tājuh), which flows by Toledo, with the Duero of northern Spain.

733 More accurately, about 115 km northeast.

734 Arabic, Wādī l-Ḥijāra (Valley of the Stones); see the article by Cristina de la Puente in *EI*^{2}, s.v. Wādī ʾl-Ḥidjāra.

735 The unpointed letters are too ambiguous to read.

736 Arabic, Saraqusṭa, about 225 km northeast of Guadalajara; see the article by M. J. Vigueira in *EI*^{2}, s.v. Sarakusṭa.

737 Arabic, Abruh; see the article by J. F. P. Hopkins in *EI*^{2}, s.v. Ibruh.

738 Arabic, Tuṭīla; see the article by Maria J. Vigera in *EI*^{2}, s.v. Tuṭīla.

(*al-baskuns*). North of this city lies a city called Huesca,[739] which borders on the (land of) a Frankish race of people called Gascons.[740] South of Zaragoza is a city called Tortosa.[741] It is the farthest of the frontier-towns of eastern al-Andalus, and borders on the (land of) the Franks. It lies on the river that flows down from Zaragoza. Traveling west from Tortosa, one reaches a region called Valencia,[742] a vast and majestic region settled by Berber tribes who give no obedience to the Banū Umayya. They have a great river in an area called Alcira.[743] From there, one travels to the region of Tudmīr, the first region (in this account). Such is the peninsula of al-Andalus and its cities.

We Return to the Account of Tāhart on the Main Road of the Maghrib

From the city of Tāhart and the area subject to Ibn Aflaḥ al-Rustamī (the traveler reaches) the principality of | a man from the Hawwāra called Ibn Masāla al-Ibāḍī, who, nevertheless, is opposed to Ibn Aflaḥ and makes war on him.[744] The city in which he resides is called al-Jabal. From there, it is a half-day's journey to a city called Yalal, near the Salt Sea. It has farms, villages, cultivated lands, fields, and trees. From the principality of Ibn Masāla al-Hawwārī (one comes) again to a principality belonging to the Banū Muḥammad b. Sulaymān b. ʿAbdallāh b. al-Ḥasan b. al-Ḥasan,[745] other than the principality that we mentioned above, which was the city of Madkara. (These Banū Muḥammad b. Sulaymān) reside in the chief city, which is called Thamṭilās. The populace of this principality consists of tribesmen from clans of all the Berber tribes, most of them being tribesmen called the Banū Maṭmāṭa.[746] They are numerous clans, having in their principality a great city called Ayzraj, in which some of them reside. The

356

739 Arabic, Washqa; see the article by B. Catlos in *EI*², s.v. Washḳa.

740 Arabic, al-Jāsqas.

741 Arabic, Ṭurṭūsha. More accurately, southeast of Zaragoza; see the article by Maria J. Viguera in *EI*², s.v. Ṭurṭūsha.

742 Arabic, Balansiya; see the article by E. Lévi-Provençal in *EI*², s.v. Balansiya.

743 Arabic, al-Shuqr. The region lies south of the city of Valencia. The modern Catalan name of the river, Xúquer, continues the Arabic. See the article by A. Huici-Miranda in *EI*², s.v. Djazīrat Shuḳr.

744 'Nevertheless,' because as an Ibāḍī, he might be expected to support a fellow member of the same sect.

745 Cf. ed. Leiden, 352, where they are called "the descendants (*wuld*) of Muḥammad b. Sulayman ..." *Wuld* and *Banū* are synonymous.

746 On this large Berber tribe, see the article by T. Lewicki in *EI*², s.v. Maṭmāṭa.

people of this city are Maṭmāṭa. Another city, controlled by a man of theirs named ʿUbaydallāh, is called al-Ḥasana (The Beautiful), if one translates the name from Berber into Arabic. Then (one continues) to the greatest and most renowned city in the Maghrib, which is called Tlemcen.[747] It is surrounded by walls of stone, which in turn have other stone walls behind them. Tlemcen has a large population and lofty palaces and dwellings. It is the residence of a man named Muḥammad b. al-Qāsim b. Muḥammad b. Sulaymān. In the environs of the city are Berber tribesmen called Miknāsa and [S ...].[748] From there (one continues) to the city named Madīnat al-ʿAlawiyyīn (City of the ʿAlids), which was under the control of ʿAlids descended from Muḥammad b. Sulaymān. Then they abandoned it, and one of the sons of the kings of the Zanāta, called ʿAlī b. Ḥāmid b. Marḥūm al-Zanātī, settled in it. From there one continues to a city called Numālata, where Muḥammad b. ʿAlī b. Muḥammad b. Sulaymān resides. The farthest part of the principality of the Banū Muḥammad b. Sulaymān b. ʿAbdallāh b. al-Ḥasan b. al-Ḥasan is the city of Fālūsan, which is a large city whose people | belong to Berber clans from the Maṭmāṭa, Tarja, Jazzūla, Ṣan- 357
hāja, Injifa and [...].[749]

After the principality of the Banū Muḥammad b. Sulaymān comes the principality of a man named Ṣāliḥ b. Saʿīd, who claims to be from (the Yemeni tribe of) Ḥimyar, but the local people say that he is a native from the (Berber tribe of) Nafza. The name of his chief city, in which he resides, is Nakūr, which is on the Salt Sea.[750] From this city, one of the descendants of Hishām b. ʿAbd al-Malik b. Marwān, along with his companions from the house of Marwān, crossed over into the peninsula of al-Andalus as they fled from the Banū l-ʿAbbās.[751] The principality of Ṣāliḥ b. Saʿīd al-Ḥimyarī extends for a ten days' journey amid cultivated lands, fortresses, villages, dwellings, fields, livestock, and fertile land. The farthest part of his principality is a city called [M ...],[752] atop a mountain, which has rivers, valleys, and cultivated lands beneath it.

From there one continues to the principality of the Banū Idrīs b. Idrīs b. ʿAbdallāh b. al-Ḥasan b. al-Ḥasan b. ʿAlī b. Abī Ṭālib—may God's peace be upon

---

747 Arabic, Tilimsān; see the article by A. Bel and M. Yalaoui in *EI*², s.v. Tilimsān.

748 The unpointed letters of the tribal name are too ambiguous to read.

749 The unpointed letters of the tribal name are too ambiguous to read.

750 On the city and its rulers, see the article by Ch. Pellat in *EI*², s.v. Nakūr (Nukūr).

751 Al-Yaʿqūbī is referring to ʿAbd al-Raḥmān b. Muʿāwiya b. Hishām, who escaped the overthrow of the Marwānid branch of the Umayyad dynasty during the ʿAbbāsid Revolution and fled into al-Andalus where he established his own kingdom, ruling from 138/756 to 172/788; see the article by Luis Molina in *EI*³, s.v. ʿAbd al-Raḥmān b. Muʿāwiya.

752 The unpointed letters are too ambiguous to read.

him.[753] The border of their principality is a place called Ghumayra, which is the residence of a man named ʿUbaydallāh b. ʿUmar b. Idrīs. Then one continues to a place called Malḥāṣ (the Refuge), because of a caravanserai there where the pilgrims coming from al-Sūs al-Aqṣā and Tangier gather. It is controlled by ʿAlī b. ʿUmar b. Idrīs. Then one continues to Qalʿat Ṣadīna, a large place in which Muḥammad b. ʿUmar b. Idrīs resides. From Qalʿat Ṣadīna to the great river called [L …][754] there are fortresses, cultivated lands, and a large region controlled by a descendant of Dāwūd b. Idrīs b. Idrīs. (One continues) to a river called the Sabū, controlled by Ḥamza b. Dāwūd b. Idrīs b. Idrīs. Then one enters
358 the chief city, called Ifrīqiyā City, on the great river called | Fez.[755] Yaḥyā b. Yaḥyā b. Idrīs b. Idrīs resides there. It is a majestic city, with many cultivated lands and dwellings. On the west bank of the Fez River, a river said to be larger than all other rivers of the world, there are 3,000 mills that grind.[756] The city known as City of the People of al-Andalus,[757] is where Dāwūd b. Idrīs resides. Yaḥyā b. Yaḥyā and Dāwūd b. Idrīs are each opposed to the other, resisting and making war upon one another. At the extreme limits of (the river) of Fez is a city called […],[758] which has been settled by the Barqasāna, a group of indigenous Berbers. Along the Fez River there are majestic cultivated lands, villages, estates, and farms on both banks. Its waters come from springs to the south, although they say that the river neither increases nor decreases. It flows into the river called the Sabū, which we have already mentioned, and the Sabū empties into the Salt Sea. The principality of the Banū Idrīs is vast and large.

---

753 That is, the Idrīsid dynasty of Morocco, ruled from 172/789 to 314/926. The Idrīsids were descendants of ʿAlī through the Ḥasanid line. See the article by D. Eustache in *EI*², s.v. Idrīsids (Adārisa).

754 The unpointed letters are too ambiguous to read.

755 Arabic, Fās; see the article by R. Le Tourneau and H. Terrasse in *EI*², s.v. Fās.

756 The text of this section is only partially legible. The original copyist omitted a large chunk of text and, upon noticing his omission, wrote the text in the margin. Unfortunately, the margin has been torn. De Goeje in his note to this passage suggested reading *lil-madīna* for *al-madīna*. This would give the meaning, "3,000 mills that grind *for* the city known as the City of the People of al-Andalus, which is where …" A city so populous as to require 3,000 mills to grind the flour for its bread is unlikely. Also, this would place the City of the People of al-Andalus on the west side of the Fez River: it is really on the east side. The translation therefore holds to the text as published, defective as it may be.

757 Arabic *Madīnat Ahl al-Andalus*. This is no doubt a reference to the quarter of Fez known as ʿAdwat al-Andalus.

758 The tear in the MS has obliterated the name.

Abū Maʿbad ʿAbd al-Raḥmān b. Muḥammad b. Maymūn b. ʿAbd al-Wahhāb b. ʿAbd al-Raḥmān b. Rustam al-Tāhartī[759] told me: Tāhart is a large, populous city located amid mountains and valleys without any empty areas. Between it and the Salt Sea is a journey of three stages on level terrain. Some of the terrain is occupied by marshy salt flats (*sibākh*) and by a watercourse called Wādī Shalif,[760] along which there are villages and cultivated lands that it inundates just as the Nile of Egypt inundates. Along it people grow safflower, flax, sesame, and other seed-plants. The river continues to a mountain called Anqabaq; then it goes on to the region of Nafza, and then it reaches the Salt Sea.

The people of the city of Tāhart obtain their water from rivers and springs, some of which come from the plain, while others come from a mountain to the south called Jazzūl. The crops of that region never suffer at all, unless afflicted by wind or cold. It is a mountainous region that stretches to Sūs. The people of Sūs call it Daran; in Tāhart, they call it the Jazzūl; | and in the Zāb, they call it 359
Aurès.[761]

Whoever leaves Tāhart by the southwest road arrives at a city called Awzkā, three stages away. It is controlled by a lineage of the Zanāta called the Banū Masra. Their chief was ʿAbd al-Raḥmān b. Ūdamūt b. Sinān. After him, power passed to his descendants, and a son of his called Zayd moved to a place called [Th ...],[762] and his descendants are (still) there. From the city of Awzkā one travels west by road to territory belonging to the Zanāta. Then one continues to the city of Sijilmāsa after traveling for seven stages or so, depending on how fast or slowly one travels. The route is through sparsely populated villages and partly through desert.

Sijilmāsa

Sijilmāsa is a city on a river called the Zīz.[763] It has neither springs nor wells. Between it and the sea is a journey of many stages. The population of Sijilmāsa is mixed; the Berbers, most of them Ṣanhāja, are in control there. Their crops are millet and sorghum. They farm with the rains because of the scarcity of water among them: if they get no rain, they raise no crops. To the city of Sijilmāsa belong villages known as those of the Banū Darʿa, among which is a city of no great size called Tāmdalt, belonging to Yaḥyā b. Idrīs al-ʿAlawī, which is

759 Al-Yaʿqūbī's informant was a minor Rustamid prince, as indicated by his genealogy.

760 Conventionally, Oued Chélif, Algeria's largest river.

761 Arabic, Aurās.

762 The unpointed letters are too ambiguous to read.

763 On this city, now mostly in ruins, located on the fringes of the desert in southeastern Morocco about 300 km southeast of Fez, see the article by M. Terrasse in *EI*², s.v. Sidjilmāsa.

overlooked by a fortress. ʿAbdallāh b. Idrīs came from Tāmdalt. Around it there are mines of gold and silver, which can be found (on the surface) like plants: it is said that the winds blow it about. A group of Berbers called the Banū Tarjā are in control of the people there.

Al-Sūs al-Aqṣā

From the city called Tāmdalt one proceeds to a city called al-Sūs, which is al-Sūs al-Aqṣā (Farthest Sūs).[764] It was settled by the Banū ʿAbdallāh b. Idrīs b. Idrīs. It has a mixed Berber population, with the Madāsa in control. From Sūs
360 one proceeds to | a region called Aghmāt, a fertile region with pasturage and fields amid plains and mountains. Its people are Ṣanhāja Berbers. From Aghmāt one continues to Māssa, a village on the sea to which commercial goods are brought. It contains a mosque known as the Mosque of Bahlūl and a *ribāṭ* on the seacoast. The sea near the Mosque of Bahlūl is (an anchorage) for stitched boats (like those) built at Ubulla that one uses to sail to China.[765]

Whoever travels south by road from Sijilmāsa toward the land of the Blacks,[766] (inhabited by) various black tribes, travels through wasteland and desert for a distance of fifty days' journey. One then encounters a group of Ṣanhāja called the Anbiya in the desert; they have no fixed dwelling. They all wrap their faces with the tails of their turbans, and this is their custom. They do not wear tunics, but only wrap their bodies in their robes. They live off camels, having neither crops nor food derived from grain.[767] Then (one continues) to a region called Ghasṭ, a cultivated valley with dwellings in it, where a king of theirs resides. He has neither religion nor religious law and raids the regions of the Blacks, who have many principalities.

---

764 On this district of southern Morocco, see the article by E. Lévi-Provençal and Cl. Lefébure in *EI*^{2}, s.v. al-Sūs al-Aḳṣā.

765 For long commercial voyages on rough seas, sailors often employed boats with relatively flexible hulls composed of planks woven together with rope rather than attached with nails or pegs. See Hourani, *Arab Seafaring*, 91–97.

766 Arabic *arḍ al-sūdān*: for Arabic geographers the term covers all of sub-Saharan Africa, not merely the modern Sudan.

767 Arabic *ṭaʿām*, usually means *food* in general, but the dictionaries note that it is often used for wheat and barley (in the Ḥijāz) or for millet (in Yemen), and that seems to be the meaning here. See Lane, *Lexicon*, 5:1854, s.v.

Colophon[768]

Thus is completed *The Book of Regions*.[769] Praise be to God, Lord of the Worlds. May God bless Muhammad the Prophet and his Pure Household. ʿAlī b. Abī Muḥammad b. ʿAlī al-Kindī al-Anmāṭī wrote it out, may God pardon him and whatever he has said. Amen! Praise be to God, who is sufficient in His benediction, and blessings on Muhammad and his Household. Work on this copy was finished the morning of Saturday, 21 Shawwāl of the year 607.[770] The work was composed by Aḥmad b. Abī Yaʿqūb b. Wāḍiḥ al-Kātib.

768 The colophon of the Munich MS is given in a note in the Leiden edition.

769 Arabic *Kitāb al-Buldān*.

770 April 6, 1211.

Fragments

A Fragments from the Lost Part of the Geography[771] 361

1. Aḥmad b. Abī Yaʿqūb, the author of *Kitāb al-Masālik wa-l-mamālik* (*The Book of Routes and Principalities*), said: There are 7,000 mosques in Basra.[772]

2. Ibn Abī Yaʿqūb mentions that the waters (of the river of Ahwāz) come from two watercourses. One rises from Isfahan and flows past the Shādhurwān of Tustar,[773] ʿAskar Mukram, and Jundīshāpūr. It has a bridge across it that is 563 paces long and is called al-Masruqān. The other watercourse rises from Hamadhān and flows on to al-Sūs; it is called al-Hinduwān. Then the two watercourses flow toward Manādhir al-Kubrā, where one flows into the other, forming one river called the Dujayl al-Ahwāz. From there it flows to al-Ahwāz and continues until it empties into the Persian Gulf near Ḥiṣn Mahdī. In the summer it dries up and the riverbed becomes a road that the caravans use. [The people of this region have a special dialect that sounds like gibberish, but the Persian language is the most common among them.][774]

3. Shiraz | is the chief city of Fārs. It is a great and majestic city in which the 362
governors reside. It is so spacious that there is not a single dwelling in it whose master does not have in it a garden with all kinds of fruits, herbs, vegetables, and everything else that grows in gardens. Its inhabitants obtain their drinking water from springs that flow into rivers that come from mountains on which snow falls.[775]

4. Al-Yaʿqūbī said: [Naṣībīn] is a great city with many rivers, gardens, and orchards. It has a large river called al-Hirmās, which has an ancient Roman

---

771 See notes 501 and 502 above.

772 Source: al-Idrīsī, *Nuzhat al-mushtāq fī ikhtirāq al-āfāq* (Leiden, 1970–1984), 383.

773 The Shādhurwān of Tustar (from Persian *shādurwān*, curtain or tapestry; halo) was an architectural marvel commented upon by many visitors to Tustar. From the description in Yāqūt, s.v. Tustar, it appears to be a steep, massive aquaduct or, at least, the above-ground portion of a larger *qanāt* that brought water from the river inside the city walls. This appears to be corroborated by modern archaeological work done in the city (see *The History of al-Ṭabarī*, XIII, trans. G. H. A. Juynboll, 227–228). *Pace* De Goeje, in his *Glossarium* to volumes 7 and 8 of the *Bibliotheca Geographorum Arabicorum*, xxvii, this has nothing to do with the Shādhurwān in Mecca, which is the low, semi-circular wall that abuts the north face of the Kaʿba also known as al-Ḥaṭīm.

774 Source: Al-Waṭwāṭ, *Manāhij al-fikar wa-mabāhij al-ʿibar*, 1:346–347. The phrase in brackets may not belong to al-Yaʿqūbī's original text.

775 Source: Al-Sharīshī, *Sharḥ Maqāmāt al-Ḥarīrī*, 3:43.

stone bridge over it. Its people are Arabs from the Banū Taghlib of Rabīʿa. Ghanm b. ʿIyāḍ al-Ghanmī conquered it in the reign of ʿUmar—may God be pleased with him—in the year 18.[776]

5. Ibn Wāḍiḥ said: The Second Qinnasrīn is Ḥiyār Banī l-Qaʿqāʿ.[777]

6. Ibn Wāḍiḥ included Martaḥwān and the district (*kūra*) of Miṣrīn in the district (*kūra*) of Aleppo.[778]

7. Ibn Abī Yaʿqūb said: Al-Manṣūr[779] built the city of al-Maṣṣīṣa during his reign—before that it had been a garrison—and al-Maʾmūn[780] built Kafarbayyā. The river Jayḥān flows between them. Over the river is a large ancient stone bridge with three arches on an area of high ground.[781]

8. Ibn Abī Yaʿqūb said: In addition to these three cities (Antioch, al-Maṣṣīṣa, and Tarsus) the Syrian Thughūr[782] also includes the city of ʿAyn Zarba, which is in the environs of al-Maṣṣīṣa.[783]

9. Ibn Abī Yaʿqūb said: The city of Malaṭya is ancient, one of the constructions of Alexander. In the lands of the Romans it is famous and borders Syria.[784]

10. Al-Yaʿqūbī said: Malaṭya is the chief city. It was ancient, but the Romans destroyed it. Al-Manṣūr rebuilt it in the year 139,[785] enclosed it with a single wall, and moved a number of Arab tribes to it. He also said: It is on level ground

---

776 Source: Ibid., 2:61. Ghanm b. ʿIyāḍ al-Ghanmī is a copyist's error for ʿIyāḍ b. Ghanm al-Fihrī, the Muslim conqueror of northern Iraq.

777 Source: Ibn al-Shiḥna, *Taʾrīkh Ḥalab*, 164. Cf. Fragments C5, C10.

778 Source: Ibid., 166. Cf. Fragment C12.

779 ʿAbbāsid caliph, r. 136–158/754–775; his rebuilding of al-Maṣṣīṣa has been noted above, ed. Leiden, 238.

780 ʿAbbasid caliph, r. 198–218/813–833.

781 Source: Ibn al-Shiḥna, *Taʾrīkh Ḥalab*, 177–178. Cf. Fragments C18 & C19. Cf. Abū l-Fidāʾ, *Taqwīm al-buldān* (Paris, 1840), 251.

782 That is, the frontier with Byzantium; see the article by C. E. Bosworth in *EI*², s.v. al-Thughūr.

783 Source: Ibn al-Shiḥna, *Taʾrīkh Ḥalab*, 182. Cf. Fragment C22.

784 Source: Ibid., 193. Cf. Fragment C26.

785 139 A.H. = June 5, 756 – May 24, 757. On the destruction of the town by Constantine VI in 133/750 and its subsequent rebuilding in the reign of al-Manṣūr, mentioned above, ed. Leiden, 238, see the article by E. Honigmann in *EI*², s.v. Malaṭya.

surrounded by the mountains of the Romans. Its water comes from springs and watercourses coming from the Euphrates.[786]

11. Ibn Abī Ya'qūb said: Ra'bān and Dulūk are two districts close to each other. 363
Dulūk is a famous ancient city and used to be populous. It has a high citadel of stone built by the Romans. It used to have an aqueduct set on arches upon which the water ascended to the citadel. In its environs there are pleasant houses carved into the stone. In its environs there are many sources of water and orchards with abundant fruit. It is said that the stopping-place of David—upon him be peace—was located here. From there he outfitted the army to attack Qūrus, and Ūrīya b. Ḥannān was killed there.[787] [The city and the citadel were destroyed and it survives today as a village inhabited by peasants.][788]

12. Ibn Shaddād said: Ibn Abī Ya'qūb mentioned [Kaysūm] in his *Kitāb al-Buldān* (*Book of Regions*) as one of the (cities of the frontier district of) al-'Awāṣim.[789]

13. Ibn Abī Ya'qūb said: Manbij is an ancient city that was conquered by treaty granted by 'Amr b. al-'Āṣ under the authority of Abū 'Ubayda b. al-Jarrāḥ. It is on the main part of the Euphrates.[790]

14. Aḥmad al-Kātib said: Adhana was built by al-Rashīd.[791] He is also the one who built Tarsus.[792]

15. Aḥmad al-Kātib said: Alexandretta[793] is a city on the coast of the Roman Sea near Antioch. Aḥmad b. Abī Du'ād al-Iyādī rebuilt it in the caliphate of al-Wāthiq.[794]

---

786 Source: Al-Sharīshī 3:62. Cf. Fragment c26.

787 Ra'bān, Dulūk, and Qūrus are towns in the border area called al-'Awāṣim. Ūrīya is Uriah the Hittite, the husband of Bathsheba, mentioned in 2 Samuel 11.

788 Source: Ibn al-Shiḥna, 219. Cf. Fragment c28. The sentence in brackets is from Ibn Shaddād (d. 684/1285), Ibn al-Shiḥna's ultimate source, not al-Ya'qūbī.

789 Source: Ibid., 221. Cf. Fragment c30.

790 Source: Ibid., 222. Cf. Fragment c8.

791 More precisely, al-Rashīd (r. 170–193/786–809) rebuilt these cities.

792 Source: Abū l-Fidā', 249. Cf. Fragment c21.

793 Arabic: Bāb Iskandarūna.

794 Source: Abū l-Fidā', 255. Cf. Fragment c25. Aḥmad b. Abī Du'ād al-Iyādī was chief judge under the 'Abbāsids starting with al-Mu'taṣim (r. 218–227/833–842) until the year 232/847,

16. Tiflis is a city in Armenia 30 farsakhs from Qālīqalā.[795] At Qālīqalā a number of large rivers have their source. The first of them is the Euphrates, which has been mentioned already. It[796] begins two farsakhs from Qālīqalā, then branches off to the west to Dabīl, [continues] to Warthān, and then empties into the Khazar Sea. The second is the Kurr,[797] which flows from the city of Qālīqalā
364 then branches off to the city of Tiflis and flows east | to the city of Bardhaʿa[798] and its hinterland. Then it approaches the Khazar Sea and joins with the Aras (al-Rass), so that they flow as one river. It is said that beyond the Aras there are 300 ruined cities. These are the cities to which Almighty God refered, along with the people of al-Rass.[799] He sent to them Ḥanẓala b. Ṣafwān, but they put him to death and so they were destroyed. Other accounts have been given about the people of al-Rass. Armenia is divided into three parts. The first part includes the cities of Dabīl, Qālīqalā, Khilāṭ, Shimshāṭ, and al-Sawād. The second part includes the cities of Bardhaʿa, al-Baylaqān, Qabala, and Bāb al-Abwāb.[800] The third part includes the city of Jurzān, the city of Tiflis, and the city known as Masjid Dhī l-Qarnayn (The Mosque of Alexander the Great). Armenia was conquered in the caliphate of ʿUthmān by Salmān b. Rabīʿa al-Bāhilī in the year 24.[801]

---

in the reign of al-Mutawakkil. He died in 240/854. Al-Wāthiq reigned from 227–232/842–847.

795 On Tiflis (Arabic, Tiflīs), see the article V. Minorsky and C. E. Bosworth in *EI*^{2}, s.v. Tiflīs; on Qālīqalā or Qālī (modern Erzurum); see the article by Halil İnalcik in *EI*^{2}, s.v. Erzurum.

796 As De Goeje noted, the sentence cannot refer to the Euphrates, which does not flow into the Khazar/Caspian Sea. Since Warthān was located on the Aras/al-Rass, which leads to the Kurr river before emptying into the Caspian Sea, it is probably that river, or a portion of it, that al-Yaʿqūbī is discussing here.

797 Modern Kura.

798 Throughout, De Goeje reads this as Bardaʿa.

799 Arabic *Aṣḥāb al-Rass* (Qurʾān, 25:38). Commentators explanded the enigmatic reference by supplying a pre-Islamic prophet, Ḥanẓala b. Ṣafwān, who warned his people (the Aṣḥāb al-Rass) not to worship an idol, but was killed, after which God destroyed their city. See the article by A. J. Wensinck in *EI*^{2}, s.v. Aṣḥāb al-Rass.

800 Bāb al-Abwāb (the Gate of Gates), or simply al-Bāb, was located near modern Derbend on the western shore of the Caspian Sea. It was a massive fortification believed to have been built by Alexander the Great, but was in fact a Sasanian foundation designed to keep their Khazar enemies penned in to the north. See the article by D. M. Dunlop in *EI*^{2}, s.v. Bāb al-Abwāb.

801 Source: Al-Sharīshī, 3:6. De Goeje adds: "Al-Yaʿqūbī is not mentioned, but the account is at least partly taken from his book." 24 A.H. = November 7, 644 – October 27, 645.

17. Aḥmad b. Abī Ya'qūb said: Armenia is in three parts. The first part includes Qālīqalā, Khilāṭ, Shimshāṭ, and everything in between. The second part includes Jurzān, Tiflis, the city of Bāb al-Lān, and everything in between. The third part includes Bardha'a, which is the chief-city of Arrān, al-Baylaqān, and Bāb al-Abwāb.[802]

18. Aḥmad b. Wāḍiḥ al-Iṣbahānī mentioned that he resided for a long time in
the land of Armenia,[803] | worked as a secretary for a number of its kings and *290*
governors, and had never seen a land more abounding in amenities or | richer in *291*
wildlife. He mentioned that the number of its principalities is 113, among them the principality of the Master of al-Sarīr[804] between al-Lān and Bāb al-Abwāb. Leading to it there are only two roads: a road leading to the land of the Khazars, and a road leading to the lands of Armenia, comprising 18,000 villages. Arrān is the first principality of Armenia, comprising 4,000 villages, most of them villages of the Master of al-Sarīr.

He mentioned that Bāb al-Abwāb is a wall that Anūshirwān[805] built and that one end of it lies in the sea. Its base extends from the sea to a point at which crossing is impossible. It extends seven farsakhs to an area of rough and rocky terrain where passage through is impossible. It is built of square carved blocks, each one no less than 50 feet [in length], and these blocks still remain.[806] The blocks were interlocked with the other blocks using pegs. In these seven farsakhs (of wall) were built seven roads, each road with a compound on it in which was garrisoned a group of Persian soldiers called the Siyāsīkīn.

He mentioned that a levy of men was imposed upon the people of Armenia to guard the wall and its gates. Each of the seven roads has a gate. The width of the wall at the top is such that twenty horsemen can pass along it without crowding one another. At the city of al-Bāb, at the Gate of Jihād, atop the wall there are two stone columns. Atop each column is the image of a lion made of

---

802 Source: Abū l-Fidā', 387.

803 De Goeje stops here and does not provide the complete text of this lengthy fragment, found in Ibn al-Faqīh, 290–292. What follows has been supplied from Ibn al-Faqīh (as did Wiet, 232–233); page references in this excerpt (in *italics* in the margin) refer to the Leiden edition of Ibn al-Faqīh.

804 A local ruler renowned for the golden throne (*sarīr*) that the Sasanian Shah Khusraw I Anūshirwān (r. 531–579 C.E.) bestowed on his ancestor. See al-Ya'qūbī, *Ta'rīkh*, 2:382.

805 Khusraw I Anūshirwān (r. 531–579 C.E.).

806 The measurement used by al-Ya'qūbī (Ar. *rijl*) here is not very common or exact. As in English, the measurement also literally means "foot," as in the appendage, so we can take take it to mean something less than 12 inches.

white stone. At the foot of the two columns are two stones with images of lions on them. Near the gate is a stone image of a man with, between his legs, an image of a fox with a cluster of grapes in his mouth. Next to the city is a cistern
292 known as the Cistern of Maʿrūf. It has stairs, | by which one can descend into the cistern when water is scarce. On both sides of the stairway are lions of stone; on one of them is a stone image of a man. At the Gate of Governance is an image of two lions, also of stone, standing outside the wall. The people of al-Bāb say that they are the talismans of the city wall.[807]

B Fragments from Other Works[808]

364 1. Muḥammad b. Aḥmad b. al-Khalīl b. Saʿīd al-Tamīmī al-Maqdisī said in his book entitled *Perfume for the Bride and Basil for the Souls*:[809] Musk is of many kinds and varieties. The finest and most expensive is from Tibet. It is obtained from a place called Dhū Samt, two months' journey from Tibet, transported from there to Tibet, and then carried to Khurāsān ... He also said: Aḥmad b.
365 Abī Yaʿqūb, a client of the Banū l-ʿAbbās, said: A group of men knowledgeable | about sources of musk mentioned to me that its sources in the land of Tibet and elsewhere are well-known. The importers build there constructions resembling a lighthouse[810] a cubit in height. The animal, in whose navel the musk forms, comes and rubs its navel against this "lighthouse" until the navel falls off right there. The importers then come at a time of year known to them and gather (the musk) as they like. When they bring it into Tibet, they must pay a tithe from it ... He also said: The finest musk comes from gazelles that feed on a grass called *al-kadahmas*, which grows in Tibet and Kashmir, or one of the two. Ibn Abī Yaʿqūb mentioned that the name of this grass is *al-kandahasah*.[811]

---

807 It was common in the medieval Near East to attribute talismanic properties (against sickness, snake-bite, infertility, etc.) to certain distinctively carved stones or ancient spolia purposely or accidentally imbedded in the fabric of city walls. Such stones were said to protect the inhabitants from all such maladies or pests.

808 The translation here returns to the Leiden edition of the *Buldān*.

809 The reading of the title as *Ṭīb al-ʿarūs wa-rayḥān al-nufūs*, for De Goeje's *Jayb al-ʿarūs* ..., is confirmed in al-Qalqashandī, *Ṣubḥ al-aʿshā fī ṣināʿat al-inshāʾ*, 2:126.

810 Arabic *manār*. The word (literally, a place for light) could denote a lighthouse, a minaret, or an obelisk, among other things, as documented by Dozy, *Supplément*, 2:744.

811 Fragments B1–B12 are from al-Nuwayrī, *Nihāyat al-arab fī funūn al-adab*, 12:1–8, the most detailed Arabic account of musk. See the article by A. Dietrich in *EI*², s.v. Misk.

2. Aḥmad b. Abī Yaʿqūb said: The finest musk is the Tibetan; after it, Sogdian musk; after Sogdian, Chinese musk. The finest Chinese musk is that which comes from Canton.[812] This is the great city that is the port of China where the ships of Muslim merchants anchor. The musk is then transported by sea to al-Zuqāq.[813] By the time it approaches the region of al-Ubulla, its scent is so strong that the merchants cannot hide it from the tithe agents. Once it is removed from the ships, its scent becomes good and the scent of the sea dissipates from it.

Next comes Indian musk, which is what is imported from Tibet to India, then carried to al-Daybul and shipped across the sea. It is inferior to the first sort.

After Indian musk comes the musk of Qinbār. This is a good musk, although it is inferior to the Tibetan in value, essence (*al-jawhar*), color, and scent. It is obtained from a land called Qinbār, between China and Tibet. Sometimes they cheat and pass it off as Tibetan.

He said: Following this in quality is the musk of the Ṭughuz-Ughuz. It is a heavy musk, tending toward black. It is obtained from the land of the Ṭughuz-Ughuz Turks. The merchants import it and try to cheat with it, but it has neither essence nor color. It is slow to grind and is not devoid of roughness.

Following this in quality is the musk of Qiṣār. It is obtained it from a little region called Qiṣār, between India and China. He said: It can approach the Chinese musk, but is inferior to it in value, essence, and scent.

He said: Then there is the musk of Khirjīz.[814] It is a musk that looks like the Tibetan and otherwise resembles it. It is yellow | with a faint scent. 366

After it comes the musk of ʿIṣmār, the weakest of all the varieties of musk and the lowest in value: the gland in which one ounce ripens produces a dirham's worth of musk.[815]

Then comes Jabalī musk, which is obtained from a region of the land of Sind in the area of al-Mūltān. It comes from large glands, is of fine color, but is weak in scent.

---

812 Arabic *Khānqū* (modern Chinese *Guangzhou*).

813 That is "the Strait"—presumably the Strait of Malacca, the only passage west from Canton in China to the Persian Gulf town of al-Ubulla.

814 The reading of this name is based on the 1964 edition of al-Nuwayrī, *Nihāyāt al-arab*. De Goeje, in his edition of the *Buldān*, printed it as "*al-Ḥarjīrī* (sic)."

815 The dirham is a silver coin of varying weight and value, and of less value than the gold dinar. Since even only a very little of the best musk could be worth many dinars, al-Yaʿqūbī is here showing just how poor in quality this variety of musk is.

He said: [The musk called] Sogdian is what is purchased by the merchants of Khurāsān from Tibet. They transport it loaded on animals to Khurāsān, then it is transported from Khurāsān to all points.[816]

3. Muḥammad b. Aḥmad al-Tamīmī said: My father related to me from his father that Aḥmad b. Abī Yaʿqūb said: Ambergris is of many kinds and varieties. Its sources are widely scattered and it varies in quality depending on its source and essence. The most excellent kind, the most profitable, best in quality, finest in color, purest in essence, and dearest in value is the ambergris of al-Shiḥr. It is what the Indian Ocean casts up on the shores of al-Shiḥr in the land of Yemen. They claim that it is cast up from the sea in lumps the size of a camel or a large boulder.

Al-Tamīmī ... said: My father also related to me from his father from Aḥmad b. Abī Yaʿqūb, who said: The wind and the force of the waves break it up and cast it onto the shore. It is boiling, so that nothing can approach it due to the intensity of its heat and boiling. After it sits for a few days and the breeze blows over it, it congeals, and the people from the coastal areas neighboring its source collect it.

He said: Sometimes the great fish called *al-bāl* (that is, the whale) comes and swallows some of the floating ambergris as it boils. Before it can settle in its stomach, the great fish dies and floats to the surface, and the sea casts it up on the shore. They cut open its stomach and the ambergris inside it is removed: this is "fish-amber" (*al-ʿanbar al-samakī*), also called "swallowed amber" (*al-mablūʿ*).

He said: Sometimes the sea casts up a piece of ambergris and a black bird like a tern[817] sees it and makes for it, hovering with its wings. When it approaches and descends on it, it becomes stuck in it with its claws and beak and it dies and decomposes, but its beak and claws remain in the ambergris. This is "beak-amber" (*al-ʿanbar al-manāqīrī*).

---

816 De Goeje adds: "It is not certain that all of this account comes from Yaʿqūbī."

817 Arabic *khuṭṭāf*. The dictionaries (Lane and Dozy) give 'swallow' as the translation, but the context implies a seabird. For *khuṭṭāf* as "tern," see al-Nijūmī, *Al-Ṭuyūr al-Miṣriyya*, 168, which gives *khuṭṭāf* as the Arabic for the genus *Sterna*. The color black suggests some sort of petrel, but the true explanation probably has nothing to do with bird beaks, but with the fact that "ambergris frequently contains the hard mandibles (beaks) of a cuttle-fish which serves as food to the spermwhale" (J. Ruska and M. Plessner in EI^2, s.v. ʿAnbar).

4. He said: After the ambergris of al-Shiḥr (in quality) comes the ambergris of Zanj, which is brought | from the land of the Zanj to Aden.[818] It is white ambergris. 367

After it comes the ambergris of al-Salāhiṭ, which is varies in quality. The best kind of Salāhiṭī ambergris is grayish-blue and very greasy. This is the kind used in perfumes called *ghāliya*.[819]

After Salāhiṭī ambergris comes the ambergris of Qāqula, which is bright gray, of excellent aroma, fine-looking, light, and slightly dry. It is inferior to the Salāhiṭī and is adequate neither for *ghāliya* perfumes nor for purification, except out of necessity. However, it is adequate for powders and plasters. This ambergris comes from the sea of Qāqula to Aden.[820]

After Qāqulī ambergris comes Indian ambergris, which comes from the inner coasts of India and is transported to Basra and other places.

After it comes the Zanjī ambergris, which comes from the coasts of the Zanj and resembles Indian ambergris and is similar to it.

This is what al-Tamīmī mentions in *Perfume for the Bride*. He ranks Zanjī ambergris after Shiḥrī ambergris, and even puts Zanjī ambergris after Indian ambergris. (Al-Tamīmī) said: From India comes a kind of ambergris called *al-kark bālūs*, named after a group of Indians known as al-Kark Bālūs who import it and take it to a place near Oman, where sea-merchants buy it from them. (Al-Tamīmī) said: As for Maghribī ambergris, it is inferior to all these kinds. It comes from the sea of al-Andalus, and merchants carry it to Egypt. It is similar in color to Shiḥrī ambergris, and so they sometimes cheat with it …

Aḥmad b. Abī Yaʿqūb said: A group of people knowledgeable about ambergris told me that it occurs in hills of various colors that grow on the bottom of the sea. The winds and the force of the sea during heavy winter rains cause it to rise up. For that reason, it is scarcely possible to get any during the summer.

5. Aḥmad b. Abī Yaʿqūb said: When the aloe wood of Khmer is ripe, it contains much water.[821]

Ibn Abī Yaʿqūb said: After the aloe wood of Qāqula (in quality) comes the aloe wood of Champa.[822] It is imported from a land called Champa in the

---

818 That is, from East Africa.

819 A fancy style of perfume, usually a heady mixture of musk and ambergris.

820 Qāqula is an unidentified port on the Malay Peninsula.

821 Following the translation suggested by Wiet, 238, n. 3. On the many varieties of aromatic aloe wood (Arabic *ʿūd*) used in medicine, perfume, and incense, see the article by C. E. Bosworth in *EI*², s.v. ʿŪd.

822 Arabic *Ṣanf*, the southeast Asian region of Champa, now in central and southern Vietnam.

vicinity of China. Between it and China stands an impassable mountain. It is the very best variety of aloe wood, and it provides the longest-lasting (scent) for clothing. There are some who prefer it over the Qāqulī aloe wood, and who consider it to be nicer, with a longer-lasting and more durable aroma. There are also some who place it higher than the aloe wood of Khmer.[823]

368 Aḥmad b. Abī Yaʿqūb said: There is also a type of aloe wood called *al-qashūr*, which is soft and blue. It has a sweeter aroma than the *qaṭaʿī* (variety of aloe wood),[824] but is less valuable. (The finest kind of Chinese [aloe wood] is a kind of it called *al-qaṭaʿī*). He said: There are also other types of Chinese (aloe wood) inferior to these types, including *al-manṭāwī* or *al-mānṭāʾī*, which comes in large pieces, smooth, black, and without knots in it. Its scent is not highly regarded, but it is suitable for medicines, powders, and digestive remedies (*al-jawārshanāt*).[825] There is a kind known as *al-jallāʾī* and a kind known as *al-lawāqī* or *al-lūqīnī*: they are comparable in value.

Al-Tamīmī said: Some people rank Chinese aloe wood differently than does Aḥmad b. Abī Yaʿqūb …

6. As for Indian spikenard (*sunbul*), Aḥmad b. Abī Yaʿqūb said: Spikenard comes in varieties, the best of which is the variety in which the rhizomes are red and "stripped" (*musallal*).[826] "Stripped" means that it has had its bark peeled and rubbed off so that the rhizomes are exposed. If one holds it in one's hand for a while and then smells it, its scent is like the scent of apples or something similar. The next variety is a type with red rhizomes tending toward white or variegated. It has a lovely scent, close to that of the first kind. The poorest variety is powdered spikenard (from) the main part (of the stem); it does not count as good perfume. As for the origin of spikenard, it is an herb that grows in India and also in Tibet. It is said that in India it grows in valleys as crops do; then it dries up and people come, harvest it, and collect it. The valleys in which this spikenard grows are said to have many snakes, so that no one can go to them

---

823 De Goeje here notes: "The passages that precede this one, on the varieties called *al-mandalī* [from al-Mandal, in India], *al-qāmurūnī* [from Kamrup, in Bengal], *al-samandūrī*, *al-ṣandafūrī* and the Chinese, are perhaps also to be attributed in part to Yaʿqūbī."

824 The voweling and meaning of this variety of aloe wood is uncertain. If it refers to a place-name, al-Qaṭaʿ or the like, it remains unidentified.

825 For Persian *al-jawārishāt*.

826 Al-Yaʿqūbī uses the word *ʿuṣfūra*, "peg" to describe the rhizomes or underground rootstalk of the spikenard plant, which were crushed and distilled into a deep amber aromatic oil. On this term, see Dozy, *Supplément*, s.v. ʿ-S-F-R.

without | tall, thick boots shod with wood or iron on his feet. They say that these snakes have horns containing a lethal poison called *bīsh*. Some say that *bīsh* is derived from the horns of the snake, but a group of experts say that it is a plant that grows in those valleys.[827] It is of two sorts: a pinkish sort,[828] tending toward yellow in color, which is the better sort, and a sort tending toward black. (The local growers) know it and guard against it, although sometimes some of them do not recognize it and, touching it, die, especially if their hand is sweaty or damp. One of the caliphs used to appoint someone over the ships coming from the land of India to al-Ubulla and other ports to inspect and test the spikenard and remove any *bīsh*. It would be removed using iron tongs: no one could touch it without dying on the spot. It would be collected in a container and tossed into the sea. 369

7. Aḥmad b. Abī Yaʿqūb said: All cloves are of one species. The best and finest are the flowers that are strong, hard, dry, fragrant, spicy-flavored, and sweet-smelling. From it come flowers and fruits. Its flowers are small, resembling the wood of the branches of hellebore, black in appearance. Its fruits are larger, resembling a date pit or olive stone. It is said that it is the fruit of a giant tree resembling the lote tree. Others say …

He said: It is imported from the leeward coast and most distant regions of India. At its places of origin there is an odor so fragrant and penetrating that they call the clove regions "The Breeze of Paradise" because of the fragrance of its odor …

8. Muḥammad b. Aḥmad al-Tamīmī mentioned in his book entitled *Perfume for the Bride*, in the chapter on *ghāliya* perfume, a great many varieties of it. We will relate from it what sorts of *ghāliya* used to be prepared for caliphs, kings, and great men. According to Aḥmad b. Abī Yaʿqūb, to prepare one of the *ghāliya* perfumes of the caliphs 100 mithqāls of rare Tibetan musk were taken and ground … This *ghāliya*, containing equal quantities of ambergris and musk, used to be prepared for Ḥumayd al-Ṭūsī and pleased al-Maʾmūn greatly. This *ghāliya* also used to be prepared for Umm Jaʿfar …[829] They also used to

827 Al-Yaʿqūbī's experts are right: *al-bīsh* is the poisonous plant aconite, better known in varieties such as wolfsbane and monkshood.

828 Arabic *khalanjī*, the color of khalanj, a kind of tree with aromatic wood. The translation "pinkish" is based on De Goeje's glossary in *Bibliotheca Geographorum Arabicorum*, 8:xix (of a color between red and yellow).

829 Umm Jaʿfar is Zubayda, a wife of Hārūn al-Rashīd and a key figure of his court.

manufacture this *ghāliya* for Muḥammad b. Sulaymān ...[830] They also used to manufacture for Umm Ja'far a variety called ambergris *ghāliya* (*ghāliyat al-'anbar*) ...[831]

370 9. A description of *rāmik* perfume and of another compound perfumes, about which al-Tamīmī related from Aḥmad b. Abī Ya'qūb that he had prepared some and that it was the most excellent of the compound perfumes. Ibn Abī Ya'qūb said: The recipe for preparing *rāmik* is: Take a nice ripe gallnut ...

10. As for the method (of mixing) *bān* oil[832] with aromatics to obtain a refined *bān*, there are is the Kufan way, and the Medinan way. As for the Kufan, Aḥmad b. Abī Ya'qūb, the *mawlā* of the 'Abbāsids, said about it: Take oil ... As for Medinan *bān*, the people of Medina cook it with perfumed aromatics ... But this oil is not fit for use in *ghāliya* perfumes because the odors of ambergris and musk are overpowered by the fragrance and sharpness of the aromatics. Kings do not use it except to anoint their hands in the winter. Women use it in their perfumes and veils.

11. As for apple water and the perfume made from it, al-Tamīmī said, from Aḥmad b. Abī Ya'qūb, about the manufacture of perfumed apple water: Take Syrian apples ...

12. A description of another royal pill to combat bad breath. Al-Tamīmī mentions it in his book, and says that he took [the account] from Aḥmad b. Abī Ya'qūb, namely ...[833]

---

830 This is probably the 'Abbāsid princeling of this name resident in al-Baṣra, a contemporary of al-Rashīd's, and renowned for his wealth.

831 This fragment is abridged.

832 This is the oil obtained from the seeds of the ben tree (*Moringa oleifera*, also called *Moringa aptera*); see the article by L. Kopf in *EI*², s.v. Bān.

833 On al-Tamīmī, see Ibn Abī Uṣaybi'a, *'Uyūn al-anbā' fī ṭabaqāt al-aṭibbā'* (Beirut, 1965), 546–548. De Goeje adds: "[Al-Tamīmī's] work, *Jayb al-'arūs wa-rayḥān al-nufūs*, on which see among others Yāqūt, 4:828, line 9 ff. ... does not appear to have survived. In the library of Paris is a part (Chapters 11–14) of his work *Murshid*, which H. D. van Gelder examined for me, and in which he found no mention of our author. Al-Tamīmī was living until at least 370/980 (Ibn Abī Uṣaybi'a, 548). Ibn Abī Uṣaybi'a (547) affirms in clear words that his grandfather, Sa'īd, was al-Ya'qūbī's companion on a journey: 'His grandfather Sa'īd was a physician and he accompanied Aḥmad b. Abī Ya'qūb, *mawlā* of the 'Abbāsids.'"

13. Aḥmad b. Abī Yaʿqūb said: The Christians of al-Ḥīra are called *al-ʿIbād* because when five of them went as a delegation to Kisrā, he said to one of them, "What is your name?" "ʿAbd al-Masīḥ," the man replied. He said to the second, "What is your name?" "ʿAbd Yālīl," he replied. He said to the third, "What is your name?" "ʿAbd Yāsūʿ," he replied. He said to the fourth, "What is your name?" "ʿAbd Allāh," he replied. He said to the fifth, "What is your name?" "ʿAbd ʿAmr," he replied. So Chosroës said, "You are all ʿAbds (*ʿIbād*)," and so they are called ʿIbād.[834] 371

14. Aḥmad b. Abī Yaʿqūb, one of the children of Jaʿfar b. Wahb, said: During his reign, al-Wāthiq distributed 5,000,000 dinars in alms, gifts, and pious donations in Baghdad, Samarra, Kufa, Basra, Medina, and Mecca. At his behest, after the fire that struck the markets of Baghdad, al-Walīd b. Aḥmad b. Abī Du'ād went to Baghdad with 500,000 dinars and distributed them to the merchants who had lost their property in the fire. Their conditions improved as a result: they rebuilt their markets in plaster and baked brick and made iron doors for their stalls.[835]

15. Aḥmad the secretary said: Aḥmad b. Ṭūlūn spent 120,000 dinars on his mosque.[836] The builders said to him, "According to what model shall we construct the minaret?" Aḥmad, who never used to fool around during his meetings, took a roll of paper and began playing with it, so that part of it came out from his hand and part of it remained in his hand. The people present were astonished. He said, "Construct the minaret according to this model." So they built it.[837] When the construction of the mosque was finished, Aḥmad b. Ṭūlūn had a dream in which Almighty God seemed to manifest Himself to the enclo-

834 Source: Al-Bakrī, *Kitāb Muʿjam mā istaʿjam*, 18. *ʿIbād* is the plural of *ʿabd* (slave of, servant of), a frequent component of names. De Goeje notes: "Perhaps this account (about the ʿIbād) is from a fuller recension of the *History* than that which Houtsma edited. For a passage praised by the Caliph al-Wāthiq in the work *Rayḥān al-albāb* (Leiden MS, f. 179 verso) is also fuller than the account cited in the text (of the *History*) edited by Houtsma (*Taʾrīkh*, 2:590)." De Goeje then provides this longer account about al-Wāthiq, which is the next account translated here (no. 14). The translator has not been able to consult the manuscript of the *Rayḥān al-albāb*.

835 That is, as a measure to prevent fires, reeds, straw, or wood were not used in the new shops. As noted above, this account, from *Rayḥān al-albāb* (Leiden MS, f. 179 verso), appears to be a longer version of the account in the surviving recension of the *History* (*Taʾrīkh*, 2:590).

836 Aḥmad b. Ṭūlūn (d. 270/884) was governor of Egypt and founder of the Ṭūlūnid dynasty of Egypt and Syria.

837 The account shows how Ibn Ṭūlūn used a roll of paper (*darj*, for the meaning see Dozy,

sure that surrounded the mosque, but did not manifest Himself to the mosque itself. Aḥmad asked the dream interpreters about it, and they said, "That which
372 surrounds it will fall into ruin, | and it will remain standing alone." He said, "Whence do you infer this?" They said, "From the words of Almighty God, *And when his Lord revealed Himself to the mountain, He made it crumble to dust*,[838] and from the words of the Prophet—God's blessings and peace be upon him—'When God manifests Himself to something, it is abased before Him.'" And it happened as they said.[839]

16. Aḥmad b. Abī Yaʿqūb the secretary reported, saying: When it was the eve of the Feast of the Fast-breaking of the year 292,[840] I recalled what this feast was like under Ibn Ṭūlūn, with its fancy dress and arms, the colorful flags and banners, the glamorous clothes, the many mounts, and the sound of horns and drums. Tears and sorrow overwhelmed me, and as I slept that night I heard a voice calling:

> Kingship, glory, and glamor
> vanished with the Ṭūlūnids' departure.[841]

17. Aḥmad b. Abī Yaʿqūb said:

> If you would know the grandeur of their kingdom,
> turn aside and enjoy the Great Square's green expanse.[842]
> Behold those palaces, what they contained;
> delight your eyes with the beauty of that garden.
> But ponder well: a lesson lies there, too,
> that tells you of the fickle ways of Time.

Supplément, 1:431) to form a cone illustrating the spiral shape of the minaret, still visible today.

838 Qurʾān 7:143.

839 Source: Ibn Taghrībirdī, 3:8. De Goeje notes: "Ibn Taghrībirdī gives this account ... from a lost part of the *History*."

840 That is, the holiday (ʿĪd al-Fiṭr) that follows the fast of Ramaḍān: 6 August 905.

841 De Goeje notes: "The text in al-Maqrīzī, 1:326, is probably from the same part of the *History*. See my *Descriptio al-Maghribi*, 20." See the modern edition: al-Maqrīzī, *Kitāb al-Mawāʿiẓ wa-l-iʿtibār bi-dhikr al-khiṭaṭ wa-l-āthār*, 2:141, citing Muḥammad b. Abī Yaʿqūb.

842 The Great Square (al-Maydān) is probably to be located in al-Qaṭāʾiʿ, the new city north of Fusṭāṭ founded by Ibn Ṭūlūn to be the seat of government. The great mosque built by Ibn Ṭūlūn was also located in it.

The murder of Hārūn pulled up their roots,
and grizzled Shaybān's head, who was their chief.
The strength of Qays availed them naught at dawn
amid a clamorous host, nor Ghassān's might.
Neither ʿAdīya, who was brave, nor Khazraj bold
were helped to victory by their brother ʿAdnān.
Egypt, like a bride, was escorted to the house of Prophethood and Guidance
and torn away from Satan's partisans.[843]

18. Similar to this is what al-Yaʿqūbī recounted, saying: | [Someone once said:] I went to the door of Ḥamdūna, the daughter of (the caliph) al-Rashīd, and Duqāq, her female client, came out. In her hand was a fan, which had written on one side: "A cunt needs two cocks more than a cock needs two cunts." And on the other side: "Just as a millstone needs two mules more than a mule needs two millstones."[844] 373

843 De Goeje found this poem cited in al-Maqrīzī, *Khiṭāṭ*, 2:136, but it appears first in al-Kindī, *Kitāb al-wulāt wa-kitāb al-quḍāt*, 250. The poem alludes to the events that precipitated the fall of the Ṭūlūnid dynasty in 292/905. Aḥmad b. Ṭūlūn, after ruling for ten years, was succeeded upon his death in 270/884 by his son Khumārawayh, who was assassinated in 282/896. Khumārawayh's son, Jaysh, was deposed by the army in 283/896, leaving his brother Hārūn, to whose assassination in 292/905 the poem alludes, apostrophizing it as having "pulled up their roots and grizzled the head of Shaybān, who was their chief" (a pun on the meaning of *shaybān*, 'gray hair')—i.e., Shaybān b. Aḥmad b. Ṭūlūn, the last of the Ṭūlūnids—as well as the murder of his nephew Hārūn—whose quasi-independent rule in Egypt was ended by invading ʿAbbāsid forces, which restored Egypt to direct ʿAbbāsid rule, an event to which the poem perhaps alludes, although this remains unclear. The poem also may be alluding satirically to the fact that Aḥmad b. Ṭūlūn, though of Turkish descent, named several of his sons after famous Arab tribes—Qays, Ghassān, ʿAdīya, Khazraj, and ʿAdnān, whose "valor availed them naught." For further details and bibliography, see the article by M. S. Gordon in *EI*[2], s.v. Ṭūlūnids; to which one should add Thierry Bianquis, "Autonomous Egypt from Ibn Ṭūlūn to Kāfūr, 868–969," in *The Cambridge History of Egypt, Volume One: Islamic Egypt, 640–1517*, 86–119; Michael Bonner, "Ibn Ṭūlūn's Jihād: The Damascus Assembly of 269/883"; and Mathieu Tillier, "L'étoile, la chaîne et le Jugement."

844 De Goeje adds: "This account, which [Muḥammad b. Aḥmad] al-Tījānī (d. after 709/1309) praises in his work *Tuḥfat al-ʿarūs* [*wa-rawḍat al-nufūs*], might come from the same part of the text (Leiden MS 330, f. 122 verso)." The translator has not been able to consult the manuscript of al-Tījānī's work, but, significantly, this passage does not appear in the published edition of the *Tuḥfa* (ed. Jalīl al-ʿAṭīya, London, 1992).

19. Describing Samarqand, Ibn Wāḍiḥ said:

Samarqand is so exalted that she is called
"the Ornament of Khurāsān" and "the Paradise of Provinces."
Are her towers not suspended
from a height that the eye cannot reach?
And below her towers are her trenches:
pits so deep that nothing can leave them.
It is as if she, encircled by her walls
and surrounded by shady trees,
Were a full moon, her rivers the Milky Way, and
her fortresses like the brightest stars.[845]

C New Fragments[846]

1. Aḥmad b. Abī Yaʿqūb recounts in the *Book of Routes* that he composed that there is a deserted house at Nahr Tīrā, and whoever (tries) to settle in it cannot stay more than a day, nor will he be able to pass the night (there).[847]

2. Aḥmad b. Abī Yaʿqūb said: The best musk in odor and appearance is that which has the color of an apple. Its odor is like that of the apples of Lebanon. Its color tends toward yellow; it is medium-sized, neither large nor overly fine. (The second best) is blacker, but similar in odor and appearance. (In the last place) is the kind that is even blacker. It is the lowest in quality and value.[848]

3. [Aḥmad b. Abī Yaʿqūb] also said:

A sudden blow was struck from the East, hurtling down
to beset the Banū Ṭūlūn.

---

845 De Goeje notes: "I do not know whence the following verses, accepted by Yāqūt, 3:136, were taken."

846 The following fragments were not included by De Goeje in his edition.

847 Idrīsī, 399. Cited by Wiet, 228, who notes that he did not verify the passage in question, having seen it at the last moment in Jaubert's translation of Idrīsī. The present translation differs slightly from Wiet's.

848 Al-Qalqashandī, 2:128. Cited by Wiet, 234. The present translation, like Wiet's, differs slightly from the reading in the Beirut edition. Also, in his translation of this fragment, Wiet included a few lines not given here that are from al-Qalqashandī, not al-Yaʿqūbī.

How can the prosperity of these poor creatures be hoped for
while Ibn Abbā oversees the secular and the sacred?
By a man of deceit and by perverse reasoning
were the precepts of justice imposed upon us.
We have seen (no one) of the family of Ṭūlūn
whom he has not ill-treated, (making him) hostage to idleness.[849]

4. Aḥmad b. Abī Yaʿqūb said:

The abode, after the dispersal of the camel-litters,
rejoices at the dispersal of its residents.
It shows no regret for its masters,
for in their departure is rest for their neighbors.
They have left, and may they not stop in some flowered garden!
and may the rain of an approaching cloud bypass them.
May they be deprived of the gush of the rain-cloud wherever they go,
and may the assault of the All-Merciful scatter them.
How heavily they weighed on the shoulders of grandeur,
and how far their hands withdrew from beneficence!
How detestable was the reign by which they thrived,
and how much it deserved the collapse of its foundations!
They did not accompany God's favors with thanks for them,
so He compensated them with the compensation due ingratitude.
Egypt is delivered of them, but O what
calumny awaits the land of Iraq![850]

5. Ibn Wāḍiḥ said: ... and the Second Qinnasrīn is Ḥiyār Banī al-Qaʿqāʿ.[851]

6. Ibn Wāḍiḥ said: ... and the subdistrict of First Qinnasrīn, which is a city on the main part of the Great Road. In it there are tribesmen from Tanūkh.[852]

7. I copied the following from the *Book of Regions* composed by Aḥmad b. Abī Yaʿqūb b. Wāḍiḥ the secretary: The subdistricts belonging to the military

849 Kindī, 251. Cited by Wiet, 245. The verse refers to the death of Aḥmad b. Ṭūlūn and the rise of the regent Ibn Abbā in 270/883.

850 Kindī, 252. Cited by Wiet, 245–246.

851 From Ibn al-ʿAdīm, *Bughyat al-ṭalab min taʾrīkh Ḥalab*, 1:74.

852 Ibid.

district (*jund*) of Qinnasrīn and al-ʿAwāṣim: the subdistrict of Antioch. It is an ancient city, of which it is said that there is no equal to it with regard to the sturdiness and impressiveness of its city walls in either the land of Islam or the land of the Romans. It has a stone city wall, inside of which are chambers (so large) that horsemen can ride into them. I have been told that the circumference of the city wall, which surrounds the city and the mountain at whose foot the city lies, is 12 Arab miles. The city of Antioch was conquered by treaty—Abū ʿUbayda b. al-Jarrāḥ arranged the treaty with them and they possess the treaty document to this day. Located there in a church called the Qusyān Church is the hand which is said to be the hand of Yaḥyā b. Zakariyāʾ—peace be upon him.[853] The city has a river called the Orontes, along which lie cultivated fields and gardens. The city also has many springs that come from the mountain and flow among the dwellings of the city, so that the people make use of the water in them as they like. The majority of its people are non-Arabs, but there are also some descendants of Ṣāliḥ b. ʿAlī al-Hāshimī and some Arabs belonging to the tribal faction of Yemen.[854]

8. Aḥmad b. Abī Yaʿqūb b. Wāḍiḥ the secretary mentioned in the *Book of Regions* while enumerating the subdistricts of the military district (*jund*) of Qinnasrīn and al-ʿAwāṣim: ... and the subdistrict of Manbij, which is an ancient city, conquered by treaty. ʿAmr b. al-ʿĀṣ arranged its treaty under the authority of Abū ʿUbayda b. al-Jarrāḥ. The city is on the main part of the Euphrates. In it is a mixture of peoples, Arab and non-Arab. There are also dwellings and palaces belonging to ʿAbd al-Malik b. Ṣāliḥ b. ʿAlī al-Hāshimī.[855]

9. I copied the following from the *Book of Regions* composed by Aḥmad b. Abī Yaʿqūb b. Wāḍiḥ the secretary, who, in mentioning Bālis, says: It is an ancient city on the banks of the Euphrates at the foot of a mountain. From it trading goods that arrive from Egypt and the rest of the land of Syria are loaded onto ships bound for Baghdad. The land tax of Bālis is administered by the tax agent

853 That is, John the Baptist.

854 Ibn al-ʿAdīm, 1:88. Ṣāliḥ b. ʿAlī was a prominent early ʿAbbāsid kinsman and governor of Syria.

855 Ibid., 1:107–108. Ibn al-ʿAdīm adds that al-Yaʿqūbī is wrong to place Manbij on the Euphrates: he is rather thinking of Jisr Manbij. Moreover, he adds, some accounts credit ʿIyāḍ b. Ghanm with the conquest of Manbij. ʿAbd al-Malik b. Ṣāliḥ was a powerful ʿAbbāsid kinsman and governor of Syria. His estate at Manbij is said to have attracted the envy of the caliph al-Rashīd.

of Diyār Muḍar, while its military and religious affairs are administered by the tax agent of the military district (*jund*) of Qinnasrīn and al-ʿAwāṣim. Its people are a mixture of Arabs and non-Arabs.[856]

10. I read in the *Book of Regions* by Aḥmad b. Abī Yaʿqūb b. Wāḍiḥ the secretary in his enumeration of the subdistricts of the military district (*jund*) of Qinnasrīn and al-ʿAwāṣim: … and the subdistrict of First Qinnasrīn, which is a city on the main part of the Great Road. In it there are tribesmen from Tanūkh; and the district of Second Qinnasrīn, which is Ḥiyār Banī al-Qaʿqāʿ. Its people are from ʿAbs, Fazāra, and other Qaysī tribes.[857]

11. Ibn Wāḍiḥ the secretary said: Maʿarrat al-Nuʿmān is an ancient, ruined city. It is populated by the Tanūkh.[858]

12. Ibn Wāḍiḥ the secretary enumerated the subdistricts belonging to the military district (*jund*) of Qinnasrīn and al-ʿAwāṣim, saying: … and the subdistrict of Martaḥwān and the subdistrict of Maʿarrat Miṣrīn.[859]

13. Ibn Wāḍiḥ the secretary said: Opposite the city of Qinnasrīn is a city called Ḥāḍir Ṭayyiʾ. In it are dwellings of the Ṭayyiʾ.[860]

14. Aḥmad b. Abī Yaʿqūb b. Wāḍiḥ the secretary mentioned it in the *Book of Regions* in his listing of the subdistricts of the military district (*jund*) of Qinnasrīn and al-ʿAwāṣim, saying: The subdistrict of Sarmīn. Its people are from the (tribal faction of) Qays.[861]

15. Aḥmad b. Abī Yaʿqūb b. Wāḍiḥ the secretary mentioned it in the *Book of Regions*, saying: The city of Kafarṭāb and al-Aṭmīm. Its people are from various tribes of the Yemen, mostly from the Kinda.[862]

---

856 Ibid., 1:123.

857 Ibid., 1:125, repeating parts of fragments C5 and C6 above.

858 Ibid., 1:129.

859 Ibid., 1:134. Ibn al-ʿAdīm adds that "these two place are subordinated to the subdistrict of al-Jazr. Martaḥwān is near Maʿarrat Miṣrīn."

860 Ibid., 1:138.

861 Ibid., 1:139.

862 Ibid., 1:141.

16. Ibn Wāḍiḥ the secretary said in the *Book of Regions*: The city of Apamea. It is an ancient Roman city, in ruins, on a large lake. Its people are from the tribes of ʿUdhra and Bahrāʾ.[863]

17. In mentioning Hama, Aḥmad b. Abī Yaʿqūb b. Wāḍiḥ the secretary said: It is an ancient city on a river called the Orontes. The people of this city are from the tribal faction of Yemen, mostly from the Bahrāʾ and the Tanūkh.[864]

18. I read in the *Book of Regions* composed by Aḥmad b. Abī Yaʿqūb b. Wāḍiḥ the secretary: The city of al-Maṣṣīṣa. The Commander of the Faithful al-Manṣūr built the city during his reign—before that it had been a garrison. The first to cross the Jabal al-Lukkām range and reach al-Maṣṣīṣa was Mālik b. al-Ḥārith al-Ashtar al-Nakhaʿī,[865] under the authority of Abū ʿUbayda b. al-Jarraḥ. There used to be a small fort there that ʿAbdallāh b. ʿAbd al-Malik built when he went to fight on the summer campaign.[866]

19. We return to the words of Ibn Wāḍiḥ: Al-Manṣūr departed for the Thughūr and he built there the great city of al-Maṣṣīṣa on a river called the Jayḥān. He transferred prisoners from all quarters and other people to the city of al-Maṣṣīṣa. The Commander of the Faithful al-Maʾmūn built a city called Kafarbayyā alongside it, so that the river known as the Jayḥān flowed between the two cities. Across the river is a great, ancient, stone-vaulted bridge. The city of al-Maṣṣīṣa is on the west bank of the Jayḥān, and the city of Kafarbayyā is on the east bank. Its populace is a mixture of peoples.[867]

20. Aḥmad b. Abī Yaʿqūb b. Wāḍiḥ the secretary said: The Commander of the Faithful al-Mahdī the son of al-Manṣūr built ʿAyn Zarba and completed it.[868]

21. Aḥmad b. Abī Yaʿqūb b. Wāḍiḥ the secretary said in his book: The city of Adhana was built by the Commander of the Faithful al-Rashīd, and completed by the Commander of the Faithful Muḥammad (al-Amīn) the son of

---

863 Ibid., 1:143.

864 Ibid., 1:150. Ibn al-ʿAdīm adds that al-Yaʿqūbī lists Hama under the subdistricts of Ḥimṣ.

865 Mālik al-Ashtar (d. 37/657) was a prominent commander involved in the conquests of Syria and Iraq. He later emerged as a supporter of the caliph ʿAlī.

866 Ibn al-ʿAdīm, 1:156. ʿAbdallāh b. ʿAbd al-Malik (d. 132/750) was a son of the Umayyad caliph ʿAbd al-Malik and a prominent commander in Umayyad times.

867 Ibid.

868 Ibid., 1:167. Al-Mahdī was ʿAbbāsid caliph from 158 to 169/775 to 785.

al-Rashīd.[869] Located there at this time because of its spaciousness are the residences of the governors of the Thughūr. It is on the river that is called Sayḥān. Its people are a mixture of clients of the caliphs and others.[870]

22. Aḥmad b. Abī Yaʿqūb b. Wāḍiḥ the secretary said in his book after mentioning al-Maṣṣīṣa, Adhana, and Tarsus: In addition to these three cities that we have mentioned, the Syrian Thughūr also include the cities of ʿAyn Zarba, al-Hārūniyya, and al-Kanīsa al-Muḥtaraqa (the Burned Church). The Commander of the Faithful (al-Mahdī) the son of al-Manṣūr built ʿAyn Zarba and completed it. Al-Rashīd built al-Hārūniyya during the reign of al-Mahdī, while he was an heir. Al-Rashīd also built al-Kanīsa al-Muḥtaraqa.[871]

23. Ibn Wāḍiḥ the secretary said in the *Book of Regions*: Tarsus is a city that the Commander of the Faithful al-Rashīd built in a plain at the foot of a mountain through which one crosses into Roman territory. The building of it took place in the year 170/786 at the beginning of his reign, at the hands of Abū Sulaym Faraj al-Turkī al-Khādim. Located there is a flowing river that comes from the mountains of the Romans until it splits up in the middle (of the city). It has a mixed population of people from every quarter of the world.[872]

24. Aḥmad b. Abī Yaʿqūb b. Wāḍiḥ the secretary mentioned in the *Book of Regions*: The Syrian Thughūr include the cities of ʿAyn Zarba, al-Hārūniyya, and al-Kanīsa al-Muḥtaraqa … Al-Rashīd built al-Hārūniyya in the days of al-Mahdī, while he was an heir.[873]

25. Ibn Wāḍiḥ the secretary said: You descend from the Jabal al-Lukkām to a city on the coast of the Green Sea called Alexandretta (al-Iskandarūna). Ibn Abī Daʾūd al-Iyādī built it in the reign of al-Wāthiq.[874]

26. I copied the following from the *Book of Regions* composed by Aḥmad b. Abī Yaʿqūb b. Wāḍiḥ the secretary: The cities belonging to the Jazīran Thughūr: Marʿash, al-Ḥadath, Zabaṭra, Sumaysāṭ, Ḥiṣn Manṣūr, Ḥiṣn Ziyād, and Malaṭya, which is the chief city. It is an ancient city, which the Romans destroyed. Abū

869 Al-Amīn succeeded his father as caliph in 193/809 and reigned until 198/813.
870 Ibn al-ʿAdīm, 1:171.
871 Ibid., 1:173, partly repeating fragment C20.
872 Ibid., 1:177–178.
873 Ibid., 1:219, duplicating material from fragment C22.
874 Ibid., 1:220.

Jaʿfar al-Manṣūr [re]built it in the year 139/756, and he set around it one set of city walls, without an external enclosure wall. He transferred a number of Arab tribes there, and so it is divided into "sevenths": a seventh for Sulaym and the rest of Qays, a seventh for the Hawāsiyya, a seventh for al-Rāʿiya and the descendants of Jaʿwana, a seventh for Taym, a seventh for Rabīʿa, a seventh for the (tribal faction of) Yemen, and a seventh for Hawāzin. Malaṭya is on level ground, surrounded by the mountains of the Romans. Its water comes from springs, watercourses, and the Euphrates.[875]

27. Aḥmad b. Abī Yaʿqūb b. Wāḍiḥ the secretary mentioned in the *Book of Regions*: The subdistrict of Sumaysāṭ. It is a city on the Euphrates. A mixture of peoples lives there.[876]

28. Ibn Wāḍiḥ mentioned in his book in the account of the subdistricts of Qinnasrīn and al-ʿAwāṣim: The two districts of Dulūk and Raʿbān are contiguous.[877]

29. Aḥmad b. Abī Yaʿqūb b. Wāḍiḥ mentioned, among the subdistricts of the military district (*jund*) of Qinnasrīn and al-ʿAwāṣim, the subdistrict of Qūrus, which is an ancient city populated by tribesmen from the tribal faction of Qays. The majority of them are of the family of al-ʿAbbās b. Zufar al-Hilālī.[878]

30. Aḥmad b. Abī Yaʿqūb b. Wāḍiḥ the secretary mentioned (Kaysūm) in his book: It is a magnificent, impregnable city. Naṣr b. Shabath fortified himself there when he rebelled, and al-Maʾmūn marched there.[879]

31. Aḥmad b. Abī Yaʿqūb b. Wāḍiḥ the secretary mentioned the following in the *Book of Regions*, while enumerating the subdistricts of Qinnasrīn and al-ʿAwāṣim: The subdistrict of al-Jūma. Located there are the sulphur springs that flow into thermal baths. The baths are at a village called Jindāris. They have a marvelous stone-vaulted building. People come there from every quarter to

875 Ibid., 1:252.
876 Ibid., 1:257.
877 Ibid., 1:259.
878 Ibid., 1:263. Al-ʿAbbās b. Zufar was a prominent tribal leader and governor under al-Rashīd.
879 Ibid., 1:265. During the Civil War (193–198/809–813) between the caliph al-Amīn and his brother al-Maʾmūn, a bandit chieftain named Naṣr b. Shabath al-ʿUqaylī at the head of some disaffected Syrian and Iraqi troops rebelled against the central government at Raqqa, before fortifying himself at Kaysūm.

bathe on account of the illnesses affecting them. It is not known whence that sulphur water comes or where it flows.[880]

32. As for what Aḥmad b. Yaʿqūb the secretary said in his book on *Routes and Kingdoms* in reproof of Egypt, namely: "It stands between a dank, putrid river abounding in malign effluvia that generate illnesses and spoil food and mountains and desiccated, barren desert in which no green thing grows because of the intensity of the dryness, and in which no water source flows ..." These are the words of a bigot that violate consensus and through the stupidity of their utterance arrive at that which hearts shun and the ears reject. Their defectiveness is sufficiently clear from the fact that he brings reproof against the Nile, for which reason and lore provide proof of excellence, and he looks with scorn at the Muqaṭṭam (mountain), which tradition cites for its noble qualities.[881]

D Passages Attributed to al-Yaʿqūbī in Ibn al-Dāya, *Kitāb al-Mukāfaʾa wa-Ḥusn al-ʿUqbā*

The following six passages are different in kind from the previous fragments included at the end of the translation of the *Geography*. The latter fragments probably derive from parts of the Geography now lost, or from a lost treatise on scents and perfumes, and therefore can be said to come ultimately from the pen of al-Yaʿqūbī, though they may have undergone some alteration when other authors cited them in their works. The following passages, however, come from a single literary work, the *Kitāb al-Mukāfaʾa wa-ḥusn al-ʿuqbā* (The Book of Recompense and Good Requital) by Abū Jaʿfar Aḥmad b. Yūsuf, known

880 Ibid., 1:478.

881 Al-Qalqashandī, 3:310. Here *baḥr* has been translated as "river" rather than "sea," as al-Qalqashandī clearly understood it as referring to the Nile. However, the text is ambiguous: al-Yaʿqūbī (or whoever the author is) may in fact be referring to the Red Sea. The passage is problematic, and the editor of al-Qalqashandī identifies the source as the now-lost *Kitāb al-masālik wa-l-mamālik* [*Book of Routes and Kingdoms*] of Ḥusayn b. Aḥmad b. Yaʿqūb al-Hamdānī, a famous geographer of the Arabian peninsula. But elsewhere when al-Qalqashandī cites "Aḥmad b. Yaʿqūb the secretary," he is clearly citing extant passages of al-Yaʿqūbī's *Buldān* (cf. al-Qalqashandī, 4:368, 369, 388, 390), which other authors also sometimes call the *Book of Routes and Kingdoms* (cf. Fragment A1). This being so, this harsh passage nevertheless does not reflect the content of al-Yaʿqūbī's section on Egypt in the *Buldān* (ed. Leiden, 330 ff.) as we have it. Perhaps, if it is indeed al-Yaʿqūbī's, then, like his poetry on Egyptian matters, it comes from a different work or a different version of the *Buldān*.

as Ibn al-Dāya, a younger contemporary who may have had contact with al-Yaʿqūbī in Ṭūlūnid Egypt—at least that is the implication of the formula by which Ibn al-Dāya introduces each anecdote: Aḥmad b. Abī Yaʿqūb (al-Yaʿqūbī) recounted to me (*ḥaddathanī Aḥmad ibn Abī Yaʿqūb*). In collections of *ḥadīth* or legal texts, this formula normally implies direct oral transmission, with preservation of the exact words of the source. In historical texts the evidence of such direct transmission and verbatim citation is not always clear, and it is even less clear in a work such as that of Ibn al-Dāya, which is not a work of Islamic jurisprudence, history, or geography. Instead, Ibn al-Dāya's book is a literary collection of historical anecdotes, arranged topically, not chronologically. It "consists of three sections containing, respectively, stories about rewards for good deeds, punishments for evil deeds, and timely escapes from difficult situations" (F. Rosenthal in *EI*², s.v. Ibn al-Dāya). Although Ibn al-Dāya implies that he heard six of these stories from al-Yaʿqūbī, who in turn had them from his father or grandfather, the literary style of these stories must be ascribed almost entirely to Ibn al-Dāya. On the other hand, the stories, if they are authentic, do show us something about al-Yaʿqūbī's interest in the ethical implications of the behavior of historical figures, an interest that manifested itself in a somewhat different way in his short work entitled *Mushākalat al-nās li-azmānihim* (The Adaptation of Men to Their Times), which focuses on how the virtues and vices of leaders, especially the caliphs, influence, for better or worse, the virtues and vices of the society as a whole. The six stories that Ibn al-Dāya attributes to al-Yaʿqūbī show how an act of benevolence can be repaid, often years later and in unexpected ways, and, conversely, how a malicious act can be punished. This mining of history for ethical content is not alien to al-Yaʿqūbī's interest in the *History* or *Adaptation*, although there is no evidence that these passages ever formed part of either work. Nevertheless, they merit presentation here as casting light on al-Yaʿqūbī's interests and those of his contemporary writers.

∴

1. Aḥmad b. Abī Yaʿqūb recounted to me on the authority of his father:[882] Yaḥyā b. Khālid b. Barmak adopted al-Faḍl b. Sahl and treated him as a son, and Yaḥyā's sons treated al-Faḍl as their brother. Yaḥyā then attached al-Faḍl to al-

882 Ed. Shākir, pp. 45–48 (No. 21). Background: The anecdote is set during the caliphate of al-Rashīd (r. 170–193/786–809), when Yaḥyā b. Khālid b. Barmak was serving as vizier.

Ma'mūn.[883] Yaḥyā b. Khālid had a good knowledge of astronomy, and al-Faḍl was also proficient in the subject. The two men agreed about what the stars foretold of the fortunes of the Barmakids, and both foresaw the happy fate that would befall al-Faḍl. It was as if each could discern his ultimate fate.

When al-Rashīd turned against the Barmakids, al-Faḍl himself was protected because of his place in al-Ma'mūn's service, but he had too little influence on al-Rashīd to help Yaḥyā and his sons. Al-Faḍl therefore wrote to Yaḥyā: "My lord, your situation grieves me, but there is little I can do to defend you so as to release him from his vow in this your crisis.[884] But I hope to do more on your behalf once I come into my good fortune."

Ibn Abī Ya'qūb continued, saying that Aḥmad b. Abī Khālid al-Aḥwal[885] related to him: "What I learned about Yaḥyā's desperate state filled me with anguish. When I recalled how well he had treated me and how generous he had been to me, I became utterly despondent. As I was in possession of 4,000 dinars, I divided it into two. Taking one half, I managed to gain entry to where they were imprisoned, and I presented it to Yaḥyā b. Khālid. He said: 'It would be wrong for us to allow you to take such a risk on our behalf or for us to promise you something from us whose fulfillment fortune will not allow. Our time is over. But if you think that our situation will improve, keep possession of your money.' I replied: 'I meant only to repay some of what I owe.'

"So he took a clean sheet of paper and wrote on it: 'Abū l-'Abbās,[886] may God keep you! This man has been steadfast throughout this trial of ours and has shown us kindness despite his despair over our fate. I would remind you of our time together, and ask that you pay him his due in my stead,[887] and lighten the debt that he has placed upon me. May God assist you and provide for you.' Then he folded the sheet, cut it in half crosswise, and said to me: 'Keep this half with you. Don't misplace it; for, if you do, much good fortune will escape you.' He then distributed the money to those persons who had suffered need because of what had befallen him. I departed from his company. He had left me with no

883 In other words, Yaḥyā b. Khālid used his influence to place his adopted son, al-Faḍl b. Sahl, in the entourage and service of al-Rashīd's son, the future caliph al-Ma'mūn.

884 This refers to al-Rashīd's vow to act against the Barmakids.

885 Another figure from al-Ma'mūn's entourage, in the service of al-Faḍl b. Sahl and later secretary to al-Ma'mūn. Note that the chronology (Aḥmad b. Abī Khālid died in 211/826–827) makes direct communication between him and al-Ya'qūbī unlikely. See the article by D. Sourdel in *EI*^{2}, s.v. Aḥmad b. Abī Khālid al-Aḥwal.

886 Addressing al-Ma'mūn by his familiar name (*kunya*).

887 That is, the debt for his kindness.

hope that he would ever regain his standing, and I had no idea of what the half sheet he had given me would mean for me.

"The authority of the Barmakids ended. Al-Rashīd died in Ṭūs, and al-Faḍl b. Sahl gained influence over al-Ma'mūn in Khurāsān and served as his deputy in all his affairs. A power struggle broke out between al-Amīn and al-Ma'mūn, and when al-Ma'mūn triumphed over his brother, al-Faḍl b. Sahl was confirmed as al-Ma'mūn's vizier. Al-Ma'mūn's heralds announced the news across all the provinces. I, meanwhile, remained unemployed and in ever greater need, for I lacked anyone to support me or take an interest in me. Then one day, while I was at home, with scarcely a scrap to eat, and wearing a shabby garment—I possessed only one dress robe that I wore when I rode out—my servant entered suddenly to announce that a group of Ṭāhir b. al-Ḥusayn's men were at the door. I put on my riding gown and let them in. Leading them was a man who, it was clear to me, held me in great esteem.

"He said: 'The commander Ṭāhir requests your presence.' I set off immediately. When I entered, he had me brought forward and showed me every honor. Ṭāhir then said: 'I received a message from the vizier,[888] may God keep him, asking that I spare no effort in preparing you for an audience with him. You have in your possession half of the note that Yaḥyā b. Khālid gave you. The vizier indicated that I was to provide you with 2,000 dinars with which to outfit yourself and your entourage properly.'

"My spirit soared and my hope returned. I took the money and set out with Ṭāhir's man. When I entered al-Faḍl b. Sahl's presence, he welcomed me graciously and asked me about the half of the note, which I produced. He whispered something to one of his servants who stepped out and then returned with a piece of paper. He joined one piece to the other and they formed a whole. When he finished reading it, he wept and said: 'May God have mercy on Abū l-'Abbās.[889] How well acquainted he was with the vicissitudes of fate, how to elicit thankfulness in their midst, and how to avoid censure!'

"Then he presented me to al-Ma'mūn. My standing rose under him until I became one of his closest officials, someone he trusted with his most important affairs."

888 That is, al-Faḍl b. Sahl.

889 Referring to Yaḥyā b. Khālid b. Barmak by his familiar name (*kunya*).

2. Aḥmad b. Abī Yaʿqūb recounted to me:[890] Al-Mahdī disapproved of Harthama b. Aʿyan's malicious treatment of Maʿn b. Zāʾida[891] and ordered that Harthama be exiled to North Africa.[892] But al-Rashīd spoke to al-Mahdī on behalf of Harthama and gradually allayed his anger. Afterward, Maʿn died; Harthama's situation improved, and he felt grateful to al-Rashīd for what he had done. The caliphate then devolved on Mūsā al-Hādī,[893] over whom Harthama gained considerable influence. At a certain point, al-Hādī decided to remove al-Rashīd as heir and assembled the notables for the appointment of his son as heir apparent. Harthama learned of this, and, recalling al-Rashīd's generous deed, he feigned illness. Al-Hādī assembled the notables and called on them to remove al-Rashīd in favor of his own son. They agreed and pledged their support.

He then summoned Harthama and asked him: "Harthama, will you swear allegiance?" Harthama responded: "Commander of the Faithful, my right hand is already taken up with my oath of allegiance to you, my left hand with the oath of allegiance to your brother.[894] So with what hand shall I swear allegiance? By God, Commander of the Faithful, do not impose on people, by exacting the oath of loyalty to your son, more than what your father imposed on behalf of your brother in exacting the oath of allegiance to him! Whoever violates the first oath will violate the second! Were it not that this assembly considers itself to be swearing under duress and secretly thinks about you the opposite of what they openly profess, they would have abstained."

Al-Hādī said to the assembly: "Shame on the lot of you! This man, my client, has told me the truth when all of you have lied to me. He has been honest with me, when all of you have deceived me!" So al-Rashīd got what al-Hādī intended for him.[895]

---

890 Ed. Shākir, pp. 61–62 (No. 29).

891 A military commander who served both the late Umayyads and the early ʿAbbāsids; see the article by H. Kennedy in *EI*^{2}, s.v. Maʿn b. Zāʾida.

892 Arabic *al-Maghrib al-Aqṣā* (the Farthest West).

893 Mūsā al-Hādī and Hārūn al-Rashīd were brothers, sons of al-Mahdī, who had designated al-Hādī as heir apparent, with al-Rashīd second in the line of succession. However, al-Mahdī had second thoughts late in his life and was about to remove al-Hādī in favor of al-Rashīd, but died before taking action. Al-Hādī succeeded to the caliphate and proceeded vigorously to suppress any possible claim to the caliphate by al-Rashīd. See the article by D. Sourdel in *EI*^{2}, s.v. al-Hādī Ilā 'L-ḥaḳḳ.

894 That is, al-Rashīd, as second in the line of succession.

895 Namely, the caliphate.

∴

3. I was informed by Aḥmad b. Abī Yaʿqūb,[896] who said that his father told him the following anecdote on the authority of his grandfather Wāḍiḥ, the client of al-Manṣūr.[897] Wāḍiḥ said: "I was in the presence of al-Manṣūr. He had summoned a man who had once served Hishām b. ʿAbd al-Malik and was questioning him about Hishām's conduct, a subject that fascinated al-Manṣūr. But whenever the man mentioned Hishām's name, he added 'May God have mercy on him,' which annoyed all of us. Finally, al-Rabīʿ[898] asked the man, 'How often are you going to invoke God's mercy upon the enemy of the Commander of the Faithful?' The man replied to al-Rabīʿ: 'The court of the Commander of the Faithful is the most appropriate place for showing gratitude to a benefactor and rewarding someone for his benevolence. Hishām adorned my neck with a necklace that only the man who washes my corpse can undo.'[899] 'And what,' asked al-Manṣūr, 'is this necklace?' The man replied, 'He adorned

---

896 Ed. Shākir, p. 66 (No. 32). Background: The anecdote is set during the reign of the second ʿAbbāsid caliph, al-Manṣūr (r. 136–158/754–75), who is portrayed as fascinated with stories about the Umayyad dynasty, which his family had overthrown. His historical interest in the previous dynasty is shown as strained when he interviews a former member of the entourage of the Umayyad caliph Hishām b. ʿAbd al-Malik (r. 105–125/724–43) who not only provides information, but expresses sympathy for his former master, angering officials at al-Manṣūr's court. Unexpectedly, al-Manṣūr rewards the man for his loyalty to his former master and his honesty.

897 The *Geography* and the *History* provide information about al-Yaʿqūbī's grandfather Wāḍiḥ. The section of the *Geography* on Baghdad (ed. Leiden, 234) states: "In fact, my ancestors were residents there, and one of them was its governor (*tawallā amrahā*)." The *Geography* (ed. Leiden, 242 and 248) states that Wāḍiḥ, along with two other dignitaries, is said to have been put in charge, governed, or administered (the language is vague) the quarter extending from the Kufa Gate (Bāb al-Kūfa) to the Syrian Gate (Bāb al-Shām). The *Geography* (ed. Leiden, 246 and 247) gives the location of Wāḍiḥ's estate. The *History* (ed. Leiden, 2:447) notes that Wāḍiḥ served as governor of Armenia and Azerbaijan under al-Manṣūr. The listing (ed. Leiden 2:462) of Wāḍiḥ as one of al-Manṣūr's officials who was a client (*mawlā*), as opposed to those who were "of the Arabs" (*min al-ʿArab*), confirms his non-Arab origins. Finally, ed. Leiden 2:477, notes that al-Manṣūr's successor, al-Mahdī, in connection with his rebuilding of the Kaʿba in 160/777, wrote to Wāḍiḥ, now serving as governor of Egypt, to "send money to Mecca and to provide tools and whatever was required in the way of gold, mosaics, and chains for the lanterns."

898 Al-Rabīʿ b. Yūnus, the chamberlain and vizier of al-Manṣūr and his two successors.

899 The collar, or necklace, represents the favor that Hishām, during his lifetime, bestowed on the speaker. Cf. the proverb cited in Lane, *Lexicon*, 7:2616, s.v. *qilāda*: "Thy beneficence is a permanent badge (*qilāda*) on my neck which day and night will not loose."

me with favor in his lifetime and relieved me of need for anyone else after his death.' Al-Manṣūr said to him: 'You have spoken well, may God bless you. By properly recompensing favors,[900] one incites to good deeds and multiplies acts of benevolence.' He then brought the man into his inner circle."

∴

4. I was informed by Aḥmad b. Abī Yaʿqūb,[901] who said that his father told him the following anecdote on the authority of his grandfather Wāḍiḥ, who said: "I heard Khālid b. Sahm, who had been a member of Marwān b. Muḥammad al-Jaʿdī's[902] inner circle, recount to al-Manṣūr how Marwān once asked him for a slave girl of his whom he loved. Marwān then falsely accused him of misdeeds, imprisoned him for a time, and took the slave girl from him. Khālid was an intelligent and courageous man, and so, when Abū Muslim gained the upper hand and routed Marwān's forces,[903] he released him from prison and promised to treat him well.

"Khālid said: 'Marwān used to laugh at the clothes of the men in black.[904] He would say, "If we were to take them prisoner, we couldn't make them look any uglier and shameful than they have rendered themselves!" But when he was forced to confront them in battle and attack them, I saw that he was frightened to engage them in combat. He said to me: "Abū Yazīd"—he had never addressed me so familiarly before[905]—"I am really frightened. Does it show on me?" I replied: "Not at all, Commander of the Faithful!" I was only trying to flatter him—in fact I was pleased by the change in his fortunes. He said, "I find that

900 Arabic *bi-ḥusn al-mukāfaʾa*, echoing the title of Ibn al-Dāya's work, *Kitāb al-Mukāfaʾa wa-ḥusn al-ʿuqbā* [The Book of Recompense and Fair Requital].

901 Ed. Shākir, pp. 83–84 (No. 43). Background: The anecdote, again told on the authority of al-Yaʿqūbī's grandfather Wāḍiḥ, illustrates how an evil action, in this case the last Umayyad caliph's wresting away a courtier's beloved slave girl, bears fruit later when the same courtier begrudges the caliph his true opinion and deliberately leads him to choose the worse of two alternatives, thereby leading to the caliph's death. The courtier, Khālid b. Sahm, survived his master's death and eventually was freed. Now, years later, at the court of the ʿAbbāsid caliph al-Manṣūr, he recounts his experience.

902 Marwān II, the last Umayyad caliph (r. 127–132/744–750).

903 This refers to the ʿAbbāsid victory over the Umayyads in 132/750.

904 That is, the ʿAbbāsids, who fought under black banners and wore black to distinguish themselves.

905 The Arabic literally says: "He had never addressed me by my *kunya* before that day." The combination of "Abū" with a name or term, typically used as an honorific, nickname, or nom de guerre, is the *kunya*.

I don't have courage to attack them." So I replied: "If that is the case, protect yourself from them by fleeing. Your horses are swifter than theirs."

'He fled, and Abū Muslim's men stopped pursuing him. When he reached his baggage train, he said to me: "I have decided to make for Byzantine territory." This, in fact, was his best option, but I begrudged him my advice and deliberately misled him. I said: "Would you have these young sons of yours and your entourage take refuge with an unbeliever who would only take heart and whose situation would be much improved? And perhaps your sons will be so taken with what they see in his realm that they turn Christian! No, you should continue on until you reach Egypt, where you will find men and horses and be able to choose what to do."

'He accepted my advice, and we set out. When we reached Egypt, he proceeded to the countryside, while I sought protection in a settled area because of a falling-out between us. He was killed at Būṣīr al-Ushmūnayn.'"[906]

5. I was informed by Aḥmad b. Abī Yaʿqūb,[907] who said that his father told him the following anecdote on the authority of his grandfather Wāḍiḥ, who said: "During the reign of al-Manṣūr, hostility developed between (the future caliph) al-Mahdī and his brother, Jaʿfar b. Abī Jaʿfar. Maṣqala b. Ḥabīb used to report to Jaʿfar displeasing things that al-Mahdī had said. Al-Mahdī could not retaliate against Maṣqala or punish him in any way, but when he became caliph, he vowed to take his life, so Maṣqala went into hiding.

"Maṣqala told me that his hiding place did not suit him, so he ventured out furtively seeking another. One of his enemies chanced upon him and shouted to the night watch,[908] 'This man is wanted by the Commander of the Faithful!' [Maṣqala said:] 'The watchmen rushed for me. I was certain that death was at hand. But just at that moment, as they held me, Maʿn b. Zāʾida passed by, so I called to him: "Master! Abū l-Mundhir! Rescue me, may God protect you." So he

906 Because *Būṣīr* was an element in several Egyptian toponyms, it was usual to distinguish them from each other, as al-Yaʿqūbī has done here: *Būṣīr al-Ushmūnayn* means 'the Būṣīr that is near al-Ushmūnayn,' which places the site in Middle Egypt, near modern El Ashmunein in Minya Governorate. There are two traditions about Marwān's death; both locate it at a place called Būṣīr, but differ as to which Būṣīr; see the article by G. Wiet in *EI*², s.v. Būṣīr or Abūṣīr.

907 Ed. Shākir, pp. 119–120 (No. 60).

908 Arabic *aṣḥāb al-arbāʿ*, the individuals charged with monitoring entry to and thus the security of urban neighborhoods.

said to the watchmen and to the man who was holding me, "Release him!" The man replied, "And what shall I say to the Commander of the Faithful?" Maʿn replied, "You will tell him that he is with me." He mounted me upon one of his pack camels and took me to his home. When his dinner was served, I ate with him and his sons. As soon as we finished, he was told that a messenger had arrived from the Commander of the Faithful. He turned to his sons and said, "Swear to me that you will not hand over Maṣqala, for he has sought my protection." They promised him as much, and he rode off. As soon as al-Mahdī saw him, he asked, "Maʿn, are you granting someone protection from me?" Maʿn answered, "Yes, Commander of the Faithful." Al-Mahdī said, "And you admit as much?" Maʿn replied: "Commander of the Faithful, I have killed for your dynasty some 30,000 enemies. Am I not entitled to extend protection under it to one enemy?" The caliph replied, "Yes, you may claim that right, and we hereby grant you his life." Maʿn said: "Commander of the Faithful, this is not how someone like you grants life! When you grant a person his life, make it, by your generosity, a life of comfort." The caliph replied, "Let him be given 1,000 dinars." Maʿn replied, "Commander of the Faithful, your gift should not be the same as the gift of your servant Maʿn, for that is the amount that I have given him." So the caliph said, "Give the man under Maʿn's protection 2,000 dinars." So I went home, 3,000 dinars in hand and free from fear.' "

∵

6. Aḥmad b. Abī Yaʿqūb told me the following anecdote on the authority of his father:[909] Jibrīl b. Bukhtīshūʿ used to assist the physicians at the court of al-Rashīd.[910] He was a man of integrity but very poor. His salary at that time was only three hundred dirhams a month. On a certain occasion al-Rashīd fainted with no previous sign of illness. The consensus of the doctors was that he would perish. When Ibn Bukhtīshūʿ was informed, he said, "There is only one treatment: they must cup him." Muḥammad al-Amīn[911] said at first, "I fear

---

909 Ed. Shākir, pp. 144–145 (No. 72).

910 Jibrīl b. Bukhtīshūʿ belonged to a distinguished Christian family of physicians. His father, Bukhtīshūʿ b. Jurjīs, was al-Rashīd's physician-in-chief until his death in 185/801. Jibrīl, the son, did not immediately succeed to his father's position, as indicated by the detail that he "was an assistant." (Arabic *kāna yakhlufu l-aṭibbāʾ* means literally, "used to come behind the physicians.") Al-Rashīd will refer to him as a young man (*ghulām*). On his career, see the article by D. Sourdel in *EI*², s.v. Bukhtīshūʿ.

911 Al-Rashīd's son and a future caliph.

that we might endanger his life." But then he said: "Now that we are in despair about his condition, the right thing to do is to try it."

They summoned the cupper. He gathered the blood into his two neck veins, while al-Rashīd lay prostrate, then extracted two cupping glasses of his blood. Al-Rashīd opened his eyes, called for food, ate, and fell asleep. When he woke up, al-Ma'mūn[912] told him how the operation had gone, and well-wishers were allowed to enter. When they finished, he addressed them: "You commanders and doctors, I appointed you to protect my life, but when a crisis befell me, only this young man, apart from God Almighty, was of any use to me. He earns little from me, while all of you earn much. So right the imbalance: let each of you give him a share of what I so graciously bestow on you, so that he receives from you proper compensation for the protection he has afforded me." The notables hastened to give Jibrīl estates, homes, and money, until he became the wealthiest man in the realm. His wealth and that of his sons increased until it came to equal that of the caliphs themselves.

---

912 Al-Rashīd's other son and a future caliph.

General Bibliography

I Primary Sources

A *Arabic Sources*

ʿAbīd b. al-Abraṣ: *The Dīwāns of ʿAbīd Ibn Al-Abraṣ, of Asad, and ʿĀmir ibn aṭ-Ṭufail, of ʿĀmir Ibn Ṣaʿṣaʿa*. Edited for the First Time, from the Ms. in the British Museum, and Supplied with a Translation and Notes by Sir Charles Lyall. Cambridge: E. J. W. Gibb Memorial, 1913.

Abū l-Fidāʾ, Ismāʿīl b. ʿAlī. *Taqwīm al-buldān*. Paris: Imprimerie royale, 1840.

Abū l-Maḥāsin [Muḥammad b. ʿAlī] al-ʿAbdarī al-Shaybī. *Timthāl al-amthāl*. Edited by Asʿad Dhubyān. Beirut: Dār al-Masīra, 1402/1982.

Abū Nuʿaym, Aḥmad b. ʿAbdallāh al-Iṣbahānī. *Ḥilyat al-awliyāʾ*. Beirut: Dār al-Kitāb al-ʿArabī, 1387/1967.

Abū Tammām, Ḥabīb b. Aws al-Ṭāʾī. *Dīwān Abī Tammām bi-Sharḥ al-Khaṭīb al-Tabrīzī*. Edited by Muḥammad Abduh ʿAzzām. 4 vols. Cairo: Dār al-Maʿārif, 1976.

Abū Tammām, Ḥabīb b. Aws al-Ṭāʾī. *Dīwān al-Ḥamāsa*. Edited by Georg Wilhelm Freytag. Bonn, 1828.

Abū Zurʿa al-Dimashqī, ʿAbd al-Raḥmān b. ʿAmr. *Taʾrīkh Abī Zurʿa al-Dimashqī*. Edited by Shukrallāh b. Niʿmatallāh al-Qūjānī. Damascus: 1980.

al-ʿAskarī, Abū Hilāl al-Ḥasan b. ʿAbdallāh. *Kitāb al-Awāʾil*. Edited by Muḥammad al-Sayyid al-Wakīl. Medina: 1966.

al-Azraqī, Muḥammad b. ʿAlī. *Kitāb Akhbār Makkah*. Edited by Ferdinand Wüstenfeld as *Die Chroniken der Stadt Mekka*, Vol. 1. Leipzig: F. A. Brockhaus, 1857–1861.

al-Bakrī, Abū ʿUbayd ʿAbdallāh b. ʿAbd al-ʿAzīz. *Faṣl al-maqāl fī sharḥ kitāb al-Amthāl*. Edited by Iḥsān ʿAbbās and ʿAbd al-Majīd ʿĀbidīn. Beirut: Dār al-Amāna, 1391/1971.

al-Bakrī, Abū ʿUbayd ʿAbdallāh b. ʿAbd al-ʿAzīz. *Kitāb Muʿjam mā istaʿjam*. Edited by Ferdinand Wüstenfeld. Göttingen: Deuerlich'sche Buchhandlung, 1877.

al-Balādhurī, Abū l-ʿAbbās Aḥmad b. Yaḥyā b. Jābir. *Ansāb al-ashrāf*. Vol. 2. Edited by Wilferd Madelung. Beirut: Klaus Schwarz, 2003.

al-Balādhurī, Abū l-ʿAbbās Aḥmad b. Yaḥyā b. Jābir. *Ansāb al-ashrāf*. Vol. 5. Edited by S. D. F. Goitein. Jerusalem: Hebrew University Press, 1936.

al-Balādhurī, Abū l-ʿAbbās Aḥmad b. Yaḥyā b. Jābir. *Kitāb Futūḥ al-buldān*. Edited by M. J. De Goeje. Leiden: Brill, 1866. Translated by Philip Khûri Ḥitti and F. C. Murgotten as *The Origins of the Islamic State*. 2 vols. New York: Columbia University, 1916–1924.

al-Balawī, ʿAbdallāh b. Muḥammad. *Sīrat Aḥmad b. Ṭūlūn*. Edited by Muḥammad Kurd ʿAlī. Damascus: al-Maktaba al-ʿArabiyya, 1939.

BGA: see *Bibliotheca Geographorum Arabicorum*.

Bibliotheca Geographorum Arabicorum. Edited by M. J. de Goeje. 5 vols. Leiden: Brill, 1870.

al-Bīrūnī, Muḥammad b. Aḥmad. *Al-Āthār al-bāqiya*. Edited by Eduard Sachau and Lutfi M. Sa'di. Leipzig: Deutsche Morgenländische Gesellschaft, 1876–1878 [reprinted 1923].

al-Bukhārī, Abī ʿAbdallāh Ismāʿīl b. Ibrāhīm al-Juʿfī. *Kitāb al-Taʾrīkh al-kabīr*. Edited by Muḥammad ʿAbd al-Muʿīd Khan. 8 vols. Beirut, 1970.

Caskel, *Ǧamharat an-Nasab*. See Ibn al-Kalbī.

De Goeje, Michael J. *Descriptio imperii Moslemici*. An edition of al-Muqaddasī, *Kitāb Aḥsan al-taqāsīm fī maʿrifat al-aqālīm*. In *Bibliotheca Geographorum Arabicorum*, 3. Leiden: Brill, 1906.

De Goeje, Michael J. *Fragmenta Historicorum Arabicorum: Et Quidem Pars Tertia Operis Kitábo ·l-Oyun Wa ·l-Hadáïk Fi Akhbári ·l-Hakáïk, Et Pars Sexta Operis Tadjáribo ·l-Omami Auctore Ibn Maskowaih, Quae Cum Indicibus Et Glossario*. Edidit M. J. de Goeje. Leiden: Brill, 1871.

al-Dhahabī, Shams al-Dīn Muḥammad b. Aḥmad b. ʿUthmān. *Mīzān al-iʿtidāl fī naqd al-rijāl*. Edited by ʿAlī Muḥammad al-Bajāwī. Cairo: ʿĪsā al-Bābī al-Ḥalabī, 1963.

al-Dhahabī, Shams al-Dīn Muḥammad b. Aḥmad b. ʿUthmān. *Siyar aʿlām al-nubalāʾ*. Edited by Shuʿayb al-Arnāʾūṭ. Beirut: 1401–1409/1981–1988.

al-Dhahabī, Shams al-Dīn Muḥammad b. Aḥmad b. ʿUthmān. *Taʾrīkh al-Islām*. Edited by ʿUmar ʿAbd al-Salām al-Tadmurī. Beirut: Dār al-Kitāb al-ʿArabī, 1409–1413/1989–1993.

al-Dīnawarī, Abū Ḥanīfa Aḥmad b. Dāwūd. *Al-Akhbār al-ṭiwāl*. Edited by Ignace Kratchkovsky. Leiden: Brill, 1912.

al-Dīnawarī, Abū Ḥanīfa Aḥmad b. Dāwūd. *Al-Akhbār al-ṭiwāl*. Edited by ʿAbd al-Munʿim ʿĀmir. Cairo: Wizārat al-Thaqāfa wa-l-Irshād al-Qawmī, 1960

Gardīzī, ʿAbd al-Ḥayy b. Ḍaḥḥak. *Zayn al-akhbār*. Tehran: Muḥammad ʿAlī ʿIlmī, 1968.

al-Hamadhānī, Ibn al-Faqīh. *Mukhtaṣar Kitāb al-buldān*. Bibliotheca Geographorum Arabicorum 5. Edited by M. J. de Goeje. Leiden: Brill, 1885.

Ḥassān b. Thābit. *Dīwān of Ḥassān ibn Thābit*. Edited by Walīd N. ʿArafat. E. J. W. Gibb Memorial Series, n.s. 25. 2 vols. London: Luzac, 1971.

al-Haythamī, Nūr al-Dīn ʿAlī b. Abī Bakr. *Majmaʿ al-zawāʾid wa-manbaʿ al-fawāʾid*. 3rd edition. Beirut: Dār al-Kitāb al-ʿArabī, 1402/1982; also 12 vols. Beirut: Dār al-Kutub al-ʿIlmiyya, 2001.

Ibn ʿAbd al-Barr, Abū ʿUmar Yūsuf b. ʿAbdallāh b. Muḥammad al-Qurṭubī. *Al-Istīʿāb fī khabar al-aṣḥāb*. Edited by ʿAlī Muḥammad al-Bajāwī. Beirut: 1413/1992.

Ibn ʿAbd al-Barr, Abū ʿUmar Yūsuf b. ʿAbdallāh b. Muḥammad al-Qurṭubī. *al-Tamhīd li-mā fī l-Muwaṭṭaʾ min al-maʿānī wa-l-asānīd*. Rabat: Wizārat al-Awqāf wa-l-Shuʾūn al-Islāmiyya, 1967–1992.

Ibn ʿAbd al-Ḥakam. *Futūḥ Miṣr wa-akhbāruhā*. Edited by Charles C. Torrey. New Haven: Yale University Press, 1922.

Ibn ʿAbd Rabbih. *Al-ʿIqd al-Farīd*. 7 vols. Beirut: Dār al-Kitāb al-ʿArabī, 1990.

Ibn Abī l-Ḥadīd, ʿAbd al-Ḥamīd b. Hibatallāh. *Sharḥ Nahj al-balāgha*. Edited by Muḥammad Abū l-Faḍl. 2nd edition. Beirut: Dār Iḥyāʾ al-Turāth al-ʿArabī, 1967.

Ibn Abī Ḥātim al-Rāzī. *Al-Jarḥ wa-l-taʿdīl*. Reprint of the Hyderabad edition. Beirut: 1271/1952.

Ibn Abī Uṣaybiʿa, Aḥmad Ibn al-Qāsim. *Kitāb ʿUyūn al-anbāʾ fī ṭabaqāt al-aṭibbāʾ*. Cairo: Dār al-Maʿārif, 1970.

Ibn al-ʿAdīm, Kamāl al-Dīn ʿUmar b. Aḥmad. *Bughyat al-ṭalab min taʾrīkh Ḥalab*. Edited by Suhayl Zakkār. Beirut: Dār al-Fikr, 1988.

Ibn ʿAsākir, ʿAlī b. al-Ḥasan. *Taʾrīkh Madīnat Dimashq*. Damascus: Maṭbūʿāt Majmaʿ al-Lugha al-ʿArabiyya bi-Dimashq, 1954–

Ibn al-Athīr, ʿIzz al-Dīn Abū l-Ḥasan ʿAlī. *Al-Kāmil fī l-taʾrīkh*. Ed. C. J. Tornberg. 4 vols. Leiden: Brill, 1868.

Ibn al-Athīr, ʿIzz al-Dīn Abū l-Ḥasan ʿAlī. *Al-Lubāb fī tahdhīb al-ansāb*. Beirut: Dār Ṣādir, 1972.

Ibn al-Athīr, ʿIzz al-Dīn Abū l-Ḥasan ʿAlī. *Usd al-ghāba fī maʿrifat al-ṣaḥāba*. Reprint of the Hyderabad edition; Beirut: n.d.

Ibn al-Athīr, Majd al-Dīn Mubārak b. Muḥammad. *Al-Nihāya fī gharīb al-ḥadīth wa-l-athar*. Edited by Ṭāhir Aḥmad Zāwī and Mahmūd M. Tanāhī. Cairo: Dār Iḥyāʾ al-Kutub al-ʿArabiyya, 1963

Ibn Badrūn, ʿAbd al-Malik b. ʿAbdallāh. *Sharḥ qaṣīdat Ibn ʿAbdūn*. Edited by Reinhart Pieter Anne Dozy as *Commentaire historique sur le poème d'Ibn Abdoun*. Leiden: S. et J. Luchtmans, 1846.

Ibn Baṭṭūṭa. *The Travels of Ibn Baṭṭūṭa, A.D. 1325–1354*. Translated by C. Defrémery, B. R. Sanguinetti, H. A. R. Gibb, C. F. Beckingham, and A. D. H. Bivar. 5 vols. London: Hakluyt Society, 1958–1994.

Ibn al-Dāya, Aḥmad b. Yūsuf al-Kātib. *Kitāb al-Mukāfaʾa wa-ḥusn al-ʿuqbā*. Edited by Maḥmūd Muḥammad Shākir. Beirut: Dār al-Kutub al-ʿIlmiyya, [1986].

Ibn Durayd, Abū Bakr b. Muḥammad b. al-Ḥasan. *Al-Ishtiqāq*. Edited by ʿAbd al-Salām Muḥammad Hārūn. Cairo: Muʾassasat al-Khānjī, 1958.

Ibn al-Fakīh al-Hamadhānī, Aḥmad b. Muḥammad. *Compendium libri Kitâb al-Boldân*. Ed. M. J. de Goeje. In *Bibliotheca Geographorum Arabicorum* 5. Leiden: Brill, 1885.

Ibn Ḥabīb, Muḥammad. *Kitāb al-Muḥabbar*. Edited by Ilse Lichtenstadter. Ḥaydar Ābād al-Dakkan: Maṭbaʿat Jamʿīyat Dāʾirat al-Maʿārif al-ʿUthmānīyah, 1942.

Ibn Ḥajar al-ʿAsqalānī, Aḥmad b. ʿAlī. *Al-Iṣāba fī tamyīz al-ṣaḥāba*. Reprint of the 1328 Cairo edition. Cairo, n.d. Also, ed. Beirut, 9 vols. Beirut: Dār al-Kutub al-ʿIlmiyya, 1415/1995.

Ibn Ḥajar al-ʿAsqalānī, Aḥmad b. ʿAlī. *Lisān al-mīzān*. 7 vols. Hayderabad: Maṭbaʿat Majlis Dāʾirat al-Maʿārif al-Niẓāmiyya, 1331–1339 [1911–1913]. Reprinted Beirut: Muʾassasat al-Aʿlāmī. 1971.

Ibn Ḥajar al-ʿAsqalānī, Aḥmad b. ʿAlī. *Tabṣīr al-muntabih bi-taḥrīr al-mushtabih*. Edited by ʿAlī Muḥammad al-Bajāwī. Cairo: Dār al-Miṣriyya lil-Taʾlīf wa-l-Tarjama, 1964.

Ibn Ḥajar al-ʿAsqalānī, Aḥmad b. ʿAlī. *Tahdhīb al-tahdhīb*. Reprint of the Haydarabad edition. Beirut: n.d.

Ibn Ḥanbal, Aḥmad b. Muḥammad. *Musnad al-Imām Aḥmad Ibn Ḥanbal*. 6 vols. Beirut: al-Maktab al-Islamī, 1985.

Ibn Ḥazm al-Andalusī, ʿAlī b. Aḥmad. *Jamharat ansāb al-ʿarab*. Edited by ʿAbd al-Salām Muḥammad Hārūn. Cairo: Dār al-Maʿārif, 1382/1962.

Ibn Ḥazm al-Andalusī, ʿAlī b. Aḥmad. *Ummahāt al-khulafāʾ*. Edited by Ṣalāh al-Dīn al-Munajjid. Beirut: Dār al-Kitāb al-Jadīd, 1980.

Ibn Hilāl al-Thaqafī, Abū Isḥāq Ibrāhīm b. Muḥammad b. Saʿīd. *Al-Ghārāt*. Edited by ʿAbd al-Zahrāʾ al-Ḥusaynī al-Khaṭīb. Beirut: Dār al-Aḍwāʾ, 1407/1987.

Ibn Hishām, Abū Muḥammad ʿAbd al-Malik. *Sīrat Rasūl Allāh*. Edited by Ferdinand Wüstenfeld as *Das Leben Muhammad's*. Göttingen: Dieterische Universitäts-Buchhandlung, 1858. Translated by A. Guillaume as, *The Life of Muhammad: A Translation of Ibn Isḥāq's Sīrat Rasūl Allāh*. Oxford: Oxford University Press, 1955.

Ibn ʿIdhārī, Muḥammad. *Al-Bayān al-mughrib fī akhbār al-Andalus wa-l-Maghrib*. Edited by G. S. Colin and E. Lévi-Provençal. 3 vols. Reprinted Beirut: Dār al-Thaqāfa, [1967].

Ibn Isḥāq: See Ibn Hishām.

Ibn al-Kalbī, Hishām b. Muḥammad b. al-Sāʾib. *Ǧamharat an-Nasab: Das Genealogische Werk des Hišām Ibn Muḥammad al-Kalbī*. Edited by Werner Caskel. 2 vols. Leiden: Brill, 1966.

Ibn Kathīr, ʿImād al-Dīn Abū l-Fidāʾ Ismāʿīl b. ʿUmar. *Al-Bidāya wa-l-nihāya fī l-taʾrīkh*. 14 vols. Cairo: Maṭbaʿat al-Saʿāda, 1351–1358 (1932–1937).

Ibn Khallikān, Abū l-ʿAbbās Shams al-Dīn Aḥmad b. Muḥammad b. Abī Bakr. *Wafayāt al-aʿyān wa-anbāʾ abnāʾ al-zamān*. Edited by Iḥsān ʿAbbās. Beirut: Dār Ṣādir, 1968–1972.

Ibn Khurdādhbih, Abū l-Qāsim ʿUbaydallāh b. ʿAbdallāh. *Kitāb al-Masālik waʾl-Mamālik*. In *Bibliotheca Geographorum Arabicorum*, Vol. 6. Ed. M. J. de Goeje. Leiden: Brill, 1889.

Ibn al-Muqaffaʿ, ʿAbdallāh. *Kitāb Kalīla wa-Dimna*. Edited by Silvestre De Sacy as *Calila et Dimna: ou Fables de Bidpai*. Paris: Imprimerie Royale, 1816.

Ibn al-Muqaffaʿ, ʿAbdallāh. *Kalīla wa-Dimna*. Edited by L. Cheikho, S. J. Beirut: Imprimerie Catholique, 1905.

Ibn al-Nadīm, *Kitāb al-Fihrist*. Ed. G. Flügel. Leipzig: Vogel, 1871–1872.

Ibn al-Nafīs, ʿAlī ibn Abī l-Ḥazm. *Sharḥ fuṣūl Abuqrāṭ*. Edited by Yūsuf Zaydān and Māhir ʿAbd al-Qādir. Cairo: Al-Dār al-Miṣriyya al-Lubnāniyya, 1991.

Ibn Qutayba, Abū Muḥammad ʿAbdallāh b. Muslim. *Kitāb al-Maʿārif*. Edited by Ferdinand Wüstenfeld as *Ibn Coteiba's Handbuch der Geschichte*. Göttingen: Vandenhoeck und Ruprecht, 1850.

Ibn Qutayba, Abū Muḥammad ʿAbdallāh b. Muslim. *Kitāb al-Shiʿr wa-l-shuʿarāʾ*. Edited by M. J. de Goeje. Leiden: Brill, 1904.

Ibn Qutayba, Abū Muḥammad ʿAbdallāh b. Muslim. *Al-Maʿārif*. Edited by Tharwat Ukāsha. 2nd edition. Cairo: Dār al-Maʿārif, 1977.

Ibn Saʿd, Muḥammad. *Kitāb al-Ṭabaqāt al-kabīr*. Edited by Edward Sachau. 9 vols. Leiden: Brill, 1905–1940.

Ibn Saʿīd, ʿAlī b. Mūsā. *al-Mughrib fī ḥulā l-Maghrib*. Edited by Zakī Muḥammad Ḥasan et al. Cairo: Jāmiʿat Fuʾād al-Awwal, 1953.

Ibn Sallām, Abū ʿUbayd al-Qāsim. *Kitāb al-Amthāl*. Edited by ʿAbd al-ʿAzīz Qaṭāmish. Damascus: Dār al-Maʾmūn lil-Turāth, 1400/1980.

Ibn Samura, ʿUmar b. ʿAlī al-Ǧaʿdī. *Ṭabaqāt fuqahāʾ al-Yaman*. Edited by Fuʾād Sayyid. Beirut: Dār al-Kutub al-ʿIlmiyya, 1981.

Ibn al-Shiḥna, Muḥammad. *Taʾrīkh Ḥalab = The History of Aleppo Known as Ad-Durr Al-Muntakhab*. Edited by Keiko Ohta. Studia Culturae Islamicae 40. Tokyo: Institute for the Study of Languages and Cultures of Asia and Africa, 1990.

Ibn Taghrībirdī, Abū l-Maḥāsin Yūsuf. *Al-Nujūm al-zāhira fī mulūk Miṣr wa-l-Qāhira*. Cairo: al-Muʾassasa al-Miṣriyya al-ʿĀmma li-l-Taʾlīf wa-l-Ṭibāʿa wa-l-Nashr, 1963.

Ibn al-Zubayr, al-Qāḍī al-Rashīd. *Kitāb al-Dhakhāʾir wa-l-tuḥaf*, ed. Muḥammad Ḥamīdallāh and Ṣalāḥ al-Dīn al-Munajjid. Kuwait: Dāʾirāt al-Maṭbūʿāt wa-l-Nashr, 1959. Translated by Ghāda al-Ḥijjāwī al-Qaddūmī as *Book of Gifts and Rarities* (Cambridge, MA: Harvard University Press, 1996).

al-Idrīsī, al-Sharīf. *Nuzhat al-mushtāq fī ikhtirāq al-āfāq*. Leiden: Brill, 1970–1984.

Ikhwān al-Ṣafāʾ. *Rasāʾil Ikhwān al-Ṣafāʾ wa-Khullān al-Wafāʾ*. 4 vols. Beirut: Dār Ṣādir, 1978.

Imruʾ al-Qays. *Dīwān*. Edited by Muhammad b. al-Faḍl Ibrāhīm. 5th edition. Cairo: Dār al-Maʿārif, 1990.

al-Iṣfahānī, Abū l-Faraj. *Kitāb al-Aghānī*. 21 vols. Cairo: Dār al-Kutub, 1927–.

al-Jāḥiẓ, Abū ʿUthmān ʿAmr b. Baḥr b. Maḥbūb. *Al-Bayān wa-l-tabyīn*. Edited by ʿAbd al-Salām Muḥammad Hārūn. 4 vols. Cairo: Maktabat al-Khānjī, 1948–1950.

al-Jāḥiẓ, Abū ʿUthmān ʿAmr b. Baḥr b. Maḥbūb. *Al-Burṣān wa-l-ʿurjān wa-l-ʿumyān wa-l-ḥūlān*. Edited by Muḥammad Mursī al-Khūlī. Cairo: Dār al-Iʿtiṣām, 1972.

al-Jahshiyārī, Muḥammad b. ʿAbdūs. *Kitāb al-wuzarāʾ wa-l-kuttāb*. Edited by Muṣṭafā al-Ṣaqqā, Ibrāhīm al-Ibyārī, and ʿAbd al-Ḥafīẓ Shalabī. 2nd edition. Cairo: Sharikat Muṣṭafā al-Bābī al-Ḥalabī, 1401/1980.

al-Kashshī. *Ikhtiyār maʿrifat al-rijāl*. Karbalāʾ: n.d.

Khalīfa b. Khayyāṭ al-ʿUṣfurī. *Taʾrīkh Khalīfa b. Khayyāṭ*. Edited by Akram Ḍiyāʾ al-ʿUmarī. 2nd edition. Damascus/Beirut: Dār al-Qalam, 1397/1977.

Khalīfa b. Khayyāṭ al-ʿUṣfurī. *Kitāb al-Ṭabaqāt*. Edited by Akram Ḍiyāʾ al-Umarī. Baghdad: [1386/1967].

al-Khaṭīb al-Baghdādī. *Taʾrīkh Madīnat al-Salām*. Edited by Bashshār ʿAwwād Maʿrūf. Beirut: Dār al-Gharb al-Islāmī, 2001.

al-Kindī, Abū ʿUmar Muḥammad b. Yūsuf. *Kitāb al-Umarāʾ* (*al-wulāh*) *wa-kitāb al-*

quḍāh [*The Governors and Judges of Egypt*]. Edited by Rhuvon Guest. Leiden: Brill, 1912.

Kuthayyir ʿAzza. *Dīwān Kuthayyir ʿAzza*. Edited by Iḥsān ʿAbbās. Beirut: Dār al-Thaqāfa, 1971.

Labīd b. Rabīʿa. *Dīwān*. Edited and translated by Carl Brockelmann as *Die Gedichte des Lebîd, aus dem Nachlasse des Dr. A. Huber*. Leiden: Brill, 1892.

al-Majlisī, Muḥammad Bāqir. *Biḥār al-anwār*. Tehran: Dār al-Kutub al-Islāmiyya, 1956–1972.

al-Maqrīzī, Aḥmad b. ʿAlī. *Kitāb al-Mawāʿiẓ wa-l-iʿtibār bi-dhikr al-ḥiṭaṭ wa-l-āthār*. Beirut: Dār Ṣādir, 1998. Also edited by Ayman Fu'ād Sayyid. London: Mu'assasat al-Furqān, 2002.

al-Maqrīzī, Aḥmad b. ʿAlī. *Kitāb al-Muqaffā al-kabīr*. Edited by Muḥammad al-Yaʿlāwī. Beirut: Dār al-Gharb al-Islāmī, 1991.

al-Masʿūdī, Abū l-Ḥasan ʿAlī b. al-Ḥusayn b. ʿAlī. *Murūj al-dhahab wa-maʿādin al-jawhar* [*Les Prairies d'Or*]. Edited by Charles Pellat. 5 vols. Beirut: Publications de l'Université Libanaise, 1966.

al-Masʿūdī, Abū l-Ḥasan ʿAlī b. al-Ḥusayn b. ʿAlī. *Kitāb al-Tanbīh wa-l-ishrāf*. Edited by M. J. de Goeje. Bibliotheca Geographorum Arabicorum 8. Leiden: Brill, 1894.

Al-Maydānī, Aḥmad b. Muḥammad. *Majmaʿ al-amthāl*. 2nd ed. 4 vols. Beirut, 1961.

al-Mizzī, Jamāl al-Dīn. *Tahdhīb al-kamāl fī asmā' al-rijāl*. Edited by Bashshār ʿAwwād Maʿrūf. Beirut: Dār al-Gharb al-Islāmī, 1983–1992.

Muḥammad b. Ḥabīb. *Kitāb al-Muḥabbar*. Edited by Ilse Lichtenstadter. Hyderabad (Deccan): Maṭbaʿat Jamʿiyyat Dā'irat al-Maʿārif al-ʿUthmāniyya, 1942.

Muslim b. al-Ḥajjāj al-Qushayrī. *Al-Jāmiʿ al-ṣaḥīḥ*. Edited by Muḥammad Fu'ād ʿAbd al-Bāqī. 5 vols. Cairo: Dār Iḥyā' al-Kutub al-ʿArabiyya, 1955–1956.

al-Nābigha al-Dhubyānī. *Dīwān*. Edited by Abū l-Faḍl Ibrāhīm. Cairo: Dār al-Maʿārif, 1977.

al-Najāshī, Aḥmad b. ʿAlī. *Kitāb al-rijāl*. Tehran: n.d.

Naṣr b. Muzāḥim al-Minqārī. *Waqʿat Ṣiffīn*. Edited by ʿAbd al-Salām Muḥammad Hārūn. Reprint, Beirut: 1410/1990.

al-Nuwayrī, Aḥmad b. ʿAbd al-Wahhāb. *Nihāyat al-'arab fī funūn al-adab*. Cairo: al-Mu'assasa al-Miṣriyya al ʿĀmma lil-Ta'līf wa-l-Tarjama wa-l-Ṭibāʿa wa-l-Nashr, 1964.

al-Qalqashandī, Aḥmad b. ʿAlī. *Ṣubḥ al-aʿshā fī ṣināʿat al-inshā*. Beirut: Dār al-Kutub al-ʿIlmiyya, 1987.

al-Qazwīnī, Zakariyā' b. Muḥammad, *Āthār al-bilād wa-akhbār al-ʿibād*. Beirut: Dār Ṣādir, n.d.

al-Rāghib al-Iṣfahānī. *Muḥāḍarāt al-udabā' wa-muḥāwarāt al-shuʿarā' wa-l-bulaghā'*. Beirut: Dār Maktabat al-Ḥayāt, 1961.

al-Rāmhurmuzī, Buzurg b. Shahriyār. *ʿAjā'ib al-Hind: Barruhu wa-Baḥruhu wa-Jazā'ir-uhu*. Edited by Muḥammad Saʿīd al-Ṭurayḥī. Abu Dhabi: al-Mujammaʿ al-Thaqafī, 2000.

al-Ṣafadī, Khalīl b. Aybak. *Kitāb al-Wāfī bi-l-Wafayāt*. Edited by Muḥammad Ḥujayrī, Otfried Weintritt, Māhir Zuhayr Jarrār, Benjamin Jokisch, and Ibrāhīm Shabbūḥ. Leipzig: Deutsche Morgenländische Gesellschaft, in Kommission bei F. A. Brockhaus. 1931–.

al-Sahmī, Abū l-Qāsim Ḥamza b. Yūsuf. *Taʾrīkh Jurjān*. Edited by ʿAbd al-Muʿīd Khān. 3rd edition. Beirut: Dār al-Kutub al-ʿIlmiyya, 1401/1981.

al-Samʿānī, ʿAbd al-Karīm b. Muḥammad. *Kitāb al-Ansāb*. Hyderabad: Dāʾirat al-Maʿārif al-ʿUthmāniyya, 1962–1982.

al-Shahrastānī, Muḥammad b. ʿAbd al-Karīm. *Mafātīḥ al-asrār wa-maṣābīḥ al-abrār*. Edited by Muḥammad ʿAlī Ādharshab. Tehran: Markaz-e Pazhūheshī Mīrāth-e Maktūb, 2008.

al-Sharīshī, Aḥmad b. ʿAbd al-Muʾmin. *Sharḥ Maqāmāt al-Ḥarīrī*. Beirut: Dār al-Kutub al-ʿIlmīya, 1998.

al-Sīrāfī, Abū Zayd Ḥasan b. Yazīd. *Akhbār al-Ṣīn wa-l-Hind*. Edited by Jean Sauvaget. Paris: Les Belles Lettres, 1948.

al-Ṣūlī, Abū Bakr Muḥammad b. Yaḥyā. *Kitāb al-Awrāq*. Edited by V. I. Belyayev and A. B. Khalidov as *Kitab al-Avrak*. Pamyatniki Kultury Vostoka, Vol. 5. St. Petersburg: Institut Vostokovedeniya Rossiyskoy Akademii Nauk, 1998.

al-Ṭabarānī, Sulaymān ibn Aḥmad. *al-Muʿjam al-kabīr* Edited by Ḥamdī ibn ʿAbd al-Majīd al-Salafī. Cairo: Maktabat Ibn Taymiyya, 1983–.

al-Ṭabarī, Abū Jaʿfar Muḥammad b. Jarīr. *Jāmiʿ al-bayān ʿan taʾwīl al-Qurʾān*. Būlāq: al-Maṭbaʿa l-Amīriyya, 1323/1905–1906.

al-Ṭabarī, Abū Jaʿfar Muḥammad b. Jarīr. *Taʾrīkh al-rusul wa-l-mulūkh*. Edited by M. J. de Goeje. Leiden: Brill, 1879–1898.

al-Ṭabarī, Abū Jaʿfar Muḥammad b. Jarīr. *The History of al-Ṭabarī, II: Prophets and Patriarchs*. Translated by William M. Brinner. Albany: State University of New York Press, 1987.

al-Ṭabarī, Abū Jaʿfar Muḥammad b. Jarīr. *The History of al-Ṭabarī, III: The Children of Israel*. Translated by William M. Brinner. Albany: State University of New York Press, 1991.

al-Ṭabarī, Abū Jaʿfar Muḥammad b. Jarīr. *The History of al-Ṭabarī, V: The Sāsānids, the Byzantines, the Lakhmids, and Yemen*. Translated by C. E. Bosworth. Albany: State University of New York Press, 1999.

al-Ṭabarī, Abū Jaʿfar Muḥammad b. Jarīr. *The History of al-Ṭabari, VII: The Foundation of the Community*. Translated by W. Montgomery Watt and M. V. McDonald. Albany: State University of New York Press: 1987.

al-Ṭabarī, Abū Jaʿfar Muḥammad b. Jarīr. *The History of al-Ṭabarī, IX: The Last Years of the Prophet*. Translated by Ismail K. Poonawala. Albany: State University of New York Press, 1990.

al-Ṭabarī, Abū Jaʿfar Muḥammad b. Jarīr. *The History of al-Ṭabarī, X: The Conquest of*

Arabia. Translated by Fred M. Donner. Albany: State University of New York Press, 1993.

al-Ṭabarī, Abū Jaʿfar Muḥammad b. Jarīr. *The History of al-Ṭabarī, XI: The Challenge to the Empires*. Translated by Khalid Yahya Blankinship. Albany: State University of New York Press, 1993.

al-Ṭabarī, Abū Jaʿfar Muḥammad b. Jarīr. *The History of al-Ṭabarī, XII: The Battle of al-Qādisiyyah and the Conquest of Syria and Palestine*. Translated by Yohanan Friedmann. Albany: State University of New York Press, 1992.

al-Ṭabarī, Abū Jaʿfar Muḥammad b. Jarīr. *The History of al-Ṭabarī, XIII: The Conquest of Iraq, Southwestern Persia, and Egypt*. Translated by Gautier H. A. Juynboll. Albany: State University of New York Press, 1989.

al-Ṭabarī, Abū Jaʿfar Muḥammad b. Jarīr. *The History of al-Ṭabarī, XV: The Crisis of the Early Caliphate*. Translated by R. Stephen Humphreys. Albany: State University of New York Press, 1990.

al-Ṭabarī, Abū Jaʿfar Muḥammad b. Jarīr.*The History of al-Ṭabarī, XVI: The Community Divided*. Translated by Adrian Brockett. Albany: State University of New York Press, 1997.

al-Ṭabarī, Abū Jaʿfar Muḥammad b. Jarīr. *The History of al-Ṭabarī, XVII: The First Civil War*. Translated by G. R. Hawting. Albany: State University of New York Press, 1996.

al-Ṭabarī, Abū Jaʿfar Muḥammad b. Jarīr. *The History of al-Ṭabarī, XIX: The Caliphate of Yazīd b. Muʿāwiyah*. Translated by I. K. A. Howard. Albany: State University of New York Press, 1990.

al-Ṭabarī, Abū Jaʿfar Muḥammad b. Jarīr. *The History of al-Ṭabarī, XXI: The Victory of the Marwanids*. Translated by Michael Fishbein. Albany: State University of New York Press, 1990.

al-Ṭabarī, Abū Jaʿfar Muḥammad b. Jarīr. *The History of al-Ṭabarī, XXII: The Marwānid Restoration*. Translated by Everett K. Rowson. Albany: State University of New York Press, 1989.

al-Ṭabarī, Abū Jaʿfar Muḥammad b. Jarīr. *The History of al-Ṭabarī, XXIII: The Zenith of the Marwānid House*. Translated by Martin Hinds. Albany: State University of New York Press, 1990.

al-Ṭabarī, Abū Jaʿfar Muḥammad b. Jarīr. *The History of al-Ṭabarī, XXIV: The Empire in Transition*. Translated by David Stephan Powers. Albany: State University of New York Press, 1989.

al-Ṭabarī, Abū Jaʿfar Muḥammad b. Jarīr. *The History of al-Ṭabarī, XXV: The End of Expansion*. Translated by Khalid Yahya Blankinship. Albany: State University of New York Press, 1989.

al-Ṭabarī, Abū Jaʿfar Muḥammad b. Jarīr. *The History of al-Ṭabarī, XXVII: The ʿAbbāsid Revolution*. Translated by John Alden Williams. Albany: State University of New York Press, 1985.

al-Ṭabarī, Abū Jaʿfar Muḥammad b. Jarīr. *The History of al-Ṭabari, XXVIII: ʿAbbāsid Authority Affirmed.* Translated by Jane Dammen McAuliffe. Albany: State University of New York Press: 1995.

al-Ṭabarī, Abū Jaʿfar Muḥammad b. Jarīr. *The History of al-Ṭabarī, XXIX: Al-Manṣūr and al-Mahdī.* Translated by Hugh Kennedy. Albany: State University of New York Press, 1990.

al-Ṭabarī, Abū Jaʿfar Muḥammad b. Jarīr. *The History of al-Ṭabarī, XXX: The ʿAbbāsid Caliphate in Equilibrium.* Translated by C. E. Bosworth. Albany: State University of New York Press, 1989.

al-Ṭabarī, Abū Jaʿfar Muḥammad b. Jarīr. *The History of al-Ṭabarī, XXXI: The War between Brothers.* Translated by Michael Fishbein. Albany: State University of New York Press, 1992.

al-Ṭabarī, Abū Jaʿfar Muḥammad b. Jarīr. *The History of al-Ṭabarī, XXXII: The Reunification of the ʿAbbāsid Caliphate.* Translated by C. E. Bosworth. Albany: State University of New York Press, 1987.

al-Ṭabarī, Abū Jaʿfar Muḥammad b. Jarīr. *The History of al-Ṭabarī, XXXIII: Storm and Stress Along the Northern Frontiers of the ʿAbbāsid Caliphate.* Translated by C. E. Bosworth. Albany: State University of New York Press, 1991.

al-Ṭabarī, Abū Jaʿfar Muḥammad b. Jarīr. *The History of al-Ṭabarī, XXXIV: Incipient Decline.* Translated by Joel Kraemer. Albany: State University of New York Press, 1989.

al-Ṭabarī, Abū Jaʿfar Muḥammad b. Jarīr. *The History of al-Ṭabarī, XXXV: The Crisis of the ʿAbbāsid Caliphate.* Translated by George Saliba. Albany: State University of New York Press, 1985.

al-Ṭabarī, Abū Jaʿfar Muḥammad b. Jarīr. *The History of al-Ṭabarī, XXXVI: The Revolt of the Zanj.* Translated by David Waines. Albany: State University of New York Press, 1992.

al-Ṭabarī, Abū Jaʿfar Muḥammad b. Jarīr. *The History of al-Ṭabarī: XXXIX: Biographies of the Prophet's Companions and Their Successors.* Translated by Ella Landau-Tasseron. Albany: State University of New York Press, 1998.

Ṭarafa b. al-ʿAbd al-Bakrī. *Dîwân de Ṭarafa ibn al-ʿAbd al-Bakrî.* Edited by Max Seligsohn. Paris: Librairie Émile Bouillon, 1901.

Ṭarafa b. al-ʿAbd al-Bakrī. *Sharḥ Dīwān Ṭarafa b. al-ʿAbd.* Edited by Dr. Saʿdī al-Ḍināwī. Beirut: Dār al-Kitāb al-ʿArabī, 1994.

al-Ṭarsūsī, Marḍī b. ʿAlī. *Tabṣīrat arbāb al-albāb fī kayfiyyat al-najāh fī l-ḥurūb.* Edited by Claude Cahen. Beirut, 1948.

al-Tawhīdī, Abū Ḥayyān ʿAlī b. Muḥammad. *Al-Baṣāʾir wa-l-dhakhāʾir.* Edited by Wadād al-Qāḍī. Beirut: Dār Ṣādir, 1988.

al-Thaʿālibī, ʿAbd al-Malik b. Muḥammad. *Laṭāʾif al-maʿārif.* Translated by Clifford Edmond Bosworth as *The Book of Curious and Entertaining Information.* Edinburgh: Edinburgh University Press, 1968.

al-Thaʿālibī, ʿAbd al-Malik b. Muḥammad. *Thimār al-qulūb*. Edited by Muḥammad Abū l-Faḍl Ibrāhīm. Cairo: Dār al-Maʿārif, 1965.

al-Thaʿālibī, ʿAbd al-Malik b. Muḥammad. *Yatīmat al-dahr wa-maḥāsin ahl al-ʿaṣr*. Edited by Muḥammad Muḥyī al-Dīn ʿAbd al-Ḥamīd. Cairo: Maṭbaʿat al-Saʿāda, 1956–1958.

al-Tirmidhī, Muḥammad b. ʿĪsā. *Sunan al-Tirmidhī wa-huwa al-jāmiʿ al-ṣaḥīḥ*. 5 vols. Beirut: Dār al-Fikr, 1983.

al-Ṭūsī, Abū Jaʿfar Muḥammad b. al-Ḥasan. *Rijāl al-Ṭūsī*. Najaf: al-Maktaba wa-l-Maṭbaʿa al-Ḥaydariyya, 1381/1961.

Wakīʿ, Abū Bakr Muḥammad b. Khalaf b. Ḥayyān. *Akhbār al-Quḍāt*. Edited by ʿAbd al-ʿAzīz Muṣṭafā al-Marāghī. 3 vols. Cairo: Maṭbaʿat al-Istiqāma, 1947–1950.

al-Wāqidī, Muḥammad b. ʿUmar b. Wāqid. *Kitāb al-Maghāzī*. Edited by Marston Jones. 3 vols. London: Oxford University Press, 1966.

al-Waṭwāṭ, Jamāl al-Dīn. *Manāhij al-fikar wa-mabāhij al-ʿibar: Encyclopaedia of Four Natural Sciences*. Edited by Fuat Sezgin and M. Amawi. Frankfurt am Main: Institute for the History of Arabic-Islamic Science at the Johann Wolfgang Goethe University, 1990.

al-Yaʿqūbī, Ibn Wāḍiḥ. *Kitāb al-Buldān*. Edited by M. J. De Goeje. Bibliotheca Geographorum Arabicorum 7. 2nd Edition. Leiden: Brill, 1892. Translated by Gaston Wiet as *Yaʿḳūbī: Les Pays*. Cairo: Imprimerie de l'Institut Français d'Archéologie Orientale, 1937. Translated by Muḥammad Ibrāhīm Āyatī as *Buldān*. Tehran: Bungāh-i Tarjumah va Nashr-i Kitāb, 1977.

al-Yaʿqūbī, Ibn Wāḍiḥ. *Mushākalat al-nās li-zamānihim*. Edited by William Millward. Beirut: Dār al-Kitāb al-Jadīd, 1962. Translated by William G. Millward as "The Adaptation of Men to Their Time: An Historical Essay by Al-Yaʿqūbī." *Journal of the American Oriental Society* 84, no. 4 (1964): 329–344

al-Yaʿqūbī, Ibn Wāḍiḥ. *Taʾrīkh*. Edited by M. Th. Houtsma as *Ibn-Wādhih qui dicitur al-Jaʿqubī Historiae*. 2 vols. Leiden: Brill, 1883. Translated by Muḥammad Ibrāhīm Āyatī as *Tārīkh-i Yaʿqūbī*. Tehran: Markaz-i Intishārāt-i ʿIlmī va-Farhangī, 1964.

Yāqūt b. ʿAbdallāh al-Ḥamawī. *Muʿjam al-buldān*. Edited by Ferdinand Wüstenfeld as *Jacut's Geographisches Wörterbuch*. 6 vols. Leipzig: F. A. Brockhaus, 1866–1873.

Yāqūt b. ʿAbdallāh al-Ḥamawī. *Muʿjam al-udabāʾ* (*Irshād al-arīb ilā maʿrifat al-adīb*). Edited by Iḥsān ʿAbbās. 7 vols. Beirut: Dār al-Gharb al-Islāmī, 1993.

al-Zabīdī, Muḥammad b. Muḥammad Murtaḍā. *Tāj al-ʿarūs min jawāhir al-Qāmūs*. Būlāq: 1307/[1890].

al-Zamakhsharī, Maḥmūd b. ʿUmar. *Al-Fāʾiq fī gharīb al-ḥadīth*. Beirut: 1399/1970.

al-Zubayrī, Abū ʿAbdallāh Muṣʿab b. ʿAbdallāh b. al-Muṣʿab. *Kitāb Nasab Quraysh*. Edited by E. Lévi-Provençal. 2nd edition. Cairo: Dār al-Maʿārif, 1976.

B Non-Arabic Sources

Chachnamah: See al-Kūfī, ʿAlī b. Ḥāmid.

DIL: see Hippocrates. *De aere locis aquis*.

[Ephraem Syrus]. *Meʿarrat Gazzē* (*The Cave of Treasures*). Edited and translated by Carl Bezold as *Die Schatzhöhle*. Leipzig: Hinrichs, 1883–1888; reprinted Amsterdam: APA—Philo Press, 1981. English translation by Sir E. A. Wallis Budge, *The Book of the Cave of Treasures*. London: The Religious Tract Society, 1927.

Euclid. *The Arabic Version of Euclid's Optics* (*Kitāb Uqlīdis fī ikhtilāf al-manāẓir*). Edited and translated by Elaheh Kheirandish. 2 vols. New York: Springer, 1999.

Fichtner, Gerhard. *Corpus Galenicum: Bibliographie der galenischen und pseudogalenischen Werke*. Berlin-Brandenburgische Akademie der Wissenschaften, September 2015. http://cmg.bbaw.de/online-publications/Galen-Bibliographie_2015-09.pdf (accessed December 28, 2016).

Fichtner, Gerhard. *Corpus Hippocraticum: Bibliographie der hippokratischen und pseudohippokratischen Werke*. Berlin-Brandenburgische Akademie der Wissenschaften, February 2015. http://cmg.bbaw.de/online-publications/Hippokrates-Bibliographie_2015_02_19.pdf (accessed December 28, 2016)

Galen. *Claudii Galeni Opera Omnia*. Edited by Karl Gottlob Kühn. 20 vols. Leipzig: Libraria Car. Cnoblochii, 1821–1833. Reprinted Cambridge: Cambridge University Press, 2011.

Galen. *On Anatomical Procedures*. Translated by Charles Singer. London: Oxford University Press, 1956.

Gold, Milton. *The Tārikh-e Sistān*. Rome: Istituto italiano per il Medio ed Estremo Oriente, 1976.

Hippocrates. *Works*. Edited and translated by W. H. S. Jones. 10 vols. Loeb Classical Library, nos. 147–150, 472–473, 482, 509, 520. Cambridge, MA: Harvard University Press, 1928–.

Hippocrates. *Aphorisms*. Stephanus of Athens: Commentary on Hippocrates' Aphorisms. Edited and translated by Leendert G. Westerink. Corpus Medicorum Graecorum, vol. 11, pt. 1–3. Berlin: Akademie Verlag, 1985, 1992, 1995.

Hippocrates. *De aere locis aquis*. Edited with German translation by Hans Diller as *Hippocratis De aere locis aquis*. Corpus medicorum graecorum, vol. 1, pt. 1, 2. Berlin: Akademie Verlag, 1970.

Hippocrates. *De aere locis aquis*. Abraham Wasserstein, Galen's commentary on the Hippocratic treatise Airs, Waters, Places in the Hebrew translation of Solomon ha-Me'ati. In Proceedings of the Israel Academy of Sciences and Humanities, vol. 6, no. 3, 185–303. Jerusalem: Israel Academy of Sciences and Humanities, 1982.

Hippocrates. *De aere locis aquis*. Fuat Sezgin et al., Galen's commentary on the Hippocratic treatise On airs, waters, places (Περὶ ἀέρων, ὑδάτων, τόπων) in Arabic translation. Publications of the Institute for the History of Arabic Science, Ser. C, vol. 65. Frankfurt am Main: Institute for the History of Arabic Science, 2001.

Hippocrates. *De aere locis aquis*. Gotthard Strohmaier, "Galen's Not Uncritical Commentary on Hippocrates' Airs, Waters, Places." Bulletin of the Institute of Classical Studies 47 (2004): 1–9.

Hippocrates. *De natura hominis*. Jacques Jouanna, Hippocratis De natura hominis, La nature de l'homme. Corpus medicorum graecorum, vol. 1, pt. 1, 3. Berlin: Akademie Verlag, 2002.

Hippocrates. *De natura hominis*. Galeni In Hippocratis De natura hominis commentaria III. Edited by Johannes Mewaldt. Corpus medicorum graecorum, vol. 5, pt. 9/1. Leipzig & Berlin: Teubner, 1914.

Hippocrates. *Galeni In Hippocratis Prorrheticum I commentaria III, De comate secundum Hippocratem, In Hippocratis Prognosticum commentaria III*. Edited by Hermann Diels, Johannes Mewaldt, and Joseph Heeg. Corpus Medicorum Graecorum, vol. 5, pt. 9/2, 195–378. Leipzig & Berlin: Teubner, 1915.

Hippocrates. *Kitāb al-Ajinna li-Buqrāṭ*. Hippocrates: On Embryos. Edited and translated with introduction, commentary and glossary by M. C. Lyons and J. N. Mattock. Arabic Technical and Scientific Texts 7. Cambridge: Heffer 1978.

Hippocrates. *Kitāb Buqrāṭ fī 'l-akhlāṭ* and *Kitāb al-Ghidhā' li-Buqrāṭ*. Edited and translated by J. N. Mattock. Arabic Technical and Scientific Texts 6. Cambridge: Heffer, 1971.

Hippocrates. *Kitāb Buqrāṭ fī 'l-amrāḍ al-bilādīya*. Edited by John N. Mattock and Malcolm C. Lyons. Arabic Technical and Scientific Texts 5. Cambridge: Heffer, 1969.

Hippocrates. *Kitāb Buqrāṭ fī ṭabīʿat al-insān*. Edited and translated by J. N. Mattock & M. C. Lyons. Arabic Technical and Scientific Texts 4. Cambridge: Heffer, 1968.

Hippocrates. *Kitāb Buqrāṭ fī tadbīr al-amrāḍ al-ḥādda*. Edited and translated by M. C. Lyons. Arabic Technical and Scientific Texts 1. Cambridge: Heffer, 1966.

Hippocrates. *Œuvres Complètes d'Hippocrate*. Translated by Maximilien P. E. Littré. 10 vols. Paris, 1839–1861.

Hippocrates. *Prognostikon*. Edited by Bengt Alexanderson as *Die Hippokratische Schrift Prognostikon: Überlieferung und Text*. Studia Graeca et Latina Gothoburgensia 17. Stockholm: Almqvist & Wiksell, 1963.

Hippocrates. *Prognosticon*. Stephanus the Philosopher: Lectures on the Prognosticon of Hippocrates. Critical text and translation by John M. Duffy. Corpus Medicorum Graecorum, vol. 11, pt. 1–2. Berlin: Akademie Verlag, 1983.

Hippocrates. *Pseudogaleni in Hippocratis De septimanis commentarium ab Hunaino q.f. Arabice versum*. Edited by Gotthelf Bergsträßer. Corpus medicorum graecorum, vol. 11, pt. 2, fasc. 1. Leipzig and Berlin: Teubner, 1914.

Ḥudūd al-ʿĀlam: V. Minorsky and C. E. Bosworth. *Ḥudūd al-ʿĀlam = The Regions of the World: A Persian Geography, 327 A.H. – 982 A.D.* London: Luzac, 1970.

al-Kūfī, ʿAlī b. Ḥāmid. *The Chachnámah, an Ancient History of Sind*. Translated from the Persian by Mírza Kalichbeg Fredunbeg. 2 vols. Karachi, 1900, 1900.

Kühn: See Galen. *Claudii Galeni Opera Omnia.*

Michael the Syrian. *Chronique de Michel le Syrien: Patriarche Jacobite d'Antioche (1166–1199)*. Translated by J. B. Chabot. Brussels: Culture et Civilisation, 1963.

M & L: See Hippocrates. *Kitāb Buqrāṭ fī 'l-amrāḍ al-bilādīya.*

Ptolemy. *Almagest*. Translated by G. J. Toomer. London: Duckworth, 1984.

Schulthess, Friedrich. *Kalīla und Dimna: Syrisch und Deutsch*. 1911–1912. Reprinted Amsterdam: APA—Philo Press, 1982.

Stephanus of Athens. *A Commentary on the Prognosticon of Hippocrates*. Edited and translated by John M. Duffy. Berlin: Akademie-Verlag, 1983.

Ta'rīkh-e Sīstān. Translated by Milton Gold. Rome: Istituto italiano per il Medio ed Estremo Oriente, 1976.

Theophanes, the Confessor. *Chronicle*. Translated by Harry Turtledove as *The Chronicle of Theophanes: An English Translation of Anni Mundi 6095–6305* (A.D. 602–813). Philadelphia: University of Pennsylvania Press, 1982.

Theophanes, the Confessor. *Chronicle*. Translated by Cyril A. Mango, Roger Scott, and Geoffrey Greatrex as *The Chronicle of Theophanes Confessor: Byzantine and Near Eastern History, A.D. 284–813*. Oxford: Clarendon Press, 1997.

II Secondary Sources

Adang, Camilla. *Muslim Writers on Judaism and the Hebrew Bible*. Leiden: Brill, 1996.

Āghā, Ṣāliḥ Saʿīd. *The Revolution Which Toppled the Umayyads: Neither Arab nor ʿAbbāsid*. Leiden & Boston: Brill, 2003.

Ahmad, S. Maqbul. "Al-Masʿūdī on the Kings of India." In S. Maqbul Ahmad and A. Rahman, *Al-Masʿūdī Millenary Commemoration Volume*, 97–112. Aligarh: The Indian Society for the History of Science and The Institute of Islamic Studies, Aligarh Muslim University, 1960.

Anthony, Sean W. "Was Ibn Wāḍiḥ al-Yaʿqūbī a Shiʿite Historian? The State of the Question." *Al-ʿUṣūr al-Wusṭā* 24 (2016): 15–41.

Arazi, Albert, Wilhelm Ahlwardt, Salman Masalha, et al. *Six Early Arab Poets: New Edition and Concordance; Based on W. Ahlwardt's The Divans of the Six Ancient Arabic Poets*. Jerusalem: Hebrew University of Jerusalem, 1999.

Arioli, A. "La rivolta di Abū Sarāyā: appunti per una tipologia del leader islamico." *Annali di Ca' Foscari* 5 (1974): 189–197.

ʿĀṣī, Ḥusayn. *Al-Yaʿqūbī: ʿaṣruh, sīrat ḥayātih, wa-manhajuhu l-ta'rīkhī*. Beirut: Dār al-Kutub al-ʿIlmiyya, 1992.

Athamina, K. "Non-Arab Regiments and Private Militias during the Umayyad Period." *Arabica* 45 (1998): 347–378.

Ayalon, David. "The Military Reforms of Caliph al-Muʿtaṣim." In David Ayalon, *Islam and the Abode of War: Military Slaves and Islamic Adversaries*, 1–39. Aldershot: Variorum, 1994.

Barthold, W. *An Historical Geography of Iran*. Translated by Svat Soucek. Edited with an Introduction by C. E. Bosworth. Princeton: Princeton University Press, 1984.

Barthold, W.. *Turkestan Down to the Mongol Invasion*. London: Luzac, 1977.

Baumer, Christoph. *Southern Silk Road: In the Footsteps of Sir Aurel Stein and Sven Hedin*. Bangkok, Thailand: Orchid Press, 2002.

Beckwith, Christopher I. *The Tibetan Empire in Central Asia: A History of the Struggle for Great Power Among Tibetans, Turks, Arabs, and Chinese During the Early Middle Ages*. Princeton: Princeton University Press, 1993.

Bianquis, Thierry. "Autonomous Egypt from Ibn Ṭūlūn to Kāfūr, 868–969." In *The Cambridge History of Egypt, Volume One: Islamic Egypt, 640–1517*, edited by Carl F. Petry, 86–119. Cambridge: Cambridge University Press, 1998.

Biesterfeldt, Hinrich. "'Eternalists' and 'Materialists' in Islam: A Note on the *Dahriyya*." In *Eternity: A History*, edited by Yitzhak Y. Melamed, 117–123. New York: Oxford University Press, 2016.

Biesterfeldt, Hinrich. "Palladius on the Hippocratic Aphorisms." In *The Libraries of the Neoplatonists: Proceedings of the Meeting of the European Science Foundation Network* "Late Antiquity and Arabic Thought," edited by Cristina D'Ancona, 385–397. Leiden: Brill 2007.

Blankinship, Khalid Yahya. *The End of the Jihād State: The Reign of Hishām Ibn 'Abd al-Malik and the Collapse of the Umayyads*. Albany: State University of New York Press, 1994.

Bonner, Michael D. *Aristocratic Violence and Holy War: Studies in the Jihad and the Arab-Byzantine Frontier*. New Haven, CT: American Oriental Society, 1996.

Bonner, Michael D. "Ibn Ṭūlūn's Jihād: The Damascus Assembly of 269/883." *JAOS* 130.4 (2010): 573–605.

Bosworth, C. E. "A Note on *Ta'arrub* in Early Islam." *Journal of Semitic Studies* 34 (1989): 355–362.

Brock, Sebastian. "Jacob of Sarug's Poem on the Sleepers of Ephesus." In *"I Sowed Fruits into Hearts" (Odes Sol. 17:13): Festschrift for Professor Michael Lattke*, edited by P. Allen, M. Franzmann, and R. Strelan, 324–330. Early Christian Studies 12. Strathfield NSW: St Paul's Publications, 2007.

Brockelmann, Carl. *Geschichte der arabischen Litteratur* (GAL). 2nd edition. Leiden: Brill, 1943–1947.

BSOAS: *Bulletin of the School of Oriental and African Studies*.

Bulliet, Richard W. *The Patricians of Nishapur: A Study in Medieval Islamic Social History*. Cambridge, MA: Harvard University Press, 1972.

Burton, John. *The Collection of the Qur'ān*. Cambridge: Cambridge University Press, 1977.

Butler, Alfred Joshua. *The Arab Conquest of Egypt and the Last Thirty Years of the Roman Dominion*. Oxford: Clarendon Press, 1902.

Chevedden, Paul E., Zvi Shiller, Samuel R. Gilbert, and Donald J. Kagay, "The Traction Trebuchet: A Triumph of Four Civilizations." *Viator* 31 (2000): 433–486.

Christensen, Arthur. *L'Iran sous les Sassanides*. 2nd ed. Copenhagen: Ejnar Munksgaard, 1944.

Christensen, Peter. *The Decline of Iranshahr: Irrigation and Environments in the History of the Middle East, 500 B.C. to A.D. 1500*. Copenhagen: Museum Tusculanum Press, University of Copenhagen, 1993.

Cobb, Paul M. *White Banners: Contention in 'Abbāsid Syria, 750–880*. Albany: State University of New York Press, 2001.

Conrad, Lawrence I. "Islam and the Sea: Paradigms and Problematics." *Al-Qantara* 23 (2002): 123–154.

Conrad, Lawrence I. "al-Yaʿqūbī." In *Dictionary of the Middle Ages*, edited by Joseph R. Strayer, 12:717–718. New York: Charles Scribner's Sons, 1989.

Cooperson, Michael. *Classical Arabic Biography: The Heirs of the Prophets in the Age of Al-Ma'mūn*. Cambridge: Cambridge University Press, 2000.

Creswell, K. A. C. *Early Muslim Architecture*. 2 vols. Oxford: Clarendon Press, 1969–1979.

Crone, Patricia. *The Nativist Prophets of Early Islamic Iran: Rural Revolt and Local Zoroastrianism*. Cambridge: Cambridge University Press, 2012.

Crone, Patricia. *Slaves on Horses: the Evolution of the Islamic Polity*. Cambridge: University Press, 1980.

Daniel, Elton L. "Al-Yaʿqūbī and Shiʿism Reconsidered." In *'Abbāsid Studies: Occasional Papers of the School of 'Abbāsid Studies, Cambridge, 6–10 July 2002*. Edited by J. E. Montgomery. Leuven: Peeters, 2004.

Daniel, Elton L. *The Political and Social History of Khurasan under Abbasid Rule, 747–820*. Minneapolis: Bibliotheca Islamica, 1979.

De Goeje, Michael J. "Über die Geschichte der Abbasiden von al-Jakubi." *Travaux de la troisième session du Congrès International des Orientalistes, St. Pétersbourg* 2 (1876): 153–166.

Dictionary of Scientific Biography. Edited by Charles Coulston Gillispie. New York: Scribners, 1970.

Donaldson, Dwight M. "Al-Yaʿqubi's Chapter about Jesus Christ." In *The Macdonald Presentation Volume*, edited by W. G. Shellabear. Princeton: Princeton University Press, 1933: 89–105.

Donner, Fred M. *The Early Islamic Conquests*. Princeton: Princeton University Press, 1981.

Donner, Fred M. *Narratives of Islamic Origins*. Princeton: Darwin Press, 1998.

Dozy, R. *Supplément aux dictionnaires Arabes*. Leiden: Brill, 1881. Reprinted, Beirut: Librairie du Liban, 1968.

Dunlop, Douglas M. "Arab Relations with Tibet in the 8th and Early 9th Century." In *Islâm Tetkikleri Enstitüsü Dergisi* (Istanbul) 5 (1973): 301–318.

Duri, A. A. "The Iraq School of History to the Ninth Century: A Sketch." In *Historians of the Middle East*, edited by Bernard Lewis and P. M. Holt. London: Oxford University Press, 1962: 45–53.

Ebied, R. Y., and L. R. Wickham, "Al-Yaʿḳūbī's Account of the Israelite Prophets and Kings." *Journal of Near Eastern Studies* 29 (1970): 80–98.

EI[1]: see *The Encyclopaedia of Islam*. 1st Edition.

EI[2]: see *The Encyclopaedia of Islam*. 2nd Edition.

EI[3]: see *The Encyclopaedia of Islam*. 3rd Edition.

Elad, Amikam. *The Rebellion of Muḥammad al-Nafs al-Zakiyya in 145/762: Ṭālibīs and Early ʿAbbāsids in Conflict*. Leiden: Brill, 2016.

El-Hibri, Tayeb. *Reinterpreting Islamic Historiography: Hārūn Al-Rashīd and the Narrative of the ʿAbbasid Caliphate*. New York: Cambridge University Press, 1999.

Encyclopaedia Iranica. New York: The Encyclopaedia Iranica Foundation. 1985–.

The Encyclopaedia of Islam. 1st Edition. 9 vols. Leiden: E. J. Brill, 1913–1936.

The Encyclopaedia of Islam. 2nd Edition. 11 vols. and Supplement. Leiden: Brill 1954–2002.

The Encyclopaedia of Islam. 3rd Edition. Leiden: Brill, 2007–.

Encyclopaedia of the Qurʾān. Leiden: Brill, 2005.

Fahd, Toufic. *Le Panthéon de l'Arabie centrale à la veille de l'hégire*. Paris: Librairie orientaliste Paul Geuthner, 1968.

Ferrand, G. "Les relations de la Chine avec le golfe Persique avant l'hégire." In *Mélanges Gaudefroy-Demombynes*, 131–140. Cairo: Institut Français d'Archéologie Orientale, 1935–1945.

Ferré, André. "L'historien al-Yaʿqubi et les Evangiles." *Islamochristiana* 3 (1977): 65–83.

Ferré, André. Trans. *L'histoire des prophètes d'après al-Yaʿqûbî: d'Adam à Jésus* Rome: Pontificio istituto di studi arabi e d'islamistica, 2000.

Finster, B., and J. Schmidt, *Sasanidische und frühislamische Ruinen im Iraq*. In *Baghdader Mitteilungen*. Berlin, 1977.

Firestone, Reuven. *Journeys in Holy Lands*. Albany: State University of New York Press, 1990.

Forand, Paul. "Early Muslim Relations with Nubia." *Der Islam* 48 (1972): 111–121.

Gabrieli, Francesco. "Documenti relativi al califfato di al-Amīn in al-Ṭabarī," RCAL [*Rendiconti della R. Accademia Nationale dei Lincei*], Ser. 6, Vol. 3, 191–230.

Gabrieli, Francesco. "Muḥammad ibn Qāsim ath-Thaqafī and the Arab Conquest of Sind." *East and West*, n.s. 15 (1965): 281–295.

Garzya, Antonio, and Jacques Jouanna, eds. *Trasmissione e ecdotica dei testi medici greci*. Naples: D'Auria, 2003.

GAS: See Sezgin, Fuat. *Geschichte des Arabischen Schrifttums*.

Ginzberg, Louis. *The Legends of the Jews*. Translated by Henrietta Szold. 7 vols. 1909–1938. Reprint, Baltimore and London: The Johns Hopkins University Press, 1998.

Gordon, Matthew S. *The Breaking of a Thousand Swords: A History of the Turkish Military of Samarra, A.H. 200–275/815–889 C.E.* Albany: State University of New York Press, 2001.

Graham, William A. *Divine Word and Prophetic Word in Early Islam.* The Hague: Mouton, 1977.

Griffith, Sidney H. *The Bible in Arabic.* Princeton: Princeton University Press, 2013.

Günther, Sebastian. "al-Nawfalī's Lost *History*: The Issue of a Ninth-Century Shīʿite Source Used by al-Ṭabarī and Abū l-Faraj al-Iṣfahānī." *British Journal of Middle Eastern Studies* 36 (2009): 241–266.

Gutas, Dimitri. *Greek Wisdom Literature in Arabic Translation.* New Haven, CT: American Oriental Society, 1975.

Gutas, Dimitri. "Platon–Tradition arabe." In *Dictionnaire des philosophes antiques.* Vol. 5/1. Paris: Éditions du Centre national de la recherche scientifique, 2012.

Haider, Najam. "The Community Divided: A Textual Analysis of the Murders of Idrīs b. ʿAbd Allāh (d. 175/791)." *JAOS* 128 (2008): 459–475.

Hassan, Zaky Mohamed. *Les Tulunides: Étude de l'Égypte Musulmane à la fin du IXe siècle, 868–905.* Paris: Établissements Busson, 1933.

Herrmann, Albert. *Die alten Seidenstrassen zwischen China und Syrien: Beiträge zur alten Geographie Asiens.* Berlin: Weidmann, 1910.

Hinds, Martin. *An Early Islamic family from Oman: Al-ʿAwtabī's Account of the Muhallabids.* Manchester: University of Manchester, 1991.

Hinds, Martin. *Studies in Early Islamic History.* Edited by Jere Bacharach, Lawrence I. Conrad, and Patricia Crone. Princeton, NJ: Darwin Press, 1996.

Hinz, Walther. *Islamische Masse und Gewichte.* Leiden: Brill, 1955.

Horovitz, Josef. *The Earliest Biographies of the Prophet and Their Authors.* Edited by Lawrence I. Conrad. Princeton, NJ: Darwin Press, 2002.

Hourani, George Fadlo. *Arab Seafaring in the Indian Ocean in Ancient and Early Medieval Times.* Revised and expanded by John Carswell. Princeton: Princeton University Press, 1995.

Huber, Anton. *Über das 'Meisir' genannte Spiel der heidnischen Araber.* Leipzig: Breitkopf & Härtel, 1883.

JAOS: *Journal of the American Oriental Society.*

Johnstone, T. M. "An Early Manuscript of Yaʿḳūbī's Taʾrīḫ." *Journal of Semitic Studies* 2 (1957): 189–195.

JNES: *Journal of Near Eastern Studies.*

Jouanna, Jacques. *Hippocrates.* Translated by M. B. DeBevoise. Baltimore: Johns Hopkins University Press, 1999.

Jouanna, Jacques. *Studies on the First Century of Islamic Society.* Carbondale: Southern Illinois University Press, 1982.

Kaʿbī, Munjī (= Mongi Kaabi). *Les Ṭāhirides: Étude historico-littéraire de la dynastie des*

Banū Ṭāhir b. al-Ḥusayn au Ḫurāsān et en Iraq au III*-ème s. de l'Hégire/*IX*-ème s. J.-C.* Tunis: 1983.

Kaegi, W. E. *Byzantium and the Early Islamic Conquests.* Cambridge: Cambridge University Press, 1992.

Kennedy, E. S., and David Pingree. *The Astrological History of Māshā'allāh.* Cambridge, MA: Harvard University Press, 1971.

Kennedy, Hugh. "Antioch: From Byzantium to Islam." In *The City in Late Antiquity*, ed. John Rich, 185–188. London: Routledge, 1992.

Kennedy, Hugh. *The Early Abbasid Caliphate: A Political History.* London: Croom Helm, 1981.

Kennedy, Hugh. *An Historical Atlas of Islam.* Leiden & Boston: Brill, 2002.

Kister, M. J. *Society and Religion from Jāhiliyya to Islam.* Aldershot: Variorum, 1990.

The Koran, trans. A. J. Arberry. London: Allen & Unwin, 1955.

Klamroth, Martin. "Ueber den arabischen Euklid." *ZDMG* 35 (1881): 270–326.

Klamroth, Martin. "Ueber die Auszüge aus griechischen Schriftstellern bei al-Ja'qûbî." Pts. 1–4. *ZDMG* 40 (1886): 189–233, 612–638; 41 (1887): 415–442; 42 (1888), 1–44.

Landberg, Carlo Graf von. Review of Houtsma's edition of the *Ta'rīkh. Critica Arabica* 1, no. 3 (Leiden: Brill, 1886): 31–53.

Lane, Edward William. *An Arabic-English Lexicon.* 8 vols. London: 1863–1893. Reprinted, Beirut: 1968.

Lassner, Jacob. *Islamic Revolution and Historical Memory: An Inquiry into the Art of 'Abbāsid Apologetics.* New Haven, CT: American Oriental Society, 1986.

Lassner, Jacob. *The Shaping of 'Abbāsid Rule.* Princeton, NJ: Princeton University Press, 1980.

Lassner, Jacob. *The Topography of Baghdad in the Early Middle Ages: Text and Studies.* Detroit: Wayne State University Press, 1970.

Lecker, Michael. "Biographical Notes on Ibn Shihāb al-Zuhrī." *Journal of Semitic Studies* 41 (1996): 21–63.

Lecker, Michael. *The "Constitution of Medina": Muhammad's First Legal Document.* Princeton, NJ: Darwin Press, 2004.

Le Strange, G. *Baghdad during the Abbasid Caliphate.* Oxford: Oxford University Press, 1900.

Le Strange, G. *The Lands of the Eastern Caliphate: Mesopotamia, Persia, and Central Asia from the Moslem Conquest to the time of Timur.* Cambridge: Cambridge University Press, 1905.

Lindstedt, Ilkka. "The Role of al-Madā'inī's Students in the Transmission of His Material." *Der Islam* 91 (2014): 295–340.

Loewenthal, Albert. "Honein Ibn Ishâk, Sinnsprüche der Philosophen. Nach der hebräischen Übersetzung Charisi's ins Deutsche übertragen und erläutert." In Fuat Sezgin, ed., *Ḥunain ibn Isḥāq (d. 260/873): Texts and Studies. Islamic Philosophy,*

17:25–226. Frankfurt am Main: Institute for the History of Arabic-Islamic Science, 1999.

Løkkegaard, Frede. *Islamic Taxation in the Classic Period, with Special Reference to Circumstances in Iraq*. Copenhagen: Branner & Korch, 1950.

Madelung, Wilferd. "New Documents Concerning al-Ma'mūn, al-Faḍl b. Sahl and ʿAlī al-Riḍā." In *Studia Arabica et Islamica: Festschrift for Iḥsān ʿAbbās on His Sixtieth Birthday*, edited by Wadād al-Qāḍī, 333–346. Beirut: American University of Beirut, 1981.

Madelung, Wilferd. *The Succession to Muhammad: A Study of the Early Caliphate*. Cambridge: Cambridge University Press, 1997.

Madelung, Wilferd. "The Vigilante Movement of Sahl b. Salāma al-Khurāsānī and the Origins of Ḥanbalism Reconsidered." Reprinted in Sabine Schmidtke, ed., *Studies in Medieval Muslim Thought and History*. Farnham and Burlington: Ashgate, 2013.

Magdelaine, Caroline. "Le commentaire de Palladius sur les *Aphorismes* d'Hippocrate et les citations d'al-Yaʿqūbī." In *Trasmissione e ecdotica dei testi medici greci*, edited by Antonio Garzya and Jacques Jouanna, 321–334. Naples: D'Auria, 2003.

Marquet, Yves. "Le Šīʿisme au IXe siècle à travers l'histoire de Yaʿqūbī." *Arabica* 19 (1972): 1–45, 101–138.

Marsham, A., and C. F. Robinson. "The Safe-Conduct for the Abbasid ʿAbd Allāh b. ʿAlī (d. 764)." *BSOAS* 70 (2007): 247–281.

Millward, William G. "A Study of al-Yaʿqubi with Special Reference to His Alleged Shiʿa Bias." Ph.D. Dissertation. Princeton University, 1962.

Millward, William G. "Al-Yaʿqubi's Sources and the Question of Shiʿa Partiality." *Abr-Nahrain* 12 (1971–1972): 47–75.

Minorksy, V. "Caucascia IV," *BSOAS* 15 (1953): 504–529

Miquel, André. *La géographie humaine du monde musulman jusqu'au milieu du 11e siècle*. Paris and The Hague: Mouton, 1967.

Morimoto, Kōsei. *The Fiscal Administration of Egypt in the Early Islamic Period*. Kyoto: Dohosha, 1981.

Morony, Michael G. *Iraq after the Muslim Conquest*. Princeton, NJ: Princeton University Press, 1984.

Moscati, Sabatino. "Le Massacre des Umayyades." *Archiv Orientální* 18, no. 4 (1950): 88–115.

Moscati, Sabatino. "Il Testamento di Abū Hāšim." *Rivista degli Studi Orientali* 27 (1952): 28–46.

Mottahedeh, Roy P. *Loyalty and Leadership in Early Islamic Society*. Princeton, NJ: Princeton University Press, 1960.

Mozaffarian, V. *A Dictionary of Iranian Plant Names*. Tehran: Farhang Moʿāser, 1998.

Nasrallah, Nawal. *Annals of the Caliphs' Kitchens*. Leiden and Boston: Brill, 2007.

Neugebauer, O. "The Early History of the Astrolabe." *ISIS* 40, no. 3 (1949): 240–256.

al-Nijūmī, al-Liwāʾ ʿAbdallāh, et. al. *Al-Ṭuyūr al-Miṣriyya*. 2nd ed. Cairo: Dār al-Fikr al-ʿArabī, 1950.

Nöldeke, Theodor. *Geschichte der Perser und Araber zur Zeit der Sasaniden aus der arabischen Chronik des Tabari*. Leiden: Brill, 1879. Reprint, Leiden: Brill, 1973.

Nöldeke, Theodor, F. Schwally, G. Bergsträßer, and O. Pretzl. *The History of the Qurʾān*. Translated by W. H. Behn. Leiden: Brill, 2013.

Nöldeke, Theodor. Review: "Ibn Wādih qui dicitur al-Jaʿqubī historiae. Pars prior historiam ante-islamicam continens. Edidit indicesque adjecit M. Th. Houtsma." ZDMG 38 (1884): 153–160.

Nöldeke, Theodor. "Zur tendenziösen Gestaltung der Urgeschichte des Islām's." ZDMG 52 (1898), 16–33.

Northedge, Alastair. *Samarra: Residenz der ʿAbbāsidenkalifen 836–892 n. Chr., 221–279 Hiǧri*. Tübingen: Universität Tübingen, 1990.

Northedge, Alastair. *The Historical Topography of Samarra*. Samarra Studies I. London: British School of Archaeology in Iraq, 2005.

Noth, Albrecht. "Iṣfahān-Nihāwand: Eine quellenkritische Studie zur frühislamischen Historiographie." ZDMG 118 (1968): 274–296.

Öhrnberg, Kaj. *The Offspring of Fāṭima: Dispersal and Ramification*. Studia Orientalia 54. Helsinki: The Finnish Oriental Society, 1983.

Pinault, Jody Rubin. *Hippocratic Lives and Legends*. Studies in Ancient Medicine 4. Leiden: Brill, 1992.

Pingree, David. "The Fragments of the Works of al-Fazārī." *Journal of Near Eastern Studies* 29 (1970): 103–123.

Pingree, David. "The Liber Universus of ʿUmar ibn al-Farrukhān al-Ṭabarī." *Journal for the History of Arab Science* 1 (1977): 8–12.

Pingree, David. "ʿUmar ibn al-Farrukhān al-Ṭabarī." In Gillispie, Charles Coulston, ed. *Dictionary of Scientific Biography* 13:538–539. New York: Scribner, 1970–1990.

Power, Timothy. *The Red Sea from Byzantium to the Caliphate, AD 500–1000*. Cairo and New York: The American University in Cairo Press, 2012.

al-Qāḍī, Wadād. *Al-Kaysāniyya fī l-taʾrīkh wa-l-adab*. Beirut: Dār al-Thaqāfa, 1974.

al-Qāḍī, Wadād. "Population Census and Land Surveys Under the Umayyads 41–132/661–750." *Der Islam* 83 (2006): 359–362.

Rabbat, Nasser. "The Dome of the Rock Revisited: Some Remarks on al-Wasiti's Accounts." *Muqarnas* 10 (1993): 66–75.

Robinson, Chase F. *ʿAbd al-Malik*. Makers of the Muslim World. Oxford: Oneworld, 2007.

Robinson, Chase F, ed. *A Medieval Islamic City Reconsidered: An Interdisciplinary Approach to Samarra*. Oxford Studies in Islamic Art, 14. Oxford: Oxford University Press, 2001.

Robinson, Chase F. "Neck-Sealing in Early Islam." *Journal of the Economic and Social History of the Orient* 48 (2005): 401–441.

Rosenthal, Franz. *A History of Muslim Historiography*. 2nd revised edition. Leiden: Brill, 1968.

Rosenthal, Franz. "'Life is Short, the Art is Long': Arabic Commentaries on the First Hippocratic Aphorism." *Bulletin of the History of Medicine* 40, no. 3 (May 1966): 226–245.

Rosenthal, Franz. "On Medieval Authorial Bibliographies: al-Yaʿqūbī and Ibn Ḥajar." In M. Mir, ed. *The Literary Heritage of Classical Islam: Arabic and Islamic Studies in Honor of James A. Bellamy*, 255–274. Princeton, NJ: Darwin Press, 1993.

Rowson, Everett K. *A Muslim Philosopher on the Soul and Its Fate: Al-ʿĀmirī's Kitāb al-Amad ʿalā l-abad*. New Haven, CT: American Oriental Society, 1988.

Rubin, Uri. "The Kaʿba: Aspects of Its Ritual Functions and Position in Pre-Islamic and Early Islamic Times." *Jerusalem Studies in Arabic and Islam* 8 (1986), 97–132.

al-Sabban, Shaykh ʿAbdalgadir Muhammad. *Visits and Customs: The Visit to the Tomb of the Prophet Hud*. Translated by Linda Boxberger and Awad Abdelrahim Abu Hulayqa. Sanaʿa, Yemen: American Institute of Yemeni Studies, 1999.

al-Sāmarrāʾī, Qāsim. "Hal kataba l-Tanūkhī kitāban fī l-taʾrīkh?" *Al-Majmaʿ al-ʿIlmī al-ʿArabī* 50 (1975), 528–551.

Sezgin, Fuat. *Ḥunain ibn Isḥāq (d. 260/873): Texts and Studies*. Ed. Fuat Sezgin. *Islamic Philosophy*, Vol. 17. Frankfurt am Main: Institute for the History of Arabic-Islamic Science, 1999.

Sezgin, Fuat. *Geschichte des Arabischen Schrifttums. Vol. I: Qurʾānwissenschaften, Ḥadīṯ, Geschichte, Fiqh, Dogmatik, Mystik bis ca. 430 H*. Leiden: Brill, 1967.

Sezgin, Fuat. *Geschichte des Arabischen Schrifttums. Vol. II: Poesie bis ca. 430 H*. Leiden: Brill, 1975.

Sezgin, Fuat. *Geschichte des Arabischen Schrifttums. Vol. III: Medizin, Pharmazie, Zoologie, Tierheilkunde bis ca. 430 H*. Leiden: Brill, 1970.

Sezgin, Fuat. *Geschichte des Arabischen Schrifttums. Vol. V: Mathematik*. Leiden: Brill, 1974.

Sezgin, Fuat. *Geschichte des Arabischen Schrifttums. Vol. VI: Astronomie*. Leiden: Brill, 1978.

Sezgin, Ursula. *Abū Miḫnaf: Ein Beitrag zur Historiographie der umaiyadischen Zeit*. Leiden: Brill, 1971.

Sharon, Moshe. *Black Banners from the East: The Establishment of the ʿAbbāsid State—Incubation of a Revolt*. Jerusalem: Magnes Press, Hebrew University, 1983.

Silverstein, Adam J. *Postal Systems in the Pre-Modern Islamic World*. Cambridge: Cambridge University Press, 2007.

Smith, Wesley. *The Hippocratic Tradition*. Ithaca, NY: Cornell University Press, 1979.

Sokoloff, Michael. *A Syriac Lexicon*. Winona Lake, IN: Eisenbrauns, 2009.

Sourdel, Dominique. *Le vizirat ʿabbāside de 749 à 936 (132 à 324 de l'hégire)*. 2 vols. Damascus: Institut français de Damas, 1959–1960.

Stannard, Jerry. "Archigenes." In *Complete Dictionary of Scientific Biography*, Vol. 1. Detroit: Charles Scribner's Sons, 2008.

Stein, Aurel. *An Archaeological Tour to Gedrosia: A Detailed Report on the Extended Investigation into the Important but Little Known Region of Gedrosia Comprising the Territories of Kharan, Makran and Jhalawan*. New Delhi: Cosmo Pub, 1988.

Stowasser, Barbara Freyer. *Women in the Qur'an, Traditions, and Interpretation*. New York: Oxford University Press, 1994.

Sykes, Percy Molesworth. *Ten Thousand Miles in Persia or Eight Years in Iran*. London: J. Murray, 1902.

Tillier, Mathieu. "L'étoile, la chaîne et le Jugement. Essai d'interprétation d'un élément de décor dans la mosquéé d'Ibn Ṭūlūn." *Der Islam* 92.2 (2015): 332–366.

Timm, Stefan. *Das christlich-koptische Ägypten in arabischer Zeit*. 7 vols. Wiesbaden: Reichert, 1984–2007.

Tomaschek, Wilhelm. "Historisch-Topographisches vom oberen Euphrat und aus Ost-Kappadokien." In *Beiträge zur alten Geschichte und Geographie: Festschrift f. H. Kiepert*. Berlin: Dietrich Reimer, 1898.

Udovitch, Abraham L. *Time, the Sea and Society: Duration of Commercial Voyages on the Southern Shores of the Mediterranean During the High Middle Ages*. Princeton, NJ: Princeton University, Program in Near Eastern Studies, 1981.

Ullmann, Manfred. *Die Medizin im Islam*. Handbuch der Orientalistik I, suppl. vol. 6/1: 24–32. Brill: Leiden & Cologne, 1971.

Ullmann, Manfred. *Die Natur und Geheimwissenschaften im Islam*. Handbuch der Orientalistik. Sect. 1: Der Nahe und der Mittlere Osten, suppl. vol. 6/2. Leiden: Brill, 1972

Ullmann, Manfred. *Wörterbuch zu den griechisch-arabischen Übersetzungen des 9. Jahrhunderts* [*WGAÜ*]. Wiesbaden: Harrassowitz, 2002.

van Bladel, Kevin. *The Arabic Hermes: From Pagan Sage to Prophet of Science*. New York: Oxford University Press, 2009.

van Ess, Josef. *Theologie und Gesellschaft im 2. und 3. Jahrhundert Hidschra: Eine Geschichte des religiösen Denkens im frühen Islam*. Vol. 3. Berlin: de Gruyter, 1992.

Vantini, Giovanni. *Oriental Sources concerning Nubia*. Heidelberg: Heidelberger Akademie der Wissenschaften, 1975.

Vasiliev, A. A. *History of the Byzantine Empire, 324–1453*. Madison: University of Wisconsin Press, 1958.

Walzer, Richard, and Michael Frede, trans. *Galen: Three Treatises on the Nature of Science*. Indianapolis: Hackett, 1985.

Watt, W. Montgomery. *Muhammad at Medina*. Oxford: Clarendon Press, 1953.

Wellhausen, J. "Medina vor dem Islam." In *Skizzen und Vorarbeiten*, IV. Berlin: Georg Reimer, 1889.

Wensinck, A. J. et al. *Concordance et indices de la tradition Musulmane*. 8 vols. Leiden: Brill, 1933–.

WGAÜ. See Ullmann, Manfred. *Wörterbuch zu den griechisch-arabischen Übersetzungen des 9. Jahrhunderts*.

Wiet, Gaston. *L'Egypte de Murtadi fils du Gaphiphe*. Paris: Imprimerie nationale, 1953.

Witkam, Jan Just. "Michael Jan de Goeje (1836–1909) and the Editing of Arabic Geographical Texts." In *Bibliotheca Geographorum Arabicorum, vol. 1*: Kitāb al-Masālik wa-l-mamālik *by Abū Isḥāq al-Iṣṭakhrī*. Leiden: Brill, 2015.

WKAS: *Wörterbuch der klassischen Arabischen Sprache*. Wiesbaden: Harassowitz, 1957–.

Wüstenfeld, Ferdinand. *Genealogische Tabellen der arabischen Stämme und Familien*. 2 vols. Göttingen: Dieterische Buchhandlung, 1852–1853.

ZDMG: *Zeitschrift der Deutschen Morgenländischen Gesellschaft*.